SAGE was founded in 1965 by Sara Miller McCune to support the dissemination of usable knowledge by publishing innovative and high-quality research and teaching content. Today, we publish over 900 journals, including those of more than 400 learned societies, more than 800 new books per year, and a growing range of library products including archives, data, case studies, reports, and video. SAGE remains majority-owned by our founder, and after Sara's lifetime will become owned by a charitable trust that secures our continued independence.

Los Angeles | London | New Delhi | Singapore | Washington DC | Melbourne

Hindu Social Organization

Hindu Social Organization

A Study of the Socio-Psychological and Ideological Foundations

Pandharinath H. Prabhu

Popular Prakashan | SAGE | TEXTS

Los Angeles | London | New Delhi
Singapore | Washington DC | Melbourne

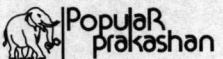

First published in 1956 by Popular Prakashan Pvt Ltd

This edition published in 2016 by

SAGE Publications India Pvt Ltd
B1/I-1 Mohan Cooperative Industrial Area
Mathura Road, New Delhi 110 044, India
www.sagepub.in

Popular Prakashan Pvt Ltd
301, Mahalaxmi Chambers
22, Bhulabhai Desai Road
Mumbai 400026
www.popularprakashan.com

SAGE Publications Inc
2455 Teller Road
Thousand Oaks, California 91320, USA

SAGE Publications Ltd
1 Oliver's Yard, 55 City Road
London EC1Y 1SP, United Kingdom

SAGE Publications Asia-Pacific Pte Ltd
3 Church Street
#10-04 Samsung Hub
Singapore 049483

Published by Vivek Mehra for SAGE Publications India Pvt Ltd, typeset in Times New Roman 10.5/12.5 pts by Zaza Eunice, Hosur, Tamil Nadu, India and printed at Saurabh Printers Pvt Ltd, Greater Noida.

Library of Congress Cataloging-in-Publication Data Available

ISBN: 978-93-860-4223-1 (PB)

To

the living memory

of our departed daughter

Mrinalini

—a promising life

cut short early;

and

To

the memory

of the author's Guru

Noshirwan A. Thoothi

who has made

outstanding contribution

towards the elucidation

of the concept of Dharma

in his book

"The Vaishṇvas of Gujarāt."

CONTENTS

Foreword by Dr. S. Radhakrishna xiii
Extracts from Preface to the First Edition xv
Extracts from Preface to the Second Edition xvii
Preface to the Third Edition xix
A Word on the Fourth Edition xxi
About the Author xxiii

Chapter 1 Prologue 1
Chapter 2 The Bases of Human Relations—The Problem of Existence and Its Implications 10
Chapter 3 The Social Psychology of the System of the Four Āsramas 47
Chapter 4 The Social Psychology of Education 65
Chapter 5 Marriage 93
Chapter 6 The Family 129
Chapter 7 Attitude Towards the Woman—And Her Place in the Society 166
Chapter 8 The Four Varnas 183
Chapter 9 Epilogue 218

Bibliography B-1
Author Index AI-1
Subject Index SI-3

"The dead, besides being infinitely more numerous than the living, are infinitely more powerful. They reign over the vast domain of the unconscious, that invisible domain which exerts its sway over all the manifestations of the intelligence and of character. A people is guided far more by its dead than by its living members. It is by its dead, and by its dead alone, that a race is founded. Century after century our departed ancestors have fashioned our ideas and sentiments and in consequence all the motives of our conduct. The generations that have passed away do not bequeath us their physical constitution merely; they also bequeath us their thoughts. The dead are the only undisputed masters of the living. We bear the burden of their mistakes, we reap the reward of their virtues."

—Gustave LeBon: *The Psychology of Peoples*
(Quoted by H. P. Fairchild: *General Sociology*, p. 346)

FOREWORD

Dr. Prabhu's book on "Hindu Social Institutions,"* is, I believe, a serious and scientific account of Hindu social organization. It deals with the many topics of education, marriage, family, the place of women in Hindu society, the system of caste, with accurate learning and great discrimination. To all those who are now engaged in the task of revitalising Hindu practices and renovating Hindu society, the book will be indispensable.

We are today in the midst of a Hindu renaissance, waiting for a new SMRITI, which will emphasize the essentials of the Hindu spirit and effect changes in its forms so as to make them more relevant to the changing conditions of India and the world. Forms which begin by being useful are soon diverted from their objects to which they owe their existence to new ones where they are no longer of any use, where they even become dangerous. The task of the wise reformer is to note the essential spirit of the institutions and reorient them so as to embody it better. For such a task a true understanding of Hindu social psychology and institutions is essential and this book provides us with a key to it.

Calcutta, August 12, 1939

S. RADHAKRISHNAN

---

* Now entitled *Hindu Social Organization*.

Extracts from
PREFACE TO THE FIRST EDITION

The problem and purpose of these studies is explained in the Prologue. In brief, it is an institutional approach to the basic social psychology of the Hindus. A work of this kind is beset with numerous difficulties peculiar to it. The task of separating and sifting the relevant and the pertinent from other material in the numerous Sanskrit texts, the difficulties in the way of correctly grasping the sense of the writers and interpreting the same in terms of contemporary expression without prejudice to the original import, and the proper assimilation and arrangement of the scattered and diffused material, are both time-consuming and labour-exacting. The author is quite conscious of the other shortcomings in this work which may be due to omission of certain aspects or points of view, other than those from which he has proceeded here, from which the Hindu social organization may also be considered in order to make a comprehensive treatise. However, he has tried to make the best of the time and the resources at his disposal, and ventures to publish what may be regarded as the nucleus around which a whole Theory of Social Organization as conceived by the Hindu may be developed and built up in time to come.

In the present work, I have often bracketed the original Sanskrit word or expression along with my translation of the same, so that the reader may judge for himself the appropriateness or relevance of my interpretation. Also, in a few cases, where the full meaning and implications of a Sanskrit term could not be adequately expressed by the English translation into one word or phrase, I have retained the original Sanskrit terms, e.g., *dharma, karma, guṇa* &c. Though I have used available English translations of Sanskrit texts, I have generally sought to give my own translations.

I have tried to avoid repetitions as best as I could; however, in a work connected with complex interpretations like the present one some repetitions became unavoidable, for the same material of statement may lend itself to be viewed from different points of view in different connections or contexts.

It is a matter of great delight for me to acknowledge my intellectual and spiritual indebtedness to my teachers, two of whom I would specially like to mention here: Mr. K. S. Parulekar not only took personal interest in the progress of my studies, but has also always favoured me with his encouragement and counsel. It has always proved instructive and delightful for me to discuss with him various problems of human life and conduct. And I owe a deep debt of gratitude to Dr. N. A. Thoothi for his personal guidance, encouragement, assurance and advice.

My indebtedness to scriptural texts and other writings is indicated specifically in the footnotes throughout the body of the work. Perhaps it could never become possible for an author to trace and identify the various sources from which his knowledge has been gradually derived and built up; and therefore my indebtedness to others must be much greater than I could possibly point out. However, I need hardly say that in regard to the views, interpretations and opinions expressed in the following pages and their shortcomings, the responsibility is entirely mine.

I am deeply grateful to Dr. S. Radhakrishnan for blessing this work with a Foreword, in the midst of and in spite of great pressure of work.

Bombay, September 1939 **PANDHARINATH H. PRABHU**

Extracts from
PREFACE TO THE SECOND EDITION

The book is an attempt, probably the first one of its kind, to discover the essentials of Hindu social thought and organization from a rather wide variety of sources and to coordinate them into a foundation frame-work for a systematic Indian sociology and social psychology. At the time that the book was first published in 1940, the subject of Indian Sociology as such was not accorded any particular attention in our Universities, excepting in one or two in which serious teaching and studies in the subject had already commenced. Since the publication of the book, however, the subject has come into its own as a full and independent paper for study in the graduate and postgraduate classes in many Universities. While the author does not wish to claim credit for the book for this change in outlook and emphasis in our Universities, the systematic presentation of Hindu social thought as attempted in the book has probably given some impetus to that outlook. At the same time, this placed a certain responsibility on the shoulders of the author which prevented him from issuing a mere reprint of the work, when the first edition went out of print some years back, without carefully revising the work. Such revision was delayed, however, from time to time, owing to the intervention of unforeseen circumstances. And now, even though he has been able to bring out this revision, he is only too conscious of the shortcomings that still exist in the work. The subject is rather vast, and perhaps every chapter of the work could be expanded into a book, and some more aspects and issues also could be included in the treatise.

It is perhaps needless to say that our reference to an 'Indian Sociology' should not be taken to imply that we believe in a number of 'sociologies', one each for its country of origin; what we merely mean to imply is that social thought in India has had its own peculiar lines of development which we have attempted to present in this work.

To the critics and readers of the first edition of this book, I am deeply grateful for the keen interest they evinced in the work and the appreciative comments they offered, in some cases spontaneously. He is particularly grateful to Professor Ramchandra D. Ranade, former Professor of Philosophy and Vice-Chancellor at Allahabad University for his kind and personal encouragement; to Professor Rao Bahadur K. V. Rangaswami Aiyengar, former Director of Sri Venkateswara Oriental Institute, Tirupati and Manindra Professor of Indian Culture at Banaras Hindu University, and to the late Professor Edward A. Ross, of Wisconsin University, U.S.A., each for carefully going through the work and sending in details his appraisal of the same.

The author was struck by the reactions which were aroused on the publication of the first edition of the work in the two sections of scholars, the 'orthodox' and the 'reformers'. Both of them have generally appreciated the work, in varying degrees; but some of the former group have tended to think that he has not been as warm and as pronounced as he should have been in upholding Hindu cultural heritage and in denouncing the Western ways; while some from the latter group have felt that he has not been as strong as he should have been in denouncing some of the aspects of our 'old' social behaviour and in pleading for fresh ideas and progress! On his own part, however, the author has never consciously entertained the notion either of upholding or denouncing any ways, Indian or Western, but has tried to present as faithful a portrayal as possible of the Hindu social thought, psychology and organization.

Bombay, April 1954

PANDHARINATH H. PRABHU

PREFACE TO THE THIRD EDITION

Advantage has been taken of the opportunity to bring out a third edition of the work and to make a few modifications in the material. The author is grateful to the readers of the book from various parts of the world who have conveyed their appreciation and comments on it to him. He is particularly beholden to the famous German social scientist, Leopold von Wiese, for honouring the work by writing a special article on it in *KYKLOS: An International Review for Social Sciences* (1955, Fasc. 1, pp. 72–84).

Bombay, December 1958 **PANDHARINATH H. PRABHU**

A WORD ON THE FOURTH EDITION

The present edition includes a few modifications, but mainly remains the same as before. In spite of the keen desire of the author to make a thorough revision, pressure of work has prevented him from undertaking the task.

Errors discovered in the last edition have been corrected in this edition and a few additions have been made.

University School of Psychology,
Education and Philosophy
Gujarat University,
Ahmedabad 9
February 1963

Pandharinath H. Prabhu

ABOUT THE AUTHOR

Pandharinath H. Prabhu studied at the University of Bombay and later in the Universities of Michigan, Pennsylvania, and Columbia in U.S.A.; in Cambridge University in England; and in the Centre d'Etudes et Recherches Psychotechniques in Paris, France. He taught at the Tata Institute of Social Sciences, Bombay; at Gujarat University where he was the first Director of its School of Psychology, Education and Philosophy from 1958–67; as Fulbright Visiting Professor at the Pennsylvania State University in 1961–62; and in the State University of New York at Oswego, N.Y. in 1969–71; as Leverhulme Visiting Professor of Psychology at the Australian National University in 1970; and as Senior Professor of Psychology and Head of the Department of Humanities and Social Sciences at the Indian Institute of Technology, Bombay (1972–75). He was Visiting Fellow at the Indian Institute of Advanced Studies, Simla (1975–77). In 1956–57 he was Senior Research Officer at the UNESCO Research Centre for South and Southeast Asia. In 1963 he was elected President of the Section of Psychology and Educational Sciences of the Indian Sciences Congress, Golden Jubilee Session.

CHAPTER I

PROLOGUE

The present study is an attempt towards constructing a picture of the Hindu social organization and institutions from the point of view of their socio-psychological foundations and implications. It will be the effort of the writer to think out and follow as closely as possible along the lines of the Hindu thought and tradition and to portray and interpret, so far as one can, both analytically and synthetically, the Hindu scriptures and theories in their proper and original perspective and setting.

It may be objected that such a study, which more or less purports to unearth the past, would prove of no use for us of the present age of science and speed. However, even if it is suspected that a study of the past institutions of India is not likely to be helpful towards the organization and control of our present social life, this has to be studied, demonstrated and proved, before the utter uselessness and sure failure of the same can be taken for granted, in the spirit of true science, devoid of prejudice. We believe that such categorical assumptions on the part of social "reformers" are as much dogmatic as are the assumptions of the "orthodox" in regard to their faith in the infallibility of the *Sastras*. For though it is quite true that some of the problems that confront our present day society may not have been even thought of by our forefathers, it is probable that similar if not the same problems may have been faced by them, and the solutions to these, as formulated by them in the past, if not in themselves useful, may at least serve to suggest solutions towards unravelling and management of the problems we have to face today. We may thus be led on to follow our ancestors in principles and spirit, if not in details, to our advantage, particularly if we discover that the spirit which goaded them to social action was inspired by proper and desirable motives and understanding. We may, to say the least about it, learn not to commit the mistakes committed by our kith and kin during the past, if we come to know how and why they came to be committed. Thus, lessons from the past may serve as caution-signals for the future. This in itself would prove to be a sufficiently adequate reward yielded by the careful study of our past social institutions, brought into existence and nurtured by our forefathers to solve the problems of their own times.

This would be, we admit, only a negative result of our study. But there will also be a positive side of such a study which cannot be gainsaid. It may, on the positive side, give us clues to future revision and reconstruction of a social order. For, the study of the past enables us to grasp the fundamental psychology behind the present problems and the attitudes that uphold or reject them due to which it has come to be what it is. We may thus be enabled to make out the causes and circumstances imbedded in the past, which led to the existence and conditions of things and events as they stand today. And, these valuable clues, conditions and causes are sure to prove themselves of great help to us in the making of and planning for our future.

We are sometimes given to regard with disdain and contempt the ideas and ideals of the ancients in the social and moral fields. We are apt to think that each new social problem must be tackled and solved afresh, and that the past is not going to be of the least assistance to us here. We may feel that the "New Generation" has new problems to be faced quite unprecedented by anything to resemble them at any time before, and fresh solutions ought to be invented in order to deal with them. The enthusiastic social worker clamours for introduction of new ideas and ideals in the social and moral fields and insists on cutting off the old ideas and ideals to the root. In this, he is forgetting the great lesson of social psychology, viz., that what has gained the very depths of the soul of a people through ages past is well-nigh impossible to be uprooted at a short notice, sometimes even by efforts carried on for several generations. The people have to be educated, and their minds prepared, for discarding older ideas that have been found to be really harmful; and they thus have to be led gradually and by degrees to favour new ideas. To be able to do this effectively, the social reformer must be able to drive home to the people the actual and real harms and evils, if there are any, wrought by a persisting past. And, there is no better way of doing this than to lay bare before the people their past traditions, trace their roots and growth, and demonstrate their results.

But this is not all. There are reasons why the enthusiastic social reformer should not clamour for introduction of newer ideas and ideals in the moral and social fields every now and then. He could ill afford to forget another great lesson of social history, viz., what has been able to stand the test of time for ages past and is yet alive and has been regulating the social order till this day may have at least some merit in it which is worthy of examination. We cannot resist here the temptation to quote at length a modern sociologist on the value and significance of the past. "The world has been a great experimental laboratory," wrote Professor Carver of Harvard University, "in the moral and social field. A great many 'new discoveries' are made in the field of morals; most of them have no survival value and they perish, or the people who try them perish, which amounts to the same thing. Once in a great while a 'new discovery' is made which happens to work. A new system of morals or a new religion is born which fits its devotees for survival, and a new moral force is introduced into the world. That is, however, a poor argument in favour of adopting every new moral idea which is proclaimed. Most of them really are wrong in principle because they won't work. Only a few have shown any survival value. Most of the 'new' ones have been tried and have been proved unworkable. If we knew as much as our great experimenters in physical science knew, we should learn not to repeat the same failures over and over again. That is one reason why persons with a historical perspective are generally conservative. At least they do not proclaim that they are willing to try anything once. A monkey is willing to do that. A real sociologist knows that many of these so called schemes have already been tried many times and have always failed."

"It is chastening for any group of mortals to know the whole story," Professor Carver proceeds to observe, "because they know then that the way they behave in their land and in their generation is not the only possible way to squeeze satisfaction out of living or necessarily the best way. They acquire a healthy, eager, inquisitive, exploring attitude towards morality. They know that morals must change to keep pace with a changing world. And so they learn the value of moral inventiveness. But they learn, too, that they cannot look very far into the future to see the far flung consequences of change. And so they learn also the value of standing pat by ancient wisdom in the matter of morals, of experimenting with care and circumspection. They know that 'whatever is' in the moral world is not necessarily right; but only possesses an actuarial probability of being right because of the fact that it has survived the best of time,—of moral selection."

On the other hand, "moral innovations we must have if there is to be progress."[1] The main reasons in favour of moral innovations are two: First, the old *mores* may be altogether unsatisfactory and may have always been such in many particulars; or/and secondly, if the human environment changes in terms of culture-contacts, the *mores* need to be modified, altered or even changed for the proper functioning of new life-values. Thus "group ways of behaving have to be altered in order to be continuously adapted to the changing life conditions a group must face."[2]

Therefore, in the present essay, we shall endeavour to visualize in details the basic conditioning factors that ruled not only the earlier phases of Indian culture and civilization, but have gone so deep into the social psychology of the Hindus that they continue to dominate his life and conduct, in a large measure, even to this day. This outlook and method may considerably save us from thoughtlessly rejecting the best of our past heritage; besides, if change is deemed necessary, we may, in the light of the insight thus acquired by us into the intricacies of our cultural fabric and psychology, be enabled to think out, devise, decide upon and adopt ways, conventions, ideas and ideals, new in themselves, yet in harmony with the spirit of the old; and even if a rejection of the old is found necessary, the synthetic attitude of detailed analysis and scrutiny which we adopt in our understanding of the old and the new will contribute a great deal towards an even and wise selection, adoption and assimilation of strange *mores* for the proper rejuvenation and nurture of the life of our people.

Moreover, a study of the social institutions and organization of the Hindus as deduced from their scriptures will give us definite glimpses of what may be called *the ideological and valuational foundations* of those social institutions. For, the *Dharma-Śāstra* and other scriptural literature of the Hindus seeks to deal not only with what is, but also with what ought to be. Not only actual individuals and actual human groups living in a particular country and during a specific period in which they were written, but also ideal individuals and ideal human relationships conceived as true and beneficial for any people, in any age and in any clime, in general and broadly, form the subject matter of the Hindu *Śāstras*. In other words, the Hindu social thinkers have given us *theories* of social institutions and organization, what they should be and ought to be. That is to say, they have thought out and portrayed social and individual ideals. And it is important for us to know this aspect of theorizing done by the Hindu social thinkers. For, it will be then that we shall be able to examine whether and how far the present Hindu social institutions conform to or deviate from their original conceptions and spirit in the actual forms they have assumed today. And, in this manner we may be enabled to grasp the fundamental spirit, the fundamental ideology, in terms of which the Hindu's social institutions were conceived, and thus may be enabled even to mark off the distance and difference between this ideology and the actualities to which the people of India have given existence and shape.

We should like to point out here that most of these basic ideas have been very widely held by all Hindus—the rich as well as the poor, the learned as well as the lay, the city men as well as the village folk. And, it is really astounding to witness this phenomenon in a country, viz., the geographical India (now divided into India and Pakistan) which is a sub-continent by itself and is so vast and varied in geographic conditions, ecology and sub-cultures for centuries past. The total population

[1] T. N. Carver: *The Essential Factors of Social Evolution*, pp. 254–256.

[2] Ibid., p. 256.

of the sub-continent equals that of China; and the population of India alone equals that of U.S.S.R. and the U.S.A. put together.[3] Writing in 1951, Kingsley Davis observed:[4]

"With now over 280 million adherents in geographical India, not to mention a few million in other places, Hinduism holds third place among the world's great religions, being exceeded in numbers only by Christians and Confucianists-Taoists.

"Because of its pervasive influence and its complex nature, there is no single criterion by which Hinduism may be defined. It can be distinguished from other religions only by multiple criteria, most of which are useless for census purposes but which nevertheless give meaning to the census figures. On the level of its *supernatural content* it possesses three outstanding characteristics: first, a doctrine of radical immanence (pantheism) which finds God in everything; second, a tendency toward tolerant syncretism, which allows it to incorporate almost any ritual or deity into its own system; and third, a complex conception of individual destiny, contained in the doctrine of *karma*, reincarnation, and *moksha*. On the level of its *social content*—that is, its manifestation in social behaviour—Hinduism becomes even more distinct. To an exceptional degree it is bound up with a specific social order, the outstanding institutions of which are the caste system, the joint family, and the rural village (themselves mutually related and inter-dependent). Indeed, since it is this order to which its supernatural content refers, the social system forms the fundamental basis of Hindu Unity."

It may also be noted here that according to the last Census taken in 1951 in India, 295 million or 82.7% of the total population of the country live in villages while 61.9 million or only 17.3% live in cities and towns. Again, in terms of population, the Hindu population constitutes about one-eighth of the whole of humanity living on earth.

Sir Herbert Risley, who was the Director of Ethnography and Census Commissioner in India for several years, was struck by this phenomenon and remarked in his book *The People of India*: "These ideas are not the monopoly of the learned; they are shared in great measure by the man in the street. If you talk to a fairly intelligent Hindu peasant about the *Paramātmā, Karma, Māyā, Mukti*, and so forth, you will find, as soon as he gets over his surprise at your interest in such matters, that the terms are familiar to him, and that he has formed a rough theory of their bearing on his own future."[5]

Therefore, the present writer's aim, in the main, will be to describe ideas, ideals and aspirations so as to re-set and reconstruct the several strata of the social structure that have been evolving in Hindu life and conduct. Social institutions will thus reveal themselves as the scaffolding around which the actual modes of living of the Hindus are being built up, organized and replenished from time to time. These social institutions, like anywhere else, have been the outcome of the necessities of life, and have had the advantage of deep social thinking behind them. In this sense, they have come into being neither haphazardly, anyhow, nor by themselves, that is to say, they are not evolved merely in the natural course of things without any deliberative bases. Further, it should not necessarily be presumed that these well thought-out institutions are against the requirements of the natural evolution of social life and institutions. Moreover, these institutions are so *vitally related to each other*, that each of them gathers its place and meaning in terms of specific *inter-relational*

---

[3] Spate, O. H. K.: *India and Pakistan*, 2nd Ed. London; Methuen, 1957, p. 97.

[4] Davis, Kingsley: *The Population of India and Pakistan*, Princeton, New Jersey, Princeton Univ. Pr., 1951, p. 178.

[5] H. Risley: *The People of India*, Thacker Spink & Co., Calcutta, Bombay, & London, 2nd Ed. 1915, p. 244.

values between them. They are devised to enable man, so far as can be, to reduce definite ideas, ideals and purposes into concrete human conduct and affairs. As such, they serve as tools for the best possible unfolding of human capacities, conduct and co-operation. In such series of infinite adjustments between the actual and the ideal, the social thinkers and the law-givers of the Hindus, whatever their failure or success, have been trying more and more to define life, its meaning and end, as also to give man new tools of life, more varied and efficient, in order that they may, by using them, live according to these ideals in actual conduct and affairs, personal and social. It is from such points of view that the problem of the basis and structure of social institutions is considered here, so that the comparative workability of these, their virtues or qualities, their shortcomings and also the causes of these may be located and defined. Along with this, a general estimate of the social system of the Hindus and of the social institutions within it in terms of inter-relations, will be made for the clear and definite apprehension of their life-designs.

While attempting this, it was occasionally found necessary to distinguish the system of the principles governing Hindu social institutions and the ideas and ideals which gave rise to them in comparison with—not mainly in order to seek or assert contradiction with—systems of ideas and ideals other than the Hindu, especially the Western. This is done in view of the fact that India's Social Heritage is being displaced by Western cultural ideals and institutions. Besides, there is a complaint by some contemporary leaders that such rejection of our own culture has been introducing and injecting into our lives, not the best of the culture of the West, but perhaps its worst. There is a great deal of truth in this complaint. But this should not mean that the Western thought, ideals, social structure and psychology are, in the opinion of the present writer, in themselves unworthy or at fault. It only demonstrates the difficulties of absorbing another intricate and historically evolved culture, life and ideas by a historic people through the media of its literature and books, rather than by living in close association and comradeship with the peoples of that culture. Intellectual understanding and fascination of *mores* of other people are admirable; but, by themselves, they prove invariably foreign to the genius of a different people that seek to absorb them.

This does not mean that there should be no cultural assimilation and contact between the peoples of the world. In fact, that is the ideal which has provoked the writer of this work to find out and study the best and the noblest of the Indian heritage in terms of the Indian social institutions and organization and the psychology underlying the same, in order that these may be conserved and preserved at their best, not merely to serve the needs of future Indian life, but also, to whatever extent, guide and direct the life of humanity at large, *so that ultimately with co-operation, goodwill and real mutual understanding, the peoples of the world, East, West, North and South, may one day learn and adopt the best from wherever it comes and by whomsoever it is offered*. It should be understood, therefore, that *the present inquiry is essentially in the nature of self-search, self-chastisement and self-guidance and not of fault-finding with other cultures, systems, valuations and outlooks*. Nor is there any presupposition that culture contact and cultural give-and-take are in themselves unworthy of assimilation. On the other hand, this is an attempt at finding out, in the midst of an anarchy of life-values and medley of points of view which not only India but the whole world has been facing in our days, what and how the thinker of old India has thought about these issues in terms of a Social Psychology, and the social institutions which expressed and served it.

On the other hand, let it be noted that the present writer believes in every people evolving a historical entity of its own, a personality, a genius, a psychology of its own, through which the nature and meaning and purpose of life unfolds itself into the so many facets that go to make the jewels of human existence. It is therefore that the present writer does not see any opposition or contradiction—in fact he does not believe that there need be any opposition or contradiction—between one theory of life and another, between one frame of mind and another, between one set of life-values and another, not only within the orbit of the life of the same people but even between the orbits of the life of different peoples, not only in the same climate but even in different climatic conditions, not only in any single period of history but even in different periods of epochs in history, not only in the same level of culture but even between different levels of culture. In view of this, therefore, this work may be taken as an attempt to provide an analytical and synthetical study of one of these facets, as an humble contribution to assist mutual exchange of thought, towards the making of a system of thought, outlook, life and understanding between the peoples of the world as members of that Great Society called Humanity![6]

* * * *

The sources of the understanding of Hindu social institutions that is attempted here are many and various. These include the Vedic literature, the Epics, the Purānic literature, the Sūtra literature, the drama, the poetry, and the vast store house of folk-tales. It may prove useful at this stage to speak a word about some at least of the sources which are being utilised in the pages that follow.

Two of the most important groups of sources dealing with ideas of great sociological significance are the epics,—*Rāmāyaṇa* and the *Mahābhārata*,—and the *Sūtras*, viz., the *Grihya-Sūtras* and the *Dharma-Sūtras*, or *Dharma-Śāstras*, as they are usually called. As for the *Rāmāyaṇa*, which deals with the earlier epoch, we may say that the best and the noblest of the Hindu traditions and ideals of the times during, before and after it was written, are worked out in the personalities of Rāma, Sītā, Lakshmana, Hanūmān and others. In a sense, this epic is a Hindu Criticism of Life. It is difficult to say how far the original *Rāmāyaṇa* has been making and moulding Hindu life and mind through history; but it is obvious that the Hindi version of Tulsidas and also other versions had and have been having a hold over millions of men and women in India. Rāma is definitely worshipped as an *Avatāra*, an incarnation of God, by them; and his life is considered as mirroring the ideal and the holy and the divine in human life, institutions, ideology, and practices.

The *Mahābhārata* is another work of immense sociological value. Though this epic describes the war fought about 1,000 B.C.,[7] and as such it is mainly concerned with the events connected with two contending families of the Kuru dynasty, it gives minute details and principles concerning the laws, life and conditions which existed and controlled human conscience and destiny during a period much before the war was actually fought. According to some authorities, the epic in its present form was

[6] Cf. The following from Professor Gardner Murphy, an eminent social psychologist of America: "Although we have been looking at cultures which historically belong to peoples with white skin, there is no reason whatever to believe that cultures remain the exclusive or distinctive property of those among whom they have developed. Western ideas and Soviet ideas are penetrating everywhere, and it is to be expected that the ideas of China, India, and of countless other nations will be deeply assimilated by our own descendants in a century or less. Perhaps the family unity and consequent security feelings so characteristic of China and Japan, the sense of oneness with nature so characteristic of India, and many other sources of strength and satisfaction can be viably grafted on into our own make-up."—Gardner Murphy: *Personality—A Bio-Social Approach to Origins and Structure*. New York, Harper & Bros., 1947, pp. 911–12.

[7] See *Camb. Hist. of Ind.*, Ed. by E. J. Rapson, Vol. I, Ch. XIII, p. 307.

being knit up by several writers between about the 4th century B.C., and the 4th century A.D., mainly in accordance with the traditions much older than when it was being written.[8] But the fact that it came to be written finally centuries after the events described therein took place, should justify the contention that at least a part of the background of the social traditions described therein must also belong to contemporary life and thought, that is, to the social conditions, beliefs and practices prevalent during the long period of about a thousand years during which the epic was forming or formed itself. And since 400 A.D. to our own days, the *Mahābhārata* has been and continues to be regarded with high reverence by the Hindu as a great authority on religious, moral and social matters.[9] Indeed, the orthodox Hindus have been regarding it as the fifth *Veda*; and, in view of this, the epic is put at least on the same level of authority as the *Dharma-Śāstras*. In fact, inscriptional evidence proves that it was classed with the *Dharma-Śāstras* as early as the fifth century A.D.[10]

The *Grihya-Śūtras* deal in the main with the domestic conduct and life of the Hindu. On the other hand, the *Dharma-Sūtras*, also known as the *Smritis*, treat mainly of the social conduct and life of the Hindu. Together, the two, mutually considered, prove to be rich sources of information for us with regard to almost every phase of life of the Hindu in the domestic, social, political, economic, moral and religious spheres. Moreover, they deal with almost all the phases of Hindu life as conceived by them. Even the minutest aspects of a Hindu's family life are described and defined by them to a degree that is astounding. Such a wealth of elaborate details is given in these scriptures that there is hardly any phase of human life, day in and day out, as the Hindu conceives it, that is left untouched by them. The *Sūtra* period is placed between about 600 B.C., to 200 B.C.,[11] But as with the *Mahābhārata* so with the *Sūtras*: the descriptions of social living and relationships narrated in these latter works also represent facts relating to a much earlier as well as of much later period, in addition to the conditions during the period in which they were composed. Indeed, many of the practices and injunctions regarding Hindu social life in the *Sūtras* have literally been functioning even in contemporary Hindu life. In fact, the spirit of the *Sūtras* may be said to be governing the general tone and tenor of the domestic and social behaviour of the Hindu, to a large extent, even to this day.

Now, the whole material and moral universe with which the individual has to deal in this world is classified by the Hindu into three big realms, viz., *Dharma, Artha* and *Kāma*, which may be translated, briefly and conveniently, as moral and ideal needs, material needs, and the needs of senses; or the moral, material and the sensual needs of man; or the needs of the soul, the needs of material prosperity, and the psycho-biological needs of the flesh. In modern terminology, these are the three principal motivating forces or urges or drives around which the whole life and conduct of man could be comprehended. And therefore, the management and conduct of his social and individual life is conceived and formulated in terms of these three, with reference to the ultimate end of life viz., *Moksha*.

---

[8] See *Camb. Hist. of Ind.*, Vol. I, Ch. XI p. 258, cf. also Dunber: *A History of India*, p. 32: Winternitz: *A Hist. of Ind. Lit.*, Vol. I (Tr. by Mrs. S. Ketkar).

[9] Says Winternitz: "The very fact that *Mahābhārata* represents a *whole literature* rather than one single unified work and contains so many and so multifarious things, makes it more suited than any other book, to afford us an insight into the deepest depths, of the soul of the Indian people." (*A Hist. of Ind. Lit.*, Tr. by Mrs. S. Ketkar, Vol. I, pp. 326–27).

And Macdonell remarks that the epic has become "so much overgrown with didactic matter that it could hardly be regarded as an epic at all, and has rather taken the place of a moral encyclopaedia in Indian literature (*India's Past*, p. 88).

[10] Macdonell: Ibid., p. 89.

[11] Dunbar: op. cit. p. 33, *Camb. Hist. of India*, Vol. I.

We shall further explain and amplify the meaning and implications of these terms in the next two chapters. In accordance with the division of the problems of life into *Dharma, Artha* and *Kāma*, we have three groups of *Śāstras* or "scientific treatises," each dealing with one of these three life-purposes in the main, viz., the *Dharma-Śāstra*, the *Artha-Sāstra* and the *Kama-Śāstra*; and the whole literature of the Hindu dealing with facts and theories of sociological value could broadly be classified under these three *Śāstras*. It is noteworthy that the consideration and treatment of all the problems under these three headings was undertaken and designated as "*Śāstra*," as a scientific pursuit, by the Hindu thinkers.

Further, as has been opined by Manu, the management and conduct of life should be conceived and formulated in terms of *harmonious co-ordination, or the proportionate aggregate of these three* (*Trivarga*) classes of life-needs, or urges, or principal motives.[12] Therefore, the three kinds of *śāstras* also have to be studied alongside with each other. They are not to be studied as separate and unconnected treatises, but as keys together to the problems of life. Moreover, the literature belonging to *any one of* these three *Śāstras* does not entirely exclude all considerations regarding the *other two*, but only deals with them secondarily. Thus, though the *Dharma-Śāstras*, for instance, deal in the main and in details with the ways and methods of *Dharma*, the other two sides of the problem of living concerning *Artha* and *Kāma* are also touched by them at many places. So it is with the *Artha-Śāstra* and the *Kāma-Śāstra*.

Of these three *Śāstras*, or sciences of life, we have already referred to the *Dharma-Śāstras* and their sociological importance. Among the second kind of these *Śāstras*, viz., the *Artha-Śāstra*, we may here refer to the *Artha-Śāstra* of Kauṭilya as one of the important sources with reference to our problem. This *Artha-Śāstra*, besides generally reasserting the earlier social codes and practices, provides new and important material for clues to understand the social changes that took place in later times. Another invaluable source of information concerning Hindu social life, psychology and civic organization is what is commonly known today as the Sanskrit literature on sex and love, which is classed under the third kind of *śāstras*, viz., the *Kāma-Śāstra*, i.e., Science of Sex.[13] Amongst the treatises on *Kāma-Śāstra*, Vātsyāyana's *Kāma-Sūtra* is perhaps the most authoritative and valuable for our purposes. This treatise attempts to give detailed information about the psychology of sex, and also such social themes as the life of the citizen (*Nāgaraka*) and his duties, and the position of woman in the Hindu family and society.

In the pages that follow, I have tried to understand and fathom the principles of living governing Hindu social mind and institutions based upon the above-named and also other important sources in the Sanskrit literature. One very surprising fact in this connection is that these various sources so generally agree with each other on fundamental facts and issues of social significance. Differences

---

[12] *Man*. ii. 224.

[13] That most eminent student and erudite scholar of the psychology of sex, Havelock Ellis, remarks that "in India sexual love has been sanctified and divinized to a greater extent than in any part of the world. 'It seems never to have entered into the heads of the Hindu legislators' said Sir William Jones long since, (*Works*, vol. ii, p. 311), 'that anything natural could be offensively obscene, a singularity which pervades all their writings, but is no proof of the depravity of their morals.' The sexual act has often had a religious significance in India, and the minutest details of the sexual life and its variations are discussed in Indian erotic treatise in a spirit of gravity, while nowhere else have the anatomical and physiological sexual characters of women been studied with such minute and adoring reverence. 'Love in India, both as regards theory and practice', remarks Richard Schmidt (*Beitrāge zur Indischen Erotik*, p. 2). 'possesses an importance which it is impossible for us (Westerners) even to conceive'."

—*Studies in the Psychology of Sex*, Random House, New York 1936, Vol. IV, p. 129.

between them, if and when any, are not only few, but they concern themselves only regarding points of minor details. And, these differences can be usually traced to historical or regional causes.

* * * *

In any discussion on the social organization and institutions of a people with reference to their ideological and psychological foundations, it would prove valuable to start with the most general of their ideas and views concerning "existence" itself. Thereafter, we may profitably attempt to grasp the fundamental ideas and ideals which govern the life of the individual in a society. This may enable us to understand the fundamental or basic psychology behind its social institutions; for the social institutions are founded more or less on the framework of the proposed or visualized solution to the problem of living. In view of this, we shall first deal generally with the Hindu view of life upon which the Hindu social institutions have been erected (Ch. ii).

Thereafter, we shall consider the Hindu way of regarding the course of an individual's normal span of life with reference to the society from the point of view of the basic ideas of existence. Here we find that man's life is conceived by the Hindu in terms of four specific stages, each of which is viewed as preparatory, not merely to the one that follows, but also to all the rest that follow it (Ch. iii). Thus, the first stage has to be conceived as preparatory not only to the three stages that follow, nor also to the living and understanding and idealization of life as a whole, but also to the meaning, place and function of this life with reference to existence before and after death. These stages are known as *Āśramas*, the first being called the *Brahmacharyāśrama* . It is connected with the system of education. It is therefore proper that the institution of education should be taken next into account before considering other institutional tools of life. In view of this, Hindu educational practices and ideals and the psychology underlying them will be our next concern (Ch. iv).

Following the lead of the *Āśrama* scheme as part of the Hindu view of life, we next propose to discuss the problem of marriage (Ch. v) which lays the foundation of the third *Āśrama*, the *Grihasthāśrama* (i.e., of the life of a family leader). And the normal consequences of marriage would be the formation of family, the care of *Grihasthāśrama*, not merely as a biological necessity, but also as a well thought-out social institution, shaped, organised and idealized by human effort, ingenuity and wisdom for ages past; so our discussion on marriage will be followed by the consideration of the institution of the family (Ch. vi).

This will naturally bring us face to face with the problem of the attitude of the Hindu towards the woman, which must be considered in the next chapter (Ch. vii). Along with this, we shall also discuss the views of Hindu social thinkers on the problem and the psychology of sex and love.

Thereafter we deal with the much vexed problem of *Varna* organisation, which has a special bearing on the Hindu social order (Ch. viii). And finally, we shall conclude our survey with a few observations, in the light of the preceding discussion on the several aspects of Hindu social organization and institutions (Ch. ix).

CHAPTER II

THE BASES OF HUMAN RELATIONS
The Problem of Existence and Its Implications

Yo devo'gnau Yo'psu
Yo Viśvam bhuvanamāviveśa
Ya oshadhīshu Yo vanaspatishu
Tasmai devāya ṇamo namah
—*Śvetāśvataropanishad*, II. 17

To the Divinity
That pervades Fire,
That dwells in water,
That penetrates the entire Universe,
To Him
That lives in medicinal herbs,
That pours life into plants
To that Shining One
I offer salutations,
I bow in reverence.

It has been generally assumed and often asserted that the ancient Hindus so much lost themselves in speculating over the abstract metaphysical problems of the ultimate nature of worldly things, that they never exerted any serious thinking in connection with the more practical and worldly problems, like those of social organization. During recent times, however, with the appearance of scholarly European, American and Indian studies in the Hindu lore of the bygone times, it is generally accepted that the Hindus did carry on a great deal of systematized speculation, apart from the purely metaphysical one, in the realms of Mathematics, Astronomy, Astrology, Engineering, Chemistry, Medicine, Grammar, Politics, Logic, Poetics, and Science of Rhetoric.* Yet, it is usually alleged, that amongst certain other intellectual pursuits, Science of Society as such did not engage the attention of the Hindu thinker. It is our purpose here to demonstrate that, in fact, they had given considerably serious attention to the problems connected with social organization, and

* See ch. iv below.

had evolved a system or scheme of social relations for securing the best possible organization of human life and conduct that they could think of. And this we are doing not primarily with a view to vindicating the Hindu thinker's capacities and achievements in this direction, but in order to discover the roots of the Hindu's social institutions and organization, without the knowledge of which no social reform and reconstruction is really possible, and also in order to see if there are any fruitful suggestions discoverable for such reform and reconstruction. The actual working out of these suggestions into a well rounded social plan to fit in with and suit modern conditions of living is a huge task by itself; and it will not be undertaken here. Nevertheless, if and when any light is possible in this direction, that in itself should be a worthwhile objective in undertaking a study of the Hindu's social heritage, such as is attempted here.

All forms of social organization, including the various social institutions, emerge out of human needs. The human needs define human interests, purposes and aspirations; and, the actual planning or devising of the different forms of social organization takes place in terms of the adjustments of human behaviour, individual and social, with these purposes and aspirations. The Hindu conception of life and its conduct, social as well as individual, is also organised in view of these considerations. And, the formation of this organization is based upon an understanding of the meaning of human existence, its needs and interests and a consequent scheme for conducting human life in accordance with that meaning. The fundamental meaning of life and existence as understood by the Hindu permeates through all the forms of social organization which are intended to regulate and direct the conduct of the individual's life. Therefore, our first task here will be to narrate and try to understand the Hindu's fundamental conceptions regarding human existence as a whole, and its purposes, its aspirations and its mission as defined in terms of these fundamental conceptions, in order that we may be able to visualize, against a proper background, the right perspective of the Hindu scheme of social organization as it has come to be formulated and as it is meant to function. We propose to state, in this chapter, this fundamental view of life as conceived by the Hindu, with reference to some of the treatises which have preserved his ancient lore and which are regarded by him as authoritative guides for the direction and management of human life and human affairs.

According to the Hindu, this life merely by itself alone would have no meaning; it has meaning only as a link,—even if the last,—in a chain of links of births in the past and in the future; it is a stage of transition from past births towards future birth or births, unless *Mokśa* or 'final liberation' is obtained within the span of this life. And, essentially, the birth of a human being is but an opportunity for him or her to free himself or herself from the bonds of this chain of births by living a life of *Dharma*,[1] as laid down by a succession of the "liberated ones" (*Muktas*) in the *Śāstras* i.e. Scientific Treatises expounding principles of *Dharma*. The soul of a man is, for the Hindu, immortal; the bodies in which he lives during the stages of transition may change. This fundamental idea persists through the whole of the Hindu lore,—from the *Vedas* to the *Samhitas*, thence to the Brahmanas, to the *Āranyakas*, the *Upanishads*, the *Sūtras*, the *Smritis*, the Epics, (viz., the *Rāmāyaṇa* and the *Mahābhārata*), the *Nitis*, the *Purāṇas*, and even the drama, the poetry, the folk-lore, with minor modifications and additions of details.

[1] The social psychological and philosophical implications of this term will become clearer as the reader proceeds through this and the next chapter, to a great extent; in a sense, however, this whole work seeks to expound the full meaning of *dharma* only.

To start with, the *Vedas* give the first form to the idea that the soul of man is immortal, though the body may be burnt away after death. In *Rigveda*-IV, 35.3, the Ribhus are described to have attained immortality (*amritattva*). At another place (RV.V.4.10) there is a prayer to Fire (*Agni*) for granting *amritattva*. In the tenth mandala of the *Rigveda*, Agni is invoked (X.16 1–6) to take the deceased to the Fathers and the Gods. And, lastly, there is an interesting *Mantra* in this *maṇḍala* (X.58. 1–2.) wherein the soul which has gone to the World of Death is recalled; and it is asked to enter into another body once more. In *Rigveda*, 1, 164.31, also, we have a mention of the notion that the soul of the dead returns frequently to this earth. In the *Atharvaveda*, this idea of the transmigration of the soul is visualized in such a realistic manner that the deceased is said to meet, after death, the souls of his wives and children (AV.xii.3.17), and his friends and parents (*Ibid*. vi. 120.3) who had died before him.[2] There is also a reference to personal immortality in the *Vedas*—a person who performs a sacrifice may be born in the next world with his entire body (*sarvatanuh*).[3]

The *Brāhmaṇas* carry the idea further. A person who practises austerities (*tapas*) retains in heaven all his bodily functions, even those concerned with the sex life (*maithuna*).[4] In the *Śatapatha Brāhmaṇa* we find a first clear statement of the theory of *Karma*, of retributive action; a sage called Bhrigu is shown the tortures which wicked persons have to undergo in hell for their foul deeds on earth.[5] "Whatever food a man eats in this world, by that same again is he eaten in the next".[6] Here is also the first statement that one who gains complete knowledge becomes one with Brahman, the highest universal principle, and is thus liberated.[7]

Again, there is the story of Nachiketa who was shown over by Yama all the abodes where the dead reap the fruits of their deeds done in this world.[8]

This germ of the idea of the immortality of the soul, coupled with the law of the deed and its retribution (*karma-phala*) is further developed in the *Upanishads*. Here, there is a clear statement of the theory of the re-birth of a soul as a result of the fruition of his deeds (*karma-phala*). The story of Nachiketa, just referred to above, is also found in the *Kathopanishad;* here the idea that the soul of the dead takes up a new body is given a clear expression. "The mortal being decays like a corn; and like a corn it is born again."[9] The *Brihadāraṇyakopanishad* says that the soul, at death, moves out and is accompanied by the person's accumulations of all actions (*karmāśaya*) during his life-time; and this *karmāśaya* determines the form which the soul has to take in the next birth.[10]

Here, in this *Upanishad*, is given an account of the symposium of several philosophers on questions of metaphysical interest. For instance, when questioned as to what happens to the soul after death, Yājnavalkya replies that man's further life is determined by his own actions (*karmas*), good actions bringing good results, and bad ones, bad results.[11] "As a caterpillar leaves the end of

---

[2] See also AV. vi, 120 I; xii, 2, 45; xviii, 3, 71; xviii, 4–9–10; and *Vājasaneya Samhitā*, xviii, 51; for this idea of transmigration of the soul.

[3] Rv. iv. 6, 1, 1; xi, 1, 8, 6; xii, 8, 3, 31; AV. xi, 3, 32 & 49.

[4] *Śat. Br.* x, 4, 4, 4.

[5] *Śat. Br.* xi, 6, 1.

[6] *Śat. Br.* xii, 9, 1, 1.

[7] *Śat. Br.* xi, 5, 6, 9; cf., Ibid xi, 4, 4, 1; iii, 10, 9, 11.

[8] *Taitt Br. iii, 11, 8, 1, ff.*

[9] *"sasyamiva martyah pchyate sasyamiva jāyate punah," Kaṭhop* i, I, 5–6.

[10] iii, 2, 13; and iv, 4, 2–6; also cf. *Chhāndo*, iii, 14, 1.

[11] *Brih. Up.* iii, 2, 13; *puṇyo vai puṇyena karmaṇā bhavati pāpah pāpena.*

one blade of grass only after it has secured its hold on another, so does this self (*ātmā*) leave the human body only after it has found out another tenement in another kind of existence; and as a goldsmith, taking a piece of gold, turns it into whatever newer and more beautiful shape he pleases, so does this self create for itself a newer and more beautiful existence, be it in the existence of the manes (*pitryam*), of the demi-gods (*gandharvam*), of the gods or of any beings that it pleases".[12] About rebirth according to one's own *Karmas*, the *Brihadāraṇyakopanishad* says: "As the soul moves out, life (*prāṇa*) moves out; as the life moves out, all the vital airs (*prāṇa*) move out after it;" his knowledge and actions and his consciousness of former births and deeds (*pūrvaprajnā*) follows him.[13] And again, "As his conduct and behaviour, so does this self (*ātmā*) become. He whose deeds have been good becomes good; he whose deeds have been evil becomes evil (*pāpah*). By the holy deeds, he becomes holy; by sinful ones, sinful. It is for this reason that they say that a person consists merely of desires (*kāma*); as his desire is so his will (*kratuh*); as his will so his deed (*karma*); as his deed, so his evolution"[14] The remedy against the cycle of deeds and births lies in becoming completely free from desire: "When a mortal man becomes free from all desires (*kāmāh*) that are after his heart, mortal as he is, he nevertheless becomes immortal (*a-mritah*) and achieves the *Brahman*".[15] So long as the person is committed to *karmas*, he must be born again. Those of good conduct (*ramaṇīya-charaṇā*) will be born as Brāhmaṇas, Kshatriyas or Vaiśyas, while those of bad conduct (*kapūya-charaṇāh*) will be born as dogs, swines or chāṇḍālas.[16] The *Kaushītaki Upanishad* goes further, and states that a soul, according to his actions and knowledge (*yathā-karma yathā-vidyam*), will take on the body of a worm, a moth, a fish, a bird, a leopard, a lion, a serpent, or man, or of any creature for that matter.[17] And the *Kaṭhopanishad* goes still further and declares that a soul may even take the form of inanimate things like plants or trees according to his deed and knowledge (*yathā-karma yathā-śrutam*[18]).

Thus the *Vedas* and the *Āraṇyakas* start with the idea of the immortality of the soul (*ātman*), though the body taken up by him is mortal and perishable. They also take the view that the soul of a person suffers in the next birth or enjoys, according as his doings in this world are bad or good. The *Upanishads*, as we saw, go even further and say that after the death of one body, the soul takes another body according to his deeds; he may even have to take to comparatively inanimate existence of trees and plants, if his deeds merit these! Freedom from this tangle of birth and death, however, can be attained by a soul with the help of the performance of proper worship and sacrifices. Such worshipper attains the region of the deity whom he has worshipped, according to one Upanishad;[19] while according to another, he achieves a complete likeness (*paramam sāmyam*) with God (*Īśam*),[20] he merges into the personality of the Divine and becomes one with it,[21] just as a river flows into

[12] *Brih. Up*. iv, 4, 3–5 (Belvalkar and Ranade's Tr., *Hist. of Ind. Phil*. p. 206).
[13] *Brih. Up*. iv, 4, 2.
[14] *Brih. Up*. iv, 4, 3–5; Ramade's Tr., *A Constructive Survey of Upanishadic Philosophy*, p. 155.
[15] *Brih. Up*. iv. 9–7, Ibid, p. 136.
[16] *Chhānd. Up*. v, 10, 7: (*śvayonim vā sūkarayonim vā chāṇḍālyonim vā*).
[17] *Kaushī. Up*. 1, 2; cf. also *Chhānd. Up. vi*. 9, 3.
[18] *Kāṭh. Up*. ii. 5, 7.
[19] (*śa ya evam etad rājanam devatāsu protam veda etāsām eva devatānām salokatām sārshṭitām sāyujyam gachchhati*)—*Chhānd. Up*. 11, 20, 2.
[20] *Muṇḍ. Up*. iii, 1, 3.
[21] Ibid. iii. 2, 7–8.

the sea, loses its name and form, and becomes one with the sea.[22] To attain this end of entering the Universal Principle (*Sarvam*) is possible for those who have renounced all passion (*vīta-rāgāh*), and who have attained peace of mind (*praśāntā*) and knowledge (jnāna-triptāh[23]).

Later literature, starting with these ideas, developed them into a whole philosophy of the *Karma* theory. Let us now see how the development of the *Karma* theory takes place, and what it implies for the Hindu.

Among the many Sanskrit works of sociological value,[24] the *Mahābhārata* grapples with the problem of *karma* along similar lines. In the *Vanaparva* section there is a long description of the blessings and enjoyments obtainable in Paradise (*svarga*): "This earth is meant for work (*karma-bhūmi*), while the next world is meant for enjoying its rewards (*phala-bhūmi*)". As soon as the rewards in proportion to deeds (*karma*) are enjoyed, the individual falls from heaven. Moreover, beyond the next world of enjoyment, there is the eternal abode (*sanātanam padam*) known as *parabramha* from whence there is no return to this world; but that could be attained only by the unselfish (*nir-mamāh*), the humble (*nir-ahankārāh*), those who have restrained their senses (*samya-tendriyāh*) and attained complete knowledge.[25] "A creature is bound by deeds (*karma*); he is liberated by knowledge (*vidyā*); by knowledge he becomes eternal, imperceptible and undecaying. Some men of little understanding eulogise *karma*, so they embrace with delight the entanglements of corporeal existence; but those who have achieved a perfect comprehension of *dharma (dharmanaipuṇa-darśinah)* do not commend *karma*, as a person drinking from a river thinks little of a well."[26] The soul (*ātman*) "is born again with its accumulated load of *karma*."[27] And, it is in consequence of a life of *karma* that one obtains pleasure and pain (*sukhadukkhe*), prosperity and adversity (*bhavā 'bhavau*); by knowledge he reaches that condition in which there is no suffering, no death, no birth and no rebirth.[28] "The acts done in the former births never leave any creature. In determining the various effects of *karma*, the Creator did see them. Man, being under the influence of *karma*, must always consider how he can atone for his *karma* and how he can extricate himself from an evil doom."[29]

The law of *karma*, moreover, explains why sometimes persons who should evidently deserve happiness and success in life as judged by their deeds in this life nevertheless meet with failures and unhappiness, while sometimes the undeserving seem to succeed. The most intelligent and diligent (*dakśāś cha mati-mantāś cha*) man may get failures in spite of great exertions during this life, but that is as a result of his past *karmas*, while the wicked during this life may seem to enjoy a happy life in this world.[30] The sage Brihaspati explains to Yudhishṭhira that after death, a man's virtuous and vicious *karmas* follow him and determine his fate in the next birth; one should, therefore, try to acquire *dharma* which alone is one's true friend in the next world, and which determines his happiness and sorrow in the next birth.[31] Nay, it determines even the particular kind of existence

[22] *Praśn. Up*. vi, 5.

[23] *Muṇḍ Up*. iii, 2, 5.

[24] *See ch. i.*

[25] *Mahā*. Vanaparva. 260, 36 (Krishnacharya's Ed.)

[26] *Mahā*. xii, 8810 ff. (—Muir: *Ori. Sans. Texts*).

[27] *Mahā Vana*. 208. 31.

[28] *Mahā*. xii, 8810 ff. Muir, op. cit.

[29] *Mahā. Vana*. 207, 19–20 (Dutt's Tr.).

[30] *Mahā. Vana*. 208, 9–12 (Dutt's Tr.).

[31] *Mahā. Anu*. 111, 11–18.

which he has to take; for the wicked may be born again as dogs, asses, worms and their like.[32] Decrepitude and death are the devourers of all creatures,—the strong as well as the weak, the tall as well as the short, except those who can escape re-birth. The soul only is eternal.[33] Every person therefore should try to attain the liberation of his soul (*mokśa*); for this world is full of difficulties and shortcomings.[34] "Whatever (*kinchit hi*) one does, he is sure to reap the fruit of his own actions. The consequences of *karma* can never be erased (*nāsti kritasya nāśah*) . . . Men's actions follow them. It is due to the influence of these *karmas* that they are born again and again.[35] Man's *karmas*, again, may be either good or evil (*śubham* or *a-śubham*), and, he is sure to reap as he sows. The people who are ignorant of this law of *karma*, severely abuse the higher powers when they are unlucky; for they do not know that their ill luck is the result of their own evil *karmas*.[36] None can be the dispenser of his own destiny according to his sweet will; the *karmas* done in the former life are seen to produce fruits in this life (*iha siddhih pradriśyate*).[37] Liberation from this cycle of births and deaths and its accompanying happiness and sorrow can be achieved when there is no more *karma*. And, to attain this end, all desire (*vāsanā*) must come to an end.[38] Moreover, what is expected to give happiness may give you grief; therefore one should try not to be swayed either by the joys or sorrows of this life.[39] "If objects of desire are renounced, they become sources of happiness; the man who follows objects of desire is ruined in that pursuit."[40] "Neither the happiness which is derived from a gratification of the senses, nor that great happiness which one may enjoy in heaven, comes up equal to even a sixteenth part i.e., a small fraction of the happiness which originates from the extermination of all desires."[41] The fulfilment of one desire leads to another desire; and so, an unending series of desires and their consequent *karmas* is created. "Contentment does not come from an acquisition of the objects of desire. The thirst for acquisition is only further increased by each fresh acquisition, like fire with new fuel thrown into it."[42] The most effective way to end the life of *karmas* is, therefore, to end all desire (*vāsanā*). Desire has its origin in the actual experience of the pleasures of the senses, touch, sight or hearing.[43] One who has never actually experienced the enjoyment given by an object, never feels the desire for that object.[44] "Therefore, to acquire happiness, a man should vow not to taste, not to touch and not to see".[45]

Here, therefore, we have in an extreme form the idea of attaining liberation (*mokśa*), from the otherwise unending cycle of birth or death, by cultivating a sense of complete detachment from worldly objects. But, the *Mahābhārata* also suggests another way of *mokśa*; and that is by following the way of one's own appointed duties (*sva-dharma*). Says Bhīshma, that universally respected

[32] Ibid. 43–130.
[33] *Mahā. Śānti*. 320, 12–13.
[34] *Mahā. Śānti*. 174, 5.
[35] *Mahā. Vana*. 208, 27–28.
[36] *Mahā. Vana*, 208, 5–7.
[37] *Mahā. Vana*. 208, 22.
[38] *Mahā. Śānti*. 174, 45, ff.
[39] Ibid.
[40] *Mahā. Śanti*. 174, 47.
[41] *Mahā. Śanti*. 174, 48.
[42] *Mahā. Śanti*. 180, 26.
[43] Ibid. 180, 30.
[44] Ibid.
[45] *Mahā. Śanti*. 180, 33.

wise man, brave soldier, and seer of the *Mahābhārata*: "The *dharmas* ordained with regard to every mode of life (meaning the different *āśramas*, about which we shall speak in the next chapter) are capable, if well performed, of leading one to heaven and to the highest fruition of Truth (*satya-phalam*). *Dharma* has numerous ways of expression (*sarva-dvāra*) and none of the practices (*kriyā*) enjoined by them fails (*viphalā*) to produce the desired effect".[46]

The dialogue between the "Dutiful Hunter" (*Dharma-vyādha*) and the Brāhmaṇa, is quite instructive in this respect.[47] The Brāhmaṇa, a man of the highest caste, had gone to this Dharma-vyādha, who was a hunter by profession, a man of lowest caste, to learn the ways of *Dharma* because despite his low birth, the latter was scrupulously observing his duties, and so deserved respect even from a Brāhmaṇa. The hunter explains how it is impossible for any person to live without doing any *karma*: Every one of us is doing something or the other every moment of his life. Even the commandment of *Ahimsā*—"not to kill any creature"—is difficult to be obeyed fully. "Man kills innumerable (tiny and imperceptible) animals that live on the ground (for instance) by trampling over them by their feet. Even wise and learned men kill many animals in various ways, when sleeping or resting. The earth and the sky are full of animal organisms which are unconsciously killed by man due to ignorance. "Do not kill"—this commandment was ordained in the days of yore by men who did not know the real facts of existence. . . Any number of things can be said as regards the *dharma* and *adharma* of our actions (*karma*). But (one thing is certain, viz., that) he who adheres to his *Dharma* (*sva-dharma-nirato*) acquires great fame".[48] Therefore, doing one's own duty (*niyata-karma*) properly, in accordance with one's *Dharma*, even if it happens to be that of killing, is also an effective way, according to the *Mahābhārata*, of attaining salvation (*mokśa*).

The soul of a man, says the Dutiful Hunter further to the Brāhmaṇa, is born again and again with its accumulated load of *karma*—the virtuous ones (*śubha-krit*) in virtuous existences (*śubha-yoni*) and the sinful ones (*papa-krit*) in sinful existence (*papa-yoni*).[49] Destiny (meaning the effect of his past *karmas* here) is all powerful (*vidhis-tu balavaān*), and it is difficult (*dus-taram*) to overcome the consequences of our past actions (*purá kritam*). His own birth in the profession of a hunter, says the Dharma-vyādha, was the fault (*dosha*) of his *karma* due to the sins committed in a former life.[50] But he would not therefore abandon the *karmas* which were proper to his profession. To abandon one's own duties (*sva-dharmam*) here in this world, is considered to be sinful; to stick to one's own *karmas* (*sva-karma-niratah*) is certainly in keeping with the *dharma*.[51] And, *karma* carried out in this manner, i.e., in accordance with one's *dharma* does not stick to or pollute the individual, even though the *karma* happens to be that of killing an animal as the case was with the Dharma-vyādha. For, as the now enlightened Brāhmaṇa said to him at the end of the conversation: "These wicked deeds being the duties of your profession, the stain of evil *karma* (*karma-doshah*) will not attach to you."[52] Men of little understanding (*alpa-buddhayah*) are overpowered with grief at heart on the occurrence of something which may not be agreeable to them, or at the non-occurrence of

---

[46] *Mahā.Śānti*. 353, 2.

[47] In *Vanaparva, Adhy*. 207.

[48] *Mahā. Vana*. 207, 30–39.

[49] Ibid. *Vana*. 208, 31.

[50] Ibid. *Vana*. 207, 2.

[51] Ibid. *Vana*. 207, 18.

[52] Ibid. 215, 11–12.

something which may be much desired by them.[53] However, nothing could be achieved by merely grieving over such things; on the contrary, it makes one all the more miserable.[54] Those wise men (*manīshiṇah*) whose knowledge has made them happy and contented (*jnāna-triptāh*) and who are indifferent both to happiness and to misery are only really happy; the foolish (*mūḍhāh*) are always discontented, the wise (*panditah*) always feel contentment (*santosham*).[55] There is no end to discontent; contentment (*tushṭih*), on the other hand, is the highest happiness (*paramam sukham*).[56] The man who becomes overpowered with dejection (*vishādah*) and whose energies abandon him when an occasion for displaying vigour presents itself, has no manliness in him (*purushārthah*).[57] The effect (*phalam*) of our actions performed by us must necessarily (*avaśyam*) manifest itself; however, no good is accomplished by giving oneself up to self-disparagement (*nirvedam*).[58] Instead of grumbling (*a-śochan*) one should try to find out the means (*upāyam*) by which one can be freed from all misery (*duhkha*).[59] The means to do this, as the Dharma-vyādha himself has pointed out above, is to follow *sva-dharma* during life.

Now even though, in general, the Hindu regards *Dharma* as the body of principles derived from *Śruti, Smriti* and *Purāṇa (śruti-smriti-purānokta*), it has been always recognised by him also that the nature of *dharma* is extremely complex; and though greatest thinkers have given their best attention to the understanding and elucidation of its principles and its manifestations, it has been also recognised that they have not been completely successful in giving a final and full account of *dharma*. It is admittedly a subtle (*sūkśma*) principle, and we mortals are not likely to understand all its ramifications (*gatim*).[60] Even the *Śrutis* differ from each other in their exposition of *dharma;* nor could we accept the word of anyone of the wise Sages as the sole authority (*pramāṇa*); indeed, the basic principles of *dharma* are unfathomably deep and so, for all practical purposes, the average man should generally follow what the great (*mahā-jana*) are doing.[61] One who, by his action, attitude and speech, shows that he has always everybody else's wellbeing at his heart and is also constantly engaged in the welfare of all others, can be said to have understood *dharma*.[62]

Before proceeding to expound *dharma*, Manu characterizes it as "that which is followed by the well-versed (*vidvān*) and accepted whole-heartedly by the good men who are ever immune to

---

[53] Ibid. 215, 18.
[54] Ibid. 215, 21.
[55] Ibid. 215, 21–22.
[56] Ibid. 215, 23.
[57] Ibid. 215, 25.
[58] Ibid. 215, 26.
[59] Ibid. 215. 27.
[60] *sūkśmo dharmo mahārāja nāsya vidmo gatim vayam*—*Mah. Ādi*. 195, 29.
bahudhā driśyate dharma śukśma eva dvijottama.—Ibid. Vana. 206–42.
[61] *tarko'partishṭhah śrutayo vibhinnā naiko munir yasya matam pramāṇam.*
dharmasya tattvam nihitam guhāyām mahājano yena gatah sa panthāh.
—*Mahābhārata*.

cf. *brikad dvārasya dharmasya sūkśmā duranugā gatik*
tasmād avāchyo kyekena bahujnenāpi samśaye—Baudh.
[62] *sarveshām yah suhrin nityam sarveshām cha hite ratah*
karmaṇā manasā vāchā sa dharmam veda Jājale.—*Mahā-Śānti*. 261–9.

feelings of hatred and disaffection towards others".[63] One who desires perfect or pure *dharma* to be realized must first fully understand not only the *śāstras* which have many aspects (*vividha*) but must also comprehend the realities of the situation coupled with inferential reasoning.[64] He alone, and no other man, can be said to have understood *Dharma*, who explores or interprets the utterances of the sages (*āshram*) and the directives of *dharma* (in the *śāstras*) by modes of reasoning (*tarka*) which is not contrary to the Vedic lore (*Veda-Śāstra*).[65] Says Brihaspati, in regard to *dharma*: No decision should be taken by mere resort to a (letter of the) *śāstras*; for, deliberations (*vichāra*) devoid of rational considerations (*yukti-hīna*) will lead to results detrimental to *dharma*.[66] And the *Mahābhārata* exhorts that in determining *dharma* and *dharma* the learned man should rely upon intelligent understanding (*buddhi*) of the situation.[67]

Every *dharma*-knowing person (*dharma-jna*), however, should steer clear of the confusion between one's *dharma* and other manifestations of *dharma*, like *vi-dharma, para-dharma, dharma-ābhāsa, upa-dharma* and *chhala-dharma*, because these aught to be considered as bad as *a-dharma* itself, so far as *his* goals and ideals are concerned. Thus, *vi-dharma* is anything that is contradictory to one's own *dharma; para-dharma* is *dharma* which is laid down for others (unlike him), not meant for oneself; *upa-dharma* consists of doctrines opposed to established morals (*pākhaṇḍa*) or of hypocrisy (*dambha*); while *chhala* is the type or form which is *dharma* in name only, not in truth.[68] What a man does to satisfy his own sweet will is *dharmābhāsa* in so far as it may be different from the *dharma* of his own *āśrama* (i.e. the order or stage of life in which he is living). Indeed, how is it possible at all that one may fail to obtain peace as long as one is following the *dharmas* which are laid down so as to be in accordance with one's own natural tendencies and aptitudes (*svabhāva-vihitah*)?[69]

And here we embark upon another important issue,—an issue which is constantly facing every human being so often in his life, and yet, on which, so far no completely satisfactory answer has

---

[63] *vidvadbhih sevitah sadbhih nityam adveshar āgibhih*
hridayenābhyanujnāto yo dharmas tam nibodhata.
—*Manu*. II. 1.

[64] *pnatyakśam chānumānam cha śāstram cha vividhāgamam*
tyayam suviditam kāryam dharmaśuddhim abhipsitā.
—*Manu*. XII. 105.

[65] *ārsham dharmopadeśam cha vedaśāstrāvirodhinā*
yas tarkeṇānusamdhatte sa dharmam veda netarah.
—*Manu*. XII. 106.

[66] *kevalam śāstram āśritya na kartavyo vinirṇayah*
yuktihine vichāre tu dharmahānih prajāyate—Brih.

[67] *tasmāt kaunteya vidushā dharmādharma-viniśchaye*
buddhim āsthāya loke'smin vartitavyam kritātmanā
—*Mahā-Śānti*. 141, 102.

[68–69] *vidharmah paradharmaś cha ābhāsa upamā chhalah*
adharma-śākhā panchemā dharmajno'dharmavat tyajet
dharmābādho vidharmah syāt paradharmo'nyachoditah
upadharmas tu pākhaṇḍo dambho vā śabdabhich-chhalah
yastvichchhayā kritah pumbhir ābhāso hyāśramāt prithak
svabhāva-vihito dharmah kasya neshṭah praśāntaye?
—*Bhāg. Purā*. vii. 15.

been offered by any social thinker,—viz., how far life is governed by fate or destiny (*daiva*) and/or how far by one's own effort or exertion (*purusha-kāra*)? The Hindu thinker's attempts to deal with this problem are highly interesting.

Yudhisṭhira desired to know which of the two—*daiva* or *purushakāra*—was more powerful (*śreshṭhataram*); and for an adequate answer to this problem, he turned to the most learned (*mahā-prājna*) Bhīshmapitāmaha who was well-versed in all the *śāstras* (*sarva-śāstra-viśāradah*).[70] In answer to the query, Bhīshma narrates the discourse between the God Brahman himself and Vasishṭha, a Sage, on the same topic.[71] One's own efforts or strivings or exertions (*purusha-kāra*), says Brahman, are like the seed (*bījam*) while destiny or fate (*daiva*) is comparable to the soil (*kśetram*); and the harvest (*sasyam*) thrives from the union of the two (*samyogāt samriddhyate*[72]). Just as without the seed, the soil though tilled does not yield any fruit, similarly without human effort, destiny does not get fulfilled (*na siddhyati*[73]). Nothing can ever be gained by depending upon fate only by a person who lacks the will to make efforts (*a-kritātmanā*); on the other hand everything (*sarvam*) can be (ultimately) attainable by effort or exertion (*karmaṇā*).[74] Man's efforts, when utilised (*kritah purusha-kāras tu*) only follow his destiny (*daivam evānuvartate*); but destiny alone by itself cannot give anything to any one who lacks efforts (*na daivam-akrite kinchit kasyachit dātum-arhati*[75]). Just as even a small fire becomes highly powerful (*mahān*) when fanned by wind, so does fate become highly potent when aided by individual exertion (*karma-samāyuktam*).[76] On the other hand, just as the light in a lamp diminishes by diminishing the supply of oil, so by the abatement of exertion or effort (*karma-kśayād*) the influence of destiny also diminishes.[77] There is no inherent power in destiny itself (*nāsti daive prabhutvam*). Just as a pupil follows his preceptor (*guru*), so does one's *karma* guided by destiny follow his personal exertions (*purusha-kārah*); where one's own exertion is displayed, there only does destiny show its hand.[78] "By the influence (*abhyutthāna*) of *daiva* and by using personal exertion do men attain bliss (*svarga*); the combined help of destiny and exertion becomes fruitful".[79] This is the conclusion at which Brahman himself arrived after carefully weighing the claims of destiny and personal exertion.

The same advice is repeated in *Śāntiparva*: Destiny and exertion depend upon each other (*anyonya-samśraya*); hence the high minded (*udāra*) engage themselves in good acts, while the impotent (*klība*) rely upon destiny. All activities which would help to promote his good should be taken up by man, whether these are harsh or mild. On the other hand, the man who is disinclined to act suffers constantly from calamities and lack of resources. Hence, unmindful of anything else, one should always display one's energy; indeed, men should attend to their good above everything else. In this regard, knowledge, bravery, alertness, strength and courage are man's five natural friends

---

[70] *Mahā. Anu*. 6, 1–2.
[71] Ibid. *Anu. adhyāya*. (The whole *adhyāya*).
[72] Ibid. 6, 8.
[73] Ibid. 6, 7.
[74] Ibid. 6, 7.
[75] Ibid. 6, 22.
[76] Ibid. 6,43.
[77] Ibid, 6, 44.
[78] Ibid. 6, 47.
[79] Ibid. 6,49.

or helpmates; the wise man uses them in this world. Other things like house, precious metal, land, wife, friends are considered as man's secondary sources of good; he may secure them everywhere.[80]

The problem of *karma* has received attention at the hands of the *Dharma-śāstras*, or what are generally known as the *Smritis*, also. *Manu-Smriti*, for instances, devotes the greater part of one whole chapter (Ch. xii) to it. The discussion may be briefly summarised as follows: All action (*karma*), in the opinion of Manu, springs from mind, speech and body (*mano-vāg-deha-sambhavam*) and produces either good or bad results. These *karmas* are the cause of the various conditions of life (*gatayah*) of man.[81] Thus, as a result of the mental sins, a person becomes a low-caste (*antya-jātī*) in the next birth; as a result of sins committed by speech, he may be born again as a bird or as a beast; while as a result of the sins of body, he becomes, in the next birth, an inanimate object (*sthāvaratā*).[82] A person who has committed wicked deeds is tortured by the God of Death (*Yama*) after death; and, after atoning for those sins, such a person is born again.[83] Every one, therefore, should understand these transitions (*gatī*) of the soul (*jīva*) according in his righteous or unrighteous conduct (*dharmato' dharmataścha*), and should always fix his mind on *dharma* (*dharme dadhyāt sadā manah*).[84] "But with whatever disposition of mind or motive (*bhāva*) he performs any action, he reaps its result in a (future) body endowed with the same quality."[85] *Karma* is therefore essentially connected with re-birth. No act whatsoever can go without its effect (*phala*) to enjoy or suffer which, as the case may be, one must be born again.

Manu, however, suggests a remedy to go out of the cycle of births and deaths (*samsāra*). That remedy lies in the attainment of the knowledge of the self (*ātma-jnāna*). This knowledge is the most blessed of all the blessed actions here in this world (*śubhānām karmnām param smritam.*)[86] Through this knowledge, immortality (*amritam*) and freedom from birth are gained.[87] All *karmas* performed in accordance with the precepts of the *Vedas* (*vaidikam karma*) are sure to bring happiness both in this world and in the next;[88] for, they include (*antarbhavati*) all (*sarvam*) meritorious acts (*dharma-karmāṇi*).[89] Now this *vaidika-karma* leads to two ways:[90] one is that of *pravritti*, that is of

---

[80] *daivam purushakāraścha sthitāvanyonya samśrayāt,*
udārāṇām tu satkarma, daivam klībā upāsate.
karmam chātmahitam kāryam tikshṇam vā yadi vā mridu
grasyate akarmaśilas tu sadānarthair akinchanah.
tasmāt sarvam vyapohyārtham kārya eva parākramah
sarvasvam api samtyajya kāryam ātmahitam naraih.
vidyā śauryam cha dākśyam cha balam dhairyam cha panchamam.
mitrāṇi sahajānyāhur vartayantīha tair budhah.
niveśanam cha kupyam cha kśetram bhāryā suhrijanak
etānyupahitānyāhuh sarvatra labhate pumān.

[81] *Man.* xii, 3.

[82] *Man.* xii, 9; cf. *Yāj.* iii, 131; and 134–6.

[83] *Man.* xii, 17–22.

[84] *Man.* xii, 23.

[85] *Man.* xii, 81.

[86] *Man.* xii, 85.

[87] *Man.* xii, 85.

[88] *Man.* xii, 86.

[89] *Man.* xii, 87.

[90] On this whole question of the *pravritti-mārga* and *nivritti-mārga* see the excellent exposition of Prof. E. I. Urwick in his book, *The Message of Plato: A Re-Interpretation of the Republic*, Methuen, London, 1920.

increase of happiness and of a continuation of mundane existence; and the other of *nivritti*, that is, of the cessation of mundane existence and thus of the achievement of supreme bliss (*naihśreyasikam*).[91] Mere meritorious action will not lead to the attainment of the supreme bliss (which is *mokśa*); it will lead, at best, to happiness during the next birth. The state of supreme bliss from whence there is no return to this mundane existence can be obtained only by attaining knowledge of the self (*ātma-jnāna*). "He who sacrifices to the self (*ātma-yājī*) equally recognising (*samam paśyan*) the self in all created beings, and all created beings in the self, becomes independent like a self-controlled and self-luminous being (*svārājyam*).[92] The real fulfilment of the mission of one's life (*janma-sāphalya*) is possible for him who exerts to the best of his abilities towards acquiring the knowledge of the self (*ātma-jnāna*) towards extinguishing his passions (*sāma*), and towards pursuing the study of the *Vedas*.[93] Steady application or discipline or austerities (*tapas*) and knowledge (*vidyā*) are the best means of obtaining supreme end of life (*nịhśreyasakaram param*); disciplined activity destroys one's blemish (*kilbisha*); and, knowledge[94] (*vidyā*) secures cessation from births and deaths (*amritam*).[95] To attain to this highest state (*param padam*) and so to be one with the *Brahman*, one must be able to recognise the self through the self (*atmānamātmanā paśyati*) in all created beings, and be just or equable in his behaviour towards all (*sarvasamatā*).[96] This is the real *dharma* of man as prescribed by Manu in the *Mānava-dharma-śāstra* in his discussion on what is *Dharma* and what is *Adharma (dharmādharmau)*.

Therefore, without causing pain to anybody, one should gradually accumulate (*samchinuyāt) dharma* for the sake of acquiring an aid in the next world.[97] For in the next world, neither father, nor mother, nor sons nor wife, nor relations stay to help him (through) (*sahāyārtham)*; *dharma*

Prof. Urwick was Director of the (then) School of Sociology and Professor of Social Philosophy in London University, Tooke Professor of Economic Science and President of Morley Memorial College, and later became Director of Social Sciences in Toronto University, Canada.

Owing to the title of the book, *"The Message of Plato"* had escaped the attention of the present author when he published the first edition of this book; but Professor Urwick himself, on noticing this author's book, was kind enough to write and draw his attention to the book. The book cannot be too highly commended. *See* A NOTE ON PROFESSOR E. J. URWICK at the end of this chapter.

91–92 *Man*. xii, 88, 91. (*'svārājya',* from 'raj' 'to rule' as well as 'to shine', following Medhātithi).

93 *Man*. xii, 92–93, cf. *Muṇḍ. Up*. iii, 2, 5, quoted before.

94 The word "Knowledge" (*jnāna, vidyā*) used by the Hindu in connection with the attainment of *Mokśa*, requires some explanation: 'Knowledge in such connection means knowledge of the Ultimate Reality—*ātmajnana*, or *brahmajnāna*,—than which there could be no higher knowledge. In a sense, therefore, one's knowledge of any particular science is no "knowledge" in the full meaning of the term for the Hindu. But in another sense, this also could be called knowledge by him, provided it is understood in its widest implication, viz., that the real and most thorough knowledge of anything whatever, be it of small things or great, must lead to the knowledge of the Ultimate Reality; and therefore, a full and complete knowledge of any particular science, will include the knowledge of everything else! Strictly speaking, therefore, for the Hindu, 'knowledge' means knowledge of the Supreme, i.e., "knowledge" in its comprehensive sense. It is the inter-relation of the finite with infinite, and you cannot know fully about the finite until you have understood its relation with the infinite also. The knowledge merely of the behaviour of finite things, i.e., of mathematics, or chemistry, as such, is still largely ignorance (*avidyā*) in this sense; it is information about only one or more isolated aspects of the Ultimate Reality.

95 *Man*. xii, 104: '*tapas=svasdharma-vrittitvam*'—Kullūka.

96 *Man*. xii, 125.

97 *Man*. iv. 238.

alone stays (*dharmastishṭhati kevalah*).[98] Single is each being born; single it dies; single it enjoys the rewards of its good deeds (*sukrutam*); single it suffers for its bad deeds (*dushkritam*).[99] Leaving the dead body on the ground like a log of wood or a clod of earth, the relations depart with averted faces; but *dharma* alone follows him.[100] During life, therefore, a person should always (*nityam*) gradually (*śanaih*) accumulate *dharma* for his aid (*sahāya*); for with *dharma* as his companion he will traverse the gloom (*tamas*) which is otherwise difficult to traverse (*dustaram*).[101] For *Dharma* speedily conducts the man, who is devoted to it (*dharma-pradhānam*), by eradicating his sins (*kilbisha*) by a life of disciplined activities (*tapas*), to the next world (*paralokam*), radiant (*bhāsvanta*) and possessing an ethereal body (*kha-śarīriṇah*).[102] *Dharma*, when violated, destroys; *dharma* when preserved protects;[103] therefore, *dharma* must never be violated, lest violated *dharma* may destroy us.[104] For, Divine *Dharma* is like a '*vrisha*' (i.e. bull), and he who would have '*alam*' ('no more') with it, i.e. would not follow it, would be considered by the gods to be a *vrishala (=vrisha+alam)* i.e. a low-born person; therefore one should never violate *dharma*.[105] The only friend (*suhrid*) who follows man even after death is *dharma*; for everything else is lost at the same time that the body perishes.[106] A person should, therefore, never turn his mind to *adharma* even though he has to suffer due to following his *dharma*; for he would find that there is quick destruction awaiting those who do not follow *dharma* and are (therefore) sinful.[107] *Adharma* practised in this world (*loka*) may not produce its fruit (*phala*) immediately like seeds sown in the earth, but it gradually accumulates and destroys the man who practised it to the root (*kartur mūlāni krintati*).[108] Once committed, *adharma* never fails to produce its effects upon him who did it; if the calamity does not fall upon himself, it falls upon his sons; and if not upon the sons then upon his grandsons.[109] For the time being he may prosper through *adharma*; and, he may also achieve success; and thereafter, he may even overpower his enemies; however, ultimately he is destroyed to the root (*samūlah*).[110] He should therefore find satisfaction (*āramet*) in the true *dharma* and conduct such as would become an Ārya.[111] Let him therefore abandon even *kāma* and *artha* if and when and where these are lacking *dharma (dharmavarjitau)*. And even *dharma* may be abandoned if and when it would cause pain in the future or is harsh or cruel to human beings

---

[98] Ibid. iv. 239.
[99] Ibid. *iv*. 240.
[100] Ibid. iv. 241.
[101] Ibid. iv. 242.
[102] Ibid. iv. 243.
[103] *dharma eva hato hanti dharmo rakshati rakshitah*—Ibid. vii. 15.
[104] Ibid. vii. 15.
[105] *vrisho hi bhagavān dharmastasya yah kurute hyalam*
vrishalam tam vidurdevāstasmāddharmam na lopayet—manu. viii, 16.
"kāmān varshati iti vrishah"—i.e. '*vrisha*' means one who pours forth pleasures, says Kullūkabhaṭṭa—commenting on the word.
[106] Ibid. viii. 17
[107] Ibid. iv. 171.
[108] Ibid. iv. 172.
[109] Ibid. iv. 173.
[110] Ibid. iv. 174.
[111] Ibid. iv. 175.

(*lokanikrishṭam*).[112] This means that the ultimate *test* of true *dharma* is not a *self-regarding* one but *other-regarding* one.

Yājnavalkya agrees with this expression of the doctrine of *dharma* and *karma* as expounded by Manu. In the opening verse of his gloss on *Yājnavalkyasmriti*, the commentator Bālambhaṭṭa says that *Dharma* and *Adharma* are the seeds of the accumulation of karma (*karmāśaya*); and that from this *karmasaya* grow the three-fold results viz: (1) *Jāti*, that is birth in the high or the low position, (2) *Āyu*, that is, the length of life, and (3) *Bhoga*, that is, the enjoyment or suffering, for every human being. *Dharma* may be said to consist in the right *karma*. Yājnavalkya says that he has been only expounding the *dharma* of the different *varnas*, of the different orders of life (*āśramas*), and other relevant topics (*itara*) in the *Smriti*.[113] The *Mitākśarā* of Vijnāneśvara further comments on this statement by saying that Yājnavalkya is considering six topics in connection with the question of *dharma*: (i) the *varna-dharma*, referring to the duties of man in relation to the four classes of men, (ii) the *āśrama -dharma* concerning the duties connected with the four stages of human life, (iii) the *varṇaśramadharma*, concerning the duties of man towards both the *varṇa* and the *āśramas* in their interrelationship with each other,[114] (iv) *guṇadharma*, regarding the duties of persons with reference to the characteristic tendencies (*gunas*) which are innate in them;[115] (v) *nimitta-dharma*, concerning the duties of man in connection with particular or special occasions (*nimitta*,[116] i.e. special duties, or duties according to exigencies, and (vi) *sādhāraṇa-dharma*, embracing duties common to all men and women as human beings,[117] i.e. general duties. These various *dharmas* describe and prescribe the right *karmas* for man. Of all *karmas*, including sacrifices (*ijyā*), rituals (*āchāra*), discipline (*dama*), harmlessness (*ahimsā*), liberality (*dāna*), and the study of the Vedas (*svādhyāya*), the highest *dharma (paramo dharmah)* of man is self-realization (*ātma-darśanam*).[118] Here, again, we come to the oft-stressed method of attaining *ātma-jnāna* for the salvation of the soul. And, it is the duty of the King to see that the various social institutions like the family (*kulāni*), the caste (*jātih*), the trade-guilds (*śreṇih*), the sects (*gaṇam*) and associations or unions like those of the artisans etc. (*jāna-padān*), who have deviated from their proper *dharma (svadharmāchchalitān-jātān*) shall be properly disciplined (*vinīya*) and set in the right path.[119]

Here we may also refer to the similar observations made by the *Śukra-Nīti*. This *Nīti* work, too, speaks of one's existence as being conditioned by his *karmas* in the previous births. "Everything in this life is founded on *daiva* (destiny, fate) and *karma*, the latter being divided into that done in previous birth or births, and that done in this one.[120] *Sukra-Nīti* thus admits *daiva* also as a factor conditioning the destiny of a person. But this is not to say that what man is and becomes has been already *in toto* decided for him by his fate, and that therefore he should not strive or make any effort

---

[112] Ibid. iv. 176.

[113] cf. also *Man*. iv. 171–81. *ante*.

[114] For example, the rule that a person belonging to the Brāhamaṇa *varṇa* and desiring to enter the *āśrama* of studenthood (*brahmacharya*) should carry a stick of *palāśa* tree, and so forth.

[115] For example, the rule that the highest duty of a king,—i.e., a Kashatriya, is to protect his subjects.

[116] For example, rules regarding observing penance for failure to carry out certain duties.

[117] For example, harmlessness, and befriending all living creatures, cf. Medhātithi and Kullūka, commenting on Manu. ii. 25.

[118] *Yāj*. i. 8.

[119] *Yāj*. 361.

[120] *śukr. Nī*. i. 97–98 (Tr. by B. K. Sarkar).

and should lead an inactive life. For, it is the weak who lead an inactive life; while those who have energy and strength can change their future destiny by work done in this birth (*ihārjita*). Thus, in the ultimate analysis, one's own actions (*karmas*) alone are the cause of his good or bad luck (*daiva*).[121]

Moreover, says the *Śukra-Nīti*, his *karmas* can determine not only his destiny (*daiva*) in the next birth, but also his mental dispositions in the next birth. A man is also inclined to virtues or vices according to the effects of his *karmas* in his former births.[122] Therefore, according to *Sukra-Nīti*, though Fate (*daiva*) is a factor in determining the destiny of man, his own *karmas* themselves have a tremendous influence over his fate. *Sukra-Nīti* is not altogether free from ambiguity in this connection. It may be that it seeks to strike a mean between two extremes; or it may be said to be stating the case of both the sides, leaving the reader to judge and decide between the two. Anyway, we see that, on the one hand it praises the philosophy of action (*paurusha*) which is born of active efforts (*karma*) in this life,[123] and denounces those who worship fate (*daiva*);[124] and, on the other hand, it opines that everything is founded on both fate (*daiva*) as well as *karma*.[125] At one place, it seems to give fate (*daiva*) a more exalted place than *karma* as the determining factor in human destiny. "The intellectual disposition is generated according as the fruits of work (*karma-phala*) make their appearance. The means and instrumentalities used also are such as are adopted to the predestined fate (*daiva*).[126]

This difficult problem has been more clearly answered in Yājnavalkya's *Smriti*. He says:—"The fulfilment of an action (*karma-siddhih*) rests between destiny and human effort (*daive purushakāre cha vyavasthitā*). Of these two, destiny is the manifestation (*abhivyaktam*) of the human effort (*paurusham*) of the past life. Some people hold that the fulfilment of an object is the result of destiny (*daiva*) only; some, of accident (*svabhāva*); some, of time (*kāla*); some, of human effort (*purusha-kāra*); but men of clear understanding (*kuśala-buddhayah*) hold, however, that the fruit (*phalam*) is the result of the combination (*samyoga*) of these. As, indeed, by one wheel alone there is no motion of the chariot, so without human effort, the destiny does not get fulfilment (*na siddhyati*).[127] *Yājnavalkya-Smriti* therefore holds, along with the *Mahābhārata*, that both *karma* as well as *daiva* are together operative in the shaping of human affairs.

We shall next consider the views of the *Yoga-Sūtras* of Patanjali on the problems of existence, of *karma* and of *mukti*, without concerning ourselves with the purely metaphysical implications of this system of thought. Even though *Yoga* has come to be regarded as one of the six systems of Hindu Philosophy, we must not forget that the chief interest of the *Yoga-Sūtras* lies, not in building up a system of metaphysics, but in devising an outlook and practices in consequence of the same, by the aid of which one could liberate oneself from the bonds of *karma (karma-bandha)* and thereafter attain liberation (*kaivalya*).[128] In this sense, Yoga is more a practical philosophy of life than a purely

---

[121] *śukr. Nī*. i. 73.
[122] *śukr. Nī*. i. 89–90.
[123] *śukr. Nī*. i. 105.
[124] Ibid. i. 96.
[125] Ibid. i. 97.
[126] *śukr. Nī* i. 91–92.
[127] *Yāj*. i, 349–51.
[128] cf. Rādhākrishnan: "The main interest of Patanjali is not metaphysical theorising but the practical motive of indicating how salvation can be attained by disciplined activity." *"Indian Philosophy,"* Vol. ii. (1927), p. 338.

speculative metaphysical system; and therefore the system has a particular interest and value in connection with our present discussion.

The word '*Yoga*' is derived from '*yuj*', 'to join', in which case it would mean joining or union of finite soul with the infinite or supreme soul (*Īśvara*) i.e. God. It implies that there is disunion, or separation (*vi-yoga*) between God and man, and that *Yoga* is an effort towards dissolving that separation. Hence the term *Yoga* has also come to mean the efforts, or the method or system of efforts by the help of which the union of God and man is effected. In fact the *Yoga-Sūtras* use the word *Yoga* generally in this latter sense, as a method involving strenuous efforts or exertions towards attaining the liberation of the soul (*kaivalya*).[129] The word is also used as a synonym for the *samādhi*—which is the last stage, among several, that the *Yogi* attains—in which case the word would be derived from the root '*yuj*' as meaning 'to go into trance or to meditate'.[130]

The word seems to have a peculiar fascination for the Hindu, since it has been used in combination with other words, by doing which the meanings of the latter are invested with a special import in each case—as in the expressions like *karma-yoga, jnāna-yoga* and *bhakti-yoga*. In these cases "*yoga*" means a "system", a "discipline".

To return to our discussion of the views of *Yoga-Sūtras*: According to Patanjali, nescience (*avidyā*) is the root cause of human suffering, including birth and death. All the 'afflictions' (*kleśāh*) of man arise out of the unreal or distorted cognition (*viparyayah*), or *avidyā* in the larger sense, which identifies *Purusha* with *Prakriti*, the ego with the body, the Mind with Matter. *Avidyā* is not absence of knowledge; it is rather false knowledge which is positively in antagonism to right knowledge (*vidyā-viparītam jnānāntaram-avidyā*).[131] It gives rise to five kinds of 'afflictions' (*kleśas*) as mentioned below:—

(i) *Avidyā*, which wrongly identifies the transient with the intransient principle, the ephemeral with the eternal, the effect with the cause, the ego with the *Purusha* i.e., the Primary Spirit from which everything has originated. This *avidyā* is the principle *kleśa* of human beings; and in the larger sense, it underlies all the other *kleśas*.

(ii) *Asmitā*, meaning the mistaken identification of the body, through which the self functions, with the self itself.

(iii) *Rāga*, which defines the inclination towards, and seeking after, things that give pleasure.

(iv) *Dveśa* which refers to the hatred of and consequent avoidance of things that cause pain.

(v) *Abhiniveśa* which relates to the love of life and fear of death.[132]

The last four are only sub-divisions or modifications (*bhedāh*) of *a-vidyā* and as such arise out of it. All the *kleśas*, therefore would be removed[133] as soon as *avidyā* itself is removed. And, the removal of *avidyā* could be achieved by right knowledge (*prajnā*) with the aid of *Yoga*.

Further, *avidyā* is the cause of all *karmas* of man on account of the *kleśas* described above. The *kleśas* are, so to say, the immediate cause of all our *karmas*—the good ones (*punya-karmas*) as

[129] cf. Ibid. p. 338.

[130] See Vasu's Intro. to *"Yoga-Sūtras of Patanjali"* Tr. by Rama Prasad. "Sacred Bks. of the Hindus," Allahabad, p. 1.

[131] Das Gupta: *"The Study of Patanjali,"* p. 99.

[132] *Pat. Yog. Sut.* ii. 3. (Rama Prasad's ed.).

[133] See Vāchaspati on *Pat.* ii. 3; and Vyāsa on *Pat.* ii, 4.

well as the evil ones (*pāpa-karmas*).[134] And the effects of these *karmas* are felt both in this life as well as after it is over.[135] They are the cause of birth (*jāti*), life-span (*āyuh*), and life-experiences (*bhogāh*).[136]

Patanjali speaks of *karmas* in terms of 'white' (*śukla*) and 'black' (*krishṇa*). The *karmas* of average man are either 'white', or 'black', or 'white-black' (*śukla-krishṇa*). The *śukla-karmas* are due to mental states only (*manasyāyattatvād*) and are not dependent upon external means (*bahih sādhanāndhīnāh*); these are study (*svādhyāya*) and meditation (*dhyāna*); these acts are free from injury (*pīḍā*) to others,—the really harmless acts. The *krishṇa-karmas* are the wicked deeds. And, the *śukla-krishṇa-karmas* partake of the character of both; these are brought about by external means, by acting kindly to some and causing pain to some others; indeed, in all cases where kindness is shown to some by the help of external means, injury is sure to be caused to some others.[137] Even in such apparently innocent actions as preparing barley for food to be given to another, it is possible that ants and other tiny or imperceptible living beings may be injured at the time of pounding the barley.[138]

Now, the three kinds of *karmas* described above are the *karmas* of the average man. But the *karmas* of a *Yogin* belong to none of these three kinds.[139] They are certainly not black; nor are they white because the *Yogin* gives up his claim to the fruit of actions (*phala-samnyāsād*);[140] he dedicates it to *Īśvara*.[141] The *Yogi* is a '*karma-samnyāsi'*—by which term is meant, *not* one who has renounced doing anything, but one who has renounced the ownership or the claims to the fruit of his actions (*phala-samnyāsa*). The *Yogi's karmas* are merely atonements of past obligations and debts; they do not create future obligations, because they are not *karmas* in the usual sense of the word; therefore, they are neither 'white' nor 'black'.

This, of course, does not involve any absence of *karma*, or inertia, as may be thought by some; in fact the actions of a *yogi* are *karmas*, performed on the attainment of discriminating knowledge (*viveka-khyātih*) which now fathoms the distinction between *Purusha* and *Prakriti*; besides, the fruits of these *karmas* are dedicated to *Īśvara*, and they are performed in His name. The Yogi does these *karmas* with the full knowledge that His (*Īśvara's*) "will be done, on earth as in heaven," and indeed, throughout the whole universe. The "fire of knowledge" (*jnānāgni*) burns down to ashes all *avidyā* and with the destruction of *avidyā*, all *kleśas* are removed right to the root;[142] thence also are the good and bad accumulations of *karmas (karmāśayah)* utterly destroyed. And as the *kleśas* and *karmas* are thus completely destroyed, the wise man (*vidvān*) becomes liberated and free even while alive (*jīvanmuktah*). The cause of all existence is rooted in distorted understanding (*viparyayah*); hence, one who is free from the affliction of unreal cognition (*kśīna-kleśa-viprayayah*) will not be born (*jātah*) again.[143]

---

[134] See Vyāsa on *Pat*. ii, 12.

[135] *drishṭādrishṭajanavedanīyah—Pat*. ii. 12.

[136] *Pat*. ii. 13.

[137] *"yadyāvat bahih sādhanasādhyam tatah sarvatrāsti kasyachit pīḍā"* Vāchaspati on *Pat* iv, 7.

[138] See *Pat*, iv, 7, and Vyāsa and Vāchaspati on it.

[139] *"karmāśuklākrishṇam yoginas trividham itareshām"*—Pat. iv, 7.

[140] Vyāsa on *Pat*, iv. 7.

[141] Vyāsa and Vāchaspati on *Pat*. iv, 7.

[142] *"samūlaghātam hatāh bhavantī"—Vyāsa on Pat*. iv, 30.

[143] Ibid.

Thus, in the opinion of Patanjali, knowledge (*jnāna*) is the only means of bringing to an end the otherwise endless cycle of *karmas* (in the sense of a force that causes re-birth) and birth, each causing the other in succession, one after the other. *The karmas do not cease with the attainment of jnāna; but they entirely lose their previous import or implication or potency for the doer.* With the attainment of *jnāna*, the *Yogi* becomes a *dharma-megha* (cloud of *dharma*), as it were, which showers down blessings upon humanity. The word 'cloud' (*megha*) probably signifies that he becomes immune, so to speak, to the 'touch' of the *karmas* or their effect. That wise man (*kuśalah*) in whom the light of knowledge has dawned (*pratyudita-khyātih*) and whose longings and desires have been destroyed (*kśīṇa-trishnah*) is not born again.[144] All others have to be born again.

So, for the *Yoga-Śūtras* of Patanjali, the end of human existence lies in the final emancipation (*kaivalya*) of the *Purusha* from the bondage of *Prakriti*.[145] But this is not the same as physical death. It consists of the destruction of *avidyā* brought about by the knowledge (*jnāna*) that *Purusha* is entirely distinct from *Prakriti*. It accrues, moreover, out of the *death of the fundamental human weakness* in each of us, and the realization that all our *karmas* have reference to the *Purusha*. That highest state of *Samādhi*, say the *Yoga-Sūtras*, wherein this realization dawns upon the *Yogī*, is called the *dharma-megha-samādhi*[146]—wherein the *Yogī*, becomes a veritable mass of all that is holy and saintly. For whatever he does then is prompted and performed by the *Purusha*,—the Holy Principle in him—which is now fully liberated from the restraining influence of *Prakriti*.

The *Purushas* are striving, through time and space, to attain to that Holiest Principle, God, or *Īśvara*, which is a distinguished (*viśeshah) Purusha*[147] and therefore distinct from other *Purushas*. He is distinguished from the other *Purushas* by the fact that He is untouched by any of the *kleśas, karmas*, and their effects,[148] to which the other *Purushas* might be subjected owing to their bondage to *Prakriti*. For Patanjali, the *Purushas*, even after they have attained *kaivalya* (absolute freedom from the bondage to *Prakriti*), are to be distinguished from *Īśvara*. For *Īśvara* never had, nor will ever have, any relation to these bondages;[149] in fact, *Īśvara* is ever free.[150] On the other hand, in the case of a *purusha* which is emancipated, the former bondage is known,[151] and even a future bondage is possible.[152]

By far the most popular and influential treatise on the problem of human existence in the Sanskrit Literature is perhaps the *Bhagavad-Gītā*—"the Song of the Lord." This treatise has secured the most honoured place in the heart of the masses as well as the classes of India not only in matters of religious behaviour but also on social and moral issues. Therefore, the *Gītā* must be considered by us an authority of very great importance for our purpose here. It answers the problem of *karma* more clearly than any other treatise has done so far.

Like others dealing with the same problem, the starting point of the *Gītā* too is the theory of *karma* and rebirth. The present stage of life is a period of transition, with past births and their

[144] Vyāsa on *Pat.* iv, 33.
[145] See *Pat.* iv.
[146] *Pat.* iv, 29.
[147] *"purushaviśesha Iśvarah"*—*Pat.* i, 24.
[148] *"kleśakarmavipākāśayairaparāmrishṭah."*
[149] *"Īśvarasya cha tatsambandho na bhūto na bhāvī."*
[150] *"sa tu sadaiva muktah sadaiva Iśvarah."*
[151] *"pūrvabandhakoṭih prajāyate."*
[152] *"uttarā bandhakoṭih sambhāvyate"*—Vāchaspati on *Pat.* i. 24.

karmas and the future lives. The soul (*ātmā*) itself as such never dies nor is it born again (*na jāyate na mriyate*); even when the body dies, the soul is not dead.[153] Just as man discards worn out clothes and puts on new ones, so the soul discards old bodies (*śarīrāni*) and takes up new ones.[154] One who is born is sure to die some day; and one who is dead is sure to take birth again[155]—unless, of course, he obtains salvation (*mukti*); but then, such a person who has attained salvation does not "die"; he is, as the word "*mukti*" implies, "freed" from birth and death. Otherwise, no one can live even for a moment (*kśaṇam api*) without doing some kind of *karma*,[156] and again, the accumulation of *karma* is sure to cause another birth.

Now if *karma* is the cause of the bondage of the individual into a chain of births and deaths (*samsāra*), it may be felt that the best remedy against this *samsāra* and its concomitant entanglements which will continue *ad infinitum* would be, according to this *karma* theory, to cease doing any *karmas* at all! This is the natural conclusion to which a partial or superficial view of the *karma* theory would lead. And, in fact, some scholars have been led to find this meaning in the *karma* theory. They have contended that the theory of *karma*, in solving the problem of existence, leads to inaction and fatality, if *mukti* has to be the end of human life. Thus, Macdonell has said: "A result of the combined doctrine of transmigration and *karma* is, it is true, to reconcile men to their fate as the just retribution for deeds done in a previous life, but on the other hand, it paralyzes action, drives to asceticism, and makes action self-regarding, since it becomes the aim of every man to win salvation for himself individually, by acquiring the right knowledge. There is consequently little scope for the development of other-regarding virtues, as each individual is intent on gaining his own salvation".[157] And Sir A. Berriedale Keith, another noted Sanskrit scholar, calls *karma* theory "essentially fatalistic".[158] It is our purpose here to show that on a complete view of the implications and meaning of the *karma* theory such a conclusion would be entirely unwarranted: and though our foregoing discussion would have partially refuted such criticism of the *karma* theory, our best authority on this point, for further discussion, would be no other than the *Bhagvad-Gītā* itself, as could be seen from what follows.

The very origin of this great treatise is worth a careful notice in this connection. Arjuna is about to resign his duty of fighting like a true soldier on the battlefield, when he sees a vast number of men, among whom were also so many of his kith and kin, who would be killed in the war. Śrī Krishṇa, however, persuades him to take up his weapons and do his duty as a soldier on the battlefield; and the whole of the *Gītā* is primarily a discourse directed to press home to Arjun this point of doing the duties of one's station, whatever may befall one. This means that the central theme around which the *Gītā* is woven is: "Do thy duty, follow thy *svadharma*, and don't ever be inactive!" The *Bhagvad-Gītā* advocates a life of action and denounces that of inaction; for "action is certainly far better than inaction".[159] The great king Janaka and others attained their salvation by following the path of action (*karma-yoga*); and, indeed, Janaka did not cease doing his *karmas* even

---

[153] *Gī.* ii, 20.
[154] *Gī.* ii, 22.
[155] *Gī.* ii, 27.
[156] *Gī.* iii, 5.
[157] Macdonell: *Lectures on Comparative Religion,* 1925, p. 67.
[158] *Keith: Religion and Philosophy of the Vedas and the Upanishads, vol*, ii, p. 596.
[159] *Gī.* iii, 8 *"karma jyāyo hyakarmaṇah."*

after attaining *mukti*.[160] So also, there was nothing in this world for the Great Krishna himself to carry out (*kartavyam*); nor was there anything for him to gain that he had not already gained; and yet he followed the path of action (*karmayoga*) because great people do set an example to mankind.[161]

However the *Gītā* ideal of activity is a qualified one. It does not advocate that *any* kind of action is preferable to inaction. Further, in carrying out the desirable actions, the *Gītā* wants that they should be carried out under a particular discipline and with reference to a specific purpose. Thus, there are two kinds of checks on the path of action in the *Gītā*. The first is the internal one, a kind of psychological discipline, in that *karmas* are to be carried out without any attachment (*a-saktah*) to them,[162] without any feeling of pleasurable or unpleasurable association (*vāsanā*), without any idea of "mine" and "thine" and of ego-involvement (*mamatva*). Blessed is the man who keeps his senses under control (*indriyāṇi manasā niyamya*) and does his *karmas* without attachment to them (*asaktah*).[163] It is impossible for any man to be without *karma* (*akarmakrit*) even for a moment.[164] Absolute cessation from activity is death. So long as a man lives, he cannot help doing *karma*; for the *karmas* that have been already credited and debited to his account will force him into more *karmas*.[165] He who is ignorant (*avidvān*) follows his *karmas* with personal attachment (*saktah*) to them, with his ego involved deeply in them. However, the man who knows (*vidvān*) should follow his *karmas* with a spirit of detachment (*asaktah*) and for collective welfare of the people (*lokasamgraha*).[166] This check, therefore, refers to the spirit, the attitude to be developed, with which man is to follow his activities throughout his life.

And then there is the second important check on man's actions, the external check. In doing his *karmas*, man is to follow his duty (*dharma*). He should not be led by his senses (*indriya*); rather, he should carry out the duties which are his *dharma*, and which he is born to do. It is better to die while following one's own *dharma* (*swadharma*), however worthless or bad (*vigunah*) it may appear; but it is dangerous to follow that of another (*paradharma*).[167] Those who follow their own duties (*sve sve karmanyabhiratah*) shall attain the fulfilment of existence (*samsiddhim*).[168] There is no sin (*kilbisham*) in undertaking activities in accordance with one's own natural propensities or aptitudes (*svabhāva-niyatam karma*).[169] Even though such *karma* seems to have faults, shortcomings or blemishes (*sadosham api*), one should not abandon it (*na tyajet*);[170] for, all *karmas* are accompanied by faults in them, just as fire is accompanied by smoke.[171] The *Gītā* explicitly declares that doing one's own *karmas* (*karma-yoga*) in accordance with *dharma* is far better than abandoning *karmas* altogether (*karma-samnyāsa*).[172] This check on man's activities refers to the problem of the kinds or types of *karmas* to be undertaken and carried out. Only the right kinds

---

[160] *Gī*. iii, 20.
[161] *Gī*. iii, 21–22.
[162] *Gī*. iii, 19.
[163] *Gī*. iii, 7.
[164] *Gī*. iii, 5: *na hi kaśchit kṣaṇamṇam api jātu tishṭhatyakarmakrit.*
[165] *Gī*. xviii, 60.
[166] *Gī*. iii, 25.
[167] *Gī*. iii, 35.
[168] *Gī*. xviii, 45.
[169] *Gī*. xviii, 47.
[170] *Gī*. xviii, 48.
[171] *Gī*. xviii, 48.
[172] *Gī*. v, 2.

of *karmas* in accordance with his natural talents, temperaments and inclinations, as suggested by the *Dharma-Śāstras* for each different type of temperamental groups, should be undertaken and carried out by him.

In the last *Adhyāya* of the *Gītā*, Śrī Krishṇa gives a more precise definition of the terms *karma-samnyāsa* and *karma-tyāga* used in this connection. By *karma-samnyāsa* is to be understood, not the abandonment of all *karmas*, but the abandonment of the claim or desire for their fruit. "By *samnyāsa*, learned men understand the renunciation of actions done with the desire for fruit (*kāmyānām karmaṇām nyāsam*); and by *tyāga*, wise men understand the renunciation of the fruit of all actions (*sarva-karma-phala-tyāgam*)[173], not of actions themselves. On the other hand, "indeed, the giving up of the *karmas* prescribed (*niyata*) by the *Śāstras* is not proper".[174] In the same strain, Śrī Krishṇa again declared: "Your duty (claimed authority) relates to the performance of your *karmas* only (*karmaṇyevādhikāras-te*), unmindful of the fruit or result (*phala*); in doing *karma*, you ought not to possess the motive of fruit (*karma-phala-hetuh*); nor should you be inclined to inactivity (*mā te sango'stvakarmaṇi*).[175] The renunciation of *karmas* through deluded understanding (*moha*) is said to belong to the *tāmasa* nature; their abandonment through fear of physical suffering belongs to the *rājasa* kind; but when they are performed without attachment (*samgam*) and also without the desire for fruit (*phalam*), then such a renunciation (*tyāga*) is *sāttvika tyāga*;[176] and, of course, it is the most desirable of *tyāgas*. "It is not possible for those who live in bodies with flesh and blood (*deha-bhritāh*) to renounce *karmas* completely; but he who renounces the fruit of *karma* (*karma-phala-tyāgī*) is verily to be called the (real) *tyāgī*.[177] And those who renounce the desire for fruit (*phalam*) of their *karma* become free from the bondage of birth (*janma-bandha*) and attain that supreme goal i.e. *mukti*.[178]

All this means that the *karma* theory so far described implies that man is born due to his past *karmas*, and that all that he has to do and has not to do, that he will do and he will not do, will react again on his past *karma* and may create tendencies for new *karmas*. The whole theory is based on the principle that every action is followed by a reaction. Nothing that is *thought or spoken* or *done* by an individual can escape being credited or debited to his account, as the case may be. One can never disown one's actions. The theory further implies that so long as man continues *karmas*, whether by body, mind or speech, he is going to be born again and again to atone for them and even to create new ones. Moreover, freedom from the round of births and deaths cannot be obtained until freedom from *karma* is obtained.

And yet, with all this, it does not at all imply,—as could be seen from our discussion,—that this freedom has to be acquired by resorting to asceticism, or by leading a life of inactivity, or a life of not doing any *karma*. It is, on the contrary, fully recognised that a life of absolute inactivity is never possible for any one, so that the question of its desirability cannot even be raised! What the

---

[173] *Gī.* xviii, 2.
[174] *Gī.* xviii, 7.
[175] *Gī.* ii, 47.
[176] *Gī.* xviii, 7–9. For the meaning of *sattva, rajas* and *tamas* as psychological qualities innate in man, see below, ch. viii.
[177] *Gī.* xviii, 11. R. G. Bhandarkar had pointed out that the insistence on *karmas* being done without any regard for the fruit is not new. The *Iśophanishad* says in the 2nd verse that "a man should desire to live a hundred years doing actions resolutely, and in that way and in no other, will action not contaminate him." cf. also *Chhānd. Up.* iv, 14, 3: *Brih. Up.* iv, 4, 23: *Maitr. Up.* vi, 20. See Bhandarkar: *"Vaishnavism, Śaivism, and Other Minor Cults,"* p. 27.
[178] *Gī.* ii, 51.

theory of *karma*, properly interpreted, implies is that only the right *karmas* should be performed, recognizing fully, that the particular position in which any individual has come to be—the birth in a particular *varna* or family (*kula*), the worldly happiness or unhappiness which surround him, and so on—is the result of his past *karmas* and not a mere accident or chance or luck. The individual has to realize this and fully understand its implications. He has to atone for, or enjoy the fruit of, his past *karmas*; but, while doing this, he should follow the path of right *karmas*; that is to say, he should follow his *svadharma*, so as to control the trends of his future *karma*. The *Gītā* insists that only thus can one counteract one's own past *karma* and safeguard himself from the future effects of *karma*.[179] The *Mahābhārata* and *Smritis*, too, agree with this basic attitude.[180] Yājnavalkya, for instance, has said that the *dharma* or *adharma* which an individual follows form the seeds of the store of his *karma*,[181] therefore, he says, he has tried to lay down the proper *dharma*, which, if followed by man, would secure salvation (*mokśa*) for him.

Evidently, such a philosophy of life is far from the uncompromising determinism or fatalism which some have tried to make of it! The fact that our deeds—whether past or present, whether mere mental, physical or both,—affect our lives, and in that sense and to that extent form part of the tendencies or forces that direct the shape of our lives is what is basically accepted by the *karma* theory. Nevertheless, the imposition of particular checks and disciplines on life and conduct further implies that it is within our power to *twist, modify* or *alter* the effects of our previous *karmas* (which now becomes our 'destiny') by better and more regulated *karmas*. This is, in fact, according to the Hindu, a rational philosophy of life, which asserts that one can never disown one's acts, once they are committed, but surely one can counteract their effects if one has the will to do so. For after all, *daiva* or destiny is *not something that has been imposed on us from without*; it is the accumulated effect of our own past doings, *a reaction of our own actions*, and as such, of our own making. But for the very reason that it is of our making, it is, or *exists*, though it is invisible (*adrishṭa*) to us, and must be accepted as a fact and reckoned with, though *it can be counteracted*. In terms of science, every *action* is followed by *reaction* (effect); but the reaction, if undesirable or undesired, can be *counteracted*. And the 'Freedom of the Will' operates in choosing the ways and means to accomplish the required counteraction. Indeed, we had the freedom of the will *previously* too, when we chose those *karmas* which have now become responsible for our present *daiva* (destiny); and therefore, virtually, it may as well be said that it *is we ourselves who have chosen our present destiny!* So, we may put it thus: If *karma* is denoted by action, its reaction, which, as reaction, is not under our control, but may, in fact, control us to some extent, is *daiva* or destiny; but there is yet the capability within us to counteract *daiva*, which is by choosing *sukarma* or *svadharma*, which, of course, naturally requires the exercise of self-control, i.e., control over our tendencies to act wrongly which are the result of our previous *karmas* and their reactions.

Here again, also, there is a considerable insistence on the principle of *self-reliance and self-dependence in regard to shaping one's own future*. Since you have been yourself entirely responsible for what you are, no one else, not even God, will help you to undo what you have done. No other power but your own self can make or mar your future.

---

[179] See above.

[180] See above.

[181] *Yāj*. i, 1.

It is a well known law of science that nothing is lost in the material realm. For the Hindu, this Law of Nature extends to the moral realm too; as with matter, so with men, since both are parts of Nature, which is a system, an organisation, a cosmos, not a chaos, and is governed by laws. To 'forgive and forget' may be a good advice for men to follow in regard to their personal or mutual relations; but Nature never forgets. She keeps a complete record of all events and activities, material and moral, and reactions must follow as necessary consequences of actions. The process is automatic so to speak. Many of us would like several of our deeds, especially, misdeeds to be forgotten by others; and men do forget many things because they have short memories. And also, men do make appeals to other men to forgive and forget. But such 'wishful forgetting' never occurs in Nature.

Further, in regard to human actions in the moral realm, according to the Hindu, the agent or the doer *himself* has to atone for or counteract the effects of his own actions. No one else will be able to help him in that regard,—not even God, or prayers or repentance, or craving for forgiveness. To expect one's deeds to be forgotten and forgiven is to expect something to happen against the very Law of God Himself. It is to think, as it were, that what has happened has *not* happened,—which is absurd! Repentance, prayers and meditation rather help to elevate one's mind on to a higher plane, to purge one's thoughts, and to motivate him to follow *svadharma*, better deeds, which if, duly executed, would make up for or atone for the blemishes of our past deeds; they cannot efface or erase the effects of those past deeds by themselves. In his analysis of the *Karma* theory, Sir Herbert Risley, himself a keen student of Hindu thought, has remarked: "Nor does the strength of Hinduism lie in its metaphysics. There are those who hold that the idea of *Karma*, the theory that on each sin as it is committed there is passed a judgment from which there is no appeal, stands on a higher plane and exercises a greater moral influence than the Christian doctrines of repentance and forgiveness of sins. The belief in a spiritual backstairs does not necessarily make for righteousness."* Man himself, therefore, according to the *karma* theory, is the master and maker of his own destiny.

Therefore, according to the Hindu view, each one of us is born to do his or her part in whatever position we find ourselves in order to undo the effects of past *karmas*, and so to behave through life that we may get *mokśa*. This means that for the Hindu, the individual is born not fully to use all his faculties, not fully to take from the world of the physical, the biological, the economical and the social existence around him as best as he can and as much as he can, which is the aim of all Western thought—of course consistent with such full opportunities to other individuals; with the Hindu, on the other hand, it is a question, not of using to the utmost, but using the just and the appropriate quantity and quality for undoing the effects of the past *karma* and for not creating a new world of *karmas* which may react either in this life or in lives to come. The *karmas* are expected to be so manipulated as not to disturb the equilibrium or the balance or the stability of the Universe. One must take out, from the world outside, only so much as is just enough for one, not more, not even less. Anything more or less might disturb the equilibrium of the system of *jagat*, and thus might entangle one into the medley of *karmas*. To be able to achieve this, we must follow our *sva-dharma* which defines our limitations and our specific duties with reference to definite, as also possible and

---

* Risley, H.: *The People of India*, 2nd Ed. by W. Crooke. Thacker, Spink, Calcutta and London, 1915. Sir H. Risley was a member of the Indian Civil Service from 1873–1910, and served as the Director of Ethnography for India.

probable situations. It is so devised as to enable one to acquit oneself just equitably. For, as the *Gītā* has said, even a little of this *karma* will be able to protect us from great dangers.[182]

So far about what is usually termed as the *karma-mārga*, the 'way of action', as a method of solving the problem of existence. But there are two other 'ways' (*mārgāh*) discussed in the *Gītā* itself for the solution of that problem, viz. *Jnāna-mārga* and the *Bhakti-mārga*. The followers of *Jnāna-mārga* would maintain that it is knowledge[183] (*Jnāna*) that leads to the goal of existence i.e. *mukti*: while the followers of the *Bhakti-mārga* maintain that it is devotion (*bhakti*) to God and self-surrender to Him that leads one to that goal. The *Gītā* has attempted to bring the three *mārgas* into harmony with each other. But before taking over this point, we shall do well to grasp the *Gītā* interpretation of *jnāna* and *bhakti* as leading to *mukti*.

We take up *Jnāna-mārga* first. The *Jnāna-marga* is discussed in the fourth *Adhyāya* and also in the seventh *Adhyāya* of the *Gītā*. Śrī Krishṇa says: "Actions pollute (*limpanti*) Me not; nor have I any desire for their fruit (*karmaphala*); he who knows (*abhijānāti*) Me to be such shall never be tied down (*badhyate*) by *karmas*. It was with this knowledge that, in ancient times, those who were desirous of attaining salvation performed actions; you also (O Arjuna), therefore, perform actions as men of old did in olden times."[184] Here, knowledge is said to be the essential means towards the salvation of man not for the purpose of dispensing with the *karmas* but for the purpose of giving the *karmas* their due meaning and value. Knowledge is essential as an auxiliary to the proper valuation of *karmas*. "Even the wise man is puzzled as to what should be done and what should not be done (*kim karma kim akarmeti*).[185] Therefore, it is essential to acquire the knowledge of the real nature of and distinction between "action" (*karma*), "forbidden action" (*vikarma*) and "inaction" (*akarma*).[186] "That man whose *karmas* are burnt away and are therefore purified by the fire of knowledge (*jnānāgnidagdhakarmā*), and, moreover, whose karmas are free from any motive or deliberate expectations of particular results thereof (*kāmasamkalpavarjitah*) is called a *paṇḍita*.[187] And, the entire (*samagram*) *karma* of such a man, whose attachments are dead, and whose mind is fixed on knowledge (*jnānāvasthitachetasah*), and who performs actions in the spirit of a sacrifice (*yajnāya*) is completely destroyed.[188]

Here we enter upon another important conception fundamental to life and existence propounded by the *Bhagavadgītā*. Man is to perform actions in a spirit of sacrifice, in a spirit of self-surrender. Actions performed without this spirit of sacrifice (*yajnārthāt anyatra*) would bind one to *karma* (*karmabandhanah*); therefore they are to be performed with that purpose, casting off all thoughts of one's own self (*muktasangah*).[189] "From food all creatures are born; from rain is food produced; rain is produced by sacrifices (*yajnāt*); and sacrifice is the result of action (*karma*). Know that all action has its source in the *Vedas*, and the *Vedas* are originated from the One (i.e. God) Who knows

182 *"svalpamapyasya dharmasya trāyate mahato bhayāt"*, Gitā, ii, 40.
183 See footnote No. 94 *ante*, for the connotation of the word "knowledge" in this connection.
184 *Gī.* iv, 14–15.
185 *Gī.* iv, 16.
186 *Gī.* iv, 17.
187 *Gī.* iv, 19.
188 *Gī.* iv, 23.
189 *Gī.* iii, 9.

no decay (*akśara*); therefore, the all-pervading *Vedas* are ever present in a *yajna*.[190] He who does not help the wheel (*chakram*) of life thus revolving here below, lives in vain, passing his life in sin and by the gratifications of the senses (*indriyārāmah*).[191]

Later, in the same *Adhyāya*, the meaning of *yajna* is further amplified. The wise man (*vidvān*), says Śrī Krishṇa, should behave completely unattached (*asaktah*), ever with the good of the people at heart (*lokasamgraham*), just as the ignorant act with self-attachment (*saktah*) to action.[192] The self-surrender must be thorough—"Dedicating all actions to Me, with a mind fixed upon the Supreme (*adhyātmachetasā*), engage yourself in battle (O Arjuna) without desire, without any notion of "mine", and (thus) without any mental grief or worry or anxiety (*vigatajvarah*)".[193] Indeed, in the next *Adhyāya*, a very wide meaning is given to this spirit of dedication, of self surrender, of *Yajna*. All our actions are to be in dedication to the Universal Spirit—"*Brahman* is the dedication (*Brahmārpanam*) and *Brahman* is the offering (*Brahmahvir*); *Brahman* is the fire (*Brahmāgnir*) *Brahman* the sacrificer (*Brahmaṇā hutam*); and *Brahman* is the destination to which he attains who meditates on *Brahman* (*Brahma-karmasamādhinā*)."[194] Therefore, "whatsoever you do, whatsoever you eat, whatsoever austerities you perform, do them as offering (*arpaṇam*) unto Me."[195] For, says the Lord, "by managing all your conduct in this manner, you will be free (*mokśyase*) from the bonds of *karma* resulting in good (*śubha*) or evil (*aśubha*) consequences or fruits; and thus attaining that state of mind which renounces (the fruit of actions) (*samnyāsayoga-yuktātmā*), you will reach *mukti* and come to Me."[196]

In this universal meaning given of *yajna*, all *karmas* are conceived as the *yajnas* performed by man, all knowledge is also *yajna* performed by him. Life itself is conceived as a perpetual *yajna*, a perpetual dedication to God, or to the Universal Being, and consequently the *karma-mārga*, or the *jnāna-mārga*, as means of attaining the end of life are conceived as *karma-yajna* and *jnana-yajna* respectively, dedicated to the *Brahman*, the Universal Being. The *Yajna* thus loses the original merely ritualistic meaning, and comes to attain a more human and also deeper and loftier significance.[197]

To return to our discussion of the *jnāna-mārga* as the means of solving the problem of life in the *Gītā:* Śrī Krishṇa, at one place, says that of all the *yajnas, jnāna-yajna* i.e. self-dedication to knowledge is far superior (*śreyān*) to that which consists of mundane activities (i.e. the *karma-yajna*); for *karma* is entirely comprehended within knowledge (*jnāne parisamāpyate).*[198] Even the sinner amongst the sinners *(pāpebhyah pāpakrittamah*) shall be able to cross (the ocean of *samsāra*) by the aid of this boat of knowledge (*jnānaplava*).[199] The fire of knowledge (*jnānāgnih*) reduces all *karmas* to ashes.[200] Indeed, there is nothing so sanctifying and ennobling in this world as knowledge.[201] To those who have their ignorance (*ajnāna*) destroyed by the knowledge of the self (*ātman*), such knowledge, like the sun, throws light on our understanding of (*prakāśayati*, i.e. reveals) That

---

190 *Gī.* iii, 14–15.
191 *Gī.* iii, 16.
192 *Gī.* iii, 25.
193 *Gī.* iii, 30.
194 *Gī.* iv, 24.
195 *Gī.* ix, 27; also of. *Bhāgawata Purāṇa* XI. iii, 38; and XI. xix, 9.
196 Gi. ix, 28.
197 We shall have occasion to speak more about this later in this chapter—see pp. 59 ff. below.
198 *Gī.* iv, 33.
199 *Gī.* iv, 36.
200 *Gī.* iv, 37.
201 *"Na hi jnānena sadriśam pavitramiha vidyate"*—*Gī.* iv, 38.

Supreme (*tat param*).[202] And those whose minds are (fixed) on That, who have their souls identified with That (*tadātmanah*), who have dedicated their all to That (*tannishṭhāh*), and who consider That as their final goal (*tatparāyaṇāh*), depart never to return, their sins being destroyed by knowledge.[203]

This 'way of knowledge' so far described may, however, be found difficult of accomplishment by the average man. To attempt to know the nature of the *Brahman* is much difficult (*kleśo 'dhikatarah*), because the unperceived (*avyakta*) goal is difficult to attain for the "embodied" (*dehavadbhih*),[204] i.e. for the human being. Therefore, another comparatively less difficult way is suggested by Śrī Krishṇa for the attainment of salvation. And that is the *Bhaktimārga*. Those who dedicate their actions to Śrī Krishṇa and holding Him as the highest goal, worship Him and meditate upon Him with their minds fixed upon none but Him (*ananyenaiva*)—of such men He becomes, without delay, the deliverer from the ocean of mortal world.[205] "That devotee (*bhaktah*) who hates no being, who is friendly and compassionate, who is free from attachment (*nirmamah*) and egoism (*nirahamkārah*), who is equally balanced in times of happiness and misery (*samaduhkhasukhah*), who is forgiving, contented, always engaged in *yoga*, self-controlled, firm of mind, and who has his mind and intellect fixed on me (*maiyyarpitamanobuddhih*) is dear (*priyah*) to Me."[206] In the opinion of Śrī Krishṇa, those who ever fix (*nityayuktāh*) their mind on Him and worship Him with the highest faith (*śraddhayā parayā*), are the greatest of Yogis.[207]

In combination with this *Bhakti-mārga* is also found, again, the doctrine of dedication of actions to which we have already referred before. "He who does actions for My sake (*mat-karmakrit*), whose highest ideal is Myself (*mat-paramah*), who is devoted to Me (*mad-bhaktah*), and who is free from attachment and enmity to any creature, comes to Me, O *Pāṇḍava*."[208] A spirit of complete dedication and self-surrender to God is the main characteristic of a *bhakta*. All possessions, spiritual or material, are to be deemed not as man's belongings but as God's; and they are to be used for Him to serve His purpose. That man is fit to attain salvation who worships (*sevate*) Him with the *yoga* of unswerving devotion (*avyabhichāreṇa bhaktiyogena*).[209]

Again, in combination with *bhakti*, we also find the eulogy of *jnāna* in the *Gītā*. By devoted love (*bhaktyā*) to God, the devotee is able to attain the knowledge of God,—what His extent is and what He is in truth (*tatvatah*); and by knowing the true nature of God, the devotee enters into Him.[210] Towards the close of the *Gītā* Śrī Krishṇa says: "He who will study this Holy Dialogue between us, will have offered unto Me the sacrifice of knowledge there is nothing better or superior (*anuttamām*)."[211]

In a previous *Adhyāya*, four kinds of devotees (*bhaktāh*) are described. "Of men of virtuous actions who worship Me, there are four types: the afflicted (*ārta*), the seeker after learning (*jidnāsuh*), the man who desires wealth or worldly happiness (*arthār thi*), and the man who knows

---

[202] *Gī.* v, 16.
[203] *Gī.* v, 17.
[204] *Gī.* xii, 5.
[205] *Gī.* xii, 6–7.
[206] *Gī.* xii, 14; also cf. Ibid.
[207] *Gī.* xii, 2; cf. also iv, 47; "Amongst all the *Yogis*, he who dwells in Me and worships Me with full faith in Me (*śraddhāvān bhajate*) is considered by Me the highest Yogi (*yuktatamah*)."
[208] *Gī.* xii, 55.
[209] *Gī.* xiv, 26. Note how the term *yoga* is suffixed to *bhakti* here.
[210] *Gī.* xviii, 55.
[211] *Gī.* xviii, 70.

(*jnānī*). Of these, the knower (*Jnānī*) who is ever possessed of steady application (*nitya-yuktah*) and whose worship is addressed to the One Being (*ekabhaktir*) excels them all (*viśshyate*); for I am exceedingly dear to the *Jnānī*, and he is so dear (*priyah*) to Me. All these are noble (*udārāh*); but the *Jnānī*, I deem to be My very Self, for he, with steady application (*yuktātmā*) resorts to Me as the goal (*gatim*), than which there is nothing better or superior (*anuttamām*)."[212]

This passage fairly summarizes the main attitude of the *Gītā* towards the "way" of *karma, jnāna* and *bhakti*. There is a clear indication here that the three "ways" are to be regarded as complementary to each other, in as much as a man of good actions (*sukritin*) wha has attained knowledge (*jnānī*) and is ever devoted to the One God alone (*ekabhakti*) will find out his salvation without delay. Thus a real synthesis of *karma, jnāna* and *bhakti* is made out here. *Jnāna* is the psychological foundation, the intellectual training, upon which the edifices of *karma* on the one hand, and of *bhakti* on the other have been established. The life of full devotion was conceived as hemmed in by a life of activity (*karma*) and a life of reflection (*jnāna*).

Thus, *bhakti*, as a means of attaining the end, is conceived as based on an intellectual foundation and not on mere emotional or sentimental one. Nor is it to be taken resort to for redress against personal afflictions, griefs, or shortages in worldly comforts. It has been defined in the *Śāṇḍilya Bhakti-Sūtras* as "affection (*anurakti*) fixed upon the Lord."[213] And, the *Bhakti-Sūtras* of Nārada say that it is in the form of the highest devotion or affection towards some one.[214] It is not, however, a mere sentimental attachment to God;[215] it is, rather, the result of a rational conviction that *Īśvara* is the goal of human existence. Even for Rāmānujāchārya, who was one of the foremost among the *bhaktimārgis, bhakti* is no mere sentimental attachment to *Īśvara*. It is attained by the devotee after passing through a long course of elaborate mental training. Its requirements are possession of the capacity of discrimination (*viveka*), freedom from attachment (*vimoha*), constant meditation of God (*abhyāsa*), doing good to others (*kriyā*), wishing well to all (*kalyāna*), speaking the truth (*satyam*), sympathy (*dayā*), non-violence (*ahimsā*), and charity (*dāna*).[216] And in his *Bhāshya* on the *Gītā*, he has pointed out that the way to *bhakti* is achieved by knowledge and action (*jnānakarmānugrihītam bhaktiyogam*).[217]

The roots and germs of the idea underlying *bhakti* could be traced back to the very ancient sources in Indian Literature, the *Vedas*. The *mantras*, the prayers, the rituals, the different invocations of Gods, with which the *karmakāṇḍa*[218] was practised in the Vedic days are some of the sources whence the later *bhakti* conception was developed. We have in the *Rigveda*, for instance,

[212] *Gī*. vii, 16–18.

[213] *Śāṇḍilya Bh. Sū*. i, 2.

[214] *Nār. Bh. Sū*. 2—*"sā kasmai paramapremarūpa."*

[215] Which seems to be the later interpretation of *bhakti*.

[216] *"Sarva-Darśana-Samgraha"*, IV—From Radhakrishnan: *Indian Philosophy*. Vol. ii, pp. 704–5.

[217] Radhakrishnan: Ibid. The same authority has drawn our attention to Svapneśvara's commentary on the word *"anurakti"* which is used to denote *bhakti*. *'Anu'* means 'after' and *'rakti'* means 'attachment'; *'Anurakti'* therefore means, according to Svapneśvara, attachment which comes after the knowledge of God.

[218] *Karmakāṇḍa* is the ritualism which was taught by the Vedas; while the later Upanishads are said to deal with what is known as *jnānakāṇḍa*—see e.g., *Siva-Samhitā*, i, 20–22. Mr. N. K. Venkatesan, however, in an article on "the Upanishads of the Atharva-Veda" in the *'Quarterly Journal of the Mythical Society'* (New Series, vol. xxvi, No. 1, July-October, 1936), points out that of the 108 Upanishads belonging to the four *Vedas*, 39 belong to the *Jnāna-kāṇḍa*, 62 belong to the *Karma-kāṇḍa*, and 7 deal with miscellaneous topics connected with the *Karma-kāṇḍa*. This means that the number of Upanishads dealing with the daily practices and rituals of the Hindus is larger than those which deal with their philosophical meditations.

this prayer to *Agni*; "Oh *Agni*, be easy of access to us, as a father is to his son."[219] Here the prayer to God proceeds upon the assumption of love or affection of God to men which is as natural as a father's love for his offspring. In a later work, viz. the *Śvetāśvataropnishad*, the very word *bhakti* is introduced, now for the first time. It tells us that unless the student has absolute faith or devotion (*parā bhaktih*) in God as well as in teacher (*guru*), he shall not be taught the sacred knowledge.[220]

It was, however, the *Bhagavadgītā* which first gave a strong impetus to the *bhakti* cult. It was made more popular later on by the *Paurāṇic* tradition, especially in *Bhāgavata Purāṇa*, the *Vishnu Purāṇa*, the *Bhakti Sūtras* of Nārada and Śāṇḍdilya, by Rāmānujācharya and other *Vaishṇavite* leaders, and the *Vishṇuprabandha*, a work in four thousand verses by the twelve *ālvārs* or saints. Rāmānujachārya, in the 11th century, invested the *bhakti* cult with fresh force. The spiritual monism preached by Śankarāchārya who flourished from about 800 A.D. onwards,[221] was considered by the Vaishnavites as opposed to their *bhakti* cult; and so, a reaction was aroused. Rāmānuja (who flourished between 1175–1250 A.D.[222]) tried to harmonize the *bhakti* principle with the belief in One Supreme Deity. Then came Madhva, Nimbārka, Rāmānanda, Kabīr, Vallabha, Chaitanya and many other teachers of religion. Madhva (1197–1276)[223] enjoined the *bhakti* of God Vishnu. Nimbārka (about the 13th century) enjoined the worship of Krishṇa and his beloved Rādhā. Rāmānanda (14th century) preached the *bhakti* of Rāma as the Supreme Diety. Vallabha (16th century) enjoined the worship of Bāla-Krishṇa, the boy Krishṇa; and, his contemporary Chaitanya preached the worship of the boy Krishṇa and Rādhā.[224] In Mahārāshṭra, the *bhakti* cult was prominently propounded by Marāṭhā saints like Jnānadeva (born about 1271 and died 1293 A.D.), Nāmdeo (about the end of 14th century), Eknāth (16th century) and Tukārām (first half of the 17th century) in the form of worship of Viṭhobā of Paṇḍharpur.[225]

Most important among the causes for the *bhakti* cult becoming so popular was that *bhakti* as a means of salvation was open to all alike—to women, to the *Vaiśyas*, and to the *Śūdras*,—nay, even to persons of the most sinful birth (*pāpayonayah*)![226] There was no distinction of race, caste, creed or sex in the way of *bhakti*. Indeed, one of the greatest saints and leaders of the *bhakti-mārga Kabir*,[227] was a Moslem by birth. The *jnāna-mārga* of the Upanishads was too restricted a path of salvation being open to the male sex and that too of the first *varṇa* viz., the *Brahmaṇas*, who only could give their full life to it. *Bhakti*, therefore, soon gained immense popularity owing to its universal appeal.

To return to the discussion of the three much debated 'paths' or 'means' of solving the problem of existence: A study of the *Gītā* reveals to us the important fact that each of these three *mārgas* has a psychological foundation. Thus, the *karma-mārgī*, who believes in 'action' as the chief *mārga* of salvation, has to acquire a certain kind of *mental discipline* in order to do *karmas* which are to serve the end of his existence. He has to abandon all sense of attachment (*asakta*, or *asamga*), to

---

[219] i, 1.
[220] *Śvet. Up*. vi, 22–23.
[221] See Macdonnell: *"India's Past"*, p. 148.
[222] Ibid. p. 149.
[223] Ibid. p. 150.
[224] Bhandarkar R.G.: *"Vaishnavism. Śaivism & Other Cults"*; and Thoothi; *"Vaishaṇavas of Gujarat"*, p. 88 ff.
[225] Bhandarkar; op. cit.; and Ranade: *"Mysticism in Mahārāshṭra."*
[226] Gī. ix, 32; cf. the Bhāgvata Purāṇa IX, xiv, 21—*"Bhaktih punāti mannishṭhān śvapākānapi sambhavāt"*
[227] Of the 16th Century.

give up all ideas of 'mine' and 'thine' (*mamatva*) and egoism (*ahamkāra*), and to perform *karmas* in a spirit of dedication to God, knowing full well that whatever he does is for the fulfilment of God's purpose and not his own, without any expectation (*āśā*) of a return of the fruit or result of that action (*karmaphala*). The psychological implications of *jnānamārga* and *bhakti-mārga* are not dissimilar to these, though in its later developments, *bhakti-mārga* degenerated even to the extent of finding erotic meaning in *bhakti*, and wavered between divine love and erotic sentiments finding expressions in the various narrations about the episodes of love between *Krishṇa* and the *Gopis* and *Rādhā*.

Our foregoing analysis of the several views on the solution of the problem of existence and the meaning and end of human life—whether it is called *mokśa, mukti* or *kaivalya*,—will be enough to enlighten us regarding the controversies which have been raging on the supremacy of one or the other of the three *mārgas*—the *karma-mārga*, or the *jnāna-mārga*, or the *bhakti-mārga*—as the most effective pathway towards *mokśa*. It has to be remembered that these three *mārgas* by no means stand in antagonism to each other. On the contrary, they are usually supposed to be working in co-ordination with each other. The difference of opinion among the philosophers lies mainly in the assertion that one of these should be taken as of the primary importance (*śreshṭha*), while the other two have to be regarded as subsidiary or auxiliary to it. In this way have arisen the *jnāna-mārga* school of thought. the *karma-mārga* school of thought and the *bhakti-mārga* school of thought. Even the *jnāna-mārga* should not be supposed to be opposed to the *karma-mārga*. It should be obvious from our preceding survey that what the *jnāna-mārga* asserts is, not that the *karmas* should be absolutely abandoned, but only that they should be executed with the fullest knowledge about the nature of existence, and therefore the fullest understanding of the nature and purpose of *karmas* themselves. A close perusal of the citations from different authorities, given in the preceding pages, will clearly show that none of these have advocated a complete abandonment of actions at all, but all of these have asserted that the *karmas* which are 'natural to one's station in life',—to use Bradley's expression,—which one is born to carry out, (*svabhāvaniyatam karma, sahajam karma, etc.*), considering one's natural propensities, tendencies and aptitudes should be carried out in accordance with one's own *dharma*.[228] And *Dharma* is defined for the individual by the *Vedas (śrutih)*, the *Smritis* (sacred tradition), the conduct of good men (*sadāchārah*) and the ultimate satisfaction of one's own conscience (*svasya cha priyamātmanah*).[229]

Early Hinduism, which was concerned with actions centred round the *yajna*, was, in a sense, an activistic religion in contrast with later Hinduism which was concerned with reflection and meditation, as in the Upanishads. The Vedic tradition said that man can return to the source of his origin by doing all the *Vedic Karmas*, by doing the duties as laid down in *Vedas*, the sacrifices, the *varna-dharma* and the *āśrama-dharma* etc., whereby salvation was promised—a sort of mechanical or routine *karmayoga*, by *doing*, not by *thinking* or *meditating; jnāna* and *bhakti*, knowledge and faith, were secondary. All the *yajnas*, the prayers, the offerings of all the nice things of life—all this was done primarily as items of *karma*. In the *Jaiminiya-Sūtras*, for instance, for all practical purposes, *Jnāna* has no place. The *Pūrva-Mimānsā* refuses to give any position to the *jnānī*. All

---

[228] Also, see *e.g. ante*, pp. 214ff., and again in Ch. viii, the story of the butcher who adhered to his *dharma*.

[229] *Man*. ii, 12; also cf. ii, 6. These are, according to Manu, the four-fold means of defining *dharma;* Yājnavalkya, who repeats all these four as the roots of *dharma (dharmamūlam)*, adds one more—"the desire which springs from a good resolution" (*Samyak samkalpajo kāmo*) Yāj. i, 8. For a fuller meaning of the term *dharma*, see also next chapter.

karmas, in its opinion, would lead to *mukti*. He who desires to reach heaven will perform sacrifices (*yajna*);[230] for sacrifices confer immortality, in the opinion of *Jaimini*.[231] Indeed, by the performance of the "*Aśvamedha*" sacrifice, (in which the horse, *aśva*, is sacrificed), one is able to conquer the world, death, sins, even the sin of murdering a Brāhmaṇa.[232]

In the Upanishadic teachings, however, *Yajna* came to be considerably looked down upon. This was the starting point of the difference between the *Pūrva-Mīmānsā* and the *Uttara Mīmānsā* schools. The *Sūtras* of Bādarāyana which belonged to the latter school and which were popularly known as the 'Vedanta philosophy', taught, in one sense, an anti-vedic *mārga*. For them, *Yajna* by itself had little meaning. The difference between the old Hinduism and the new Hinduism was the difference between a life around *Yajna* and a life without *Yajna*. The old Hinduism is a life of active optimism, in a sense. It was concerned with attempts at earning power. The particular institution of monasticism, of self-suffering, is absent in Old Hinduism. Life was regarded as a striving of purposes through several elements which were to be won over with the help of *Yajnas*. In a sense, therefore, it is the *Upāsanā*, the control of a deity with a kind of magical charm by which it was propitiated and subdued, that the old Hinduism concerned itself with. Thus old Hinduism was an activistic type of religion as opposed to reflective one. Even when reflection was attended to, it was carried in terms of, and to promote, action. The magico-religious rites of the Vedic Aryans following in what they called the *karma-kāṇḍa* (field of activity), centred round the *Yajna-kuṇḍa*, or *Agni-kuṇḍa*, that is the Fire-place. Fire was the medium, a kind of agent, between man and God. It was through Fire (*agni*) that man performed a *yajna* offering the best things that he could afford for the Gods—milk, ghee, grain and cattle.[233] All life was thus revolving round the *Yajna-kuṇḍa*. The life of activity was conceived as lying in and through sacrifice and giving away what was very dear to man, his necessities of life. The life of the individual, of the family (*kula*), of the village (*grāma*), of the community, was centred round the sacrificial fire.

However, this early phase of Hinduism, known as the *karma-kāṇḍa*, was so much overdone that the *karmas* grew into mere routine ritualism. This ritualism soon came to be looked down upon with contempt by the time the *Upanishads* appeared. It was attacked and corrected by later meditative and reflective life. The contempt of *yajna* ritualism, e.g., is thus expressed: "These boats in the form of *yajna* are weak (*adriḍhā*); those fools who regard these, performed by the eighteen persons (the host, the hostess and sixteen priests) as yielding blessings are certain to attain old age and death."[234] And again, "these boats of *Yajna* are fragile—think not over the many words of the scriptures, for they will bring you fatigue. What shall I do with these? For they cannot secure immortality for me. Grant me, O Lord, that knowledge which has secured immortality for thee."[235]

Therefore the Upanishadic seers set themselves to the task of discovering a new method of reaching salvation. This was done, not by completely discarding the *yajna*, but by giving a new interpretation to it. *Yajna* had now to be in terms of the inner life, not in terms of the external and formal ritual observances Contemplation of the nature of the ultimate reality, *Brahman*, was therefore, a way to realizing *mokśa*; and so *Yajna* was reinterpreted in terms of *jnāna*. Thus, the

---

[230] *"Yajate svargakāmah"*.

[231] *"Yajaterjālampūrvam"* and *"Apāma sommamrito babhūma"; etc.*

[232] *"Sarvānlokānjayatī, mrityum tarti, pāpmānam tarati, brahmahatyār; tarati, yo'śvamedham yajate", etc.*

[233] cf. Thoothi: *"The Vaishṇavas of Gujarāt."* p. 32.

[234] *Muṇḍ.* Up. ii. 7.

[235] See Thoothi: *"The Vaishṇavas of Gujarāt"*, p. 34.

Yajna-paramparā, the tradition of the *yajna*, was kept alive, but re-oriented, though in a different garb now.[236]

This meaning of *yajna*, in terms of the spiritual and reflective life, was elaborated by the Upanishads and was given a fresh impetus by Sankarāchārya and the teachers of his school who came after him. They interpreted, accordingly, the *Vedas*, the *Upanishads*, the *Gītā* and the *Bādarāyaṇa Sūtras* in the light of the *jnāna-mārga*. In the period of early Hinduism, *yajna* had been a means to an end superior to itself and there were attempts to rationalize a life of *Yajna* in terms of superior purposes, aims, and destiny of life. All this living spiritualism of early Hinduism is missing in the later period starting from the Upanishads in which philosophical reflections were carried out. Śankarāchārya and his followers merely meditated upon and discussed philosophical problems, which is a characteristic also of Buddhism and Jainism. On the meditative side, the Upanishadic teachings were considerably supported by the Buddhistic and the Jaina schools of thought. *Śankarāchārya* takes up the *Vedic* tradition, the *Upanishadic* tradition, and the Bauddha and Jaina traditions and tries to harmonize all of these and secure a balance between the *Vedas* and the *Upanishads*, the *Gītā*, and the *Bādarāyana-Sūtras* (i.e. the *prasthāna-trayī*). It may be remembered that Śankarāchārya was popularly known as *Prachchhanna-Bauddha*, a *Bauddha* beneath the surface or at heart, in view of the fact that for him, as in Buddhism, both the world (*jagat*) as well as worldliness (*samsāra*) were illusion (*mithyā*). On the other hand, in spite of the injunctions of their founders, both the Buddhistic and the Jaina traditions set up by their followers take up practically to the *karma* doctrine. In Jainism, for instance, meditation itself resolved into a matter of ritualistic observance; thus, a Jain is expected, for instance, to read or recite a particular *grantha* (religious book) for a particular number of times every day.

Now, the re-interpretation and re-orientation of *yajna* in terms of *jnāna*, as pronounced by the *Upanishads*, Śankarāchārya and others, was again carried to such an extreme extent that it became almost incompatible with the every-day life of an average man. The extreme form to which *jnāna-yajna* philosophy led was of asceticism and renunciation of a life of activity (*karma-samnyāsa*). The eulogy of *jnāna* at its extreme tended to result in a wholesale condemnation of *karma*. In order to raise the one to its loftiest and to indicate its distinctive merit, the other was placed at the lowest in estimation. Also, like *karma* in the earlier days, *jnāna*, too, soon became formalistic and fossilized, giving rise to a relish for outward forms of ascetic life. The extreme ascetic implications of the *jnāna* cult must have caused a great deal of dissatisfaction among the masses of India. It was too much to ask the average man to believe that world and worldliness (*jagat* and *samsāra*) were all false (*mithyā*), on the ground that they were all appearance (*māyā*).

Therefore, there emerged a new social need, a social demand, which had to be satisfied and Hinduism had to be again re-interpreted to suit the needs of the average man in India. In the new re-interpretation, account had to be taken of the past heritage (*paramparā*) of India; that could not be discarded *in toto*. The extremes and mistakes of the past, too, had to be avoided. Both the interpretations of the past,—the one in terms of the *karma-yajna* as well as the other in terms of *jnāna-yajna*—were, as we have seen, expressions of the social needs of their own times. Dissatisfied with the one as a solution of the problem of existence, the Hindu mind discovered the other; but then this latter was soon found incompatible with the actual every-day life of the Hindu. Therefore, the

[236] There are instructions regarding this *jnāna-yajna* in the Upanishads, e.g. in *Chhānd. Up*. iii. 17, 1–14; and in *Taitt. Aran*. x. 48; 64; *Śat. Br*. xi, I, i. seq.

new interpretation of Hinduism had to be such as to take into account the life that has to be lived by the common man, and yet possess the dignity and majesty of a philosophy in order to be able to replace the philosophy of *jnāna-mārgīs*. The *karma-mārga* had taken into account the common man's life, but soon failed to satisfy the Hindu with loftier ideas and ideals, who must have felt that what the *karma-mārga* resulted into was too mundane and low an aim of life. The *jnāna-mārga*, on the other hand, proved rather too lofty and impracticable an ideal, one far too removed from the day-to-day realities of life for the average individual to approach. Both these kinds of mistakes of the past had to be avoided now. And yet, the past tradition (*paramparā*) had to be kept alive as far as possible; in fact, the new philosophy had to draw upon the past *paramparā* itself.

All this was sought to be achieved by the introduction of the *bhakti* principle, especially by the thinkers of Vaishnavite school, mainly at the instance of the *Bhagavadgītā.* The *Gitā* accepted the heritage of the past in that *yajna, karma, jnāna, samnyāsa, dharma* and even *bhakti* itself, were taken up and absorbed by it; but each of these was invested with a newer meaning, more compatible with the every-day life that is lived, and therefore more human. *Yajna* was inter preted as a discipline in self-surrender to the will of God (*Iśvarārpaṇa* or *Brahmāpaṇa*); *karma* was placed in opposition to *akarma*, inactivity, and made acceptable in life so far as it was actuated in accordance with the *dharma* of a man. *Jnāna* was explained as instrumental in acquainting man with the knowledge of the greatness and the glory of God and Godliness; this was necessary in order to establish the existence of a Supreme Authority which is the be-all and end-all of everything, and thus to impel man to cultivate a spirit of activity in His name and for His sake without desire or expectations of its result, (i.e. to *karma-samnyāsa* in its true meaning of *karma-phala-samnyāsa*). And *bhakti*, towards which all these converge, with unswerving faith (*śraddhā*) as its foundation, is the very pinnacle of the philosophy of life expounded by the *Gītā.* It elevates and carries forward the old *Yajna* tradition (*Yajna-paramparā*) towards a living and ever-new interpretation. Life itself was conceived as a perpetual *yajna*, a perpetual surrender to God's purpose, not in terms of the libations of ghee, milk, butter, cattle, or grain (ie. *vaidikam karma*), nor in terms of mental contemplation (*jnāna*), but in terms of giving up the entire self of man,—body, mind, intellect, heart and possessions. Truest and fullest living means the complete surrender of everything (*sarvārpaṇa*);—that is the real *yajna*, the full *yajna*. And, all along, it is in this line of thought that the Hindu did, and does even today look upon life as a *Yajna* to be performed in terms of *bhakti*, of course in spite of and in the midst of human frailties.

Thus, it is the *yajna-paramparā* that is sought to be interpreted by all Vedic writers, Upanishadic writers, the *Bhagavadgītā* and the Bhāshya-kāra Āchāryas. The *Yajna-paramparā* is at the root of all Hindu scriptures and of the Hindu social psychology too. A very pointed instance of the persistence of this *paramparā*, social heritage or tradition, is the fact that even today, the term *yajamāna* (sacrificer) is very commonly used to denote the head of the house, or the householder, or the husband of a woman, according to the context in which it appears, at least in Mahārāshṭra, of which the present writer has personal knowledge. The term *yajamāna*, thus, has become synonymous with the term householder, or the chief of the family, as the case may be. This is how the socio-religious heritage of the Vedic India has persisted in the cutural consciousness of the Hindu even to this day.

Now, a close scrutiny of all the several philosophies of life presented hitherto will disclose to us more of the psychological unity behind them in spite of the historical differences of opinion and the ritualistic additions incidental in the course of their development. All these views are based on a certain attitude of mind which is fundamental in the midst of all the divergencies. Let us attempt to understand this attitude.

In the first place, in considering the problem of existence, of life, we must, according to the Hindu way of thinking distinguish between the 'means' and the 'end'. The 'end' has been variously named as '*mukti*', '*mokśa*', or '*kaivalya*', though in fundamentals the general meaning of all these terms is the same. The reader must have already noticed this similarity; and, as we proceed, we will further see how it is the same in all cases. The 'means' have also been variously conceived as *jnāna, karma* and *bhakti*. And here again, we have seen that though these differ from each other, none of them is exclusive or even independent of the other two. The important point is that these 'means' have to be made use of in accordance with *dharma*. So that, in one word, *dharma-samchaya* (accumulation of *dharma*) would be the means to attain the meaning and the end of human existence, viz. *mokśa*.

And here we come to the main point of our inquiry, the psychology behind the 'end' and the 'means':

The first issue that the Hindu thinker raises here is: What is the end or the ultimate goal of life? Through one birth or several, whatever man has come to be has an origin. Why should he be born at all? Now, the Hindu believes that man is born and exists in accordance with the wish of God (*Īsvara*), of the Universal Principle, of the Primal Cause; and that he is to that extent separated, as it were, from it. And from birth to birth, all the struggles that he goes through and the means that he employs, are the means to go back to the source of his existence. We are all born to fulfil the will of God. All sparks that radiate from him must naturally desire to return to the original source. The whole problem seems to be reduced to this, that the whole universe is a process, first of evolution,—of the Many being evolved out of the One; and then of involution,—the Many trying their best to go back to the origin from which they came. From the point of view of this life of *samsāra*, there is involution; from the point of view of the One, the *Iśvara*, there is evolution. From Infinity, thus, finite souls appear and strive, with struggles and efforts, ultimately with a view to reach the Infinity;—this is the end of existence. And, the birth of the sort that we get, in the view of the Hindu, is bound to keep us as finite and away from the infinite. It is therefore that we seek to be free from birth. However, we also get in Hindu Philosophy the theory that births are opportunities to serve the Infinite,[237] that births themselves are thus also means towards the end, that dealings in space and time are necessary implemental factors which we should welcome, in so far as they give us opportunities to be one with the Infinite!

But, it may be asked: Why should it be said that freedom from birth is salvation, is life found? The Western mind misinterprets such a theory in terms of not only death of this life, but of all existence. The Hindu's answer to this lies in another theory altogether. The Hindu feels that the things of life and world and worldly relations are fetters in the way of his freedom. And therefore, the fact of the birth which brings him in contact with these is, for him, the main cause of this difficulty, fundamentally because he feels a sense of separation (*viraha* or *viyoga*) from the One, the Universal Principle, while he really wants to merge into the One. Therefore, he finds himself divided between this longing to merge in the Universal and the problems of life, viz., world and worldliness (*jagat* and *samsāra*). In his best mood he compares these two opposite attractions, these two desires, these two longings, and declares that if he wants to reach the one, he must abandon the other. This birth, then, is an opportunity to be one with, or to belong to, or to be united with, or to be about (according to the various philosophies) God. Otherwise, ordinarily he would be satisfied with what he gets of the world and

[237] As with the Vaishṇavaites, especially, Vallabhāchārya. See, Thoothi: *Vaishṇavas of Gujarāt*, pp. 93 ff.

worldliness, or seek more of it. Unless, therefore, that longing, that pang, that desire to go out of one's self to the source of his being is aroused, the problem of salvation has no place for an individual.

So, the problem of life, the problem of existence, is to return back, or to be alongside with, or to be one with the original source of existence. It is not to die, but to become deathless (*amara*); and, to be *amara* does not mean that one dies for ever, but one becomes free from births and deaths, that is to say, one becomes immortal. And, this sense of separation from the original source of life by the individual lies, thus, at the root of his search for salvation in terms of *mukti* as cessation of births and deaths, as cessation of relation between the individual (*jīva*) and worldliness (*samsāra*).

All the institutions, social or personal, are, in view of these considerations, further means of *Dharma-samchaya* and are calculated to secure this end of *mukti* for the individual. The four *āśramas*, the *varṇa*-organization, education, marriage, family, personal and social conduct—all these are means in this sense, to the one end, and must be followed in accordance with *dharma*. The finite personality itself is also a means towards the end. The finite personality is the object which is sought to be developed, birth by birth, *āśrama* by *āśrama*, stage by stage, day by day, throughout this life, throughout his connection with the various social institutions, throughout his private life, towards realising the one end, viz., *mokśa* from whence there is no return to this worldly or any existence of a transient nature (*anitya*).

It is on these fundamental considerations that the various *dharmas*—the *varṇa-dharma*, the *āśrama-dharma*, the *kula-dharma*, etc. are founded. The basis of *āśrama-dharma*, for instance, lies fundamentally in so helping the individual, each personally training himself up along such lines, that though he may have to live in, with and along with society, that is to say, world and worldliness (*jagat* and *samsāra*), he may so formulate and work out his career as to acquit himself equitably in the social universe,—which is only a part of the larger universe,—and in the world and worldliness, without being affected by these, so that when the time comes, the individual may, out of this training and discipline, be enabled to cast away these social bonds, go into himself, and find himself out (*ātma-jnāna*), and thus secure the salvation to achieve which this birth is an opportunity and the things of life in it are so many instruments of salvation.

The whole system of *āśrama-dharma* has this note of direction; the whole system of *varṇa-dharma* is based on such fundamental conception; and all other qualitative *dharmas*, like *manushya-dharma* (*dharma* for human beings), *nitya-dharma*, (usual *dharma*), *naimittika-dharma* (unusual *dharma*), *kula-dharma* (family *dharma*), *strī-dharma* (woman's *dharma*), *purusha-dharma* (man's *dharma*), *sādhārana-dharma* (normal or common *dharma*), *āchāra-dharma* (*dharma* of good conduct), *vyavahāra-dharma* (*dharma* of everyday dealings or day-to-day affairs), *guṇa-dharma* (*dharma* according to one's characteristic abilities), *deśa-kāla-dharma* (*dharma* according to the place-and-time or environmental and temporal relevance), *rāja-dharma* (*dharma* of the ruler), *putra-dharma* (*dharma* of the son), *pitri-dharma* (*dharma* of the father), *pati-* and *patnī-dharma* (*dharma* of the husband and of the wife), *guru-dharma* or *āchārya-dharma* (*dharma* of the teacher), *śishya-dharma* (*dharma* of the pupil), and even *āpad-dharma* (*dharma* in times of calamity or emergency) and so forth,—each one of which refers to the respective role that an individual may have to take on at different times during the course of his life,—are all within the orbit of this fundamental chord of Hinduism, viz., that all *dharmas* and *karmas* can be so adjusted and apportioned that ultimately they will enable the individual to be free from his *karmas* and bring him face to face with the ultimate *dharma*, to cultivate and practice which alone he took birth. In the following pages we shall attempt to elucidate and explain this with reference to the different social institutions and aspects of social organization.

A NOTE ON E. J. URWICK AND HIS *THE MESSAGE OF PLATO*

Edward Johns Urwick (b. June 20, 1867; d. Feb. 18, 1945) was Director of the (then) London School of Sociology and Social Economics 1904–10; Tooke Professor of Economic Science at King's College, London, 1907–14; Professor of Social Philosophy at the University of London, 1921–24; President of Morley Memorial College, 1903–23; Director of the Department of Social Science and Administration* in the London School of Economics, 1910–23; came to Toronto, Canada, in 1924 where Professor R. M. MacIver, who was at the time Head of the Department of Political Economy at the University of Toronto, persuaded him to accept a Special Lectureship at the University. Two years later, when Professor MacIver went to Columbia University, Urwick was appointed his successor as Head of the Department of Political Economy. In 1928 he became the Director of the Department of Social Science, which is now called the School of Social Work, at the University of Toronto. He retired from the University in 1937, and continued as Emeritus Professor for some time. He was a Fellow of the Royal society of Canada, and the author of *Studies of Boy Life in Our Cities* (1904), *Luxury and Waste of Life* (Dent, London, 1906), *A Philosophy of Social Progress* (Methuen, London, 1912, 2nd. Ed. Rev. 1920), *The Message of Plato* (Methuen, London, 1920), *The Social Good* (Methuen, London, 1927), *The Values of Life* (Univ. of Toronto, Canada, and Ox. Univ. Pr., London, 1948), and many important papers and articles including *Modern Industry*: *A Short Analysis of Some Outstanding Dangers in the Present Situation, Freedom in Our Time* (1933), *Liberalism True and False* (1938), *Social Philosophy and Social Work* (in *Training for Social Work*, pub. by Univ. of Toronto, 1940), *The Building of the Community* (in *Social Welfare*, 1936). The interested reader may find his social thought and philosophy admirably summarized by J. A. Irving in his "Introductory Essay" to Urwick's posthumously published *The Values of Life*. The facts mentioned above are taken from Mr. Irving's "Essay".

Lest this may give an impression to the reader that Urwick was a mere "social philosopher",—by which term is understood, by many, an arm-chair speculator whose thinking is far removed away from the actual realities,—we quote below a few relevant passages from Mr. Irving's "Essay":—

"Urwick made an enduring contribution to education for social work . . . . he helped to establish courses for the preparation of social workers at the Universities of Liverpool, Edinburgh, Birmingham, and Glasgow—before similar courses were instituted even in American Universities. He maintained that the training of social workers should be soundly based on the social sciences, a principle now generally accepted. Of Urwick's contribution to the foundation of schools of social work an English authority has written: 'He has done more than any other individual to shape the development of standards of training in London and throughout the country" . . . .

". . . . Perhaps his greatest contribution consisted in his provision of a philosophy of social work. Owing to American influence, there has been an insistent clamour in Canada for new and ever newer "techniques" in social work. Urwick was always calling social workers back to basic realities and principles; it is significant that one of the most recent trends is a return to his position. . . . . It is no wonder that . . . . one still hears in Toronto references to Professor Urwick as the 'soul' of social work . . . . During his sixteen years' residence in Toronto, Urwick made significant contributions to

* It may interest the reader to note that on the title page of *The Message of Plato* (1920), Urwick's designation appears as "Head of the Ratan Tata Department of Social Science and Administration, University of London."

the life and thought of the larger Canadian community, serving as committee and board member of several organizations . . . . ”

As has been noted on p. 31, footnote no. 90, *The Message of Plato* had escaped the notice of the present writer when he published the first edition of this book at the end of 1939; but Professor Urwick himself was kind and gracious enough to write to the publishers asking them to draw his attention to it. Soon after, this author had an opportunity to present a summary of Urwick's *The Message of Plato* in a paper on *A Survey of Research in Indian Sociology During Twenty-Five Years*: 1917–42, (in the volume entitled *Progress of Indic Studies*—1917–42, pub. by the Bhandarkar Oriental Research Institute, Poona, 1942), to which the reader may be referred. The book itself, however, must be read in the original, for Urwick presents his theses with such force, brilliance, beauty of language and expression, elevating thought, all of which will be missed in any summary of the work. And, it is not necessary to agree with Urwick's view that Plato borrowed his thought from Vedanta, in order to derive edification and enjoyment from a perusal of the book.

Commenting on the *Message of Plato* in his “Essay”, Mr. Irving remarks:—

“. . . . The uniqueness of Urwick's interpretation of Plato consists in the effort to show—without, it must be admitted, a sound basis in scholarship—that the *Republic* can only be adequately understood in terms of the religious thought of ancient India, more specifically in terms of Vedantism . . . . (He made) two large assumptions, both of which may be seriously challenged: that there was in pre-Alexandrian times a fairly direct contact between India and Greece; and that the influence was profoundly felt by Plato . . . .”

“It is maintained . . . . that Plato is best understood as a disciple of Pythagoras, and Pythagoras is best understood in terms of Vedantism. Nine of the twelve chapters of *The Message of Plato*, accordingly, are devoted to a detailed analysis of the *Republic* with the object of showing Plato's debt to ancient Indian philosophy. In this stimulating and often brilliantly written re-interpretation of the *Republic*, Urwick considers that Bks. I-IV treat of the prepation of the soul and give an account of what the Vedas call “the lower path”; Bks. V-VII treat of spiritual realization, or of the Path of Religion; and the last three Books discuss the dangers of the lower path. . . . .

“The significance of Urwick's study of Plato consists, however, in its dynamic affirmation of religious idealism rather than in the success or failure of the attempt to establish inter-relations between Indian and Greek philosophy. He was . . . . too much of a realist not to see clearly that the experience, the common sense, the science, and even the religion of the modern Western world were in fundamental opposition to the supreme spiritual values he had discovered in Plato and in the Vedic literature. A reassessment of contemporary values was much more important than a formal defence of his position, and in this reassessment Urwick reviewed and found wanting, to a greater or less degree, modern man's belief in Christianity, science, progress, and civilization. . . .”—“The Social Philosophy of E. J. Urwick”, in E. J. Urwick: *The Values of Life*, pp. xi–lxv.

It is very interesting to note that The Very Rev. Dr. W. R. Inge, Formerly Dean of St. Paul's, England, remarks in his *Mysticism in Religion* (p. 99): “Urwick in his excellent book *The Message of Plato*, in which he shows the close resemblance between Indian thought and the Platonic tradition, contrasts ‘the two paths’ which are open to our choice, the ‘path of divine knowledge’ and the ‘path of pursuit’ which the Indian thinks the Western nations have chosen to follow. The upper path brings into play powers of the soul which are dormant on the lower. These powers are often ignored or refused hearing. ‘Our thought is so little religious, it is concerned so wholly with the path of pursuit, in attainments and achievements and satisfactions in this world and the things of it, that we are almost content to identify religion with the goodness of the lower path—a religion of morality touched with emotion and linked to occasional worship, which satisfies us because it can be made compatible with a virtuous worldliness'."—W. R. Inge: *Mysticism in Religion*, Hutchinson's University Library, The Senior Series, London, 1943.

In the Preface to this book, Inge observes (pp. 7–8): ". . . . I have quoted a saying of Whitehead, that if Christianity and the Asiatic religions both show signs of weakness, one reason may be that they have remained too much aloof from each other. It is a reproach to us* that with our unique opportunities of entering into sympathetic relations with Indian thought, we have made very few attempts to do so. The Germans have done more work on Indian Philosophy than we have. I am not suggesting that we should become Buddhists or Hindus, but I believe that we have almost as much to learn from them as they from us."

* i.e., the Britishers.

CHAPTER III

THE SOCIAL PSYCHOLOGY OF THE SYSTEM OF THE FOUR ĀSRAMAS

Dharmo viśvasya jagatah pratishṭhā
loke dharmishṭham prajā upasarpanti
Dharmeṇa pāpam apanudanti dharme sarvam pratishṭhitam
tasmad dharmam paramam vadanti
—*Mahāhnārāyaṇopanishad*, 22.1

Dharma is the mainstay of the entire moving world. In the world, people approach the most ardent follower of *Dharma*. They shake off sin by *Dharma*. Everything is established in *Dharma*. Hence they say that *Dharma* is supreme.

Na rājyam ñaiva rājā cha na daṇḍyo na cha daṇḍikah
Dharmeṇaiva prajāh sarve rakshanti sma parasparam
—*Mahābhārata*.

Neither the state nor the king, neither the mace (by which the authority punishes law-breaker) nor the mace-bearer govern the people; it is only by *Dharma* that people secure mutual protection.

The Hindu *śāstra-kāras* (i.e., those who have written the *śāstras*, the scientific treatises) have taken man into account as a social being with reference to four broad factors that influence his life and its conduct: He is considered in relation to: (i) *deśa*, (place, region) which may be said to be the regional approach to the study of society; (ii) *kāla* (time) which, we may say, constitutes the historical approach to the study of society, (iii) *śrama* (effort) which takes into account man with reference to his nurture and development in the contemporary environment; and (iv) *guna* (natural traits), which refers to the natural inherent psycho-biological equipment of man.

The importance and significance of 'place' and 'time' or geography and history in the activities and behaviour of man has been acutely recognised by the Hindu thinkers; and the Royal Sage (*Rājarshi*) Bhīshma teaches us, indeed, that *according to the conditions, demands and exigencies of the time-and-place* (deśa-kāla), *what is otherwise* dharma *may become* adharma, *and what is* adharma *may become* dharma,[1] *for the time being*. Evidently, however, it is not possible to visualize and anticipate

[1] *Mahā Śānti*. 78, 32.

all the probable variations of the locale (*deśa*) and the times (*kāla*) which human beings are likely to be confronted with, and hence, it may be said, no generalizations have been attempted by the *Dharmaśāstra-kāras* regarding men's conduct under conditions such as may be peculiar to these two. Indeed, the recognition of *deśa* and *kāla* as significant factors affecting *dharma* itself is a tacit acceptance by the *śāstra-kāras* of the fact that despite their attempts at canalizing and regulating man's conduct of life and behaviour through *dharma*, this is not to be taken as a rigid, static principle but has to be allowed a certain flexibility, a modifiability, a dynamic potentiality for its operation to suit the conditions dictated by the locale and the times. And, moreover, to speak of *dharma* itself becoming *adharma* and *vice versa* according to the times and the locale is really to speak of much more than just allowing the possibility of modifications in *dharma;* it is to ask men to be prepared for such complete and radical changes in *dharma* which may even be contradictory to the generally sanctioned *dharma* practices in order to suit the exigencies of the times and the conditions, if the latter necessitate such changes. It is in view of the impossibility of visualizing the emergencies of the locale and the times that the *śāstra-kāras* have not attempted to dwell on the *dharmas* of *deśa* and *kāla*, while the *dharmas* of *śrama* and *guṇa* have been discussed in such details by them.

And so, in the present work, we have attempted to make an investigation into the Hindu social thought under the last two headings, i.e. on man as a social being in connection with his nurtural development (*śrama*), and in connection with his natural endowments (*guṇa*). Here we may note that in substance, all the Hindu sages agree that any plan or scheme of social organization which aims at the best functioning of every human being as a social unit, must, in the first instance, take him into account from these two aspects: First, it must consider man as a social being with reference to his training and development in the natural and social environment in order to enable him to fulfil the final aim of his existence; and secondly, this has to be co-ordinated with another scheme which studies man with reference to his natural endowments, dispositions and attitudes. The first of these is the problem undertaken in the scheme of the *āśramas;* the second is thought out in the scheme of the *varṇas*.

The two organizations of the *Āśrama* and the *Varṇa (varṇāśrama-vyavasthā)*, which, to put it briefly, refer to the problems of the *nurture* and the *nature* of man, rightly serve as the cornerstones of the Hindu theory of social organization. And, we may also note here that the scheme of the *āśramas* as thought out and devised by the Hindu is a unique contribution in the whole history of the social thought of the world, without even a parallel to it in any other thought-system, excepting, perhaps, to some extent, in Plato's *The Republic*.* The same may be said to be true to a great extent of the *varṇa*-organization also.†

* As has been already noted in the Appendix to ch. ii, Professor E. J Urwick concludes in his book *The Message of Plato* that Plato borrowed the ideas he has expressed in his dialogues from India's Vedic thought. He has advanced several arguments in favour of this view.

† Cf. the special review article by the well known German sociologist Leopald von Wiese on "DIE KLASSISCHEN GRUNDLAGEN DER SOZIAL ORGANISATION DER INDER" ("The classical Basis of the Social Organisation of the Hindus") in *Kykios*, Fasc. 1, 1955, pp. 72–81. The original article is in German, with summaries appended in German, English and French.

L. von Wiese was the first among Western Sociologists to have given space in a sociological system to a discussion of *dharma* as a principle governing social life in his German works, *Beziehungslehre* (1924) and *Gebildelehre* (1929) which have been adapted and amplified by Howard Becker and published in English as *Systematic Sociology*, by L. von Wiese and H. Becker, pp. 772, Wiley, New York, 1932. Pitirim Sorokin of Harvard is another important sociologist who has been giving careful attention to the early Indian thought, as is evidenced in some of his recent publications. (See bibliography.)

Now, both the schemes of the *āśrama* as well as the *varṇa* presuppose, and are fundamentally based upon, a certain point of view in regard to the problem of life and its conduct, upon a certain basic outlook, a certain *philosophy* of life; this fundamental philosophy of life was the topic of our first chapter. There we have discussed the ways in which the problem of existence and human destiny was conceived by the Hindu, and how attempts were made to arrive at a basis for the solution of that problem. In this chapter and in those that follow, we shall attempt to find out how, on such basis, the whole superstructure of the Hindu social institutions has been planned and erected so as to give effect to the principles enunciated in the first chapter, within the orbit of the practical day-to-day life of the Hindu. In other words, in the first chapter, we dealt with the *theory* of the problem of life and its solution, while in this chapter and in the chapters that follow, we are going to consider the *practices* based on that theory, by following which the ideals preached by the theory could be realized.

And here lies, broadly speaking, what appears to be one of the main distinctions between the Hindu way of understanding, tackling and solving social problems and the Western way. In the West, generally speaking, the social sciences, as such, of to-day are mainly built up straight in terms of the relations between man and man, and between man and his environment. Rarely, if at all, would the social scientist take into consideration the more fundamental questions of the ultimate human values, of the ultimate aim and fulfilment of man's existence, of the basic social philosophy which does and should govern the super-structure of social practices, conduct and institutions and take such basic ideas and concepts as the starting points in his discussion. This is particularly true of the social scientists who are working in the field of economics and politics; and it is also true to a considerable extent of even those who are working in the field of general sociology, barring very rare exceptions like P. Sorokin, who is now considered to be "out of fashion" in sociological circles in his country by some of his colleagues just because he is interested in such problems. Of course, some sort of a social philosophy will always be found implicitly underlying any sociological discussion, but it is not given a conscious and deliberative consideration, it is not explicitly discussed and taken as the basic starting point in the modern treatises on social organization. Modern social scientists, *qua* social scientists in general, are on the contrary inclined to consider such questions of ultimate values as of more or less "speculative" nature, of "meta-physical" interest; on the other hand, they concern themselves directly with the "actual" and "factual" interactions between man and man and between man and his environment. These are their starting points, and also the main themes of discussion.

A pointed attack against the "philosophical" approach to social studies on the bases of ethical values was made by Ēmile Durkheim, Lucien Lévy-Bruhl and their school in France at the end of the last century and in the beginning of this century, among others. These writers vigorously advocated the "scientific" approach of studying "social facts" in the social sciences, which seems to have meant, for them, exclusion of any consideration of the ultimate and higher values of human life. We do not propose to enter here into the controversy of "social philosophy vs. social science", but the interested reader may profitably peruse the relevant writings of Durkheim and Lévy-Bruhl, and the spirited attack on their position by Simon Deploige* who himself quotes a large number of relevant excerpts from them.

---

* Simon Deploige: *The Conflict Between Ethics and Sociology*, Tr. by C. C. Mitter. B. Herder Book Co., London, 1938.

See also the present writer's article on *"Fact and Theory in the Social Sciences"* in the *Socio-Economist*, Bombay, Vol. II, ii. 1940.

In sharp contrast with such attitude, the Hindu, in his *śāstric* discussions of social life and practices, first raises the fundamental question of the significance of man's existence on earth, gives consideration to basic questions of the relation between man and the possible ultimate purpose and fulfilment of his existence, and, upon such bases, seeks to define and formulate his relations with every other thing, person, event and circumstance in the world. Thus, for the Hindu, the individual's relations with the Ultimate Principle or the Universal or Primal Cause defines his relations with other men, with his family, with the group or society in which he lives or with which he comes in contact, with his village and his country,—and, indeed, with the entire animate and inanimate creation!

And this general statement of the case applies to the *Āśrama* theory which we propose to discuss in this chapter, reserving the discussion of the *Varna* theory for a later chapter (See ch. viii). The whole of the life of an individual is, for the Hindu, a kind of schooling and self-discipline. Now, during the course of this schooling, he has to pass through four stages,—four grades of training, as it were,—called the *Āśramas*. And, in regard to the *āśramas*, too, every item and stage and phase has to be defined in terms of the already defined relations between man and God. Here, therefore, practically we start with supernatural basis; upon this, we erect the superstructure of man's earthly career. The earthly existence has thus to be defined primarily in terms of *dharma;* and *dharma* has to be interpreted in the concrete in terms of *karma*. The *āśrama* scheme, therefore, defines our *dharma* in and through a life of worldliness, of *samsāra*, before it, and beyond its pale; and, in practice, it seeks to delineate the implications of *dharma* in terms of *karma*.

In this connection, the following, from a review of one of the recent books of Sorokin, by Dr. William L. Kolb of Tulane University, may be of interest to the reader: "Who reads Sorokin?" asks Dr. Kolb, and answers the querry thus: "Whatever the answer to that question, sociologists generally are not included in the attentive group. To be sure *Social Mobility* and *Contemporary Sociological Theories* are frequently cited by Sociologists and are used by them in teaching and research. But the *Dynamics* and all its progeny, among which can be included the book under review, (viz., *Social Philosophies in an Age of Crisis*) are lost in sociological limbo. They are no longer even criticised, simply ignored. Sorokin is concerned with the study of 'the how and why, the whence and whither, of man, society, and humanity'."

"However," adds Kolb, "Sociologists as professional men are not concerned with these problems. The mistaken use of Weber's dictum of no value judgements, the pressure of the sources of research funds and perhaps a deeply rooted sense of despair conspire at the level of applied social research to confine the social scientists to problems which accept the present social order and its movement as a given, thus closing the door to the development of a sociology of possibility. At the theoretical level, as Reinhard Bendix has shown in a recent issue of *Commentary*, the image of man conceptually developed renders a value system based on human dignity and reason utterly irrelevant. Thus why read Sorokin; why even bother to criticise him?"

On the other hand, Kolb points out that this very attitude of neglect by the intellectuals of our times in understanding and analysing values may itself be an indication of the degeneration of our society: "Contemporary social science is profoundly symptomatic of what the philosophers of history regard as the decline of our society. Its scientistic concentration on human manipulation represents an extreme form of the reduction of the human being to pure object."

Kolb therefore admonishes the above current tendency among Sociologists. "To ignore the contemporary philosophers of history is to risk the loss of our sociological souls, because, in the right or wrong fashion they are grappling with the essential problem of the moral and practical significance of social science in our contemporary society." (Review by William L. Kolb. of A. Sorokin's *Social Philosophies in an Age of Crisis*. The Beacon Press, Boston, 1950, in *The American Sociological Review*, 16,2, [April 1951], pp. 267–68).

In order to understand the psycho-moral basis of the *āśramas* proper, it is advisable that we should look into the theory of the *purushārthas* which concern themselves with the understanding, justification, management and conduct of affairs of the individual's life in relation to the group, in and through the *āśramas*. The *purushārthas* are four, viz., *dharma, artha, kāma* and *mokśa*. We speak of these *purushārthas* as the 'psycho-moral' bases of the *āśrama* theory, because, on the one hand, the individual receives a psychological training through the *āśramas* in terms of lessons in the use and management of the *purushārthas;* while, on the other hand, in actual practice, he has to deal with the society in accordance with these lessons. It is in the light of the understanding of the meaning and place of the *purushārthas* in the *āśrama* scheme that we shall be able to comprehend the right method, way and outlook for the management of each of the *āśramas*.

It is usual to translate these terms *dharma, artha, kāma* and *mokśa* in English by such words as morality, wealth, desires or passion, and salvation respectively. But the Sanskrit terms are potent with deeper meanings than these English words singly convey. Thus, the word *dharma* is derived from the Sanskrit root '*dhri'* meaning 'to hold together, to preserve'.[2] The social implications and meaning of *dharma* as a principle for maintaining the stability of society is brought out by Śrī Krishṇa in three verses in the *Mahābhārata:* In advising Arjuna as to what is *dharma* he explains that "*dharma* is created for the well-being of all creation",[3] and further that "all that is free from doing harm to any created being is certainly *dharma*; for, indeed, *dharma* is created to keep all creation free from any harm"[4]. Śrī Krishṇa proceeds, next, to give a still more comprehensive view of *dharma:* "*Dharma* is so called because it protects (*dhāraṇāt*) all; *dharma* preserves all that is created. *Dharma*, then, is surely that principle which is capable of preserving the universe".[5] *Artha*, on the other hand, is to be understood as referring to all the means necessary for acquiring worldly prosperity, such as wealth or power. And *Kāma* refers to all the desires in man for enjoyment and

---

[2] For the several stages of meaning through which the word has passed from the Rigvedic period onwards, see P. V. Kane: *"History of the Dharmaśāstras",* Section I, pp. 1–4.

[3] *Mahā Karṇa.* 69, 57. *"Prabhavārtham cha bhūtanām dharma-pravachanam kritam."*

Also *Mahā. Śānti.* 109; 10. *"Prabhavārthāya bhūtānām dharma-pravachanam kritam/Yas syāt prabhava-samyuktas sa dharma iti niśchayah.*

[4] Ibid. 58; *"Yas syād ahimsāsamyuktas sa dharma iti niśchayah/ahim sārtham cha bhūtānām dharma-pravachanam kritam."*

[5] Ibid. 59; *"dhāraṇād dharma ityāhur dharmo dhārayate prajāh/yas syād dhāraṇa-samyuktas sa dharma iti niśchayah."*

Also. *Mahā-Sāntī.* 109–11:—

Dhāraṇād dharmam itāyahur dharmeṇa vidhritāh prajāh
Yas syāt dhāraṇa-samyuktas sa dharma iti nischayah.

And in *Mahā-Karṇa* 119–59:—

Dhāraṇād dharma ityāhur dharmo dhārayati prajāh

And in *Vaiśeshika Sūtras*:—

Yato abhyudaya-nihśreyasa-siddhih sa dharmah

And in *Matsya Purā.* cxlv (145), 47:

Dharmeti dhāraṇe dhātur mahattve chaivam uchyate
adhāraṇe mahattvo vā dharmah sa tu niruchyate

satisfaction of the life of the senses, including the sex drive to which the word *kāma* more prominently refers.[6] The term refers to the native impulses, instincts and desires of man, his natural mental tendencies, and finds its equivalent, we may say, in the use of the English terms "desires", "needs", "basic or primary motives", "urges", or "drives" and the collective use of the term "*kāma*" would refer to the totality of the innate desires and drives of man.* The term is also often used in a broader sense to include socially acquired motivation too. *Dharma, artha* and *kāma*, therefore, refer respectively to the moral, material and mental resources, accessories and energies available to man.

Of these three, *artha* and *kāma* refer to two of man's earthly belongings, while *dharma* stands on a higher level. At its lowest level of manifestation, *kāma* is understood in the sense of pure sex drive, and is said to be one of the six 'enemies' of human being.[7] But it is equally true that a human being-cannot conduct his life without *artha* which constitutes the material means of living, and *kāma* which helps the propagation of the species. Therefore, it is needed that the correct quality and quantity, the place, and the time of *artha* and *kāma*, have to be determined and laid down by the wise sages. This is done in terms of *dharma*, which defines, for man, the proper quantum, place and season, for the right functioning of *artha* and *kāma*. By attending to his *dharma*, therefore, a person is able to live a proper life even though it may be lived in terms of *artha* and *kāma*. As Vidura says: "It is by the help of *dharma* that the sages have been able to cross the world. The stability of the universe depends upon *dharma; artha* and *kāma*, too, depend for their proper management upon *dharma. Dharma* is the foremost of all; *artha* is said to be middling: and *kāma*, it is said by the wise, is the lowest of the three. Therefore, we should conduct our lives with self-control; paying major attention to *dharma*".[8]

In the opinion of Manu, the good of humanity lies in a harmonious management or co-ordination of the three (*trivarga*), viz., *dharma, artha* and *kāma*. Says he: "Some declare that the good of man consists in *dharma*, and *artha*; others opine that it is to be found in *kāma* and *artha*; some say that *dharma* alone will give it; while the rest assert that *artha* alone is the chief good of man here below (on earth). But the correct position is that the good of man consists in the harmonious co-ordination of the three"[9] Now this advice, the commentator Kullūka explains, is meant for those who weigh the issue from the viewpoint of the immediate and worldly objectives of life. But, from the point of view of the final purpose and meaning of life, *mokśa* alone would prove to be the best guide.[10] With reference to the supreme end of *mokśa*, therefore, the other three immediate objectives of life become but the means for the attainment of that end.

---

[6] cf. the discussion on the *purushārthas* in Dr. Thoothi's *"The Vaishnavas of Gujarāt"*, pp. 44–45.

* Though many social psychologists would use the terms "drives" and "motives" interchangeably, some would like to distinguish between the two. See T. M. Newcomb: *Social Psychology*, pp. 80–83.

[7] *Kāma, krodha, lobha, moha, mamada and matsara*—passion or lust, anger, greed, temptation, conceit and jealousy are the six 'enemies' (*shaḍ-ripu*) of man.

[8] *Mahā. Śanti*. 167, 6–9: *"dharmeṇaivarshayas tīrṇā dharme lokāh protishṭhitāh/dharmeṇa devā vavridhur dharme chārthah samāhitah //7// dharmo rājan guṇah śreshṭho madhyamo hyartha uchyate/kāmo yavīyān iti cha pravadanti manīshiṇah //8// tasmād dharmapradhānena bhavitayam yatātmanā."*

[9] *"dharmārthāvuchyate śreyah kāmārthau dharma eva cha /artha eveho vā sreyas trivarga iti tu sthitih /Man*. ii, 224. *On 'Trivarga'* Kullūka comments: *"dharmārthakāmātmakah parasparāviruddhas trivarga eva purushārthatayā sreya iti viniśchayah/*

[10] *"evam cha bubhukśūn pratyupadeso na mumukśūn/mumukśūṇām tu mokśa eva śreya iti shashṭhe vakśyate.*

Now, as we shall see in our discussion of the *grihasthāśrama* (Ch. VI), *artha* and *kāma* have to be practised by the individual with reference to one or more other individuals. So also, the practice of *dharma* cannot be possibly conceived as existing apart from the relation between the individual and the group,—except when the *dharma* directed is entirely in the interest of the *mokśa* of the individual, as in the case of the *samnyāsin* (the recluse), in whose case *artha* and *kāma* become transformed and get merged into *mokśa*. Thus, on the whole, the *purushārthas* are concerned both with the individual as well as the group. They enunciate and justify the *kinds* of relation between the individual and the group; they define the *just* relations between activities of the individual and those of the group; they also state explicitly and by implication, the improper relations between the individual and the group with a view to enabling the individual to avoid them. Thus, the *purushārthas* control both the individual and the group, and also their inter-relations.

Here, it is to be remembered that when we refer to *artha* and *kāma* as *purushārthas*, we refer to them in their proper proportions, that is to say, only in the best sense of these words. *Artha* refers to the problem and activities connected with the finding, making, gathering, conserving and organizing of the material necessities of life and all that accompanies the same. Similarly, *kāma* refers to the sex and the reproductive aspect, its understanding, its right functions, its obfunctioning, its organization and management both with reference to the individual and the group. As we have pointed out above, *Kāma* in the wider sense refers to all the innate desires and urges of man. *Dharma* seems to be the arbiter, the conscience keeper, the director, the interpreter, of the properties that govern the right functioning and management of the relations between the inner man and the outer man, and between the individual and the group. *Dharma* is, therefore, the holder of the balance in terms of which *artha* and *kāma* have to be dealt with, weighed, practised and apportioned.[11] *Mokśa*, on the other hand, seems to be concerned mainly with the individual. It refers, perhaps, to the appeal of the inner man to the individual, unaffected by the group. It is perhaps too personal an outlook that defines the struggle and hope and justification within the individual for *Mokśa*. But, from the Hindu's point of view, we must also remember, that the inner personality of the individual, at its best, is identified by him not only with the group, nor only with the society, nor with the nation, nor the race, nor even with the entire human race, but with the whole creation, animate and inanimate, seen and unseen, which includes all these and is still much more than all these! This will be amply evident from our discussion on the problem of *mokśa* in the previous chapter. In the light of these considerations, the goal of *mokśa* does not possess the narrow individual outlook, for the Hindu. *Nor is it to be pursued exclusively and directly by an individual unless and until he has duly satisfied all his social debts (riṇāh) or obligations*.*

And now let us turn to the theory and practice of the *āśramas* proper. The word *āśrama* is originally derived from the Sanskrit root *śrama* 'to exert oneself'; therefore, it may mean, by derivation (i) a place where exertions are performed, and (ii) the action of performing such exertions.[12] Literally, an *āśrama* is a 'halting or resting place'. The word therefore signifies a halt, a stoppage, or a stage in the journey of life just for the sake of rest, in a sense, in order to prepare oneself for further journey. The *āśramas*, then, are to be regarded as resting places during one's journey on the way to final liberation which is the final aim of life. The four stages of life, says Vyāsa in the

[11] For a discussion of the implications of the concept of *dharma on* similar lines, see also, Thoothi: *"The Vaishṇavas of Gujarāt"*, Ch. II.

* See pp. 86–87 below.

[12] Hastings: *"Encyclopaedia of Religion and Ethics"*—Art. on *"Āśrama"* by P. Deussen.

Mahābhārata, form a ladder or flight of four steps. That flight attaches to *Brahman*. By ascending that flight one reaches the region of Brahma.[13] Whichever of the above be the original meaning of the word, the historical development of the *āśrama* scheme as an institution and the social implications within it include all the interpretations given above. Each of the *āśramas* is a stage of life in which the individual has to train himself for a certain period, and exert himself within the circuit of the same in order to qualify himself for the next.

The *āśramas* are four in number: (1) the *brahmacharya*—that of a student, (2) the *grihastha*—that of a married man, the house-holder, (3) the *vānaprastha*—that of retired life in the forest, after abandoning the home, preparatory to complete renouncement of worldly relations, and (4) the *samnyāsa*—the life of complete renunciation of worldly relations and attachments.

Attempts have been made to show that in the beginning there were only three *āśramas*, that originally the *vanaprastha* and the *samnyāsa āśramas* formed only one order, and that these came to be distinguished from one another in later times.[14] Thus the *Chhāndogya Upanishad* mentions three orders of life according to *dharma (trayo dharmaskandhā)*: (1) the householder's order, where one is expected to perform sacrifices (*yajnah*), study (*adhyayanam*) and charity (*dānam*); (2) the order of the recluse, wherein one is expected to perform penances (*tapas*); and (3) the order of a perpetual or life-long (*atyantam*) student residing permanently in the house of a teacher (*āchārya-kula-vāsī*). All these three (*sarva ete*) reach the worlds of bliss (*puṇyaloka*) after death; but any of these three who is established in *Brahman (brahmasamstho)*[15] attains immortality (*amritatvam*)[16] Dr. Modi also refers to two other passages from *Manusmriti* where a positive assertion that the scheme of *āśramas* consists of three *āśramas* is made.[17]

---

[13] *Mahā-Śānti.* 242, 15: *Chatuspadī hi nihśreṇī brahmaṇyeshā pratishṭhitā/etāmāruhya nihśreṇīm brahmaloke mahīyate.*

[14] See *"Proc. and Trans, of the Seventh All Indi. Ori. Conf."* Baroda. Dec. 1933 (1935) pp. 315–16, Art. on *"Development of the system of Āśramas"* by Dr. P. M. Modi. See also *"Vedic Index"* by Macdonell and Keith, Vol. I, pp. 68–69; and C. V. Vaidya: *"History of Sanskrit Literature"*. Vol. I. Section ii, pp. 180. ff., Poona (1930).

[15] *"trayo dharmaskondhā, yajno' dhyayanam dānamiti prathomah, tapa eva dwitīyo, ācharyakulavāsī tritrīyo, atyantamātmānamāchār yakule' vasādayan/sarva ete puṇyalokā bhavanti brahmasamstho' mritatvameti// Chhāndo. Upa.* ii. 23, 1.

[16] See Modi: op cit.

This passage, however, may be interpreted in a different manner. For, Dr. Modi has taken the word *'brahma-samsthah'* as an adjective qualifying the three orders mentioned prev ously in the passage. The word, on the other hand, may have been used independently to denote an order by itself. It is in this manner that Prof. Ranade has interpreted the last sentence from the passage quoted above as referring to the *samnyāsa āśrama* as the fourth *asrama*.".. We are told", says he, "that he alone who lives in Brahman *(brahmasamstho)*—referring probably to the life of the *somnyāsin.*—attains to immortality. When we re-arrange these orders", he further adds, "we find that the foundations of the future *āśrama* system are already to be found firmly laid even in such an old Upanishad like the Chhāndogya"—*"A Constructive Survey of Upanishadic Philosophy"*, (Poona, 1926), pp. 60–61.

[17] *"ta eva hi trayo lokās ta eva traya āśramāh/ta eva hi trayo vedās ta evoktās trayo'gnayah"*—Man: ii, 230:— "There are three Worlds, three- *Āśramas*, three *Vedas*, as also there are said to be three Fires."

And, *"Yasmāt trayo'pyāśramiṇo ijnānenānnena chānvaham/grihasthenaiva dhāryante tasmājjyeshṭhāśramo grihi/* Man. iii, 78.

Dr. Modi considers that in the latter verse, the force of *'api'* is intended to include all the *āśramas* in existence; and therefore, for him, the passage means that all the three *āśramas* including the *grihasthāśrama* itself are dependent upon *grihasthāśrama*. The commentator Kullūka on *Manu*, however, has interpreted *trayo, pyāśramiṇo' as*

Now, even though in early literature we find, as in the *Chhāndogya Upanishad* quoted above, a mention of the three phases of life viz., the student, the householder, and the hermit, yet it was not enjoined that these must be followed compulsorily one after the other. A man, it seems, could become a householder after he finished his student's life, or he could live the life both of a student and a householder together, or he could turn to the hermit's life after he finishes his student's career, without marrying.[18] This means that the *samnyāsi's* stage need not necessarily be preceded by the *grihastha* phase. The four stages comes to us in sequential form from later *Upanishads* like the *Jābāla*, according to which the order of the student must precede that of the householder, and that of the householder must be followed by the order of the hermit (*vānaprastha*), while the order of the wandering or begging ascetic (*parivrājaka or bhikśu*) must be preceded by those of the householder and the hermit.[19]

In trying to identify the three *āśramas* mentioned in the *Chhāndogya Upanishad* with the four traditional ones, one can say that a system of three *āśramas* rather than four could find justification from another point of view also. There is a view according to which the *samnyāsa* state was not regarded as an *āśrama* proper; it was rather considered as outside the meaning, and therefore beyond the limits, of an *āśrama* as in the *Śvetāśvatara Upanishad*, wherein the *samnyāsi* is said to be above all the *āśramas (atyāśramin)*[20]; as such, he is no longer a "social personality"; he is devoid of any family bond; he is a homeless wanderer, begging, without any belongings or property of his own; and such a one bears the name of *sam-nyāsin*, that is, a person who has made complete (*som*) renunciation (*nyāsa*) of everything.[21] And, we may also point out that even in the later development of the *āśramas* into a scheme of four stages, the personal identity of the man who ends with the *vānaprastha* stage and enters into the *samnyāsa* stage ceases to exist altogether both for himself and for the rest of the world in a formal way too. In fact, such a person is actually supposed to have been dead, the usual death ceremonies (*antyeshṭi*) being actually performed by his kinsmen; and the *samnyāsin* is said to have been born out of the ashes and the flames of the funeral pyre of the dead person. Such a person, in fact, even abandons his personal name and the family surname by which he was known before he took up *samnyāsa*, and actually adopts a new name by which he comes to be known thereafter. And, since the man is supposed to be dead, and his body is taken to have been already burnt away and the death ceremonies performed, his actual death after the *samnyāsa* is accepted by him has to be by the special rites of what is known as *samādhi*, and not by the *antyeshṭī* death rites meant for the ordinary man.

Now, according to the Hindu Dharma-Śāstra, each individual should normally pass through these four phases of life, one after the other, (*kramaśah*), and live in them in accordance with the *śāstras* if he desires to obtain salvation (*mokśa*).[22] After passing from *āśrama* to *āśrama*, and after offering the sacrifices with senses under control (*jitendriyah*), comprehending and realizing

---

"the three *āśramas* other than the *grihasthāśrama" (grihasthavyatiriktās trayo'pyāśramiṇo)*; these depend upon *grihasthāśrama* for their support.

[18] See *Chhānd. Up*. ii. 23. 1 (already quoted above); v. 10; viii, 15: Br. *Lp*. iii. 8. 10; iv, 2, 22; *Taitt. Up*. i, II. cf. Ranade. *"A Constructive Survey of Upanishadic Philosophy"*, pp. 60–61; Keith; *Religion and Philosophy of the Veda and the Upanishads"*, vol. ii. p. 587.

[19] *Keith*. Op. cit. pp. 587–8. See *Jābāla. Up*. iv.

[20] *Śvet. Up*. vi. 2.

[21] *Keith*: Op. cit. p. 589.

[22] *Man*. VI. 88; also see *Gau*. iii, l; *Āpa*. ii, 21, 2.

the limitations and futility of a life dependent upon alms and offerings (*bhikśābalipariśrāntah*), if one goes forth as a wandering mendicant (*parivrajan*) and dies thereafter, he becomes blessed; that is, as explained by Kullūkabhaṭṭa, such a person attains *mokśa*.[23] However, before entering the last phase viz., the *samnyāsa*, he has to pass through the three previous phases of life in their proper order; besides, he has to satisfy himself that he has carried out the duties and obligations laid down for each of the *āśramas;* and he has also to see that he has duly given his dues in connection with the social obligations or the three "debts" (*riṇas*).[24] These three *riṇas* are: (1) the debt to the *rishis* (*rishi-riṇa*), (2) the debt to the ancestors (*pitri-riṇa*), and (3) the debt to the Gods (*devariṇa*).[25] Now these three debts could be vicariously satisfied, respectively, (1) by studying the *Vedas* in accordance with the rules laid down for the study (*vidhivad*), that is to say, by passing through the *brahmacharyāśrama*, (2) by begetting sons in accordance with the *dharma* (*darmatah*), i.e. by going through the *grihasthāśrama*, and (3) by offering sacrifices according to one's capacity (*śaktitah*), i.e. by performing the duties of the *vānaprasthāśrama.*[26] After carrying out these duties in the first three *āśramas*, one should apply one's mind exclusively towards the attainment of *mokśa*.[27] It is opined that the man who fails to carry out any of these obligations due to him during the first three *āśramas* is not entitled even to try to attain *mokśa*; and Manu says that he who seeks *mokśa* without fulfiling his duties in the first three *āśramas* will sink low to damnation (*vrajatyadhah*).[28]

There are differences of opinion among different authorities concerned as regards the particular age at which one is expected to enter each of the *āśramas*, and the period of life he is expected to spend in it. Different ages at which a man is expected to enter the *grihasthāśrama* have been prescribed by different authorities; and, moreover, for different *varṇas*, again, different ages at which an individual may enter the *brahmacharya* stage i.e. the first *āśrama;*, of education and studies, are given.[29] After the prescribed course of education is completed, the young man enters the *grihasthāśrama*; this iṣ bound to be obviously in the maturity of youth, when he has completed all the requirements of *brahmacharyāśrama*, and is fit to marry. And, he is expected to retire from the *grihasthāśrama* after playing his part as a member of the *āśrama*, in the proper manner (*vidhivat*);[30] this happens when his skin gets wrinkled, when his hair turns white, and when he sees the sons of his sons; he has now to take to a life in the forest; he may leave his wife to the care of his sons, or he may take her away alongside with him.[31] In the forest he has to live the simplest life: receiving alms, performing sacrifices, and studying the *Vedas* and the *Upanishads*.[32] After having thus spent the third part of (a man's natural term of) life in the forest, he may live as an ascetic during the

---

[23] *Man*. vi, 34, and Kullūkabhaṭṭa's commentary on it; (*mokśalābhādbrahmabhūtarddhyatiśayam prāpnoti*). cf. also *Bau*. ii, 17, 15–17.

[24] *Man*. vi, 35 cf. *Yāj*. iii, 57.

[25] *Man*. iv, 257.

[26] *Man*. iv, 36.

[27] Ibid.

[28] *"Anadhītya dvijo vedān anutpādya tathā sutān/anishṭvā chaiva yajnaiścha mokśam ichchhan vrajatyadhah"*/and also *"Riṇāni trīṇyapākritya mano mokśe niveśayet/anapākritya mokśam tu sevamāno vrajatyadhah." Man* vi, 35 and 37. cf. also *Yāj*: iii, 56; *Bau*. ii, 34; Apa. ii, 24.

[29] See next chapter.

[30] See chapter V and VI.

[31] *Man*. vi, 1–3; also *Mahā. Śānti*. 244, 4.

[32] *Man*. vi 5 ff; *Yāj*: iii, 45; *Viś*. xciv. 1–3.

fourth part of his existence, abandoning all attachment to worldly objects and relations (*tyaktvā samgam.*)[33]

The *Kāma-Sūtras* of Vātsyāyana point out, in this connection, that as the natural span of the life of a human being is supposed to be a hundred years (*śatāyaur vai purushah*), one should divide this period into childhood (*bālya*), youth (*yauvana*) and old age (*sthāvira*). In childhood, the individual should acquire education (*vidyā-grahana*); in youth he should seek to satisfy his natural craving for enjoyment and pleasure (*kāmam*); while in his old age he should seek *dharma* and *mokśa*.[34] But, Vātsyāyana adds, that owing to the uncertainty of life (*anityatva*), one should follow these viz., *vidyā, kāma, dharma* and *mokśa* as they come to him at any period of life (*yathopapādam seveta*);[35] this is to say, one has to pursue each of these, not to the exclusion of the rest, but whenever he gets opportunities to practise any of these, he should properly avail himself of the same, in whatever *āśrama* he may be. According to Vātsyāyana, in fact, one should pursue all the three *purushārthas (trivarga)* viz. *dharma, artha*, and *kāma*, together in proper adjustment with each other, without any one of these coming in the way of the other.[36] This is also the tone in which Manu has advised that the real good of man consists in the harmony or aggregate of the three *purushārthas (trivarga)*.[37]

Of the four *āśramas*, the first two will be treated here only in brief, as they will be described in details in the chapters that follow;[38] on the other hand, we propose to discuss the *vānaprastha* and the *samnyāsa āśramas* rather more fully in this chapter, so as to give us an idea of the kind of discipline and training which the individual is expected to undergo in these *āśramas*.

The *upanayana* ceremony introduces the young boy into the *Brahmacharyāśrama*.[39] After the course of studies is over in accordance with the *dharmas* laid down for the *brahmachāri*, he takes a bath, symbolic of his completion of that *āśrama* course; so he now becomes a *snātaka* i.e. (one who has taken the bath).[40] He now becomes fit to enter the next *āśrama* viz., the *grihasthāśrama*. The ceremony of returning back home from the teacher is called *samāvartana*. In the *grihasthāśrama*, the individual has to fulfil his obligations (*riṇas*) to the members of his family, to his deceased ancestors, to strangers and to gods, in order to become fit to enter the next *āśrama* of *vānaprastha*.

Now, in the *vānaprasthāśrama*, as the name itself suggests the individual has to leave the shelter not only of the family (*kula*) and of the home (*griha*), but of the village (*grāma*) too; he must go to the forest (*vana*) and live there, all the while striving to bring under control his senses of enjoyment (*niyatendriyah*)[41] in the following manner: He has to eat vegetables and fruits only;[42] he is not to touch sweet things or meat,[43] he must never accept fruits or roots grown in the village even when he is extremely hungry (*ārto' pi*).[44] For his clothing he has to use the deerskin or the bark of a tree.[45] He

---

[33] *Man*. vi, 33.

[34] *Kāma*, i, ii, 1–6.

[35] Ibid.

[36] *"Anyonyānubaddham parasparasyānupadyāttakam seveta."*

[37] *Man*. ii, 224.

[38] For *"Brahmacharyāśrama"*, see Ch. IV. *infra*; and for '*grishasthāśrama*' see chs. V and VI *infra*.

[39] See *Śān. Gr. Sū*. II, i ff; *Gobh. Gr. Sū*. II, 10 ff; *Ap. Gr. Sū*. IV, 10, 1 etc.: Āśv. Gr. Sū. I, 20, 11, ff; etc.

[40] *Śān. Gr. Sū*. III, 1 ff; *Gobh. Gr. Sū*. III, 4, 7 ff; *Āp. Gr. Sū*, V, 12–13. *Āśv. Gr. Sū*. III, 8, 9, etc.

[41] *Man*. vi, 4; also *Yāj*. iii, 45; *Gau*. iii, 27.

[42] *Man*. vi, 5; also *Yāj*. iii, 46.

[43] *Man*. vi, 14.

[44] *Man*. vi, 16; cf. *Yāj*. iii, 46.

[45] *Man*. vi, 6.

should make no deliberate attempts to obtain comforts; and, he has to lead a celibate life, sleeping on the floor, residing under a tree, without any attachment to where he happens to reside.[46] Yet, he has to continue the performance of the five great sacrifices (*mahā-yajna*) which he used to perform in the *grihasthāśrama*, in the proper manner,[47] and has to offer to the fullest for sacrifices; and out of whatever he collects for eating, he has to offer to the guests who may visit him, according to his might.[48] Besides, he should utilize his time in studying the *Upanishads* and the *Śrutis*, and practise penances (*tapas*) for the purging of his body, as also in order to elevate his soul up to higher and higher levels.[49] Thus, he must devote himself heart and soul to his studies and meditation; at the same time, he has to lead a life of self-control and friendliness and charity to others—a life wherein though he never accepts charity from others *(nityam anādāta),* he bears a compassionate attitude towards all creatures (*śarvabhūtānukampakah*).[50] If the individual dies while he is pursuing his life in the *vānaprasthāśrama* in this manner, he is expected to reach the region of *brahma*[51]—that is, he attains *mokśa*, as the commentator Kullūkabhaṭṭa, on *Manu-Smriti*:,[52] explains.

But if he survives the *vānaprasthāśrama*,[53] the individual has to enter the last *āśrama* of *samnyāsa*, casting off all attachment (*samgam*) with the world.[54] Manu also permits the individual to enter this *āśrama* immediately after the *grihasthāśrama*.[55] Commenting on this *śloka* of Manu, Kullūkabhaṭṭa quotes from *Jābāla Śruti*: "One should complete *brahmacharya* and enter *grihastha's* order, after that he should enter *vānaprastha*, and thence he should take to *samnyāsa*: or else, he may take to *samnyāsa* directly after *brahmacharya*, or after the grihastha stage is completed."[56] Yājnavalkya, too, takes the same view by allowing a person to take up the *samnyāsāśrama* either after the *vānaprasthāśrama*, or directly after he has done with the *grihasthāśrama*.[57] The man who has entered the *samnyāsārama* should possess nothing; he must always move about all alone without being dependent upon any one for help or support;[58] he could beg alms only once in a day; and he should not feel dispirited when he fails to procure alms nor should he feel elated when he is able to procure it.[59] Indeed, he should care neither for living nor death.[60] By restraining his senses, by casting away the love and hatred within himself, and by living a life of harmlessness to living beings, the *samnyāsī* becomes fit to achieve immortality—that is, as Kullūka explains, to attain

---

[46] *Man*. vi, 26; *Yāj*. iii, 51 and 54.
[47] *Man*. vi, 5.
[48] *Man*. vi, 7.
[49] *Man*. vi, 29–30.
[50] *Man*. vi, 8. cf. *Yāj*. iii, 48.
[51] *Man*. vi, 32.
[52] On *Man*. vi, 32; *Mokśamāpnoti ityarthah*.
[53] *"Yasya tu maraṇābhāvastasyāha*" says Kullūka, before starting to comment on the next section on *Samnyāsa*.
[54] *Man*. vi, 33.
[55] *"Ātmanyagnīn samāropya brāmaṇah pravrajed grihāt"—Man*. vi. 38.
[56] *Yathā Jābālaśrutih-'Brahmacharyam samāpya grihī bhaved, grīhi bhūtvā vanī bhaved, vanī bhutvā pravrajet; itarathā brahmacharyādeva pravrajed, grihādvā vanādvā.'*
[57] *Yāj*. iii, 56; also in *Bau*. ii, 17, 18–28; *Viś*. xcvi, 1–2. Vijnāneśvara's commentary on *Yāj*. iii, 56 quotes the same passage from *Jābālaśruti* which is quoted above.
[58] *Man*. vi, 57.
[59] *Man*. vi, 57.
[60] *Man*. vi, 45.

mokśa.[61] All the sins of the man who passes through the *samnyāsāśrama* in this manner are washed off and destroyed,[62] and thus he attains the ultimate end or goal of existence (*paramām gatim*)—which end is again explained by Kullūka as the same as "*mokśa*."[63]

The *Mahābhārata* describes the duties and obligations of the *āśramas* in almost similar terms.[64] And Kauṭilya too, summarizes them in his *Artha-Śāstra* in a like manner.[65] Kauṭilya further adds that it is the duty of the King to see that his subjects abide by the rules made obligatory for persons following each of the four *āśramas*. He asserts that the violation of the codes of behaviour for the *āśramas* as well as for the *varṇas* would lead to a confusion of the *varṇas* and *āśramas* and thence to a chaotic state of the society (*samkara*)—such that the world (*lokah*) would thereby come to an end.[66] On the other hand, he adds, if all people follow these regulations, the world would certainly progress.[67] The *āśrama* and the *varṇa* schemes are thus conceived as means not merely towards furthering the best ends of social organization, stability and equipoise, but also of social progress.

Apart from the special duties concerned with the life of the individual in each of the *āśramas*, there are certain obligations of a general or universal nature; these are considered as part of the duties of every human being without reference to the *āśrama* to which he belongs. Thus, according to the *Smritis*, to whatever *āśrama* a man may belong, he should with diligence and assiduity (*prayatnatah*) practice the following ten characteristic features of a proper life of *dharma*:[68] Steadiness, forgiveness, self-control, abstention from appropriating anything belonging to others, purity, control of the sense organs, correct discernment, knowledge, truthfulness, and absence from anger.[69] Kauṭilya, too, has said that harmlessness, truthfulness, purity, absence of spite, abstinence from cruelty and forgiveness are the duties common to all human beings.[70]

Of all the *āśramas*, however, the *grihasthāśrama* is given a very high place of honour. The *Mahābhārata* is quite emphatic in this connection. Thus we are told in the *Śantiparva*, that once Yudhishṭhira became so disgusted with the ways and affairs of the world that he proposed to take to the *samnyāsī* mode of life; but eventually he was pursuaded to remain in the *grihasthāśrama* by the wise counsels of his brothers, wife, and the wise Dvaipāyana Vyāsa himself.[71] The story was narrated to him of how "certain little-witted, well-born Brāhmaṇa youths, before attaining manhood,

---

[61] *Man*. vi, 60; Kullūka's commentary is: *"mokśayogo bhavati."*

[62] *Man*. vi, 85.

[63] *Man*. vi, 96; Kullūka's commentary is *"paramām gatim mokśalakśndn prāpnoti."*

[64] See *Mahā. Śānti. Adhyāyas* 61 (11 to 17 *ślokas*); 191–192; 241–245; 268–275; 353–355; Anu. 141 (where the Great God [*Maheśvara*] is said to have explained to his consort *Umā* the duties of the four *āśramas*).

[65] *Artha*. p. 7 (Śāmaśāstry's Tr.).

[66] *"Svadharmassvargāyānantyāya cha/tasyātikrame lokassamkarāduchchhidyeta/tasmātsvadharmam bhūtānām rājā na vyabhichārayet/svadharmam samdadhāno hi pretya cheha cha nandati//" Artha*. I, iii. 8, 6–7, Śāmaśāstry's Tr., Op. cit., p. 7.

[67] *"Vyavasthitāryamaryādah kritavarṇāśramasthitih/trayyā hi rakśito lokah prasīdati na sīdati//"*Ibid.

[68] *Man*. vi, 91.

[69] *"Dkritih kśamā damo'steyam śaucham indriyanigrahah/dhīrvidyā satyom akrodhho daśakam dharmalakśaṇam"*. Similarly, *Yaj*. iii, 66:—*Satyam asteyam akrodho rhīh śaucham dhīr dhritir damah/samyatendriyatā vidyā dharmah sarva udāhritah", cf.* also *Vasx*. 30.

[70] *Sarveshām ahimsā satyam śaucham anasuyā'nriśamsyam kśamā cha/Artha*. I, iii, 8, 4.

[71] *Mahā, Śānti. Adhyāyas* 11 ff. The explanatory title of *adhyāya* 11 is: *"Yudhisṭhiram prati gārhasthyasya śreshṭhyopapādanam"*, i.e.: "Exposition of the superiority of *Grihasthāśrama* Yudhisṭhira."

forsook their homes and came to the woods for leading a forest life."[72] Indra felt pity for them, and taught them that "Asceticism is attainable by leading the life of a householder (*kuṭumba-vidhīnā*) upon which the proper management of everything depends (*yasmin sarvam pratishṭhitam*).[73] In fact, says Indra, "the life of a householder itself only (*ayam eva*) is very superior and sacred, and gives scope for fulfilment (of life's mission)."[74] We are told that on hearing these beneficial words full of *dharma*, those "ascetics" abandoned the idea of Renunciation saying—'This is not meant for us now,'—and started living like householders.[75] After all his relatives did their utmost to dissuade Yudhishṭhira from taking up *samnyāsa*, the Dvaipāyana Vyāsa himself advised him to follow the counsel of his brothers and wife of not abandoning his post as a member of the *grihasthāśrama.* For, in the opinion of that sage, the highest *dharma*, as sanctioned by the *śāstras*, consists in a training through the duties and living the full life of a householder.[76] The householder is the support of birds, animals and various other creatures;[77] "he, therefore, who belongs to that mode of life, is superior to all."[78] In this *āśrama*, moreover, can the three *purushārthas*, *dharma, artha* and *kāma*, exist together and can be used towards the end of *mokśa*.[79] In fact this mode of life is considered as the very basis of all the others.[80] The other three *āśramas* "derive from this *āśrama* the means they live upon, the offerings they make to the departed manes and the gods, and, in short, their entire support."[81] All the obligations of life, the individual and social, all the three 'debts' (*riṇas*)—the debt to the gods (*devariṇa*), the debt to the manes or ancestors (*pitri-riṇa*) and the debt to the sages (*rishi-riṇa*)—could be satisfied by a person living a full life in the *grihasthāśrama*.[82] So also, the trust vested in us by the Creator could be executed in this *āśrama* by the proper begetting of off-springs in the family.[83]

And the *Smritis*, too, bestow the highest praise upon the *grihasthāśrama*. Just as all living creatures subsist by receiving support from air, so all the *āśramas* subsist by receiving support from the *grihastha*; and since men in the three other *āśramas* are daily supported by the householder with sacred knowledge and food, the householder's is the leading *āśrama*.[84] As rivers, great and small, find a resting place in the ocean, even so men of all *āśramas* gather their stability and support at the hands of the householder.[85] "And, in accordance with the precepts of the *Veda* and the *Smriti*, the

---

[72] *Mahā. Śānti*, 11, 2.

[73] Ibid. 11, 21.

[74] Ibid. 11, 15. *"Siddhikśetram idam puṇyam ayam evāśramo mahān/"*

[75] Ibid. 11, 27. *"Tataste tadvachah śrutvā dharmārtha-sahitam hitam/utsrujya 'nāsti iti' gatā gārhasthyam samupā-śritāh."*

[76] *Mahā. Śānti*. 23. 2 *"Śāstradrishṭah paro dharmah sthito gārhasthyam āśritah."*

[77] Ibid. 23, 5.

[78] Ibid. 23, 50. *"Grihasthenaiva dhāryante tasmāchchhreshṭho grihāśramī"*.

[79] *Mahā. Śānti*. 191, 10: *"Dharmārthakāmāvāptirhyatra."*

[80] Ibid. 191, 10: *"Taddhi sarvāśramāṇām mūlam udāharanti."*

[81] Ibid. 191, 10: *"Teshāmapyata eva bhikśā-bali-samvibhāgah pravar tante."*

[82] Ibid. 191, 13. *"Api chātra yajnakriyābhir devatāh priyante, nivāpena pitaro, vidyābhyāsaśravaṇadhāraṇena rishayah, apatyotpādanena prajāpatir iti"/*

[83] Ibid.

[84] *Man*. iii: *"Yathā vāyum samāśritya vartante sarvajantavah/tathā grihastham āśritya vartante sarva āśramāh// Yasmāt trayo 'pyāsramiṇo jnānenānnena chānvaham/grihasthenaiva dhāryante tasmājjyeshṭhāśramo grihī//"* 78.

[85] *Man*. vi. 90: *"Yathā nadī nadah sarve sāgaram yānti samsthitim/tathaivāśramiṇah sarve grihasthe yānti samsthitim"/*

householder is declared to be superior (*śreshṭha*) to all of them; for he supports the three."[86] He who desires imperishable bliss in heaven and permanent happiness here, must strive through this *Āśrama* with great care and effort; for it is difficult to be practised by men with weak faculties.[87]

Now, this special eulogy bestowed upon the *grihasthāśrama* should not be misunderstood; we must try to comprehend its meaning in its proper perspective. The *grihasthāśrama* is glorified, not in terms of absolute superiority of the *āśrama* over all the others, but from a particular angle of vision and with reference to the particular position which that *āśrama* occupies in the scheme of life. The *Śāstrakāra's* praise for the *grihastha* as the best *āśrama* emanates, we must not fail to notice, from the point of view of the "social values" of the *āśramas*. Otherwise, in general, since each *āśrama* is regarded as an essential stage for the development of the individual, it is the best in its own place, and any comparison of merits between them on absolute grounds would be surely beside the point. But, from the point of view of a particular aspect, viz. the aspect of social valuation, the *grihastha* is exalted on the grounds of its lending support to the other three *āśramas*, the scope it affords for the practice and cultivation of all the three *purushārthas*, viz., *dharma, artha* and *kāma*, as well as of its direct contact with the society and the consequent direct contributions made by it to the society. On the other hand, from the point of view of the acquisition of knowledge by the individual, the *brahmacharyāśrama* would evoke the highest praise; while from the point of view of individual salvation, the *samnyāsāśrama* would take the place of honour.

It is quite possible to maintain, on the other hand, on the strength of the foregoing high compliments paid to the *grihasthāśrama*, that of all values, social values were regarded as of supreme importance by Hindu *Śāstrakaras*, the Hindu writers on social life like the *Smriti*-writers and the Epic-writers. This interpretation is further confirmed by one or two statements already quoted above, which specifically compare the *grihasthāśrama* with the next two *āśramas* by asserting that in this *āśrama* could be achieved the merits that are achievable in the other two *āśramas* too! Thus, it is said that in the *grihasthāśrama* alone can the three *purushārthas* be practised together, and the three *riṇas* could *all* be discharged satisfactorily. May we say that such a view of the *grīhasthāśrama* was due to the fact that the Hindu *Sāstrakāras* perhaps found that it was, in practice, not always possible, or was exceedingly difficult, for the average individual to follow the course of all the four *āśramas* one after the other, considering the actual average life-span of man,—which would be in most cases much less than one hundred years,—and that therefore, they wisely suggested that one can hope for salvation even if he continued in the *grihasthāśrama* till the end of his life, provided that he discharged in that *aśrama* the three *riṇas* and practised the three *purushārthas* in the manner prescribed?

In the light of our description of the theory and practice of the *āśramas* given above, let us try to find out the significance and position of the *purushārthas* as envisaged in the *āśrama*—scheme: In the *brahmacharyāśrama, dharma* is the predominating *purushārtha; dharma* has to be learnt up in all its aspects and ramifications; and it has to be practised particularly as a check upon *kāma* and *artha*, because these latter two are far from the objectives of the young trainee; besides, the ultimate value of *mokśa* has to be learnt during this *āśrama*.

---

[86] *Man.* vi. 89: *"Sarveshāmapi chaiteshām vedasmritividhānatah/grihastha uchyate śreshṭhah sa trīnetānbibharti hi"//*

[87] *Man.* iii. 79: *"Sa samdhāryah prayatnena svargam akśayam ichchatā/sukham chehechhatā nityam yo'dhāryo durbalendriyaih//".*

In the *grihasthāśrama*, both *artha*, and *kāma* become the fields of the personality of the individual who has already acquired a knowledge and practice of *dharma*, and who has studied the value and place of *mokśa* for his own self-realisation. Here, let it be admitted that *kāma* and *artha* are part of the essential heritage of both the human individual and races. In this sense, *artha*, and *kāma* form what may be called part of the natural, physical and psycho-physiological apparatus for the functioning of both the group and the individual. We must observe, however, that this apparatus may be, and as a natural history of facts, has been and is being misused and misfunctioned by individuals and races. Now instead of demanding a total repression of this apparatus by damning them as merely base and worthless, the Hindu seers have taught that *artha* and *kāma* shall, on the one hand, be wisely directed into proper life-functions, as prescribed by *dharma*, and shall, on the other hand, be controlled from misfunctioning or disfunctioning as prescribed and proscribed also by *dharma*. In this way, *artha* and *kāma* have been so placed in the *āśrama* scheme, each in terms of *dharma*, that both of them may, by right functioning, contribute their necessary quota for the upkeep, stability, growth and development of the human race consistent with the personality of each of the individuals whose conscious self-control and self-direction carry the seeds of the race and its cultural heritage through history.

Thereafter, in the *vānaprasthāśrama, dharma* and *mokśa* become the main concern of life, *dharma* occupying the primary position. And, in the *samnyāsāśrama*, *mokśa* occupies the supreme position in the *samnyāsi's* mind; in fact, his *dharma* now becomes identified with *mokśa*. Of course, throughout the *āśrama* scheme and throughout life in every and any phase, *mokśa* always lurks as the ultimate aim, permeating sometimes explicitly, sometimes implicitly, underneath and defining the course of the other three viz. *dharma, artha* and *kāma* also.

Like the tradition of *dharma* (*dharma-paramparā*) the tradition of *yajna* (*yajna-paramparā*) also persists and permeates through the Hindu scheme of life, through the *āśramas*. In terms of *yajna*, all the four *āśramas* must be considered as four kinds of *yajna*. The nature, practices and the forms of the *yajna* in each of the *āśramas* are obvious. It is, in fact, a part of the theory of the *āśramas;* as such, *yajna* must of necessity be the spirit that hovers over every stage of the life of a person in any of the *āśramas*. (For the concept and implications of *yajna*, see ch. ii.).

Thus, in the *brahmacharyāśrama*, the individual has to surrender his life of sense (*indriya*), mind (*mana*), and intellect (*buddhi*), that is to say, all the intellectual and emotional apparatus,—to the handling of and moulding by the adept (*guru*). Therefore, in this *āśrama*, on the one hand, a sort of a *yajna* of the lower self has to be practised, in the sense that the student (*brahmachārī*) has to undergo all sorts of lessons in self-control imposed upon him by his preceptor (*guru*); and on the other hand, as he has also to acquire knowledge from his *guru, jnāna-yajna*, i.e. *yajna* or 'sacrifice' in terms of devotion to and practice of learning has also to be increasingly practised by him.

The *grihasthāśrama* proves another kind of field for a life of *yajna*. At its best, it is, in a sense, the fully dedicated life. Here it is one's duty to practise *artha* and *kāma* in terms of *karmas* in strict accordance with the *dharmas*, the meaning and value and the justification of which he has learnt in the first *āśrama*. He can partake of *artha* and *kāma*, of the material and the physical pleasures available on earth, but without any feelings of covetousness, greed or lust, taking only his due share in these pleasures in strict accordance with the *dharmas* of this *āśrama*. The *grihastho's* life has also to be a continuous stream of giving (*dāna*)—a life of self-less service and dedication of his best and utmost for his elders, children, wife (who also is his sharer in his service to others) and other members of his family (*kula*), his dependents and strangers (*atithi*), through his acts of fulfilling his social obligations (*riṇas*). Here in the home, he has to bear in mind and practise the parting advice given by his *guru* in the preceding *āśrama* that he has to give his dues to the mother, to the father, to the teacher and to the strangers (*mātri-devo bhava, pitri-devo bhava, āchārya-devo bhava, atithi-devo bhava*). The devoted service of and for these is considered the same as the service of God. Here, therefore, a *karma-yajna* consistent with and in accordance with *dharma* has to be practised as fully as possible by the individual.

In the third *āśrama*, the beginnings (*ārambha*) are made for the yielding of the self for the final *yajna* which is expected to be performed in the last *āśrama*. The individual now gives up his fields of *artha* and *kāma* by leaving his near and dear ones, his family (*kula*), his village (*grāma*), and by abandoning his belongings and possessions; he now goes out into the forest (*vana, araṇya*), where by meditation and service of others, he trains himself up for the execution of the final *yajna* that awaits his soul-pouring in the *samnyāsāśrama*, the last *āśrama*.

And, this last *āśrama* provides the fullest opportunities for the self-expression and self-expansion of the individual in terms of the final *yajna*. This consists of a complete offering of the self (*ātmāhuti*) wherein the self, out of a will and purpose to be perfect, surrenders all that was nearest and dearest to his lower ego, in order that thereby and thereafter he may be enabled to be one with the real self, the *ātmā*. In both these last *āśramas* a kind of *bhakti-yajna* has to be practised in that the dedication to God is complete, the entire self of the individual having been now surrendered to God (*sarvārpaṇa*). Again, the individual becomes, in a sense, a *jnānī bhakta* when he takes to *samnyāsa*; for he has undergone the schooling and discipline from stage to stage, *āśrama* to *āśrama*, realizing more and more that he belonged not to this *samsāra* nor that this *samsāra* belonged to him; thus, now fully realizing the place and meaning of the self in the midst of *samsāra* he brings himself face to face with the final aim of all existence, viz., *mokśa*, in this last *āśrama*.

The *āśramas*, then, as we have already said, are regarded as schools of life at several stages of human existence, devised and organized towards the best likelihood for the individual to attain the end of *mokśa*, in accordance with the theory of the ultimate nature of things, or in accordance with the conception of existence and its relation to the Ultimate. During these different stages of life, the functions of the group and the individual are both different and definite with regard to each other. Thus, during the first *āśrama*, the function of the group is to look after the individual. On the other hand, as far as the individual is concerned, this may be said to be natural, neutral phase. In the second *āśrama* the individual has to look after the group; he is the trustee and manager of the social estate, of the social *mores*, and of the three *riṇas*. The group here is interested in giving him and taking from him the fullest opportunities, social, economic, physical and spiritual, so that the individual may and should best satisfy these obligations. The third *āśrama* is, once more, a largely neutral phase from the point of view of the individual, as well as of the group. Here, on the part of the individual, efforts have to be made to yield up his responsibilities in the midst of power and pelf, and thus, by and by, to take to a life in accordance with the best lessons acquired in the *brahmacharyāśrama*, viz., of going into one's self and finding the truth out for oneself. The feeling of separation from the Ultimate or God begins to make itself felt at this stage. Even then, however, the individual is pledged to the young and the junior that he shall serve them, the family and the group, as a counsel occasionally advising them, rather than as a manager of their estate which position he had to undertake in the second *āśrama*. In this third *āśrama* and in the fourth, the function of the individual is to deal with the supernatural, with the life within; and the function of the group becomes gradually thinned out till in the fourth, it comes to almost nil. And in the last stage, the individual who is now completely free from any social obligation, has to help himself in the search of the self (*ātma-chintana, ātma-jnāna*).

And the justification of such a scheme of the functions and interdependence of the group and the individual in the first three *āśramas* and their independence from each other in the fourth *āśrama* is to be taught during the first stage of life, the *brahmacharya*; and the management of the whole scheme is to be organized, supported and established by the group as well as the individual in the second stage, the *grihasthāśrama*. In the first stage, the group rears, protects and gives the best of its heritage to the individual. In the second stage, the individual yields his best and most for the efficient and harmonious functioning of group life, consistent with the dictates of his own conscience; here, the individual seeks to make the group the chief medium and instrument for the upkeep and growth of his personality. In the third stage, the individual, giving up the close attention formerly required of him to manage the affairs of group life, starts on a preliminary journey for self-search. While, in the fourth stage, the individual retires altogether from group activities and seeks to know and find and realize the self that hides within the core of his being.

CHAPTER IV

THE SOCIAL PSYCHOLOGY OF EDUCATION

In the second chapter we attempted to study the fundamental attitude of the Hindu towards the problem of living which is at the basis of all Hindu social institutions. In the third chapter, we considered how the general frame-work of the social institutions was visualized and established in the theory and practice of the *āśramas*, which is probably a unique way of considering and solving social problems, without a parallel in the whole history of social thought of the world.

In this chapter, we shall discuss the first of the four *āśramas*, viz., the *brahmacharyāśrama* which concerns itself with the management of education as a social institution. In this connection, we shall consider the institution as a socio-psychological phenomenon, rather than discuss the purely psycho-physiological techniques of education or training process which is generally understood to be the subject-matter of what is known as "Educational Psychology" today. Our principal concern will be to look into the social-psychological implications and outlook involved in the Hindu methods and discipline of education.

It is well recognised that the outlook and methods of education prevalent in a society have a far-reaching significance and influence upon the other social institutions of that society. It is also recognised that this significance and influence is not just one-sided, but of a mutual nature; that is to say, the system of education prevalent amongst a people influences as also is itself influenced by the society which it serves and by its *mores*. Education is the principle instrument, in the hands of a social group or an assemblage of social groups, by means of which it passes on and hands over to the individual (and thus to itself), the traditions, disciplines and culture it has gathered through long and continual endeavours of the race towards making the best and most of the gift of human life. Thus it seeks to train the individual to adjust himself to the ideas and ideals which have gathered meaning and value and respect from the best and the noblest that have made the history of the society. It is evident, therefore, that amongst all the social institutions, the system and outlook of education is of primary significance. "Conceivably a people could dispense with religion, as the U.S.S.R. has tried to do; conceivably a state might refuse to distinguish fixed forms of sexual union as marriage. But education is indispensable to any society, for without it there would be lost all the accumulated knowledge of the ages and all standards of conduct. Education is the social economy that forestalls such wastage."[1]

Our main concern here, therefore, will be to study the social aspects and implications of the Hindu system of education and to discover the psychological reactions of the same on the individual and the society in relation to each other.—How far, in what respects, and with what results does the Hindu educational system affect the relations of the individual with the society in which he "lives and moves and has his being"? What are the socio-psychological foundations of this influence of

[1] R. H. Lowie: *Social Organization*, London: Routledge, 1950, p. 194 ff following Count's article on *"Education"* in the *Ency. Soci. Sc.*

education upon the individual and upon the group?—These shall be some of the issues we shall have to raise, and into which we shall have to probe. After stating the views of the Hindu sages on these points, we shall endeavour to evaluate the same.

Before starting to inquire about the problem of the Hindu education system, it would be advantageous for us if we consider some of the social principles which should generally underlie every educational system. By 'education' is meant here what Dewey has called "formal or institutional education."[2] This is a regular programme of training, as, for instance, carried out by schools and colleges to-day. For, in one sense, we are being educated every moment of our life, from birth till death. Consciously and unconsciously, we may be said to be learning every moment of our life. But it has been recognized that since the behaviour of an individual is likely to have vital reactions on the community of which he is a member, he should be given for a specific period in his early years a regular training calculated to equip him to adjust himself to and to serve the community. Students of human nature of all times have urged that some sort of a deliberate training of the individual is absolutely essential in order to enable the individual to adjust himself to the complex social environment in which he finds himself. From Plato, Aristotle and Plutarch down to Pestalozzi, Rousseau, Herbart and Spencer, in the West, all have pointed out that nature unaided by training and discipline cannot accomplish all that is demanded of an individual in this direction.[3] If we bear these remarks in mind, they will be sufficient to give us an idea of the social functions which an educational system is expected and actually has to serve.

In this connection Dr. Nunn observes: "Every scheme of education being, at bottom, a practical philosophy, necessarily touches life at every point. Hence any educational aims which are concrete enough to give definite guidance are correlative to ideals of life, and, as ideals of life are eternally at variance, their conflict will be reflected in educational theories."[4] And yet it seems that we can formulate certain social principles which are, or must be, common to all educational systems. For, the real conflict is reflected not so much in what the aim of education should be, but in the ways and means employed in education, and in emphasizing some aspect or other of education. It is therefore not too difficult to get at a general idea of the social functions of education.

"The primary function of the educational system," as Panunzio has pointed out, "is to transmit a knowledge of the forms and skills society regards as indispensable to its survival and improvement. That system regularizes the knowledge-transmitting activity; inculcates the folkways and the *mores*; trains the young to fit into the established cultural scheme, aims to aid the individual in the development of personality and aptitudes; and sets forth the broad lines which the society believes must be followed in order to survive and improve."[5] Along with imparting knowledge and skills, education also transmits the particular system of moral, social and cultural values of the group, and thus undertakes the indoctrination of both the rational and the emotional elements which make up the adult individual. Education, understood primarily as the induction of the maturing individual into the life and culture of his people, is the most vital of all institutions and embraces all other institutions.[6] Understood in this sense, education "is essential to both the renewal and the growth

[2] Dewey. *"Democracy and Education,"* pp. 7–11.

[3] O'Shea: *"Social Development and Education"*, pp. 248 ff.

[4] Nunn: *"Education; Its Data and First Principles,"* p. 2.

[5] C. Panunzio: *"Major Social Institutions,"* New York, Macmillan 1939, p. 242.

[6] R. H. Lowie: *Social Organization*, London, Routledge, 1950, p. 194, following Count's article in the *"Encyclopædia of Social Sciences"*.

of human society. In its absence the achievement of man would be limited by the powers and to the experiences of the individual, and what is known as culture could not develop."[7]

The chief aim of education is thus to furnish the individual with such necessary equipment for living that he may be enabled to reduce to a minimum the operation of those of his personal interests which conflict with the interests of the group or the society, so as to live in harmony with the group life and its ideals, and even to raise high and exalt the social and moral practices and codes which the group considers as conducive to the healthy and proper growth of its members. Each one of us has innate tendencies and impulses, some of which, if given unrestrained freedom and expression, might come into clash with the best interests of the society; therefore, one of the main purposes of education should be to train the individual in curbing these in the interests of the society. As Sumner has expressed it, education transfers the *mores* to the individual; that is, "He learns what conduct is approved or disapproved; what kind of man is admired most; how he aught to behave in all kinds of cases; and what he aught to believe or reject."[8] In this sense, education may be said to be the process *par excellence* to socialise the individual. Says Young, though in a slightly different context, "Unfortunately, much of our earlier educational psychology (i.e., in its modern western development) failed to recognize that *all learning is essentially social*."[9] Looked at from this point of view, the main problem of education would consist "either in repressing in some manner such of the child's native impulses as are out of alignment with contemporary social practices, or transferring these impulses into tendencies that will bring the individual into harmony with the customs, ideals and institutions of civilized society."[10]

Now, the problem of the socialisation of the individual must be understood and evaluated in its proper perspective. An individual may be said to have been socialised when, and to the extent to which, he has attained harmony with the purposes, aims and ideals of the group of which he is a member as also of humanity at large. For, we must remember that from the larger view-point we cannot possibly think of a particular limited group or tribe or clan apart from or opposed to other human groups or mankind as a whole. Particularly, if we are concerned with the most universal meaning of the aim of education as the theory, method and institution devised and planned for the proper socialisation of the individual, then, we must understand the term 'socialisation' in this wider sense. Of course, there is a narrower sense in terms of which socialisation would mean 'making of a good citizen' in the context of a particular country or province or some such thing. But this cannot form the universal aim of education; for, the ideals of citizenship may vary.

And, here we come to the distinction between aims of education as they *should* be, and as they have been and *are* being actually conceived by the different systems of education. In many educational systems, the aims of education are formulated with reference to the satisfaction of certain ideals of a particular group at a definite period in its history. "There can be no universal aim of education if that aim is to include the assertion of any particular ideal of life, for there are as many ideals as there are persons. Educational efforts must, it would seem, be limited to securing for every one the conditions under which individuality is most completely developed—that is, to enabling him to make his original contribution to the variegated whole of human life as full and as truly

---

[7] Art. by G. S. Count on *"Education"* in the *Ency, Soci. Sc.*, p. 403.
[8] Sumner: *"Folkways"*, p. 638.
[9] K. Young *"Sociology,"* 2nd. Ed., New York, American Book Co., 1942, p. 361. (Italics in the original).
[10] O'Shea: op. cit p. 249.

characteristic as his nature permits; the form of contribution being left to the individual as something which each must, in living and by living forge out of himself."[11]

This interpretation of the socialisation of the individual by means of education suggests another very important function of education which may be called the *individual* function of education as distinguished from its *social* function. This individual function consists in the development of the personality of an individual. In this sense, education should provide the necessary machinery, training and opportunity to the individual in order that the potentialities within him may be nursed and developed, even to the extent that the group may thereby grow in stature and breadth of its outlook and vision. Much has been made, by most writers on the subject, of education as the chief instrument in the operation of the process of socialisation as compared to its value in the development of personality. Thus, Ellwood remarks that "the systems of education may work under the fiction that they exist for the training and development of the individuals as such, regardless of the social life; but their real purpose must be to control the process by which individuals acquire habits; so that as adults, they will be efficient in carrying on the social life, and will co-ordinate their activities harmoniously with the group."[12] "Systems of education", the same writer observes at another place, "have not been created for the training and development of the individuals as such, but rather to fit the individuals for membership in society, that is, to control the process by which they acquire habits, so that they shall advantageously co-ordinate their activities with those of the group."[13] In a similar strain, Dr. Williams opines that "Education must lead to the formation of convictions for civic and political action, to the end that every citizen may become, within the limits of his capacity, an effective agent for progress."[14] It will be evident from this that there is a growing opinion among writers on this subject that the value of education lies in its ability to direct the capacities and powers of the individual towards the proper functioning and stability of the social group to which he or she belongs.[15]

It must be borne in mind, however, that education can be said to have an equally great value, if not greater, in as much as and to the extent to which it provides a means for the intellectual development of the *individual* as such. And this aspect of the value of education requires as much attention on the part of our educationists as the other aspect of socialisation has already received and has been receiving even to this day. True education helps the cultivation not only of character, habit and discipline of mind, but also of the intellect, the reason, and the critical and discriminating faculty. Without the development of the faculty of intelligent appreciation, discrimination and judgment, man would be no more than a tool, a machine which acts, be it for the good of the society or otherwise, without understanding *how* his actions are good or bad, and in what respects they are going to affect the social order. Besides, a truly educated individual is not always expected to be led blindly by the society; in fact, he may at times also lead the society. He must be able to weigh, to discriminate and to appreciate, and possess sufficient courage and personality to follow his own reason.

Any sound theory of education, we may therefore say, must not separate the intellectual faculties of the individual from his behaviour towards the society. The two react closely upon each other;

---

[11] Nunn: op. cit. pp. 5–6.

[12] Ellwood: *"Introduction to Social Psychology"*, p. 110.

[13] Ellwood: *"Sociology in its Psychological Aspects"*, p. 186.

[14] Williams: *"The Foundations of Social Sciences"*, p. 115.

[15] See also Judd: *"Psychology of Social Institutions"*, Ch. XVIII; Young: *"Social Psychology"*, pp. 239 ff. Williams: *"Principles of Social Psychology"*, pp. 366 ff.

and education must try to lay the foundations of individual's social behaviour upon an appeal to his or her own powers of reasoning and intellect, and not upon the mere fact of social approval or disapproval. The appeal to the individual's reason or intellect, moreover, will receive welcome consideration or will fall short of it and be turned down under the pressure of a social bias, according as the individual's intellect has been allowed an independent development or not. It is the task of true education to help the growth of the individual's intellect by keeping it independent and uninfluenced by external prejudices and biases of any kind. Such a development of the individual on the intellectual side would enable him to judge every action or idea on his own and free from any social or other bias. This is what is most likely to result in the development of the personality of the individual members of the group. The system of education which aims at development of the individual's personality endows him at the same time with the power of rational appreciation. Such a system prevents that conservative and orthodox attitude of mind, which shuns the acceptance of any new ideas in the social and moral fields, and which pursues the traditional path merely because it offers the line of least or no resistance. For, such a type of education enables one to judge any idea or act on its own merits. Actions based on such educational equipment will be actions backed by intellect and reason, rather than mechanically followed by the individual.

Moreover, the development of the personality of individual members of the group will also help the growth of real social progress. Society will, under such conditions, refuse to remain satisfied by blindly following a social bias when it may be irrational to do so; it would, in fact, incessantly endeavour to break away from old biases and thus lead itself onwards and upwards towards a life based and built on a will that conforms with reason. This aspect of education, viz., of personality-development of the individual as such, therefore, is as much important as the other aspect of social harmony which has been much stressed by writers on the subject. In fact, real education has value both in so far as it develops the individual personality as well as it "socialises" the person and thus enables him to keep in harmony with the material and moral framework of the group to which he belongs. The proper ideal of education must envisage a co-ordination of these two aims. It is our contention that such should be the true sociopsychological basis of any educational theory.

After this introductory discussion on the problem and aims of education in general, we may now proceed to study the sociopsychological bases of the Hindu educational theory, and see how the Hindus have tried to solve the problem of education.

In the Hindu home, every male[16] child belonging to the Brāhmaṇa, Kshatriya and Vaiśya *varṇna* started his educational career with the observation of certain rites and rituals grouped under the name of the *upanayana* ceremony. The earliest reference to this *upanayana* ceremony seems to be in the *Atharva-Veda*, where the sun is described as a Brāhmaṇa student approaching his *āchārya*[17] (teacher) with firewood (*samidh*) and alms.[18] The *Śatapatha Brāhmaṇa* describes a student named Uddālaka approaching his teacher with *samidhs*, and requesting him to be accepted as

[16] Female education will be dealt with later in this chapter.

[17] *Āchārya* is the word most often used in the *Grihya-Sūtras* and other early literature (see e.g. Mān. G.S.I. 2, 10; Āśv. O.S.I. 19, 1, etc.) The *Smritis* have used both *āchārya* and *guru* to denote the teacher (see e.g. Man. ii,-69; 140; 145; 191–218; 225–226; etc. Yaj. i-15; 26; 33; 51, etc.). In Man. ii, 191, for instance, we have both the words *āchārya* and *guru* used simultaneously to denote the same person. Other words denoting a teacher are *adhyāpaka, upādhyāya*.

[18] A. V., xi, 5.

a *brahmachārin* for tuitions under him.[19] And the *Brihadāraṇyakopanishad* declares that such a request to the teacher by the student has to be preceded by the words *'Upaimyaham bhavantam'*, i.e., 'I am approaching you, Sir.'[20] The teacher then inquires about the name, birth and family of the student, as Satyakāma Jābāla was asked when he approached Gautama Hāridrumata.[21] All these formalities, and many others, which we shall enumerate as we proceed, had to take place with the observance of due rites (*vidhi*), as was done by Śaunaka, for instance, when he approached Angiras, to learn.[22]

The *Śatapatha Brāhmaṇa* describes some of the rites thus: The *āchārya* places his right hand upon the head of the pupil (*Śishya*), thus symbolizing the imparting of the very core of his own personality to the pupil (*tena garbhī bhavati*); and on the third night, such personal inner splendour (*garbha*) of the teacher is supposed to enter the very core of the pupil's whole being; thereafter, on being taught the *Sāvitrī Mantra*, the pupil becomes a true Brāhmaṇa.[23]

The *Grihya-Sūtras* and the *Smritis* have given elaborate descriptions of these and various other rites to be performed at the *Upanayana*.[24] A gridle (*mekhalā*) has now to be tied round the waist of the young boy to be initiated. This girdle is to be made of *munja* grass in the case of a Brāhmaṇa, bow-string in the case of a Kshatriya, and woollen thread in the case of a Vaiśya.[25] The boy is then to be given a staff (*daṇda*)—of *palāśa* or *bilva* wood for the Brāhmaṇa boy, of *nyagrodha* wood for the Kshatriya, and of *udumbara* wood for the Vaiśya.[26] Or, in the alternative, it is also laid down that any sort of staff may be used by a boy of any *varṇa*.[27] Thereafter, the sacrificial cord (*yajnopavīta*) is adjusted round his body.[28] The *āchārya* then inquires after the name, family and other particulars of the boy, and asks him whether he is seriously desirous to undertake the vow of *brahmacharya* under his instructions.[29] After the student asserts his willingness to observe the *brahmacharya*, the *āchārya*, "grasping down, with the span of his right hand, the student's right shoulder, touches the part of his chest behind which his heart lies with the words: 'May I be dear to thy inviolate heart'."[30] He further adds: "Under my will I take thy heart; my mind shalt thy mind follow; in my word shalt thou rejoice, with all thy heart; may Brihaspati, (the Lord of Learning), join thee to me."[31] Then, calling the boy by his personal name, the āchārya declares "Thou art the *brahmachārin* of *kāma*."[32] And then the *Sāvitrī mantra* is recited by the *āchārya* to the student.

---

[19] Śat. Br. xi, 4, 1, 9.

[20] *"Upaimyaham bhavantam iti vāchāha smaiva pūrva upayanti"*—Brih. Up. vi, 2, 7.

[21] Chhānd. Up. iv, 4, 4.

[22] Muṇḍ. Up. i, 1, 3.

[23] Śat. Br. xi, 5, 4, 12; with Śat. Br. xi, 5, 4th Brahmaṇa, which gives a description of the rites of accepting a pupil by a teacher, cf Śan. Gr. S. ii, 1 ff.; Āśv. G.S. i, 20, ff; Pār. G.S. ii, 2, 17 ff.; etc.

[24] See Āśv. G.S. I, 19 seq.; Śān G.S. II, 1 seq., III, i; IV, 5. seq., Āpa. G.S. IV, 10 seq., etc. Man. ii; Yāj. 1. 14. ff etc. Some of these texts use the word *'upanāyana'*, but as Vijnāneśvara on Yāj. i, 14 has explained this word means the same thing as *'upanayana'*.

[25] Śān. G.S.: ii, I, 14–17; Āśv. G.S. i, 19, 12, Pār. G.S. ii, 5, 21–23; also Man. ii. 42.

[26] Śān. G.S. ii, I, 18–30; Āśv. G.S. i, 19, 13; Pār. G.S. ii, 5, 25–27; Āp. G.S. v, ii, 16.

[27] Śān. G.S. ii, I. 24; Āśv. G.S. i, 20, I, Pār. G.S. ii, 5, 28; Go. G.S. ii, 10, 14, Āp. G.S. v, ii, 17; etc.

[28] Śān. G.S. ii, 2, 3. etc.,

[29] Śān. G.S. ii, 2, 4 ff; Pār. G.S. ii, 2, 17, ff; etc.

[30] Śān. G.S. ii, 3, 3; cf. Āśv. G.S. i. 20, 10.

[31] Śān. G.S. ii, 4, 1; Āśv. G.S. i, 21, 7.

[32] Śān. G.S. ii, 1–3; Pār. G.S. ii, 2, 7–10; Āpa, iv, 11, 8–10, etc.

The *upanayana* sacrament (*samskāra*) is virtually regarded as the second birth of the young boy (*kumāra*).[33] Till the *upanayana* is not passed through, every child is considered nature-born and, as such, as good as a *Śūdra*; therefore, any child that had not gone through the *upanayana* rite did not enjoy the full rights of an *Ārya*. After *upanayana*, he becomes a *dvija*, a twice-born.[34] And, indeed, he is now born a second time, as it were,—born into a new world of activities, duties, responsibilities and expectations and aspirations for all of which he has now to begin training and equipping himself.

These elaborate rituals and ceremonies, centering round the *upanayana* have a great social significance which is worth noting in this connection. They create an atmosphere of dignity and seriousness about the particular occasion; therefore, they serve to impress the minds of the persons or group taking part in the ceremonies with the deep significance attached to the occasion. It has been pointed out that the primitive tribes also had noted the social importance of ceremonials of which they took advantage when they initiated their young folk in the art of archery, or hunting.[35] Speaking of the elaborate ceremonials of this nature, Dr. Nunn observes: "The value of these consists not in themselves, but in what they symbolise. In brief, their biological utility lies in their power of arousing in actors and spectators, as often as they are repeated, states of feeling and emotion that are frequently of great social importance."[36] Both of them feel the weight and importance of the particular duties and responsibilities entrusted to the initiated young; and the interest shown by the spectators is an index of the social significance of the occasion.

Regarding the age of the pupil at which he is to commence his studies, there are differences of opinion among the Hindu Śastrakāras. Some authorities, for instance lay down that the Brāhmaṇa, the Kshatriya and the Vaiśya student should be initiated at the ages of eight, eleven and twelve respectively.[37] Yājnavalkya adds that the *Upanayana* may also be carried out at any convenient time according to the family custom (*yathākulam*).[38] But it is advised by some of these that the students who desire to speed up their educational attainments should start their studies a little earlier: the Brāhmaṇa in the fifth year of his age, the Kshatriya in the sixth, and the Vaiśya in the eighth.[39] The authorities concerned also laid down the minimum and maximum age limits in each case by saying that the *upanayana* may be performed at any time between the eighth and the sixteenth years of age for the Brāhmaṇa boy, between eleventh and twenty-second for the Kshatriya boy, and between twelfth and twenty-fourth years for the Vaiśya.[40] Those who do not get initiated within the age limits as mentioned above, become *patita-sāvitrīka*, i.e., lose their right of learning the *Sāvitrī* verse;[41] they become *vrātyas*, by thus losing this right; and such individuals are censured by Āryas (*ārya-vigarhitāh*).[42] The Śūdras were not to go in for learning according to these authorities.

[33] Āpa. i, I, I, 15; Gau. i, 8; Vis. xxiviii, 37–40; Vas. ii, 3–5; Man. ii, 148; 64.

[34] E.g.; Śat. Brāh. xi, 5, 4 etc.

[35] Nunn: *"Education; its Data and First Principles"* (1935), pp. 75–76.

[36] Nunn: op. cit.

[37] Śan. Gr. Sū. ii, 1, 1–9; Āśv. Gr. Sū. i. 19, 1–7; Pār. Gr. Sū. ii, 5, 36–38; Go. Gr. S. ii, 10, 1–4; also in *Smritis*: Man. ii. 36, Yāj. i, 14, etc.

[38] Yāj. i, 14: so again Pār. Gr. Sū. adds that *upanayana* may also be performed at any time according as it is considered auspicious by different families—Pār. G. S. ii. 2, 1–4.

[39] Man. ii, 37. cf. Āp. i, 1, 19–20; Gau. i, 6.

[40] Śān. Gr. Sū. ii, 1, 1–9; Āś. Gr. Sū. i, 19, 4–7; Par. G.S. ii, 5, 37–38; Go. ii 10, 3–4 etc; and, Man. ii, 38, etc.

[41] San. Gr. Sū. ii, 1, 8; Āśv. G.S. i, 19, 8; Pār. G.S. ii, 5, 39; Go. G.S. II, 10, 5.

[42] Manu. ii, 39; Yāj. i, 38.

From the difference in the respective ages prescribed for the three different *varṇas*, some writers have inferred that this emphasizes the supposed intellectual superiority of the Brāhmaṇa who was considered to be ready to begin the study at a younger age than his non-Brāhmaṇa fellows. But if we recall here an earlier remark, made at the beginning of this chapter, that an educational scheme touches life at every point and is a practical philosophy of life, we shall be able to see that the real explanation of this distinction should lie in another direction altogether. Of the three *varṇas*, the Brāhmaṇa's main duties centred round teaching and learning, according to the Hindu theory of *varṇa* of which we shall have to speak in more details in a later chapter.[43] The Brāhmaṇa boy was supposed to have come of a family, the members of which adhered to their duties of teaching and learning; and therefore, it would be quite natural to expect a hereditary predisposition as well as environmental facilities for a Brāhmaṇa child to develop tendencies to learn earlier owing to his family and social surroundings than it could be for the Kshatriya and Vaiśya children who were born and bred up in totally different surroundings. And, as to the Kshatriyas and Vaiśyas, the age when each of these is allowed to start studies is very nearly the same, which fact goes to support the above contention. Moreover, as the Brāhmaṇa's duties of life were centred around learning and teaching the earlier he started to learn, the better it would help him to become a master of as much knowledge as possible. Besides, he had also to spend a longer period in studenthood.

With the performance of the *upanayana* ceremony of the boy, his first lessons in simple living and developing 'frustration tolerance', so to speak, begin, irrespective of the position or status of the family in which he is born. In all humility and with a reverential attitude the initiated pupil had to start begging alms for his teacher. The *Satapatha Brāhmaṇa* says of the student who is required to do this: "Having made himself humble, as it were, and having become devoid of shame he begs alms."[44] He may start begging food from his mother, sister or other female relatives who are not likely to refuse.[45] He has then to announce (*nivedya*) the same to the *guru*, and with his permission, should help himself with it.[46] The student is expressly forbidden from accepting from anybody anything but alms (*bhikśā*).[47]

Next, there are rules about taking meals prescribed for the student. Manu says that he should take meals only twice a day, once in the morning and once in the evening, and must abstain from taking a third meal between the two.[48] He has to avoid over-eating (*atibhojanam*) because it causes ill-health (*anārogyam*), shortens the duration of life (*anāyushyam*), prevents acquisition of the spiritual merit (*apuṇyam*), will not lead to heaven (*asvargyam*) and is condemned by men.[49] According to *Hārīta* also, overeating as well as eating spoilt or stale food causes ill-health, is hostile to longevity and to the attainment of the celestial region and virtue; besides it is condemned by the society and should therefore be avoided.[50] The student should never eat flesh (*māmsam*) or honey (*madhu*).[51] He is also

[43] See Ch. VIII.
[44] Sat. Br. xi, 3, 3, 5. (Tr. by J. Eggeling).
[45] Man. ii, 50; also Śān. G.S. ii, 6, 4–6; Āśv. G.S. i. 22, 4–7.
[46] Śān. G.S. ii, 6, 7; Man. ii, 51; Yāj. i, 35.
[47] Vyāsa. i, 32.
[48] Man. ii, 56; ch. Bau. i, 8, 14.
[49] Man. ii, 57.
[50] Hār. i, 61 (Tr. by M. N. Dutt) 8.
[51] Man. ii, 177; Gaut. ii, 13; Āp. 1, 2, 2, 23.

advised not to eat stale sweet.[52] He is ordered not to eat beetle leaf.[53] Says the *Mahābhārata*: "Eating morning and evening is an ordinance of the Gods. It is ordained that no one should eat anything between these periods."[54]

About the dress of the student, Manu has said that a Brāhmaṇa student shall wear a piece of hempen cloth, a Kshatriya student shall wear a piece of silken cloth, while a Vaiśya one shall wear a piece of woollen cloth, just enough to cover the body. So also each of these three have to put on upper garments (*uttarīya*) made of the skins of antelope, of the *ruru* (a kind of deer), and of the goat, respectively.[55] In the opinion of Vasishṭha, the Brāhmaṇa student should wear a piece of cloth dyed with madder, and the Vaiśya student should wear a piece of cloth dyed with turmeric or made of raw silk.[56] Another piece of thread or threads, considered sacred (*yajnopavīta*), is also to be worn by the student; it is suspended from the left shoulder and comes to the bottom of the right arm, and is made up of three strings of cotton for the Brāhmaṇa student, of hempen thread for the Kshatriya, and of woollen thread for the Vaiśya.[57] We must note that the *higher* the *varṇa* to which the student belonged, the *less luxurious* piece of garment in regard to its quality is to be worn by him.

The staff, which the student is to hold, should be straight, unburnt, pleasing in appearance (*saumya-darśanah*), and not likely to create terror in any person (*an-udvega-karah*);[58] for it is intended merely as a security of the student's safety and not for deliberately offensive purposes. It is also required of the student that he should not indulge in such luxuries as anointing (*anjanam*) the eyes, using scents, and using umbrellas and shoes (*upānachchhatra-dhāraṇam*).[59] He is not to embellish or adorn his body with ointments etc. (*abhyagam*); nor is he to enjoy dancing (*nartanam*), music and playing on the instruments (*gīta-vādanam*), or take part in gambling (*dyūtam*), or useless gossipping (*janavādam*).[60] He is to preserve his vow (*vratam*) of *brahmacharya;* he is not to talk with women more than necessary.[61] He is to speak the truth, be modest and possessed of self-control, and keep free from lust (*kāma*), anger (*krodha*) and greed (*lobha*).[62] He has also to behave without causing any harm (*himsanam*) to any being.[63] In short, as Gautama puts it, he has to keep his tongue, arms and stomach under control and discipline.[64]

Thus the Hindu student was being trained in the habits of simple life, no matter to what family he belonged. Williams has rightly observed that young children should be taught to think not of what they *can have* but of what they *can do without*. "Then, as men and women", he proceeds, "will they be free to give themselves to high aims untempted by the material side of life."[65] In India, whatever the social position or status of the students' families,—whether they came from rich or from poor

---

[52] Man. ii, 177; Yāj. i. 32; Vis. xxiii, 11.
[53] Parā. i, 50.
[54] Śānti. 193, 10.
[55] Man. ii, 41.
[56] Vas. x.
[57] Man. ii, 44; Vis. xxvii, 19.
[58] Man. ii, 47.
[59] Man. ii, 178–9; Yāj. i. 32 Gaut. ii.
[60] Man. ii, 177–9; Ap. i, 1, 1, 2–23 to 3–24; Gau. ii, 135, 16, 22; Yāj. i, 32.
[61] Ibid.
[62] Ibid.
[63] Ibid.
[64] Gau. ii, 22.
[65] Williams: *"Principles of Social Psychology"*, p. 378.

families,—they had to take up the same mode of life. In the *Mahābhārata* and the *Rāmāyaṇa*, there are several instances showing how even princes had to undergo the same rigours of the student's life along with their poorest brother-students. Śrī Ramachandra, the hero of the *Rāmāyaṇa*, and his brothers,—all sons of the King Daśaratha,—had to undergo these hardships of the life of a student. And in the *Śrimad Bhāgavata*, we have, for instance, the story of princes Balarāma and Krishṇa following the hard life of the student along with their poor fellow student Sudāmā at the *āśrama* (hermitage) of *guru* Sāndīpani of Avanti.[66] So again, in *'Raghuwamśa'* we have a description of the peaceful atmosphere and the simple mode of living at the *āśrama* of *Kula-pati* (Rector, Principal) Vasishṭha;[67] we are told that King Dilīpa, accompanied by Queen Sudakshiṇā, went to the *āṣrama* with a very small retinue of attendants, in order that there should be no disturbance to the quiet atmosphere of the *āśrama*;[68] and, on their arrival at the *āśrama*, these royal guests were provided with only the rural (*vanyam eva*) means of living for the night's stay—viz. a hut made of leaves (*parṇa-śālā*) and beds of *kuśa*-grass.[69]

The student has to rise up early in the morning before sunrise. "If the sun rises, seeing him asleep out of wilful laziness, let him mutter the *gāyatrī mantra* and fast for a whole day",[70] as a penalty. He is not to sleep during day time at all.[71] He should offer the *sandhyā* prayer and rite twice daily—early in the morning and in the evening.[72] Says Bhīshma in the *Mahābhārata*: "The Sun-God should always be adored. One should not sleep after sunrise. Morning and evening the prayers should be offered, sitting with face turned towards the East and towards the West, respectively."[73] The student should take his bath every day.[74] The first duty (*āditah*) of the *guru*, on the completion of the preliminary rites of the *Upanayana* of the student (*śishya*), was to instruct him in the rules of personal cleanliness (*śaucham*) and of proper conduct (*āchāram*).[75] The *āchārya* says to the initiate: "You are a *brahmachārī;* do the service; do not sleep in daytime; with devotion to the *āchārya*, study the Veda."[76]

One unique thing to be noted about the student's life in Hindu India was that he had to live in the premises of the hermitage (*āśrama)* of the *guru*. The *Chhāndogya Upanishad* speaks of the student as residing with the family of, or in the neighbourhood of the *āchārya* (*āchārya-kulavāsin, ante-vāsin*).[77] The term *antevāsin* with reference to the student is also mentioned in the *Brihadāraṇyaka* and the *Taittirīya Upanishad.*[78] The *Smritis* too prescribe rules for the student's residence at the *guru's* house. We have already referred to the story of Balarāma and Krishṇa's education at the *āśrama* of *guru* Sāndīpani, and Rāmchandra's and his brother's education at Viśwāmitra's *āśrama.* And,

---

[66] See Bhāg. x, 80, 34 ff.

[67] See *Raghuvamśa*, Canto. i, 35–95.

[68] Ibid. i, 37.

[69] Ibid. i, 94–95.

[70] Man. ii, 220.

[71] Āb. i, 1, 2, 24.

[72] Man. ii, 222; Yāj. i, 22; 25.

[73] Śānti. 193, 8.

[74] Man. ii, 176, etc.

[75] Man. ii, 69; Yāj. i, 15.

[76] Āśv. G.S. i, 22, 2: *Brahmachāryasyupo'śāna, karma kuru, divā mā svapsir, āchāryādhīno vedam adhīshveti"*/Also cf. Śāt. Br. xi, 5, 4, 5; Śān. G.S. ii, 4, 5.

[77] Chhānd. Up. ii, 23, 2; and iii, 11, 5.

[78] e.g. Brih. Up. vi, 3, 7; Taitt. Up. i, 11, 1.

there is something indeed that could be said in favour of this system of the ancient Hindus giving the boy up to the absolute care of the teacher, during the period of his education. In the family, the young boy is likely to come in close contact with persons who may be of a less moral calibre than his parents would desire for his company. It is also probable that the boy may come in contact with environment and surroundings which would not be conducive to his free and healthy moral and mental development. Further, there are likely to be some family prejudices and beliefs whose impress upon the child at an early age may obstruct the free and proper development of his faculty of reason. Under the Hindu system, the raw material of the child was given over, for proper emotional and intellectual shaping, to the care of the expert who was particularly equipped for his special task, who was a man as well known for his learning as for his high character, and whose main duty in life was to teach and train. The young child was placed in the hands of the *guru* at an age when his attitude towards things and persons around him was not yet formed and fixed. At this stage, his mind is so flexible and so much likely to be influenced by those who possess authority over him that it should be the duty of the parents to place him under the care of a tried person of a high moral character. Ross has observed: "The hackneyed metaphors, 'potter's clay', 'wax tablet', 'bent twig', 'tender osier', are so many ways of emphasizing the high suggestibility of the child. The mark of the young mind is an absence of fixed habits, of stubborn volitions, of persistent ways of acting. The staunch personality that can plough through counter-suggestions as tremorless as an iron-clad in a flight of arrows we look for only in the adult. The child gradually builds it as a worm builds its wormcast—out of material taken in from without. And this original dependence on surroundings holds true alike of the martyr and of the milk-sop, of moral hero and of weakling. They differ only in their power to form fixed habits."[79]

Therefore, childhood is an age when utmost precaution has to be taken in selecting the *environment* in which the child is to be brought up, as well as in selecting the *person* under whose influence he is to be brought up. It is the formative period of life; and the process of suggestion as well as of imitation play greatest part during this period of one's life. The greater part of an individual's character is due to the various impressions his mind has received during childhood. Further, we also know how the modern psychoanalyst often traces the cause of an adult's mental disorder to some event which has left its stamp upon his mind during his more tender years. Under the Hindu system of education, the young boy had to live with his *guru*, often far away from his nearest relations, so that his absolute mentor and guide was the *guru* alone. And, he was kept in an environment free from temptations, an environment of simplicity, of natural surroundings.

This system, again, can claim another advantage to its credit. It avoided any occasion of conflict between the teacher and the family, such as are, for instance, met with in the modern school.[80] The school-child finds itself divided between two kinds of interests,—the one is the tendency to follow the family and other attitudes he has been acquiring during the time he is spending with his family, and the other is the tendency to develop the power of independent learning.[81] This conflict of the two interests also was avoided in the Hindu system by leaving the child entirely in the custody of the *āchārya*.

[79] Ross: *"Social Control"*, p. 163.

[80] See e.g., Williams: *"Principles of Social Psychology"*, pp. 367 ff.

[81] Ibid.

Rightly, therefore, have the Hindu sages spoken of the *āchārya* as the "spiritual father" of the pupil.[82] The *āchārya* in his turn was to regard the pupil with all the affection due to a son.[83] Unless the *āchārya* took a real paternal interest in his pupil, he would not be able to wield a deep moral influence upon him; and, therefore, to that extent he would also be unable to mould his character properly. The opening prayer which both the teacher and the pupil sing together, according to the *Taittirīya Upanishad*, is this: Almighty! Do protect us both, together; give food for both of us at the same time; may both of us apply our energies towards acquisition of knowledge in harmony and co-operation; may our studies be illustrious and brilliant; may there never be any feeling of estrangement amongst us two! Peace! Peace! Peace!!![84]

It is highly interesting, and also instructive, to note here how the concept of *viḍyā* ('knowledge' or 'learning' or 'lore' or 'science') gradually developed and became more and more comprehensive and inclusive as the Hindu pioneered and developed newer and newer 'lores' or 'sciences'. To begin with, all learning, all *viḍyā*, consisted of the three *vedas* (*trayī*, i.e. the trio), the *Rig-Veda*, the *Yajur-Veda*, and the *Sāma-Veda*, to which very soon the fourth *Atharva-Veda* was also added. Learning and scholarship, then, meant proficiency in these *Vedas*. As new vistas of knowledge were gradually opened up and new branches of knowledge emerged and were developed by the Hindu, the concept of *viḍyā* also became wider and wider; but still the tendency was to trace the roots and sources of the new knowledge to the *Vedas*, which was reflected in the Hindu's regarding the *Vedas* as the fountain source of all knowledge and the other newly emerging branches as their secondary and derivative offshoots. In fact, according to the tradition, the term *veda* also means *shaḍ-anga veda*, i.e., *veda* with six "limbs" (*anga*) or branches, viz., *Śikshā* (Phonetics), *Kalpa* (Rules for *yajna*), *Vyākaraṇa* (Grammar), *Nirukta* (Etymology), *Chhanda* (Prosody), and *Jyotisha* (Astronomy). Therefore, when the Hindu wanted to refer to 'learning' or 'knowledge' he still referred to the *Vedas*, which, now by implication included the four *vedas* and all other available knowledge also.

However, he must have felt that this way of conceiving relationship between the new branches of learning and the *Vedas* was not altogether convincing or satisfactory, particularly when the new lore or branch came to achieve such great advances, development, systematization and specialization, as in the cases of Medicine (*Āyurvidyā*=Science of the Life) and Archery (*Dhanur-vidyā*=Science of the Bow); and so he went to the extent of exalting these new *vidyās* themselves by suffixing the term, *veda* to them, which now came to be known as *Āyur-Veda* and *Dhanur-Veda*. In the Sanskrit literature, mention is often made, in describing the scope and extent of the field of knowledge available for the inquisitive student, of the fourteen *vidyās* (sciences) and sixty-four *kalās* (arts); and though we have no evidence that all of these *vidyās* acquired the exalted designation of *vedas*, yet, the trend indicated in the names like *Āyur-Veda* and *Dhanur-Veda* is clear. It is necessary to bear all this in mind whenever we come across terms like *Veda-pāraga*, proficient in the *vedic* lore, or learned in all the *vedas;* or *mantravid*, proficient in the *mantras;* and so on.

In this connection, it may also be mentioned that the term *Veda* is derived from *vid*, to know; and Jaimini, in his *Pūrva-mīmāmsā* notes that its subject-matter consists of *Dharma* and *Brahma*, which

---

[82] Ath. Veda. xi, 5, 3; Ait. Br. i, 1; Man. ii, 170; Gaut. i, 1, 10; Vas xxviii, 38–9. Mahā. Vana. 180, 34; etc.

[83] Praśna Up. v, 8; Āp. i, 2.

[84] Taitt Up. ii, 1: *"Om! sahanāvavatu, sahanau bhunaktu, sahavīryam karavāvahai/tejasvināvadhītam astu mā vidvishāvahai/ Om! Śāntih! Śāntih! Śāntih!"* The same prayer is repeated in Ibid. iii, 1.

could be understood only through the *Veda*.[85] Again, the term *Mantra* is derived from *manana*, thinking, cogitating, and so means an instrument or vehicle of thought.[86]

Traditionally, mention is often made in Sanskrit literature (including the drama, the story and the poetry) of fourteen sciences (*vidyās*) and sixty-four disciplines of arts and crafts (*kalās*); but occasionally reference is made to a larger number of sciences and arts also. Among the sciences, e.g., are mentioned the following: the three (or four) *Vedas, Itihāsa-purāṇa* (history), *Vyākaraṇa* (Grammar), *Bhūta-vidyā* (demonology), *Kshātra-vidyā* (Military Science, Science of War), *Vākovākyam* (Science of Disputation, Dialectics), *Tarka-śāstra* (Science of Reasoning or Logic), *Śikshā* (Phonetics), *Nirukta* (Etymology), *Chhandas* (Prosody or Metrics), *Nakshatra-vidyā* (Science of Stars or Astronomy), *Jyotisha* (also Science of Luminaries or Astronomy), *Rāśī* (=*Gaṇitam*, i.e., Arithmetic), *Ekāyāna* (=*Niti-śāstra*, i.e., Science of Ethics and Politics), and a few others also.[87] Among the arts, Vātsyāyana gives a list of sixty-four (see below), and many other writers refer to or mention this number, but some also refer to a larger number.[88] In the *Chhāndogya Upanishad*, for example, Nārada tells Sanatkumāra that he has studied the sciences, a list of which he mentions;[89] most of these are referred to in the list above; and therefore, he asserts he is truly a *mantra-vid*; but yet he admits that he feels far from satisfied because he has still not learned the Science of the Soul, *Ātma-vidyā*, and therefore is not an *Ātma-vid*, i.e., learned in the science of the *Ātman* (soul).[90]

The teacher's duty towards his pupil was to impart to him "truth exactly as he knew it".[91] The function of the teacher was to lead the pupil from the darkness of ignorance to the light of knowledge.[92] The teacher from whom the pupil receives the *upanayana* sacrament (*samskāra*) is called an *āchārya*.[93] And Āpastamba explains the word thus: "He from whom the student gathers (*āchinoti*) his *dharmas* is the *acharya*".[94] The *āchārya* must never get wearied of instructing his pupil, and must also, as a teacher, try to maintain a high standard in respect of his own academic attainments.[95] The *Gopatha Brāhmaṇa* narrates the story of a certain teacher named Maitreya who closed his *āśrama* and dismissed his students as soon as he discovered that he was not conversant with a particular subject; and, thereafter, he started to acquire a knowledge of that subject.[96] The *āchārya* must not only love his pupil like his own son, but must also give full individual attention to him while teaching; and he must not withhold any part of the sacred knowledge from him: "Loving him like his own son, and full of attention, he (the teacher) shall teach him the *Dharma-Śāstra*, without keeping away anything from the whole *dharma*. And, he shall not use him for his own purposes to the detriment of his studies, except in times of distress".[97] The *Mahābhārata* as well as the *Rāmāyaṇa* give us numerous instances of teachers of very high moral character and learning, like Viśwāmitra, Vasishṭha, Sāndīpanī, Dronāchārya, Kripāchārya and others.

---

[85] *Dharma—brahmaṇī Vedaikavedyā.*

[86] Yāsk in *Nirukta*, vii, 3, 6.

[87] See *Chhāndogya* Up. vii, 1; Śat. Br. iv, 6, 9, 20; xi, 5, 6, 8; etc.

[88] *Kāma*. i, iii, 1–15; also in *Śukra-Nīti;* Bhāg. Purā. x, 45, 36; Rāmā. i, 9.

[89–90] Chhānd. Up. vii, I.

[91] Muṇḍ. Up. i, 2–23; Praśna Up. vi, 1; Chhānd. Up. vii, 16, 7.

[92] Āp. i, 10, 11.

[93] Gau. i, 9: Āpa. i, 1, 1, 13.

[94] Āpa. i, 1, 1, 13.

[95] Man. ii, 73; Sār. Gr. S. iv, 8, 12, 16–17.

[96] Gop. Br. i, 1, 31.

[97] Āp. i, 2, 8, 25–26.

On the other hand, a very high degree of reverence to the teacher was expected of the student. *Manu-Smṛiti* says that within the sight of his *guru*, the student shall not sit carelessly or at ease.[98] Again, in the presence of his teacher he was always to eat less, wear less valuable dress and ornaments, and rise earlier and go to bed later.[99] Wherever people defame his teacher, whether justly or falsely (*parīvādo nindā vāpi*), there the student must cover his ears, or depart from that place, rather than hear it.[100] By censuring his teacher, though justly, he will become (in his next birth) an ass; by falsely defaming him he will become a dog.[101] Now, these and such other rules were not intended to create a servile attitude in the pupil towards the teacher; they were meant only to cultivate an attitude of deep reverence for the teacher in the breasts of the students. Yājnavalkya explains such rules by saying that the student should "wait upon (*upāsīta*) the *guru* for the sake of learning (*svādhyāya*). He should also be all attentive to him (*samāhitah*). He should always promote his *guru's* interest (*hitam*) by all acts of body, mind and speech" (*mano-vāk-kāya-karma-bhih*).[102]

In *Mahābhārata* we have several instances of strict obedience of the teacher's word by the pupils. The *Mahābhārata* says: "The father and mother only create body. On the other hand, the life which one acquires from the *guru* is divine. . . . The *gurus* always treat their disciples with great affection. The latter should, therefore, revere their *gurus* duly. . . . The *guru* deserves greater respect than either the father or the mother".[103] These and such other rules were intended to infuse a spirit of high reverence in the pupil's heart towards his teacher. The reason is obvious. Unless the teacher is regarded with deep reverence as well as deep affection by the pupil, he would not succeed in carrying the psychological influence over the pupil such as is necessary for the proper mentor and the guide. Childhood, as Ross puts it, "is the hey-day of personal influence",[104] and the Hindu child was therefore placed under the influence of a "picked person" and an expert intellectual leader of a high moral standard. Such great, selfless, intellectual leaders are a rarity at any time and in any country. At any rate it would be certainly impossible to find such an intellectual leader in every family. To the sole care of one of these few great men was the student in ancient India entrusted for his moral and intellectual training. The *Mahābhārata* points out that "if the *guru* happens to be unwise, the disciple cannot possibly behave towards him in a respectful or proper way; if the *guru* is possessed of purity and good conduct, the disciple also succeeds in acquiring conduct of the same kind".[105]

The moral influence of the teacher upon his pupil must have acquired an added weight due to the fact that the teacher charged no fees to the pupils or their parents for his labours. Teaching for a stipulated fee (*bhṛitakādhyāpakah*), as well as being taught for a stipulated fee (*bhritakādhyāpitah*), have both been severely denounced.[106] After the young student has finished his course of studies, however, he may offer a gift (*guru-dakshiṇā*) to his *guru*, according to his own means, before he

---

[98] Man. ii, 198; also Gaut. ii, 14–15; Āp. Gr. S. i, 1–21; Sār. Gr. Sū. iv. 8, 5, 7–11.

[99] Man. ii, 194; 198; also Gau. ii, 21; Āp. Gr. S. i, 4, 22–28: Mahā. Ādi. 91.

[100] Man. ii, 200.

[101] Man. ii, 201.

[102] Yāj. i, 26–27; cf. also Man. ii, 191 '*Kuryād adhyayane yatnam āchāryasya hiteshu cha.*'

[103] Śānti. 108–18, 21 and 24.

[104] Ross, op. cit., p. 164.

[105] Mahā. Anu. 105, 3: *"Na guravakrita-prājne śakyam śishyeṇa vartitum/guror hi dīrgha-darśitvam yat tachchhishyasya Bhārata//.*

[106] Man. iii, 156; cf. Yāj. i, 220; Mahā. Śānti. 260.

leaves the *guru's* house.[107] But such a gift, as the *Vājasaneya Samhitā* points out, does in no way signify an adequate return in exchange of the knowledge received; it is only a mark of honour and respect to the teacher.[108] There is an instance in the *Mahābhārata*, for example, of *guru* Droṇa being presented with gifts by Bhīshma for accepting the tutorship of the Kaurava princes.[109] But such gifts to the teacher were regarded as *honoraria* paid to the *guru*, as an expression of respect for one who was very often himself a man with little or no financial possessions.

The poet Kālidāsa has given a pertinent instance in this connection: Varatantu, the *guru*, was urged by Kautsa, the *śishya*, to accept some fee (*guru-dakshiṇā*) from him after his course of studies (*vidyā*) was over (*samāpta*). Varatantu, however, refused to think of any payment in return for the knowledge he had imparted, for, indeed, he looked upon Kautsa's attention and devotion (*bhakti*) to him as the fee itself. But Kautsa's obstinate insistence provoked him into anger, and he demanded "four and ten crores of money, according to the number of lores"—i.e., the fourteen lores (*vidyās*)—that were taught by the *guru*,[110] so as to indicate to Kautsa that the teacher's obligations to the pupil are unrepayable by money. This story clearly indicates that accepting fees for tuitions was regarded as immoral by the teachers of ancient India. Learning was thus never used in India as a means of earning material gains.

Free tuitions had another very important significance in the Hindu educational system. It meant that the education of the Hindu child never depended upon the financial position of the family into which he was born. The gates of the Temple of Learning were open to all, prince and pauper, alike. Nor did the quality of education suffer owing to lack of capacity to spend money over it. Education was thus not dependent nor controlled by external factors like financial beneficiaries, ruling authorities, or political systems. In fact, as we have already seen, even the Kings had to be humble when they approached an educational institution or *āśrama* for a visit.

Knowledge was not only never given with any material motive behind it, but it was also never acquired with such a motive. There were no material prizes offered to pupils for excellence shown in their lessons except perhaps the expression of admiration by the teacher. There were no competitive examinations marking the gradations of the students' abilities. To acquire knowledge for its own sake was the sacred duty (*dharma*) of every one; and no one went to learn with a view to furthering or increasing material prospects. Absence of any material motive in learning must have been a great psychological asset in keeping the Hindu educational system free from many of the evils that would otherwise have beset it. For, it was the firm belief of the Hindu sages that once a material motive is let in as an end into the educational system in one way or the other, it would set into motion the interplay of a variety of complex economic forces into the system which, along with those who taught and learnt under it, would be very adversely affected as a consequence. On the side of the teachers, there would be created a rivalry and competition amongst them to obtain as large a number of students as possible, since that would pay them more, and the efficiency in imparting education would deteriorate to that degree. On the side of the students, there would be created a rivalry and a spirit of competition amongst them also to win prizes and other material awards; and this spirit of rivalry amongst the students is most detrimental to the real cause of education. For then, learning will have value for the students only in so far as it is able to yield laurels

[107] See Man. ii, 245; Yāj. i, 51; Āsv. Gr. S. iii, 9, 4; Gobh. Gr. S. iii, 4, 1–2, etc.
[108] Vāj. Sam. xix, 30.
[109] Mahā. Ādi. 141–44.
[110] *Raghuvamśa*, Canto. v, 20–21.

and prizes and other gains, and will, therefore, be pursued only with the material motive in view. The temptations of material profit would be too great and too enticing to keep the pure, disinterested intellectual joy in learning alive. "Spontaneous and disinterested desire for knowledge", says Russell, "is not uncommon in the young, and might be easily aroused in many in whom it remains latent. But it is remorselessly checked by teachers who think only of examinations, diplomas and degrees".[111] The Hindu system of education was never allowed to suffer from motives of any kind of material prospect or of a spirit of rivalry and competition; and utmost care was taken to keep alive lofty ideals in the breasts of the learners. The pursuit of knowledge was carried on as one's part of the inherent, natural duties (*dharma*) of man.

To achievements in learning (*vidyā*) is due the highest honour, according to the Hindu, more even than to achievements in wealth (*vittam*) or to elderly relationship, or to age.[112] Manu tells us the story of a young boy (*sisuh*) named Kavi who taught his elder relatives and used to call them "little sons" (*putrakā*) since he excelled them in knowledge. These relatives complained to the Gods about Kavi's audacity; but the Gods gave their decision in favour of young Kavi.[113] For, a learned man, though young, has to be respected and honoured by virtue of his learning.[114] Bhīshma advises that before giving a maiden in marriage, inquiry must first be made as to the educational qualifications of the suitor.[115] So again, a maiden coming from a family where the Vedas are not studied is regarded as unfit for marrying.[116] Every twice-born person (*dvijanman*) is by sacred duty bound to study the Vedas together with their inner essential meaning (*rahasya*); at the same time such a person must undergo the disciplines and obey the rules (*vratāh*) laid down for a *brahmachārin*, (that is, for one belonging to the "order" of a student).[117] It was well recognised that education was the foundation upon which the whole edifice of the moral culture of the individual was to be built. A person belonging to the *dvija varṇas*, i.e., to any of the first three *varṇas*, who failed to do his duty of studying the Vedas would be degraded to the śūdra *varṇa*.[118] In this connection, it may be pointed out that as early as in the times of *Yajur-Veda*, at least, Vedic knowledge was possible to all classes including the Śūdras, and even the non-Āryans.[119]

There were many other matters of discipline imposed upon the Hindu student. As soon as the initiation ceremony of the student was over, the first duty of the *guru* was to instruct his new pupil in the rules of personal cleanliness and of good conduct.[120] The young boy must learn to befriend all living beings.[121] A striking feature of the Hindu system of education was that the training in character-building proceeded side by side with the development of the intellect of the student. The moral culture of the student was not separated from his intellectual culture. "Grateful, non-hating, intelligent, pure, healthy, non-envious, honest, energetic,—such a student should be taught,

---

[111] Russell: *"Why men Fight"*, p. 174.
[112] Man. ii, 136; Yāj. i, 126; Mahā. Vana. 133, 11–12.
[113] Man. ii, 151, 53; also in Baudh. i, 3, 47.
[114] Man. ii, 156; Gaut. vi, 21. 23; Yāj. i, 115.
[115] Mahā. Anu. 44, 3.
[116] Man. iii, 7; Yāj. i, 54. See Ch. on *'Marriage'* below.
[117] Man. ii, 165.
[118] Man. ii, 168; Vis. xxviii, 36; Vas. iii, 2.
[119] Yajur. xxvi, 2: *Yathemām vācham kalyāṇīmāvadāni, janebhyah brāhmaṇā-rājanyābhyām śudrāya chānāryāya cha svāya chāraṇāya*. (svāya = of one's own (group); *chāraṇa = Vaiśya; rājanya = Kshatriya*).
[120] Āśv. Gr. i, 22, 2; Man. ii, 69; Yāj. i, 15.
[121] Man. ii, 87, Vas. xxvi. 11.

according to *dharma*".[122] Indeed Manu would say that one who completely governs himself (*suyantritah*), though he knows the *Śāvitrī mantra* only, is better than he who knows all the Vedas but who cannot control himself.[123] No amount of knowledge can help one whose heart is contaminated with evil ideas (*(vipradushṭa-bhāva)*).[124] On the other hand, he whose speech and thought are pure and ever perfectly guarded, gains the full benefit which is attainable by the study of the Vedas.[125] "The wise man", says Manu, "should strive towards controlling (*samyama*) his organs (*indriya*) which run wild among alluring sensual objects (*vishya*), just as a charioteer controls his horses.[126] The organs are: the five faculties of sense (*buddhīndriyāṇi*), viz., the ear, skin, the eye, the tongue and the nose; the five organs of action (*karmendriyāṇi*)—viz., the anus, the organ of generation, hands, feet and the organ of speech; and the eleventh—the mind, which is both an organ of sense as well as of action. When the mind (*manas*) is controlled (*jita*), all other organs are controlled.[127] For Manu, man incurs guilt undoubtedly (*asamśayam*) through the attachment of his organs to sensual pleasures. But he is sure to attain the aim of his life (*siddhim*) if he keeps these under complete control (*samyama*).[128] On the other hand, desire (*kāmah*) is never extinguished by the enjoyment of the desired object; it grows only stronger like fire fed with clarified butter.[129] One must, therefore,—and especially the student must, (because Manu is dealing with the life of a student [*brahmacharyāśrama*] in this section)—try his utmost to subdue the urges for sensual pleasures (*vishaya*). And the best way to subdue and keep under control the organs which are attached to sensual pleasure is, not by mere abstinence (*asevā*) from them, but by constantly engaging oneself in the pursuit of studies (*jnāna*).[130] Mere repression of desires is not so much effective in achieving self-control as the purposeful engaging of one's mind in the pursuit of better and more desirable things would prove to be. Manu indeed declares that "not a single act here below appears to have been done by a man free from *kāma*; for whatever he does, it is the result of the prompting of *kāma*"![131] What every one has to take care of is to see that these desires or *kāmas* are directed in the proper manner, and towards proper ends. This is the purpose of education,—to train the young student to direct his energies towards right activities.[132]

Kauṭilya also has declared that the main purpose of education is the control of the organs of sense.[133] "Absense of discrepancy (*avipratipatti*) in the perception of sound, touch, colour, flavour, and scent by means of the ear, the eyes, the tongue and the nose is what is meant by the control of the organs of sense (*indriyajayah*)" says Kauṭilya. "Strict observance of the precepts of sciences

---

[122] Yāj. i, 28; *"Kritajno'drohi medhāvī śuchih kulyo'anasūyakah/adhyāpya sādhuśoktāptasvārthadā dharmatastvime//*Also, cf Man. ii, 109.

[123] Man. ii, 118.

[124] Man. ii, 97.

[125] Man. ii, 160: *"Yasya vāng-manasī śuddhe samyagupte cha sarvadā/sa vai sarvam avāpnoti vedāntapagatam phalam."*

[126] Man. ii, 88.

[127] Manu. ii. 90–92.

[128] Man. ii, 93.

[129] Man. ii, 94.

[130] Man. ii, 96.

[131] Man. ii, 4; *Akāmasya kriyā kāchit driśyate neha karhichit/ yad yaddhi kurute kinchit tattat kāmasya cheshṭitam//* also, Man. ii, 2. See also our discussion on the *purushārthas* in Ch. III, *supra*.

[132] Man. ii, 3 and 5.

[133] Artha. i, iii, 12, 1–2.

(*Śāstrānushṭhānam*)", he further proceeds, "also means the same; for the sole aim of all sciences is nothing but control of the organs of sense (*kritsnam hi śāstramidam indriyajayah*)[134]; whosoever is of reverse character, whosoever has not his organs of sense under control, will soon perish, though he possesses the whole earth bound by the four ends' of the world." The young student is, therefore, enjoined to "abandon lust (*kāma*), anger (*krodha*), greed (*lobha*), vanity (*māna*), conceit (*mada*), and overjoy (*harsha*)".[135] Says the *Mahābhārata*, also: "Knowledge of the *śāstras* is said to bear fruit when it produces modesty and virtuous conduct".[136] And the *Śukra Nīti* similarly observes: "The mind covetous of the meat of enjoyable things, sends forth the senses—sound, touch, sight, taste and smell; any of these five by itself is sufficient to cause destruction. Therefore, one should check the mind; for when the mind is controlled, the senses are conquered".[137] The student ought to keep himself away from gambling (*dyūtam*), idle disputes (*jana-vādam*), back-biting or talking scandals (*parīvādam*), and lying (*anritam*). So also has he to abstain from looking at and touching women (*strīṇām preksanālambham*), and from hurting others.[138] It was well recognised that mere knowledge without a proper discipline and training in self-control would prove of little avail to a person who desired to promote his own happiness and progress as well as of those around him.

Thus, the teacher's duty under the Hindu system of education was to help to cultivate the moral culture of his pupil *along with* his intellectual culture. The harm that results, in our own times, out of the separation of the moral from the intellectual development of the young boys is expressed thus ably by John Dewey: "The much lamented separation in the (modern) schools, of intellectual and moral training, of acquiring information and growing in character, is simply one expression of the failure to conceive and construct the school as a social institution, having a social life and value within itself".[139] "It is false psychology", says R. B. Cattell, "to draw any sharp distinction between character training and the acquisition of knowledge. Habits of behaviour, such as honesty, fair play, tidiness, etc., have been produced under experimental conditions; and it has been found out that they only maintain themselves in the field in which they were taught. This means that a boy who has learned fair play and honesty on the playing fields of Eton may yet show no signs of them on the Stock Exchange."[140] And in this connection, the problem of "transfer of training", i.e. the carry-over of the attitudes developed during the early period of training to the later actual situations in life, is one of the biggest problems in all educational systems. Mere class instruction and lecturing on general principles like "honesty is the best policy" does not lead the trainee to observe honesty when it actually comes to behaving in a given situation. Character training depends for its lasting effect on learning through experiencing and *doing*. Besides, example is always better than precept in character training. Therefore, every efficient scheme of education must always find an adequate place for the moral training of the young *along with* the courses devised for their intellectual training; and, it must also be placed in the hands of teachers who are intellectual as well as moral leaders themselves. In the words of Sir T. P. Nunn: "The school must be thought of primarily not as a place where certain knowledge is learnt, but as a place where the young are initiated in

[134] Artha: Ibid,Tr. by Śāmasāstry, p. 10.
[135] Artha: Ibid, Tr. by Śāmasāstry, p. 10.
[136] Mahā. Sabhā. 5, 112.
[137] Śukra. p. 195–6 (Sarkar's Tr.).
[138] Man ii, 179; also Āp. i, 3. 17–24.
[139] Deway; "*Moral Principles in Education*", p. 15
[140] Cattell: "*Psychology and Social Progress*", p.374

certain forms of activity namely, those that are of greatest and most permanent significance in the wider world. Those activities fall naturally into two groups: In the first, we place the activities that safeguard the conditions and maintain the standard of individual and social life; such as the care of the health and bodily grace, manners, social organization, morals and religion; in the second, the typical creative activities that constitute, so to speak, the solid tissue of civilization; these are, the arts, the sciences, and literature."[141]

In the Hindu scheme of education both these aims of education were thought out by the Hindus, in their own way, as *inseparable* complements that made one whole system. This is so forcefully expressed by the *Taittirīya Upanishad* when it declares: Justice (*ritam*), reading and teaching have to be practised together; truth (*satyam*), reading and teaching have to be practised simultaneously; sublimation (*damah*) or self-control, reading and teaching have to be carried on together; tranquility of mind (*śamah*), reading and teaching have to be practised at the same time; the worship of sacred fires, reading and teaching have to be practised side by side; burnt offerings, reading and teaching have also to be carried on side by side; nay, even the duties and obligations towards strangers and guests (*atithayah*), duties as a human being (*mānusham*), duties of begetting offspring and those towards descendants, have to be practised by man in conjunction with his studies and teaching.[142]

In all writings on the life and programme of the student, the Hindu Śāstrakāras have laid the greatest emphasis on the importance of the virtue of celibacy (*brahmacharya*) in the development of the moral culture of a student. The powers of *brahmacharya* have been described to be so great that the *Rig Veda* declares that by virtue of it, a King is able to rule his kingdom efficiently, the gods themselves were able to attain immortality, and Indra was able to achieve the position of the chief of Gods.[143] Some authorities would forbid the young student even from "looking at or touching women".[144] Kauṭilya, speaking about the duties of a prince-student, says that he should observe celibacy till he becomes sixteen years of age.[145] "Let him always sleep alone"; says Manu, "let him never waste his manhood; for he who voluntarily emits his manhood, breaks his vow (*vratam*)".[146] This quality of *brahmacharya*, of celibacy, was thought to be so very essential for a student, that in the course of time, this Sanskrit word itself has come to acquire the very meaning of studenthood; the word *brahmacharya* has thus become synonymous with "studenthood". Every student, in order to increase the spiritual prowess (*tapovridhyartham*), must observe *brahmacharya* till he completes his studies.[147] It was thought to be incumbent upon the student to cultivate habits of purity of thought and action, as well as of the body.

One of the very important considerations with regard to a system of education is the place, value and method of punishment in that system. Should every lapse on the part of the pupil be met with

---

[141] Nunn: *Education: Its Data and First Principles*, pp. 242–3.

[142] *Tatt. Up*. Śikshā. Vallī, 9: *"Ritam cha svādhyāya-pravachane cha, satyam cha svādhyāya-pravachane cha, damaś cha svādhyāya-pravachane cha samaś cha svādhyāya-pravachane cha, agnayaś cha svādhyāya-pravachane cha, agnihotram cha svādhyāya-pravachane cha, atithayaś cha svādhyāya-pravachane cha, mānusham cha svādhyāya-pravachane cha, prajā cha svādhyāya-pravachane cha, prajanaś cha svādhyāya-pravachane cha, prajātiś cha svādhyāya-pravachane cha."*

[143] Rig. xi, 5–19.

[144] Man. ii, 179; and Gop. Br. i, 2, 1–8.

[145] Arth. p. 19.

[146] Man. ii, 180.

[147] See Tait. Ār. ii, I; Man. ii, 175; Yāj. i, 33; Kām. Sū. i, ii, 2–3; Pāras G.S. ii, 5, 12; Gobh. G. S. ii, 1, 16; etc.

by the rod? Should the fear of punishment for ever loom large before the horizon of the student's vision in order to prevent him from committing mistakes? Or should his native love for the right and hate of the wrong be aroused and cultivated by a sympathetic appeal to his heart and he be thus convinced that it would be in his own best interest that he should never commit a wrong again? The Hindus have answered this question in favour of sympathetic treatment in dealing with the pupil; though, according to them, the rod may be of some use at times, if properly applied. Manu is quite emphatic on this point; and Gautama and āpastamba agree with him: "Created beings", says Manu, "must be instructed in what concerns their welfare without giving them pain; and sweet and gentle speech (*vākchaiva madhurā ślakshṇā*) must be used by a teacher who desires to abide by what is *dharma*".[148] At other places, he has said that the teacher may beat his pupil, if he has committed a fault (*aparādha*), with a rope or a stick; but this can be done only on the back, and never on any of the noble parts of the body (*uttamānga*); but, even this can be done, again, only with a view to correct or improve the student (*śishṭyartham*), and with no other motive.[149] Similar observations with regard to the use of the rod are made by the Gautama, Vishṇu and in the *Mahābhārata*.[150]

The social bearing of the use of the rod for correcting the young is quite apparent. Locke has expressed it in these words: "If the mind be curbed and humbled too much in childhood, if their spirits be abashed and broken much by too strict a hand over them, they lose all their vigour and industry, and are in a worse state than the former. For, extravagant young fellows that have liveliness and spirit, come sometimes to be set right and so make able and great men; but dejected minds, and low spirits are hardly ever to be raised, and very seldom attain to anything. To avoid danger that is on either hand is the great art; and he that has found a way to keep up a child's spirit easy, active, and free, and yet at the same time to restrain him from many things he has a mind to, and to draw him to things that are necessary to him;—he, that knows how to reconcile these seeming contradictions, has, in my opinion, got the true secret of education".[151] O'Shea has shown, by giving instances of the use and spare of the rod in different countries of Europe and America, how in actual results the rod is ineffective as a measure of corrective.[152] In France, for instance, corporal punishment was absolutely prohibited while in Germany it was the most used, in public schools. But the German student, as soon as he left the school and joined the University where the control at the point of the rod was taken off, got into more riotous moods than his French brother.

What is essential for the real discipline of the student, therefore, is more a habit of *self-control than a control imposed from without*. Control from without leads to fear of the control if the fault or mistake is discovered, and therefore, the student may be driven to acts of concealment to avoid the control; it may at best prevent recurrence of mistakes as long as the fear of that control from outside exists; and at worst it may create a psychological framework of a hesitating and halting disposition in the future man. Self-control, on the other hand, is bound to be permanently effective in the individual. It is the basis of the strength of character and firmness of mind upon which, ultimately, effective and well-regulated conduct must depend; and this is entirely opposite of the hesitating and irregular conduct which is the outcome of direction and control from without by the help of fear.

---

[148] Man. ii, 159; and Gaut. ii, 42; Ap. i, 8. 25–30.

[149] Man. viii, 299–300 and 164.

[150] Gaut. ii, 42; Vis. lxxi. 80–81; Mahā. Anu. 104, 37.

[151] Quick: *"Locke on education"*. p. 46;–Quoted by O'Shea: Op. cit. p. 260. (The above quotation is slightly modified, as the original one is in old English.)

[152] O'Shea: Op. cit., pp. 346ff.

We thus see that the Hindu student had to learn habits of simple life, honesty, modesty and cleanliness. He had to undergo a discipline in self-control. He was by his *svadharma* bound to be friendly to all living creatures. He was to avoid bad company. In the matter of his material needs, he was to remain satisfied only with what was absolutely necessary for his bodily upkeep, whether he was a king's son or a pauper's. Under the roof of the Guru's abode, all students had the same status with reference to each other; and every one of them had to observe the same rules of discipline and of simple living. One would very much like to see this principle of equality of treatment, and habits of simple living being introduced in the modern schemes of education. As for equality of treatment, *though it is absent today where it is most needed, it is conspicuously present where it ought not to be so at all: Equality of treatment in regard to the material needs of the young students has given place to equality of treatment in regard to their intellectual needs in a sense that is quite undesirable.* Education, especially in the modern class-room, is based on standardization. It cannot proceed unless it takes for granted that all the students in the class possess the same or about the same intellectual abilities, the same capacities to grasp, the same mental outfit, and the same intellectual needs also. All this is as injurious and unwise as anything could be! And, proceeding upon this assumption of equal abilities and equal interests, the whole class is made to go through the self-same intellectual exercises, without regard to the personal differences of interests and abilities between the members of the class. Any scheme of education which is based on such a fundamentally false and dangerous psychological assumption must necessarily tend to retard the progress of the inherent capacities of students who may be above average in the class, while others who are below that average might continue to progress only in their inability to keep pace with the class! At best, such a system of education may yield its fullest and best advantages to the child of average intellect only. In all probability, it has been devised with reference to some vague notion and basis of "average ability". The Hindu educator of old times, however, believed strongly in individual attention to the pupil, regarded every student as his own son, and made full allowances for individual differences in learning abilities between those different young men that came to him to learn and to know and to do. We have several instances of how the Hindu student was, each with reference to his own talent, personally attached to the teacher—as for example, in the relations that existed between Droṇāchārya and the Kaurava princes, and between Paraśurāma and Karṇa, in the *Mahābhārata;* between Viśvāmitra and the sons of King Daśaratha in the *Rāmāyaṇa;* and between Vasishṭha and his pupils in *Raghuvanśa* (Canto I).

It stands to reason to infer that education in ancient India was free from any external control like that of the State or the Government or any party politics. It was one of the King's duties to see that the learned *puṇḍits* pursued their studies and their duty of imparting knowledge without interference from any source whatever. So also, education did not suffer from any communal interest or prejudices in India.[153] Again, there were no fixed curricula of studies that bound down the student

[153] The deportation of the great scientist, Albert Einstein, along with many others, from Germany because he belonged to a race different from that of the dominant political party illustrates how education has been influenced by party politics in modern times. The *"Nature"*, a leading British Scientific journal, gives a report as to how another great man of science of Germany, and himself a Nobel Laureate, Professor Lenard, was influenced by the political views of the Government and denounced any "intellectual follower of a Jew". [See *"Nature"*, No. 3422 Vol. 135, (June 1, 1935), p. 919].

Some more instances illustrating the unhealthy influence of politics on Education are also given by Professor Newlon of the Teachers' College, Columbia University. Writing on "Forms of Repression" upon teaching in the

or the teacher. So that there was no censorship or limitation laid down in the matter of the quality or variety of courses to be studied or taught according to the individual needs or tastes of the pupils. Anything worth knowing, and everything that was known by the teacher, could be taught by the teacher and learnt by the student. The teacher, as we have already seen, was to explain truth exactly as he knew it; he was enjoined not to keep back any knowledge from his student. He never worked under the influence of any person, institution or sect. And yet he was a person always honoured, respected, and listened to even by the King; and no one, not even the King, could domineer over him. He was not "employed" as a subordinate by any other higher authority. He taught because it was his duty to teach. He accepted such pupils as he liked, often after a "test" to find out the seriousness of the purpose of the prospective pupil. He was not controlled by the King, or the State, or by any other organization in regard to the content or the method of teaching. And it is to this kind of long tradition that the teacher in India owes the respect paid to him, even to this day, by the average Hindu, despite the fact that the present day economy and politics has tended to effect a considerable shift in emphasis in one's notions of status, prestige and social eminence.

Nor was the student in Hindu India dominated by the particular ideas and prejudices which ruled his family. We have seen how during the course of his education, the *guru* becomes his sole mentor. True education, remarks Sumner, "means a development and training of all useful powers which the pupil possesses, and repression of all bad prepossessions which he has inherited".[154] If a real development of the useful powers of the child is the aim of education, it is essential that his mind should be kept beyond the influence of any family prejudices and family biases, for, these are likely to be founded more on family conveniences rather than upon rational convictions. Among the prepossessions of the child, there are also instinctive prepossessions, apart from the specific family traits. Of these instinctive prepossessions or the original or primitive instincts of the man as they

U. S. A., he observes: "Repression takes various forms. Reference has already been made to the growing tendency to legislate the content of the curriculum—to compel by law the study of particular subject-matter . . . or to delimit severely the areas of study . . . ."

"If any reader questions the reality of this problem, he is referred to Dr. Howard Beal's study of freedom of teaching in the United States". (The study by Beale is, "*Are American Teachers Free?*", Scribner's, 1936). . . . "Or he is referred to numerous instances of dismissal, such as the dismissal of Professor Turner and others from the University of Pittsburgh and Professor Carrothers from the University of Ohio for political activities: this list could be extended indefinitely; instances might be included of dismissal of teachers in the last twenty years in almost every State in the Union because they dared to make controversial social problems the subject of study in their classrooms or because of their alleged dangerous political views."—Ch. X: "Freedom of Teaching," pp. 268 ff., in "*Teacher and the Society*", (First Yearbook of the John Dewey Society). Appleton-Century, London and New York, 1937.

Recently Mr. Bertrand Russell, one of the most famous thinkers and reformers of today and a writer of some well-known books on social philosophy and metaphysics, has been "judicially pronounced unworthy to become a Professor" in America. And, Mr. Russell brandishes this on the title page of one of his recent books, "*The Meaning of Truth*", (Allen & Unwin, London, 1940), in the list of titles and qualifications under his name as the author!

During recent years, there have been quite a number of instances of University teachers in the U. S. A. being dismissed for suspected sympathies with Communism or with "un-American activities"!

Our references to German and American conditions above should not lead the reader to imagine that it is only in these countries that the freedom of teaching is repressed. Especially, it has been possible to refer to the American conditions so pointedly because, obviously, American scholars feel free to take up and discuss openly any infringement of or encroachment upon the teachers' freedom by their government or educational authorities, and hence such information is comparatively more readily available in published literature of the U. S. A.

[154] Sumner: *"Folkways"*, p. 634.

are called, the sex instinct is the most powerful; it is found to be the most potent source of a greater part of the psychic energy of an individual.[155] Now, psycho-analysts tell us that a natural instinct cannot be completely destroyed by repression. On the contrary, such attempts at its repression may lead to certain mental deficiencies, distortions and other harmful effects which go deep into the make up of the child who may have to suffer due to them in later years. The most effective way to control the sway of this natural instinct is to divert the child's psychic energies to other proper channels. "In years before puberty", aptly observed Professor Tansley, "almost any direction can be impressed upon the developing mind by appropriate and sufficiently severe training."[156] By insistence on *brahmacharya* in deed and word as well as in thought, the Hindu system of education attempted to keep the student's psychic energies in proper directions. Further, throughout the day, the student was kept engaged either in studies, or in doing some personal or religious duties, or in bringing food or wood for fuel, or in some way or other helping himself or his *guru* or guests (*atithi*). Purity of body, mind and thought was always insisted upon by the teacher in regard to the day-to-day behaviour of the student, not merely by injunctions, but by keeping him occupied in activities conducive to the development of good moral and intellectual habits and also by his own example. Besides, his environment was kept free from all mundane affairs and temptations and complex human relationships and interests. The best part of the student's energies was thus directed towards studies and the formation of good habits.

* * * *

The Hindu scheme of education which we have portrayed so far seems to have been formulated with reference to the sons of India only; there seems to have been no place in that scheme for the daughters of India. It seems, however, that in the Vedic India women were able to achieve educational attainments similar to what men could achieve. The eighth and the tenth *maṇḍala* of *Rigveda* describe the man and his wife participating in sacrificial arrangements and performing the recitations of *mantras* together.[157] Brahmin girls were taught *Vedic* lore, and Kshatriya girls were taught the use of the bow and arrow.[158] In the *Kaushītaki Brāhmaṇa* there is mentioned a lady named Pathyāvasti who obtained the title of *Vāk* (Learned Lady) after finishing her course of studies.[159] A lady named Gandharvagrihītā is spoken of as having specialized in a certain branch of knowledge (*viśeshāvijnā*).[160] So also, in the *Brihadāraṇyaka Upanishad* there are references to education of women and to highly educated women of early India. For instance, a certain ritual is mentioned for the father who desires his daughter to become a *paṇḍitā*, that is, a learned scholar;[161] so also, in

[155] A. G. Transley's *The New Psychology and Its Relation to Life*, (Allen & Unwin, 11th imp., 1929), esp. ch. vii gives an account of psycho-analysis which is extremely lucid and fascinating and at the same time scientific for the general reader. Calvin S. Hall's *A Primer of Freudian Psychology* (*A mentor* book, pub. by the New American Library, 1955) is a concise and accurate presentation of Freud's theories.

[156] Tansley: *"The New Psychology"*, p. 96.

[157] Rig. viii, 31, 5; 94; 10.

[158] Rig. i, 112, 10; x, 102–2.

[159] From Muir's *"Original Sanskrit Texts,"* Vol. v, p. 388.

[160] In Kaush. Br. ii, 9; and in Ait. Br. v, 29.

[161] Br. up. vi, 4–17.

the second chapter, we find Yājnavalkya's wife Maitreyī discussing with her husband some problems of the deepest philosophical import, like the destiny of the soul after death;[162] and in the third chapter, a lady named Gārgī Vāchaknavī is one of the learned participants in the debate held at King Janaka's Sacrificial Assembly.[163] Besides, two ladies named Ghoshā and Lopāmudrā are spoken of in the *Rigveda Samhitā* as being *Mantradrika*, that is to say, well-versed in the *mantras*.[164] Then, particular *mantras* are enjoined to be recited by the wife, according to *Áśvalāyana Śrauta Sūtra*;[165] which means that the wife was expected to know some *mantras* at least. According to this and other *Sūtras* it seems that every housewife must have had education; for, otherwise, she would be unable to participate at a sacrifice as described by them.[166]

Patanjali, in his *Mahābhāshya*, refers to the lady scholars of his times who were well-versed in the "*Mimāmsāśāstra*", a work written by a lady called Kāśakritsnī; and these women were known as *Kāśakritsnā Brāhmaṇīs*.[167] Patanjali also distinguishes the word *upādhyāyā* from *upādhyāyānī: Upādhyāyā* is a lady teacher under whom one studies; while an *upādhyāyānī* is the wife of an *upādhyāya* or a teacher.[168] Similarly, the lexicon *Amara-Kosha* too points out that the term *upādhyāyā* refers to a lady who is herself able to give learned discourses.[169] The *Amara-Kosha* also distinguishes two other terms of like connotations, *āchāryānī* and *āchāryā: āchāryānī* refers to the wife of an *āchāryā* (male teacher); but *āchāryā* refers to a lady-teacher, who could lecture on *mantras*.[170] Patanjali also mentions women who were spear-bearers (*saktikis*). It is reasonable to infer from this, that there must have been quite a number of women who underwent all the courses of studies and became learned professors, and also women who chose to learn the art of fighting, for otherwise it is not possible for the terms like *Kāśakritsnā Brāhmaṇīs* denoting a whole class of women teachers, and also the terms *upādhyāyā* and *āchāryā*, to have originated.

In the Epics, there are several references to educated women. In the *Rāmāyaṇa*, Rāmachandra, the hero of that epic, finds his mother in the act of offering oblations with the necessary *mantras*, when he goes to bid farewell to her preparatory to his journey to the forest.[171] Tārā, the wife of Vāli, is referred to as a lady who had learnt *mantras* (*mantravid*).[172] Hanūmant, when he is unable to find Sītā in the city of Lankā, feels sure that he would be able to meet her at the time of sunset on the bank of the river; for Hanūmant knows for certain that she was sure to come there to perform her *sandhyā* (evening prayers and oblations which are accompanied by the repetition of *mantras*).[173] And, in the same epic, we are told that *Ātreyī* studied in the *āśrama* of teacher Vālmīki along with Rāma's sons Lava and Kuśa. In the same manner, the *Mahābhārata* supplies us with instances to show that women acquired learning in those days like men. A lady named Śivā was learned in the

[162] Ibid. ii, 4.
[163] Ibid. iii, 6–1.
[164] Rig. Sam. I, 179 and ix, 30–40.
[165] Āśv. Śrauta. Sū i, ii; *Vedam patnyai pradāya vāchayet.*
[166] Go. G.S. i, 3, 14–15; Kh. G.S. i, 5, 17.
[167] Pat. iv, 1, 140.
[168] Ibid. iii, 322.
[169] *Upādhyāyā svayam vidyopadeśinī.*
[170] *Syād āchāryāpi svata-svayam mantra-vyākhyātrī.*
[171] Ayodhyā 20, 15.
[172] iv, 16–12.
[173] Sundar. 15, 48.

Vedas (*Vedapāragā*).[174] In the *Udyogaparva*, queen Vidulā gives a long discourse to her son who ran away from the battlefield, on the dharma of a Kshatriya. Another lady, princess Sulabhä lectures on the principles and methods of *yoga, samādhi* and *mokśa* to King Janaka.[175] In the Vanaparva again, King Virāṭa is found employing a woman named Brihannaḍā as a tutor in the fine arts—dancing, music and painting—to the ladies of the palace. The *Bhāgawata Purāṇa* tells us that the daughters of Dākśayaṇa were proficient in philosophical and religious studies.[176] In his *Arthaśastra*, Kauṭilya has mentioned women archers (*strīgaṇaih dhanvibhih*).

Similarly in the poetic and dramatic literature, we find actual references to ladies who were able to read and write, and in some cases at least, were even learned. In the drama called *Śākuntalam* of Kālidāsa, for instance, Śakuntalā is said to have written a love letter to her lover. In the same poet's *Raghuvamśa*, the wife of King Aja is described as his own dearest disciple in the literary and fine arts (*priyaśishyā lalite kalāvidhau*). In another poem of his called the *Meghadūta*, the heroine of the poem is described as composing poems when the pangs of separation from her lover become unbearable to her. In Bhavabhūti's drama *Mālatī-Mādhavam*, a lady called Kāmandakī is mentioned as a student studying along with the boys. So again, in the *Kāvyamīmamsā* of Rajaśekhara are mentioned some learned ladies,—viz. Śīlabhaṭṭārikā, the poetess who was well-known for ease and grace of style and harmony of sound and sense;[177] Devī, who continued to occupy the hearts of her readers even after her death;[178] Vijayānkā, the Goddess of Learning (Saraswatī) incarnate who was next only to Kalidāsa;[179] Vikalanitambā, whose poetry was extremely sweet; Vijjikā who was also Saraswatī incarnate; Prabhādevī, who was adept in all the arts; and Avantisundarī, the wife of the poet himself,—she was a writer on the science of poetics.[180] As late as in the times of Śaṇkarāchārya (b. 788 A.D.), when there was a debate between him and another great scholar Maṇḍanamiśra, in regard to the opposite philosophical systems which they held, Maṇḍanamiśra's wife was appointed as the sole judge before whom the contestants argued their cases,[181]—a debate which was of momentous significance in the history of Indian philosophical thought in determining which of the two schools of thought was superior, in which Śankarāchārya was adjudged victorious.

The "*Samskāraprakāśa*" of Vīramitrodaya says that in former times (*purā*), there were two kinds of women: (1) the *Brahmavādinīs* who continued acquiring knowledge of the *Vedas*, sacrificing, and begging alms in their own homes; and (2) the *Sadyovadhūs* who married as soon as they

[174] Vanaparva.

[175] Mahā. Śānti. 321.

[176] Bhāg. Purā, iv, 1–64.

[177] *śabdhārthayo samo gumphah pānchālī vrittir ishyate.*
Śīlabhaṭṭārikā vachi Bāṇoktishu cha yā sadā.

[178] *sūktīnām smarakelīnām kalānām cha vilāsabhūh,*
probhur Devī kavī lāṭi gatāpi hridi tishṭhati.

[179] *Saraswatīva karṇāṭī Vijayāṇkā jayatyasau,*
yā vaidarbhagirām vāsah Kālidāsād anantaram.
nīlotpala-dala-śyāmām Vijayānkām ajānatā,
vrithaiva Daṇdināpyuktam sarva-śuktā Saraswatī.
—from *Śūkti-Muktāvalī.*

[180] See Venkatesvara: *"Indian Culture through the Ages"*, Vol. i, (1928), p. 293.

[181] *Śankara-dig-vijaya, VIII*, 51: *vidhāya bhāryām vidushīm, sadasyām vidhīyatām vāda-kathā sudhīndra.*

attained the marriageable age.[182] Then he proceeds to quote some now well-known verses, from *Yama-Smriti* and *Hārīta-Smriti*, in his support; these verses also record that in former times (*purā*) ladies used to go through the ceremony (*sams-kāra*) of initiation (*maunjī-bandhanam*) and enter the order of *Brahmacharya*; but, it is added, that these women had to pursue their studies under the guidance of the father, uncle or brother only, and of no other person.[183]

But if we turn to the other *Smritis*, we find a different rule laid down for women in regard to the initiation sacrament. In the opinion of Manu, the marriage ceremony (*vaivāhiko vidhih*) of a maiden is equivalent to the initiation ceremony of a boy; and serving her husband (*patisevā*) and staying with him is equivalent to the boy's service of the *guru* and residence in his *āśrama*.[184] On the other hand, however, Manu and Yājnavalkya also expect every housewife to keep accounts of the family income and expenditure.[185]

According to the scheme detailed out by Vātsyāyana, women are to be taught the sixty-four *kalās* or arts of life, of which he has given a list.[186] The list includes such items as music, painting, knowledge of the language current in the country (*deśabhāshāvijnānam*), and even the game of dice (*dyūtaviśeshah*) and other indoor physical games (*krīḍā*). Vātsyāyana discusses the question whether women should be taught these, though the content of his scheme of education for women is, as we have seen above, different from that of men.

Thus, both Manu and Vātsyāyana seem to think that the women's sphere of action lies in the home and that their education, therefore, must be such as to help them in securing comfort for the husband and for the other members of the family. Hence, though in the early vedic period women were able to secure the same education as men on equal terms, later on, it seems, that the content and also mode of the education for the two sexes came to be differentiated. Woman's services to the society seem to have been conceived as concerned with, in and through the home and the family. Due to this, it may be said that on the whole, in the later history of Hindu civilization, the Indian woman has had much less chances of education as compared with the chances man was accorded.[187]

* * * * *

The above review of the salient features of the Hindu educational system will prove sufficient to impress upon our minds how it functioned as a social organization calculated to create,—so far as males at least were concerned—strong personalities whose reason was sought to be kept ever awake, whose mental powers and capacities were well-developed, whose understanding of the meaning of life, in general and in detail, was founded on a broad basis unaffected by any political,

[182] See '*Viramitrodayah*' of Mm. Pt. Mitra Misra. Ed. by P. N. Sharma (Chowkhamba Sanskrit Series), Benares, (1919) Section on '*Stryupanayana*' pp. 402–5.

[183] *Purā kalpe tu nārīṇām maunjī-bandhanam ishyate/adhyāpanam tu vedānām sāvitrī vachanam tathā//pitā pitrivyo bhrātā vā nainam adhyāpapayet parah/svagrihe chaiva kanyāyā bhaikshacharyā vidhiyate//*The same quotations from Hārīta and Yama are also given by Mādhavāchārya on *Parāśara-somhitā* (Bom. Sansk. Ser. Vol. I, pt. ii, pp. 82–84).

[184] Man. ii, 67; cf. Yāj. i, 13.

[185] Man. v. 150; Yāj. i, 83; cf. also Vis. xxv, 5–6.

[186] Kām. i, iii, 1–15; cf. also Śukra Nīti.

[187] See also Ch. vii, *infra*.

family or secular interest, and whose intellectual impulse to learn was kept pure and alive, unsullied by any pecuniary motive.

There have been no definite rules prescribed as to the period for which a student is expected to continue his studies under the guidance of his teacher. Manu, for instance, lays down that the *vrata* of studentship may be observed for thirty-six years, or for half the time or for one-fourth of the time, or, in the alternative, till the student has perfectly learnt the Vedas.[188] On the eve of his departure for home after completing his studies, the teacher advised the student in these words, according to the *Taittirīya Upanishad*: "Speak the truth, follow *dharma*, never, swerve from thy own studies. Having pleased the *āchārya* with a gift of his choice, you should now marry and see that you do not break the family lineage. Never swerve from truth and *dharma*. Take good care of your welfare (*kuśala*). Do not miss any opportunity of success or prosperity (*bhuti*) in life. Do not miss your duties towards gods and ancestors. Regard your mother as your god, the father as god, the teacher as god, the guest as god; and as such, pay their dues to them. Do such deeds only as are regarded unblameable by people and not others; and emulate respectfully only those actions of ours which are praiseworthy and not others".[189]

Thus, the fundamental lesson in *brahmacharyāśrama* was in answer to the quest: What is *Dharma*? In this *āśrama*, the pupil is taught his *dharma*, primarily as a pupil so far as his studies (*adhyayana*) are concerned, but also with reference to the future man in him, who is to go out into the society as a *grihastha*, the householder, the social man, the gentleman. The reading, writing, arts, sciences, and other studies also have to be consistent with the *dharma* laid down for man. He is to keep under control *artha* and *kāma* completely in accordance with his *dharma* in the *brahmacharyāśrama*. In fact, in this *āśrama, dharma* is the only immediate aim for the pupil, and his whole behaviour and conduct (*āchāra*) is in terms of *dharma* only. The rules and definitions of such behaviour are known as *vratas*, which include study proper as *one* of them, the various other rules of conduct constituting the rest of them. We have described these throughout this chapter.

After the student has completed his course of studies, he leaves the place of the *āchārya* and journeys back home; this is called *Samāvartana* (returning back).[190] He is now to take a bath (*snāna*) symbolizing his 'washing off' as it were, of the *brahmacharya vrata*, and is therefore known as a *snātaka*.[191]

The *brahmachārī* has to fulfil all *vratas* of *brahmacharyāśrama* before he passes on to the next *āśrama*.[192] In fact, some scriptures speak of three kinds of students, who have completed their career of *brahmacharyāśrama*: (1) the *vidyā-snātaka*,[193] (2) the *vrata-snātaka*, and (3) the *vidyā-vrata-snātaka*. The *vidyā-snātaka* is one who ends his student's career as soon as his studies

---

188 Man. iii, 1: cf. also, Āśv. G.S. i, 22, 3: Pār. G.S.: ii, 5, 13–15; Yāj. I, 36 Āpa. i, 2, 12–16.

189 Taitt, Śikśā, Vallī. 9: *Vedamanūchya āchāryo'ntevāsinam anuśāsti: satyam vada, dharmam chara, svādhyayān mā pramadah/āchārāya priyam dhanam ārhitya prajā-tantum mā vyavachchhetsih/satyān na pramaditavyam, dharmān na pramaditavyam, kuśalān na pramaditavyam, bhūtyai na pramaditavyam, svādhyāya-pravachanābhyām na pramaditavyam, deva-pitri-kāryābhyām na pramaditavyam/mātri-devo bhava, pitri-devo bhava, āchārya-devo bhava, athithi-devo bhava/yānyanavadyāni karmāṇi tāni sevitavyāni, no itarāṇi/yānyasmākam sucharitāni tāni tvayo'pāsyāni, no itarāṇi.*

190 Śān. G. S. ii, 18 1–4; etc.

191 Śān. G. S. iii, 1; Pār. G. S. ii, 6, 1 Āpa. G. S.: v, 12, 1; Man. iii 4; Yāj. i, 51; etc.

192 Man. G. S. i, I, I: *"Upanayanāt prabhriti vratachārī syāt."*

193 Pār. G. S. ii. 5, 32; cf. Man. iv, 31; Āp. i, 30, 1–3; Kullūka, on Man. iii, 2, quotes a similar passage, describing the three kinds of *snātakas* as above, from Hārīta.

are finished but before he has been able to fulfil the *vratas* laid down for the *brahmachārī*. The *vrata-snātaka* is one who has fulfilled all the *vratas* satisfactorily, but has not completed all the studies. The *vidyāvrata-snātaka*, on the other hand, is one who ends his student's career after completing the course of his studies as well as fulfilling his *vratas*.[194] The implication seems to be that one who has completed both his *vidyās* as well as *vratas* is a better *brahmachāri* than one who has completed either only.

* * * * *

We may close this chapter with the following quotation from the *Śatapatha Brāhmana* which quite admirably sums up the main virtues and aims of education as conceived by the Hindus:

"Now, then, in praise of learning: Learning and teaching are a source of pleasure to man; he becomes ready minded, or mentally well equipped (*yuktamanah*) and independent of others, and day by day he acquires prosperity. He sleeps peacefully; he is the best physician for himself; and (peculiar) to him are restraint of the senses, delight in steadiness of mind (*ekārāmatā*), development of intelligence, fame" and, last but not the least in importance, "the task of perfecting the people".[195]

[194] Pār. G. S. ii, 5, 32–35.

[195] *Śat. Br*, xi, 5, 7, 1: The above translation is slightly modified from that of J. Eggeling, in S.B.E. Vol. xliv, p. 99.

CHAPTER V

MARRIAGE

In spite of the fact that many authoritative works on India and Indian life are seeing the light of the day, some writers in the West still seem to be persistent in their ignorance about India, or in their method of gathering information about India from unauthoritative quarters and refusal to choose first-hand sources of information. There is yet a lamentable ignorance prevailing in the West regarding the Hindus and their ways and the realities of Hindu social psychology; and this can be said to be the case even among some of the eminent social anthropologists, who have shown no hesitation in making wild generalizations about India and her people on fragmentary or partial information.

For instance, Robert Briffault's essay on "Sex in Religion"[1] refers to India as a place "where the harvest festival is a signal for general license, and such general license, is looked upon as a matter of absolute necessity. Men set aside all conventions and women all modesty and complete liberty is given to the girls."[2] The same essay gives us other novel pieces of information about India: "In many parts of India, 'the Brāhmans play the part of thorough-bred stallions, upon whom it is incumbent to ennoble the race and cohabit with virgins of inferior caste. The venerable personage scours the town and country, the people give him presents of money and stuff; they wash his feet, drink the dirty water and preserve the rest. After a repast of dainty meals, he is conducted to the nuptial couch, where crowned with flowers, the virgin awaits him'. The first child is accordingly held particularly sacred, and is spoken of as 'born by the grace of God".[3] Here is another piece of information from the same source: "In India the amount of rain is thought to be proportionate to the number of marriages that have taken place during the season."[4] In the same strain, Professor Paolo Mantegazza says this about the Hindus: "In some countries (*sic!*) of India the creditor has the right to demand the debtor's wife, whom he enjoys until the whole debt has been paid. If the woman remains with him several years, and if the debt has been paid in the meantime, the children born in this period are divided between the creditor and debtor . . . ."[5] He gives, again, only a fraction of a truth when he says that "The Laws of Manu allow a son to be begotten *per procura*"[6]; but this needs a number of qualifications which are mentioned in the Laws of Manu and others.

---

[1] In *Sex in Civilization* edited by Calverton and Schmalhausen, New York, p. 34.

[2] Mr. Briffault does not name the authority upon which he relies for this curious piece of information, though he evidently gives this as a quotation from somebody.

[3] Ibid. p. 44.

[4] Ibid. p. 45.

[5] *Sexual Relations of Mankind* (Anthropological studies of Professor P. Mantegazza, of the University of Florence). Privately issued by The Anthropological Branch of Falstaff Press. Tr. by James Bruce. Pub: Anthropological Press, New York. 1932.

[6] Ibid.

It is really surprising that such opinions based on incorrect reports should find place in the works of eminent writers. "Unfortunately", as Professor B. Malinowski has so pointedly remarked in his excellent article on "marriage" in the *Encyclopaedia Britannica*, "we find too often in ethnographical accounts generalities and stock phrases such as that 'the wife is regarded as the personal property of the husband', as 'his slave or chattel', or else again we read that 'the status of the wife is high'. The only correct definition of status can be given by a full enumeration of all mutual duties, of the limits to personal liberty established by marriage, and of the safeguards against the husband's brutality or remissness, or, on the other hand, against the wife's shrewishness and lack of sense of duty".[7]

In this chapter, we shall try to present the Hindu view of marriage; and this, in conjunction with the basic attitude towards the family organization and concepts of family duties as indicated in chapter iii, and the discussion of the Hindu conception of the rights and duties of the husband and the wife in the family treated in the next chapter, will give us a clear idea of the real status of each of them with reference to the other.

The term 'marriage' has been often used to denote a social institution* complete by itself.[8] But Sumner has drawn our attention to the fact that the word does not truly denote a perfect social

---

[7] *Ency. Brit.*, Vol. 14, (14th Ed. 1929), p. 945.

[8] Westermarck: "*History of Human Marriage*", vol. i, p. 26.

* Even though it is not necessary for us, at this place, to go into the details of the analysis of the meaning and implications of the term "institution", the following brief note on the subject may be made, just to show how difficult it is to precisely define the characteristics of several of the social categories like "social institutions" which are so frequently used by us and with which we are so familiar:

One of the earliest systematic attempts to come to a precise understanding of the term "social institution" is by Hertzler (see: J. O. Hertzler: *Social Institutions*, McGraw-Hill, N. Y., 1929). After quoting various suggested definitions by writers prior to the book, the author gives a summary of the pertinent characteristics gathered from them of the term "Social Institution" (pp. 2–7). Despite this, LaPiere and Farnsworth have been led to remark that "Hertzler in his book . . . . . fails after two hundred and fifteen pages to arrive at a clear-cut definition of his title phrase!" (R. T. LaPiere & P. R. Farnsworth, *Social Psychology*, 2nd Ed., McGraw-Hill, N. Y., 1941, p. 302, footnote.)

See also: Gillin J. L. & J. P.: *Cultural Sociology*, Macmillan, New York, 1948, pp. 313–26, for a brief outline of the silent features and characteristics of social institutions. Other fuller treatises on the subject, in addition to Barnes' mentioned below, are:—Panunzio, C: *Major Social Institutions* Macmillan, N. Y., 1939; Ballard, L. V.: *Social Institutions*, Century, N. Y., 1936.

Sociologists like Harry Elmer Barnes (*Social Institutions*, Prentice-Hall, N. Y., 1942) would use the term "institution" in a very broad sense, to refer to anything which is socially established. Thus, according to Barnes, "social institutions represet. 'he social structure and machinery through which human society organizes, directs and executes the multifarious activities required to satisfy human needs." (p. 29). He also quotes Hamilton's definition with approval, as a comprehensive definition of social institution: "Institution is a verbal symbol which, for want of a better word, describes a cluster of social usages. It connotes a way of thought or action of some prevalence and permanence, which is embodied in the habits of a group or the customs of the people . . ." (Article "Institution" in the *Ency. Soci. Sc.*, by W. H. Hamilton).

On the other hand, the sociologist Maclver (*Society*, Macmillan, London, 1949) would use the term "institution" to mean "*the established forms or conditions of procedure* characteristic of group activity", and would distinguish it from another term, "association", which is used synonymously with it (p. 15). "An association", says MacIver, "*is a group organized for the pursuit of an interest or group of interests* in common" (p. 12). "Associations are the means or agencies through which the members realize their similar or shared interests" (p. 14).

"When we are considering something as an organized *group*, it is an association; if as a form of *procedure*, it is an institution. Association denotes membership, institution denotes a mode or means of service" . . . . "Every

institution. "Although we speak of marriage as an institution, it is only an imperfect one. It has no structure. The family is the institution, and it was antecedent to marriage. "'Marriage' has always been an elastic and variable usage, as it now is . . . . In fact the use of language reflects the vagueness of marriage, for we use the word 'marriage' for wedding, nuptials or matrimony (wedlock). Only the last can be an institution".[9] As a social institution, marriage is a part of, and should be included in, the family; and even though in a theoretical treatment it precedes considerations about the family, it is actually intended as a preparation for, and, therefore, the supplement of the study of the more inclusive institution called the family.

Similar considerations generally apply also to the discussion of the Hindu *vivāh* (marriage), and *kuṭumba* (family). For, the *vivāha* is in essence a ritual and a formality, of course, very important, through which an individual has to go, to be able to start his or her life in the *Grihasthāśrama* i.e. the householder's life. The meaning of *vivāha* refers mainly to the ceremony of 'carrying away' the bride to the house of the bridegroom (*vi+vah*=to carry). But the term has long since come to be applied to the whole of the wedlock ceremony.

As a social institution, marriage has been defined by Westermarck "as a relation of one or more men to one or more women which is recognized by custom or law, and involves certain rights and duties both in the case of the parties entering the union and in the case of the children born of it".[10] Such a definition of marriage once more indicates that certain aspects of the family itself are also included in its connotation. Indeed, it would be impossible to study the problem of marriage without at the same time involving ourselves into the discussion of some important and fundamental questions relating to the institution of the family. When Westermarck, for instance, points out that "marriage is something more than a regulated sexual behaviour", and that "it is an economic institution, which may in various ways effect the proprietory rights of the parties",[11] he refers more to the issues connected with the structure and function of the family than to marriage itself. Any discussion of the institution of marriage, therefore, must necessarily include also some of the vital problems connected with the institution of the family. And let us state at the outset that all these considerations are equally true of the Hindu social institution of *vivāha*.

Among the Hindus, *vivāha* is generally considered as obligatory for every person; because, in the first place, the birth of a son is said to enable one to obtain *mokśa*. "To be mothers were women created, and to be fathers men; therefore, the *Vedas* ordain that *dharma* must be practised by man together with his wife".[12] *Vivāha* is one of the *śarīra-samskāras* (sacraments sanctifying

---

association has, with respect to its particular interests, its characteristic institutions." Thus, family, which is an association, has marriage as its institution; it also has the home, the family meal together, and so on, as its institutions. The school or college, as a body of teachers and taught, is an association; the education system is an institution (p. 16). After having given a critical analysis of the two terms, however, MacIver sounds a note of warning that this distinction should not be rigidly understood. "One note of caution is required . . . . These established forms of procedure are clearly methods used by *groups* of men: whether they are enacted instruments of associations or the unofficially developed patterns of community practice, institutions *in life* cannot be separated from those who follow their ways. Thus investigation of social reality always includes reference to both human institutions and human groups. However, if the focus is *institutional*, as we have defined it, it centers upon the procedures themselves." (p. 17).

[9] Sumner: "*Folkways*", pp. 348–9.

[10] Westermarck: op. cit. p. 26.

[11] Ibid. p. 26.

[12] Man. ix, 96: *Prajanārtham striyah srishṭāh santānārtham cha mānava/tasmāt sādhāraṇo dharmah śrutau patnyā sahoditah.*

the body) through each of which every man and woman must pass at the proper age and time (see next Ch. on Family); Manu considers it as a social institution for the regulation of proper relations between the sexes.[13]

Again, it is believed that one's progency is considerably connected with and instrumental to happiness both in this world as well as hereafter.[14] "He only is a perfect man, who consists of his wife, himself and his offspring".[15] There is the story in the *Mahābhārata* of a lady who remained single because she could not find her equal to marry; she then devoted her life to the practice of hard penance till old age with a view to obtaining *mokśa*. But the sage Nārada rebuked her for remaining unmarried; he told her that it was impossible for her to gain the ultimate bliss as long as she was not sanctified (*asamskritā*) by marriage rites.[16] Moreover, the birth of a son is conceived to be particularly contributory towards helping the father to execute his obligations which are due to the departed ancestors (*pitri-riṇa*)[17]—one of the three basic social obligations (*riṇas*), each of which every Hindu is in duty bound to fulfil. For a full understanding of these *riṇas* or obligations, the reader is referred to chapter iii, and also chapter vi on the family.

The Hindu Śāstrakāras are especially particular about the *vivāha* of a woman, though it is also enjoined that every male should marry. For, a "wife is the very source (*mūlam*) of the *purushārthas*,* not only of *dharma, artha* and *kāma*, but even of *mokśa*. Those that have wives can fulfil their due obligations in this world (*kriyā-vantah*); those that have wives, truly lead a family life; those that have wives can be happy; and those that have wives can lead a full life (*śriyānvitā*)".[18]

Most particular care, however, has to be taken to perform the *vivāha* of maidens as soon as they attain the marriageable age. A girl who continues to stay in her father's home more than three years after attaining puberty, is called a *vrishalā* or a *śudrā* i.e., a very low type; and the father or other guardian of such a girl who is not careful enough to give her in marriage in proper time is said to be incurring a great sin.[19] If her elders fail to arrange her marriage within the proper time, it is permissible for such a young lady to take the whole responsibility upon herself of choosing her life-mate and enter into wedlock with him; she has to wait for three years only after puberty, for some responsible elder to arrange for her marriage, but no more.[20] Vātsyāyana, too, advises a young maiden who has attained youth (*prāpta-yauvanā*) to select a husband for herself and get married without waiting for the assistance and permission of her elders.[21]

---

[13] Man. ix, 25; *Eshoditā lokayātrā nityam strīpumsayoh śubhā.*

[14] Ibid.; also Āśv. G.S. i, 6, ff; Baudh. ii, 9, 16, 10; Āp. ii, 9, 24; 9.

[15] Man. ix, 45: *etāvāneva purusho yajjāyātmā praieti ha/viprāh prāhustathā chaitad yo bhartā sā smritānganā//* The Commentator Kullūka quotes from Vājas. Br.: "That man who does not win a wife is really half (*ardho*); and he is not the full man (*asarvo hi tāvad bhavati*) as long as he does not beget an offspring (*prajāyate, etc.*)." Also cf. Āp. ii, 14, 16; and Brih. Smri. xxiv, 11.

[16] Mahā. Śalya. 52.

[17] Man. x, 106; Baudh. ii, 6, 11, 3; Vas. xi, 48 etc. See also Ch. III.

* For the meaning and analysis of *purushārthas* as the psycho-moral bases of social organization in terms of motivating forces of human activity, see ch. iii.

[18] Mahā. Ādi. 74, 40–41.

[19] Man. ix, 93; 90; Yāj. i, 64; Vis. xxiv, 41; Vas. xvii, 67–68; Baudh. iv, 1, 11, 14; Nār. 25–26; Gaut. xviii, 23; Parā. vii. 6. Brihas. Smr. xxiv, 3, speaks of punishing such relatives.

[20] Ibid. (all); and Mahā. Anu. 44, 16–17.

[21] Kāma. iii, iv, 36.

This brings us to the various forms of the Hindu marriage. The expression "form of marriage" is generally applied to the numeric variation in the partners in marriage, as Malinowski puts it. Accordingly, the forms of marriage usually listed are monogamy, polygamy, polyandry and group marriage.[22] But in dealing with the Hindu *vivāha*, we shall use the expression "form of marriage" conveniently to denote *the method of consecrating a marriage-union*. The forms that are enumerated are:[23]

(1) The *Brāhma* form, consisting of the gift (*dānam*) of a daughter by the father, after decking her with ornaments, to a man, learned in the *Vedas*, and of a good character (*śrutiślavān*) whom the bride's father himself invites.
(2) The *Daiva* form, involving the gift of the daughter as above, to a priest who duly officiates at a sacrifice, during the course of its performance.
(3) The *Ārsha* form, wherein the father gives his daughter in marriage to the bridegroom, after receiving a cow and a bull, or two pairs of these from the bridegroom, in accordance with requirements of *dharma* (*dharmatah*) and not in any sense with the intention of selling the child (*na tu śulkabuddhyā*,—says Kullūka). In other words, the gift of cow and bull is to be made as a token of gratitude to the man who offers his daughter to the groom to enable him to fulfil his *grihasthāśrama* obligations.
(4) The *Prājāpatya* form, in which the father makes a gift of the daughter, by addressing the couple with the *mantram* "may both of you perform together your *dharma*" (*sahobhau charatām dharma*), and has done due honour to the bridegroom.
(5) The *Āsura* form: In the four forms mentioned above, the important point to be noted is that it is the father (or a person in his place) who makes a gift (*dāna*, or *pradāna*) of the bride to the bridegroom. But in the *Āsura* form, the bridegroom has to give money to the father or kinsman of the bride, and thus, in a sense purchases the bride.
(6) The *Gāndharva* form, wherein the mutual love and consent of the bride and bridegroom is the only condition required to bring about the union (*ichchhayānyonyasamyogah*). Neither the father nor the kinsmen need have a hand in bringing about the marriage. As will be seen below, such marriage may be subsequently consecrated by going through the sacred rites of *vivāha*.
(7) The *Rākshasa* form is described as "the forcible abduction of a maiden from her home, while she cries and weeps, after her kinsmen have been slain or wounded and their houses broken." It is the capture of the bride by force.
(8) The *Paiśācha* form is one in which the man seduces, by stealth, a girl who is sleeping, intoxicated, or disordered in intellect.

In all the *Smritis*, the descriptions of the forms of marriage are much the same as described above.[24] *Manu-Smriti* further declares that of these forms, the (1) *Brāhma*, (2) *Daiva*, (3) *Ārsha*, (4) *Prājāpatya*, (6) *Gāndharva* and (7) *Rākshasa*, are lawful, while the two forms (5) *Āsura* and

---

[22] *Ency. Brit.*, art "Marriage", vol. 14 (14th Ed. 1929), p. 949.

[23] Man. iii, 27–37; Yāj. i, 58.

[24] See Yāj. i, 58–61; Vis. xxiv, 18–28; Gaut. iv, 6–15; Vas. 17–35; Baudh. i, 20, 1–21; Āp. ii, 11, 17–21; The Āśv. G. S. gives the eight forms in this order: *Brāhma, Daiva, Prājāpatya, Ārsha, Gāndharva, Āsura, Paiśācha and Rākshasa.*

(8) *Paiśācha* are unlawful and should never be practised (*na kartavyau kadāchana*).[25] According to the *Aśvalāyana Grihya Sūtra*, the first four of the above forms bring purification (*punāti*) to twelve, ten, eight and seven ancestors respectively, on both the sides; no such merit is described to be due to the remaining four.[26]

The most approved form of marriage is of course the gift of the maiden, by the father or other guardian, to the bridegroom, i.e., any one of the first four forms. The father, the grandfather, the brothers, the kinsmen, and the mother, in the order in which they are mentioned here, have the right to give a young maiden in marriage, provided the giver be in balanced physical and mental conditions (*prakritisthah*), i.e. not insane etc.[27]

The first qualification needed in a young man for marriage is the fulfilment of his obligations of the student's life. He must have studied, in due order, the three *Vedas*, or two of them, or at least one, without violating any of the rules of the order of studentship (*aviplutabrahmacharya*) i.e. the first of the four orders (*āśramas*) of life.[28] The *Kāma Sūtras* also follow the *Smritis* on this point; a person who has completed his course of studies should then enter the householder's order (*gārhasthya*), and lead the life of a citizen.[29] In Vātsyāyana's opinion, only such an educated youth (*śrutawān*) had a right to marry.[30]

The bride to be selected must not have been already given to any one before, and she must be a virgin.[31] Love directed to a girl who is already accepted by another (*paraparigrihītā*) would be censurable.[32]

Sumner characterises this demand for virginity in the maiden to be married as an "appeal to masculine vanity", and as "a singular extension of the monopoly principle.[33]..." "In the development of the father family," he proceeds, "fathers restricted daughters in order to make them more valuable as wives. Here comes the notion of virginity and pre-nuptial chastity. This is really a negative and exclusive notion. . . His wife is to be his from the cradle, when he did not know her. Here then, is a new basis for the sex-honour of women and the jealousy of men. Chastity for the un-married meant—no one; for the married—none but the husband."[34]

The Hindu *Śāstrakāras* emphasis on pre-nuptial chastity, however, does not seem to have been one-sided, in favour of the female only. The Hindus demanded pre-nuptial chastity on the part of the male as well, in the form of *brahmacharya vrata*, as we have seen above. Evidently, they were not one-sided in their valuation of chastity, but placed equal value on the pre-nuptial chastity of the boy as they did on the virginity of the maiden. This is further evident from the elaborate rules laid down for the conduct of the *brahmachāri*—i.e. every young man's conduct till his marriage, which we have seen in the previous chapter.

---

[25] Man. iii, 24–251; also cf. Mahā. Anu. 44, 9.

[26] Āśv. G. S. i, 6, 1–8.

[27] Yāj. i, 63–64.

[28] Man. iii, 2; Yāj. i, 52; Medhātithi expands the meaning of Man iii, 2, by saying that one who was well educated can have the right to be a householder: And Āśv. G. S. i, 5, 2 says '*buddhimate kanyām prayachchhet*" i.e., the daughter should be given in marriage to an intelligent (meaning here, educated) person.

[29] Kām i, 4, 1: *grihītavidyah . . . gārhasthyam adhigamya nāgaraka-vrittam varteta.*

[30] Kām. iii, 1, 2: *Śrutavān śīlayet/.*

[31] Kām. iii, 1, 1: *ananya-pūrvā*; Yāj. i, 52: *ananya-pūrvikā* Gaut. iv, 1; Vis. xxiv, 9; Vas. iii, 1.

[32] Kām. i, 5, 2.

[33] Sumner: "*Folkways*", p. 358.

[34] Sumner: "*Folkways*", p. 359.

There are certain rules of endogamy and exogamy laid down in the *Dharma-Śāstras*, for regulating the Hindu marriage with a view to controlling the choice of mates. According to these, the endogamic rule states that marriage must take place between persons of the same *varṇa.*[35] If a person directs his love towards an unmarried girl of his own *varṇa* in accordance with the injunctions of the *śāstra*, his action deserves public (*laukikah*) fame, (*yaśasyah*) and good progeny (*putrīāyah*). Any other way of love would meet with social disapprobation (*pratishiddhah*).[36] We may note, here, that in practice the law of endogamy has come to play a very important part with reference to the later *jātis* within each of the *varṇas;* according to this, the endogamic circle is restricted within the orbit of each of the *jātis*. This means that members of the same *varṇa* who at the same time did not belong to the same *jāti*, could not marry each other as before.

The exogamic rules relating to Hindu marriage form a very complicated subject. The three terms, *gotra, pravara* and *sapiṇḍa*, used in connection with the laws of exogamy, have undergone so many changes, additions and modifications in their meaning and implications through the ages since their origin, that it becomes well-nigh impossible to find out their original implications. We need not go into the problems of the origin and history of the institutions called *gotra* and *pravara;* for our purposes we shall content ourselves with a very brief general discussion of these terms so as to bring out their social import and relation to marriageability among the Hindus.

So far as the paternal side is concerned the problem is dealt with in terms of *gotra;* and, with reference to the maternal side it is ordained that a person shall not marry a woman who is a *sapiṇḍā* on his mother's side,[37] upto the sixth degree in ascending or descending line; this means that *sapiṇḍā* relationship ceases to exist with the seventh degree in ascending or descending line between two individuals with reference to their maternal relatives.[38]

Next, we take up the *gotra*: It has been pointed out that *gotra* probably meant 'herd';[39] and, later on it came to denote the 'family' or the 'clan'.[40] The *gotra* of a family is said to be named after the *rishi*-ancestor who founded the family in the immemorial past. It is said that originally there were few *gotras* in existence. But, later on, as the population went on multiplying, more and more persons attained fame as *rishis* on account of their achievements; and subsequently, additional *gotras* came to be formed after the names of these new *rishis.*[41] Whatever may have been the origin of *gotra*, the exogamic rule relating to the Hindu marriage according to the *Grihya-Sūtras* and the *Dharma-Śāstras* is that no man shall marry a maiden from within his own *gotra.*[42]

Closely connected with the *gotra* is the other term *pravara*. *Pravara* literally means 'invocation' or 'summons.'[43] It can be traced back to the cult of the fire-worship amongst Indo-Aryans. The *Purohita* (priest), officiating at a sacrifice to *Agni*, used to recite the names of his famous *rishi*

---

[35] Man. iii, 4; Yāj. i, 52; Kāma, iii, 1, 1; etc.

[36] Kāma. i, 5, 1–2; etc.

[37] Go. G. S. iii, 4, 4–5; Hir. G. S. i, 17, 2; etc: and Man. iii, 5; Yāj. i, 53; Bau. ii, 37–38; Vis. xxiv, 9–10; Mahā. Anu. 44, 18; etc.

[38] Man. v, 60; Bau. i, 11, 2; Vis. xxii, 5; Vas. iv, 17–18.

[39] From '*go*'—cow, *gotra* may have come to mean "a collection of cows." See *Vedic Index*, i, p. 235.

[40] *Vedic Index*, i, 235.

[41] Mahā. Śāanti. 297, 17–18 says e.g.: *Mūlagotrāṇi chatvāri samutpannāni Bhārata/karmato'nyāni gotrāṇi samutpannāni Pārthiva/ nāmadheyāni tapasā tani cha grahaṇam satām//*

The grammarian Pāṇini has explained *gotra* as "the descendants from grandsons onwards"—iv, 1, 162.

[42] See footnote 37, above.

[43] *Vedic Index*, ii, p. 39.

ancestors when invoking *Agni* to carry libations to the Gods; therefore, the *pravara* came to denote the series of such ancestors of the persons who had in former times invoked *Agni*.[44] Now, evidently the list of ancestors has had its social bearings: for, by and by, *pravara* came to be associated with the various *samskāras* of domestic and social nature, the most important being the *vivāha*;[45] and it is laid down by some of the authorities that a man shall not marry a woman who can be traced from any of the ancestors as mentioned in his *pravara*.[46]

On the whole, therefore, these exogamic taboos are designed for the restriction of free marital relationship. Their psychological origin lies in the horror of incest and the consequent incest-taboo which aims at preventing sex relations between parents and offsprings, and between brothers and sisters. The *Dharma-Śāstras* have declared that sex relations with mother, or with sisters by the same mother or by the same father, or with the daughter, or with the wife of a son, is a heinous sin (*mahā-pātaka*).[47] The *Vishṇu Smriti* declares that for a person who has committed such a heinous crime, there is no other way of expiation but burning himself by throwing himself into the fire.[48] In the course of time, however, strict adherence to the requirements of all these exogamic laws must have been found so difficult, for one reason or another, that some of the *Dharma-Śāstras* have sought to modify these rules by making them more limited in their operation. Thus, according to these, persons related with each other beyond five degrees on the mother's side and beyond seven degrees on the father's side are allowed to marry.[49]

There is no known society which does not restrict marriage relations by some kind of exogamic and endogamic rules. In the first place, sex relations between parent and child,—father and daughter, mother and son,—and between brother and sister, are almost universally forbidden;[50] this restriction is known as the incest taboo. And, in several societies the restriction extends to more remote blood relations. It is not necessary for us to go into the details of whether the incest taboo is based on an

---

[44] Ibid.

[45] For some historical details relating to the terms *gotra, pravara*, see K. Rangachari: Art. on "*Gotra* and *Pravara*" in *Proc. and Trans. of the Third Ori. Conf., Madras* (1924), pp. 635 ff; C. V. Vaidya: Art. on "*Gotra and Pravara* in *Proc. and Trans. of Ori. Conf. Poona* (1919); P. V. Kane: Art. on "*Gotra and Pravara in Vedic Literature*" J.B.B.R.A.S.; New Series Vol. xi, 1–2, Aug. 1935, p. 1 ff. None of these, however, have been able to arrive at any satisfactory solution of the problem.

[46] E.g., Mān. G.S. i, 7, 8; Gaut. iv, 2; Vas. viii, 1; Yāj. 1, 53. How and why *pravara* came to be associated with these exogamic rules is almost impossible to ascertain. For apparently there is no connection between *gotra* which denotes the ancestry of a person, and *pravara* which denotes the ancestry of some *purohita* of one of his ancestors. It might be that in those ancient times when the Hindu sacrificer (Yajamāna) acted himself as the priest (purohita) reciting the various *mantras* for himself, he used to invoke Agni by the name of his *gotra-rishi* as well as by some other ancestors who had attained fame as *rishis* (venerable sages); in that case, the *gotra* and *pravaras* are obviously related to each other as being all paternal ancestors of the sacrificer. However, later on when priesthood came to be established and certain experts used to officiate at the sacrifice on behalf of the *Yajamāna*, it is probable that the officiating priest invoked *Agni* in the name of *his* own ancestors, and so these came to be the *pravara-rishis* for the sacrificer too. The connection between *gotra* and *pravara*, once established in the more ancient past when the sacrificer himself used to be the priest, was, however, thoughtlessly supposed to be still holding true, and was allowed to continue.

[47] Man. xi, 59; Yāj. iii, 231; Vis. xxxvi, 4–7; Gaut. xxi, 1; Bau. ii, 2, 13; etc.

[48] Vis. xxxiv, 1 f.

[49] Vis. xxiv, 10; Vas. viii, 2; Gaut. iv, 3–5.

[50] Ogburn, W. F. & Nimkoff, M. F.: *A Handbook of Sociology*: Kegan Paul, London, 1947, p. 462 gives some exception to this rule where brother and sister marriages were allowed in some ruling classes.

instinctive or natural feeling of abhorrence, or is due to social conditioning from early childhood.[51] Suffice it to say that the customs of most of those peoples, who extend the incestuous taboo further than first degree relationship, by several rules of exogamy, reveal that the fear of resulting defective progeny seems to underlie such a prohibition.[52] And the prohibition of consanguinous marriages may be carried to such an excess, as in China and in some parts of India, as to forbid marriage of two persons bearing the same surname.[53]

The fear of the possible harmful effects of inbreeding if such marriages are freely allowed seems to have, however, a scientific justification based on eugenical considerations.[54] The union of man and women closely related by blood ties is a union of similar hereditary traits, and if the ancestry of the two is good, their offspring will receive, so to speak, a "double dose" of the good traits of their ancestors. At the other extreme, however, if the stock of each carries some undesirable traits or others from their ancestry, the offsprings are likely to be doubly the sufferers for it. But usually it is difficult to trace the ancestral historical details of each family much backwards, and it often happens that some undesirable trait which was *latent* or *recessive*, and therefore, was not known in the ancestry now makes itself manifest because of the "double dose" in the case of consanguinous marriages, e g. feeble mindedness, of which there are instances in the offsprings born of cousin-marriages. And this risk is too great to take. It is in view of such difficulties that it is necessary to take the precaution on the genetic side, of ascertaining the hereditary traits of the parties, to be on the safer side.*

---

[51] See e.g., Young, K.: *Sociology*, American Bk. Co., N. Y., Second Ed., 1949, p. 316, and footnote 7; Panunzio, C.: *Major Social Institutions*, Macmillan, 1939, pp. 167–168.

[52] Popenoe, P.: *Modern Marriage*, Macmillan, New York, Second Ed., 1941, p. 103.

[53] Ibid. pp. 103–4.

[54] Ibid. pp. 104–5.

* See also Panunzio: *Major Social Institutions*, pp. 167–8. After discussing briefly the different suggested causes or explanations of the exogamic and incest taboo, viz., the magical, the instinctive, the rational, the common-sense, and the social explanation, Panunzio dismisses all of them as unsatisfactory: "None of these explanations is satisfactory: and as in the case of all origins, no valid explanation is available."

"Endogamy is easily to be explained," says Dr. R. H. Thouless, "as a result of the tendency of social groups to become segregated. There is, for example, a strong tendency for different social classes and different religious bodies to form endogamous groups within our own culture. Still stronger is the endogamous tendency amongst different racial groups within the same area. Thus the whites and blacks in the U.S.A. and in South Africa remain on the whole sharply distinct groups because there is a strong pressure on the members of each group to choose a mate from inside that group." "Since all explanations of exogamy must be speculative," Thouless goes on to observe, "there is no reason why we should not add a new speculation. If members of small groups in a large society choose their mates from within their own small group, the result will be segregation of each small group into a separate class. Such segregation is a source of weakness to the larger social unit of which these groups are parts. It is clear that exogamy will check this tendency to segregation, and perhaps that is its essential social purpose. . . . . The greatest disunion in a society through the formation of segregated groups would take place if all families became segregated through always marrying their own members. This may be an explanation of the universality of the prohibition of brother-sister marriage. It also may be an explanation of the occasional relaxation of this prohibition (such as the brother-sister marriage of the Pharaohs), since in a ruling family social segregation is desired."—R. H. Thouless: *General and Social Psychology*, Univ. Tutorial Press, London, 3rd Ed., 1951, pp. 137–8.

For an excellent discussion on the whole subject of incest taboo and the various explanatory theories of the same, see G. P. Murdock: *Social Structure*, chs. 10 and 11, pp. 285–322 (Macmillan, New York, 1949).

There are other rules, in addition to exogamy and endogamy, regarding qualifications for fitness to marry, laid down by the *Dharma-Śāstras*. Thus, Manu gives a list of types of families, girls from which should not be accepted for wedlock, even though the families may be "ever so great, or rich in kine, horses, sheep, grain or other property." These families are:

(1) One which neglects the *dharmas*, i.e. their personal and social duties and obligations according to the śāstras;
(2) One in which the *Veda* is not studied;
(3) One in which no male child is born;
(4) One, the members of which (a) have thick hair on their body; or (b) are subject to any of the following: hemorrhoids, pthisis, weakness of digestion, epilepsy, and white or black leprosy.[55]

The third and fourth types of families have to be avoided due, it is evident, to biological considerations. They suggest that the *smritikāras* were impressed by the influence of heredity on man. A maiden from a family in which there is a hereditary disease prevalent of the type mentioned above is quite likely to be a victim of that disease herself; and she is sure also to pass it or its tendency on to her progeny.

Similar considerations of the influence of heredity seem to prevail with the *smritikāras* when they prescribe certain other qualifications for the bride. Thus, a man must not marry a girl with reddish hair, or one who has a redundant or extra bodily limb, or who is sickly, or has no hair or too much hair on the body, nor should he marry one who is garrulous or has red eyes.[56] One must "not marry a girl who is vicious, unhealthy, of low origin, ill brought-up, talks improperly, inherits some disease from mother or father, is of masculine appearance.... has hairy legs, or thick ankles.... or red eyes.[57] He must not marry a maiden who has no brother, or whose father is not known; for, in the former case, there is the likelihood of her being made an "appointed daughter"; i.e. her son may be adopted by her father, in order to continue his family line; and so, she may remain son-less herself; and in the latter case, there is a likelihood of the young man's committing the sin of marrying either a *sagotrā* or a girl born of illicit union.[58] In short, says Manu, a man should marry a maiden free from any bodily defects, with agreeable name, with the majestic gait of a *hamsā* or elephant, with a moderate quantity of hair on the body and head, with small teeth and delicate limbs.[59] Vasishṭha sums up the directions by saying that the maiden must come of a good family and faultless lineage.[60]

Now, even though these precautions and regulations should normally be observed as best as possible, it is recognized that there would be exceptional cases in which there may be an excellent girl (*strī-ratna*—a jewel of a girl) born in a low family; and in such a case, she should be accepted in marriage by the man, just as a health-giving elixir is acceptable even though it may be prepared

[55] Man. iii, 6–7; cf. also Yāj. i, 54; and Vis. xxiv, 11.
[56] Man. iii, 8; cf. Vis. xxiv, 12, 16.
[57] Vishnu Purā. iii, 10.
[58] Man. iii, 11; cf. Yāj. i, 53.
[59] Man. iii, 10; says Āśv. G.S. *'buddhi-rūpa-śīla-lakshaṇa-sampannām arogām upayachchheta'*.
[60] Vas. i, 38.

out of poisonous ingredients, or gold is acceptable even though it may be available from mud and mire, or superior knowledge acceptable even though it could be had from a man of low position.[61]

The qualifications listed above apply on the bridegroom's side also, by analogy (*atideśa).*[62] He must not only possess these qualifications, but, in addition, he must be one whose powers of virility are carefully ascertained.[63] And Nārada declares that the bridegroom is fit to be married "if his collar-bone, his knee and bones are strongly made, if his shoulders and his hair are also strongly made, if the nape of his neck is stout and his thigh and skin strong, and if his gait and voice is full of vigour",[64] the young man has also to undergo an examination with regard to his virility.[65]

Vātsyāyana takes a similar point of view into consideration with regard to most of the qualifications which he thinks are necessary in the bride-to-be. Thus he advises: "Let him give up a girl who, when the wooers come to woo (*varaṇe*), is found asleep, or in tears, or not at home. Let him also shun these sixteen types: (1) a girl with an uncouth name (*apraśastanāmadheyā*), (2) One who has been kept in concealment (*guptā*), (3) One who is betrothed to another man, (4) One with red hair, (5) One with spots on the face, (6) A masculine woman (*rishabhā*), (7) One with a big head, (8) A bandy-legged woman (*vikaṭā*), (9) One with a rather too broad forehead (*vimuṇḍā*), (10) One ceremonially impure (*śuchidūshitā*), (11) One born of improper marriage (*sāmkarikī*), (12) One who has menstruated (*rākā*),[66] (13) One who is or has been pregnant, (14) An old friend, (15) One who has a younger sister much handsomer than herself, and (16) One that hath a moist hand.[67] The girl, further, must have both of her parents alive; she should be younger than the man by three years at least; she should belong to a family (*kula*) of good character (*ślāghyāchāra*), of good means and large (*dhanavati pakshavati*), with many relatives who are attached to each other with affection (*sambandhipriye sambandhirākule*).[68] She should have many relatives both on the father's side as well as on the mother's side.[69] She should possess beauty (*rūpa*) as well as good conduct (*śīla*); and she should be one with auspicious marks on her body (*lakshaṇa*). She must have neither more nor less than the proper number of any physical limbs like teeth, nails, ears, hair, eyes and breasts; and must have a healthy constitution free from any disease.[70]

Manu does not speak much about the bridegroom's qualifications on the biological side as Yājnavalkya and Nārada have done.[71] Vātsyāyana, on the other hand, specifically says that the bridegroom also must possess similar qualities described above for the bride; and, in addition, he must have completed his course of studies.[72]

---

[61] Kauṭilya in *Arthaśāstra: vishād apyamrutam grāhyam amedhyād api kānchanam, nīchād apyuttamām vidyām, strī-ratnam dushkulād api.* Also, Man. ii, 238.

[62] Yāj. i, 54: *etair eva guṇair yuktah.*

[63] Yāj. i, 35: *Yatnāt parīkshitah pumstve.*

[64] Nār. xii, 9.

[65] Nār. xii, 8.

[66] This probably means one who is just passing through the period of three days menstruation, for Vātsyāyana is more liberal than others in his views on marriage.

[67] Kām. iii, 1, 11–12; Peterson's Tr., *J.B.B.R.A.S.*, xviii, p. 117, cf. *Rati-śāstra*, viii.

[68] Kām. iii, 1, 2.

[69] Ibid. (*prabhūta-mātā-pitri-paksham*).

[70] Ibid.

[71] Yāj. 55; Nār. xii, 16. 18. (See *supra*).

[72] Kām. iii, 1, 2: *tathāvidha eva śrutavān śīlayet.*

Vātsyāyana shows a truly psychological insight into the problem, again, when he points out that marriages between persons of unequal social status are not likely to be happy unions. "Social games such as filling up '*bouts rimés*', marriages and social intercourse (*samgatam*) generally, should be with a man's equals, not with those either above or below him. A man marries above him (*uchcha-sambandhah*) when he marries a girl only to be treated by her and her friends as a servant ever afterwards; no man of spirit will do that. He marries below him (*hīna-sambandhah*) when he and his people lord it over the girl; that is a bad marriage; it too is censured by the good".[73] Inequality of social status between the two parties to a marriage union is thus likely in all probability to be a cause of disparity between the relations of the two with each other. True love-union can arise only between social equals. "Where the love between husband and wife adds lustre to both, and where it is a source of joy to families of both,—that is the only type of marriage which is worthy."[74] Vātsyāyana adds, however, that in any case, one should at least take precaution not to marry a bride from a status lower than his own. "Let a man marry above him, and walk humbly ever afterwards; but on no account let him do, what all good men disapprove of, viz., marry beneath him."[75]

Even though Vātsyāyana goes into such details about the principles that should guide the selection of the bride as well as the bridegroom, he seems to be conscious of the fact that it would ordinarily be rather difficult for every person to make a scrutinizing search into so many details while making the selection of a bride or of a bridegroom. He therefore gives one simple test, as if to make up for the possible deficiencies of inadequate information, viz. "He will be a happy husband who marries the woman on whom his heart and eyes are set".[76] He quotes Ghoṭakamukha on the point as saying that a man should direct his love or attention (*pravrittih*) towards that girl by marrying whom, he feels, he would be satisfied, and would not incur the censure of those in similar social circumstances as his.[77] Or perhaps—which seems to be the more correct interpretation of his view,—*Vātsyāyana* wants that in addition to the several other qualities in the parties to a marriage, mutual attraction between the two should also be looked upon as an essential condition to bring about the marriage.

Let us now consider the rites and ceremonies (*vidhi*) to be performed at the *vivāha*. In describing the ceremonies and rituals connected with the *vivāha*, all the texts concerned refer to the bride as being given away (*dāna*) by the father or her guardian in the family, who invites the bridegroom.[78] The bridegroom goes to the bride's home[79] where the *vivāha* is to take place. The description of these rites, therefore, may be said to refer to the *Brāhma* form of *vivāha*; and these have come down to us even to this day from ancient times. In this connection, the *Āśvalāyana-Grihya-Sūtra*[80] tells us that there are, indeed, variations in the observation of wedding rites with peoples of different

---

[73] Kām. iii, 1, 22–24. The Tr. is Peterson's in *J.B.B.R.A.S.*, xviii, (1890–94), p. 117.

[74] Ibid. iii, 1, 25.

[75] Ibid. iii, 1, 26.

[76] Ibid, iii, 1, 14: *Yasyām manaś-chakshushor-nibandhanam tasyām riddhir netarān ādriyeta ityeke.* Peterson, op. cit., thinks that Vātsyāyana is quoting here from Āp. G.S. i, 3, 20.

[77] Kām. iii, 1, 3: '*Yām grihītvā kritinam ātmānam manyeta na cha samānair nindyeta tasyām pravrittir iti Ghoṭakamukhah*'.

[78] All these ceremonies are described, e.g., in Āśv. G.S. i, 7, 1, seq.; Pār. G.S. i, 5, 1, seq.; Āpa. G.S. ii, 4, 10, seq.; Gobh. G.S. ii, 1, 13, seq.; Khā. G.S. i, 3, 5, seq.; etc.

[79] Śān. G.S. i. 12.

[80] The different *Grihya-Sūtras* belong to different *śākhās* (branches) of the *Vedas* and are followed by the different groups of Hindus according to the *śākhā* to which these groups belong. Thus, e.g., those who belong to the *Rigveda*—and these predominate—follow the authority (*pramāṇa*) of the *Āśvalāyana Grihya-Sūtra* for all their *samskāras* including the *vivāha*; those belonging to the *Āpastamba śākhā* of the *Yajurveda* follow the *Hiraṇyakeśi*

regions and villages (*janapada-dharmā grāma-dharmāścha*). However, it proceeds to tell us what is commonly accepted by all.[81] Of these rites, the *kanyā-dāna*, the *vivāha-homa*, the *pāṇi-grahaṇa*, the *agni-pariṇayana*, the *aśmāro-haṇa*, the *lājā-homa*, and the *saptapadī*, each succeeding in the order given here, are important and involve several implications of a social nature. We now propose to give the salient features of each of these below, in order that these social implications may be properly unfolded:

The first of these is the *kanyā-dāna* (i.e giving away of the maiden) ceremony performed by the father (or other guardian in his place); he pours out a libation of water,[82] symbolizing the giving away of the daughter (*dāna*) to the bridegroom;[83] the groom accepts (*pratigriṇhāti*) the gift; he then recites the *kāma-sūkta* (Hymn to Love) verse which runs thus:

Who offered this maiden?
To whom is she offered?
*Kāma** gave her (to me),
That I may love her.
Yea, Love is the giver,
And Love the acceptor.
Enter thou, (Oh my bride,) the ocean of love.
With love, then,
I receive thee.
May she remain thine,
Thine own, O God of Love![84]
Verily, thou art, (oh my bride),
Prosperity itself,
May the Heaven bestow thee,
May the Earth receive thee.

Thereafter the father of the bride exhorts the bridegroom not to fail the girl in his pursuit of *dharma, artha* and *kāma*,[85] and the groom replies, three times, that he shall never fail her in these.[86]

Next comes the *vivāha-homa* rite: This requires that, having placed a mill-stone to the West of the fire (which is kindled symbolically as a divine witness and sanctifier of the *samskāra*), and having deposited a water-pot to the north-east of the fire, the bridegroom has to offer oblations, the

---

Grihya-Sūtra; those belonging to the *Sāmaveda* would follow the *Gobhila Grihya-Sūtra*; and so on. In general, however, the main *samskāras* and the modes of their operation are, in principle, almost the same in all the *Grihya-Sūtras*.

[81] Āśv. G.S. i, 7, 2: *Yattu samānam tad vakshyāmah*.

[82] Āśv. G.S. i, 6, 1, etc.

[83] In modern times, all these scriptural rites (*vaidika vidhi*) of the *vivāha* from *kanyā-dāna* onwards are preceded by some other rites which are more or less of a customary (*laukika*) nature. Thus, in Mahārāshtra, for instance, all the rites from *kanyā-dāna* onwards start after the bride and groom garland each other in the presence of a large gathering invited to witness, or rather, to declare in their presence, that *vivāha* is to take place between the bride and the groom.

* i.e. the God of Love.

[84] *Om! ka idam kasmā adāt, kāmah kāmāyādāt, kāmo dātā, kāmah pratigrihītā, kāmam samudramāviśa, kāmena tvā pratigrihṇāmi, kāmaitat te/vrishṭirasi, dyaustvā dadātu, prithivī pratigrihṇātu/,* etc. The *mantra* is in Taitt. Br. II. ii, 5, 5–6; cf. also Āśv. Śrau. 5, 13.

[85] '*dharme cha arthe cha kāme cha nāticharitavyā tvayeyam.*'

[86] '*. . . . Nāticharāmi, nāticharāmi, nāticharāmi*'.

bride participating in the offering by grasping the hand (of the groom) that makes the offering.[87] This is followed by the *pāṇi-grahaṇa* rite (i.e., "holding the hand"); here the bridegroom stands facing the west, while the bride sits in front of him with her face to the east; he now seizes her hand while reciting the following Vedic mantra:[88]

I take thy hand in mine,
Yearning for happiness;
I ask thee
To live with me
As thy husband,
Till both of us,
With age, grow old.
Know this,
As I declare,
That the Gods
Bhaga, Aryamā,
Savitā and Purandhī
Have bestowed thy person
Upon me,
That I may fulfil
My *Dharmas* of the householder
With thee.[89]

This is followed by the *lājā-homa* rite in which the bride offers the sacrifice (*homa*) of fried grain, which is poured in her hands by her brother or a person acting in her brother's place (*bhrātris-thāno vā*) to the Gods Aryaman, Varuṇa, Pūshan, with Agni as the intercessor on her behalf, in order that these four may be pleased to release (*munchatu*) her from the bonds (*pāśa*).[90]

After the *mantra* is recited, the rite of *agni-pariṇayana* (i.e. walking around the sacred nuptial fire) follows; here three times the bridegroom leads the bride (*trih pariṇayan*) round the nuptial fire and waterpot, keeping their right sides towards both of them (*pradakshinam*) and he reciting the *mantra* thus:

This I am,
That art thou;
—That indeed, art thou,

[87] Āśv. G.S. i, 7, 3; etc.

[88] This seizing of the hand is to be done in one of the three ways, according to some *Grihya-Sūtras*: The groom holds the bride's whole hand from the hairside (*romānte*) including the thumb if he desires both male and female offsprings; on the other hand, if he desires only male offspring, he seizes the thumb only; while, if he desires female offsprings, he holds her fingers, leaving the thumb free.—See Āśv. G.S. i, 7, 3–5, and Āpa. G.S. ii, 4, 12, 15.

[89] Āśv. G.S. i, 7, 3; etc. the *mantra* is in Rig. x, 85, 36:—*gribhṇāmi te saubhagatvāya hastam mayā patyā jaradashṭiryathāsa/ bhago aryamā savitā purandhirmahyam tvādurgārhapatyāya devāh//* cf. also Ath. Ved. xiv, 1, 50; Pār. Gr. S. 1, 6.

[90] Āśs. G.S. i, 7, 8–15; etc.

This, yea, this I am.
I the heaven,
Thou, the earth;
I the *Sāman* (i.e. music, song, rhythm),
Thou, then, the *Rik*, (i.e. the poetry, the verse),
Let us marry,
Let us marry here."[91]
Let us join together,
And beget our little ones.[92]
Loving each other,[93]
Desirous of moral splendour[94] (or spotless career),
With genial minds and hearts,[95]
Thus, yea thus,
May we live
Through a hundred autumns.[96]

At the end of each round there is another supplementary rite which is performed by the bride; that is called the *aśmārohaṇa* (mounting the stone). Here, with the helping hand of the groom, she treads on the stone as he recites the following:

Mount up this stone;
Like a stone
Be firm.[97]
Overcome the enemies,
Tread over the foes,—
(—the many difficulties through *samsāra!*—),
Down,
Even as you tread over
This stone.[98]

Thereafter, he loosens two locks of her hair (*śikhe*) which have been previously tied, with the *mantra*:

I release thee, now
From Varuṇa's bondage (*pāśād*).[99]

---

[91] *'tāveva vivahāvahai'*.
[92] *'prajām prajanayāvahai'*.
[93] *'sampriyau'*.
[94] *'rochishṇū'*.
[95] *'sumanasyamānau'*.
[96] Āśv. G.S. i, 7, 6; Śān. G.S. i, 13, 4. ff.; Pār. G.S. 1–6.
[97] *Aśmaiva tvam sthirā bhava.*
[98] Āśv. G.S. i, 7, 7; etc.
[99] Ibid. i, 7, 16–7, etc.

Then follows the most important rite in the whole *samskāra*, viz. the *saptapadi* rite (*sapta*—seven; *pada*—step) near the nuptial altar; the bridegroom leads the bride for seven steps, in the northeastern direction; and he recites the relevant part of the following *mantra*, as they walk each of these steps:

> Let us pray together,
> For life-sap, as we tread one step along,
> For life-power, as we tread two steps together,
> For wealth more abundant, as we go on three steps with one another,
> For happiness in life, as we walk four steps together,
> For offsprings, as we move along five steps together,
> For a long-wedded-life[100] as we pledge six steps together.
> Be thou now my life-mate as we walk up seven steps together.
> Thus do thou go together with me for ever and for ever.
> Let us thus acquire many many sons, and long may they live, we pray.[101]

We may note here that the bride is said to have been given over to the groom by the gods, Bhaga, Aryama, Savita and Purandhi.[102] Some of the *Grihya-Sūtras* include another *mantra*, also taken from the Vedic text, which says that the bride is given over to man by three gods who were her first three husbands, viz., Soma, Gandharva and Agni; the *mantra* recited before the nuptial fire is: "Soma had acquired thee first as his wife; after him the Gandharva acquired thee, thy third lord was Agni; and, the fourth is thy human husband. Soma has given thee to the Gandharva, the Gandharva gave thee to Agni. Besides thee, O wife, Agni has (as good as) given wealth and children[103] to me". Yājnavalkya is perhaps interpreting this very Rigvedic *mantra* when he says that the God Soma conferred purity (*śaucham*) upon the woman, Gandharva bestowed upon her a sweet tongue (*śubhām girām*), while Pāvaka (i.e. Agni) bestowed upon her perfect purity (*sarvamedhyatvam*).[104]

After the above *vivāha* rites are duly carried out at the bride's parents' home, the wedded couple start out on their journey to the bridegroom's home; and this is also to be done ceremoniously and with due rites. The father's parting words to the bride are the following *mantra*:

> "Now from the noose of Varuna, I free thee, wherewith most blessed Savitar, hath bound thee.
> In the realm of the Right, to the world of virtuous action, I give thee up uninjured with thy consort.
> Hence (i.e. from the father's house), and not thence (i.e. from the husband's house), I set thee free.

---

[100] The word is *'ritubhyah'* literally meaning 'seasons'. But, as expressed in a previous *mantra* above (*jīveva śaradah śatam*) it seems mean 'long life' here too.

[101] Āśv. G.S. i, 7, 19: *'isha ekapadyūrje dvipadī rāyasposhaya tripadi māyobhavyāya chatushpadī, prajābhyah panchapadī, ritubhyah shaṭpadi, sakhā saptapadī bhava, sā māmanuvratā bhava, putrānvindāvahai bahūnste santu jaradashṭaya iti'*, etc.

[102] See *supra*. Also, in Man. ix, 95, and Kulluka's commentary thereon.

[103] E.g. Pār. G.S. i, 4, 18: The mantras are Rig. x, 85, 39–42:—*punah patnīm agniradad ayusihā saha varchasā/ dīrghāyur asyā yah patir jīvāti śaradah śatam//somah prathamo vivide gandharvo vivida uttarah/tritīyo agnis te patis turīyas te manushyajah/somo' dadad gandharvāya gandharvo' dadad agnaye/rayim cha putrānschādadagnir mchyamatho imām//cf.* also Ath. Ved xiv. 1, 47–8.

[104] Yāj. i, 71.

I make thee softly fettered there,

That, O bounteous Indra, she may live blest in her fortune and her sons."[105]

On leaving her parental home, the bridegroom helps the bride to mount the vehicle as he repeats the following Vedic *mantra*:

"Let Pūshan take thy hand and hence conduct thee;

may the two Aśvins on their car transport thee.

Go to the house (*griha*) to be the household's mistress (*griha-patnī*), and speak as Lady to thy gathered people."[106]

The nuptial fire is to be constantly carried along with the bridal pair during this journey.[107] And again, when their destination is reached, the groom helps the bride to alight down from the car.[108] Next follows the rite of *grihapraveśa*; (*griha*=home; *praveśa*=entry); in this, the groom conducts the bride into the house.[109]

The groom's father (or another person in his place) now addresses the following benedictory *mantras* in welcoming the bride:

"Happy be thou and prosper with thy children here;

be vigilant to rule thy household in this home.

Closely unite thy body with this man, thy lord. So shall ye,

full of years, address your company.

Dwell ye here; be ye not parted; reach the full time of human life.

With sons and grandsons, sport and play, rejoicing in your own house."[110]

Thereafter, the nuptial fire is established in its proper place in the home; and the newly-wedded couple offer oblations to it (*hutvī*), when the groom recites these *mantras*:[111]

"So may Prajāpati bring children forth to us; may Aryaman adorn us till old age come nigh.

Not inauspicious enter thy husband's house; bring blessings to our bipeds and our quadrupeds.

Not evil-eyed, no slayer of thy husband, bring weal to cattle, radiant, gentle-hearted.

Loving the Gods, delightful, bearing heroes, bring blessings to our quadrupeds and bipeds.

Oh bounteous Indra, make this bride blest in her sons and fortunate,

Vouchsafe to her ten sons, and make her husband the eleventh man.

Over thy husband's father and thy husband's mother bear full sway.

---

105 Rig. x, 24–25: *pra tvā munchāmi varuṇasya pāśād, yena tvā badhnāt savitā sushevah/ritasya yonau sukrutasya loke' rishṭām tvā saha patyā dadhāmi/preto munchāmi, nāmutah, subaddhām amutas karam/yatheyam indra mīḍhvah suputrā subhagā satī//*. (The metrical tr. in the text is modification of Griffith's).

106 Āśv. G.S. i, 8, 1; etc. The *mantra* is in Rig. i, 85, 26:—*Pūshā tveto nayatu hastagrihyāśvinā tvā pravahatān rathena/grihān gachchha grihapatnī yathāso vāśinī tvam vidatham āvadāsi/* (The tr. in the text is slightly modified from Griffith's).

107 Āśv. G.S. i, 8, 5: "*Vivāhāgnim agrato'jasram nayanti*"; etc.

108 Āśv. G.S. i, 8, 3; etc.

109 Āśv. G.S. 1, 8, 8, etc.

110 The verses are in Rig. x, 85, 27 and 42:

.... *'iha priyam prajayā te samridhyatām asmin grihe gārhapatyāya jāgrihi/ena patyā tanvam samsrijasvādhājīvrī vidatham āvadāthah// ihaiva stam mā viyaushṭam viśvam āyur vyaśnutam// krīḷantau putrair naptribhir modamānau sve grihe//*cf. also, Ath. Ved. xiv, 1, 22.

111 Āśv. G.S. i, 8, 9, etc.

Over the sister of thy lord, over his brother, rule supreme. So may the Universal Gods, so may the Waters, join our hands, May Mātariśvan, Dhātar, and Deshṭrī together bind us close."[112]

Then follows the rite of looking at the polar star Arundhatī at sunset by the bride: Here, the groom shows her the star, known also as *dhruva* (firm) because of its permanently fixed position in the heaven, while he recites the verse:

"Firm (*dhruva*) be thou, thriving with me"[113]

After the ceremony of *griha-praveśa* is thus completed, the couple are asked to give up all pungent or saline food, to wear ornaments, to sleep only on the floor and observe continence (*brahmacharya*), till three nights are over.[114] Vātsyāyana says that after the marriage ceremony is over, the couple should sleep on the ground for three nights and eat food devoid of pungent flavour or salt (*kshāra-lavaṇavarjam*); for one week they should take bath to the accompaniment of music and auspicious tunes, put on ornaments, eat together, visit and pay respects to relatives and actors (the latter, perhaps means visits to the theatre to enjoy the stage-performances together);—these observances are meant for all the *varṇas*, says Vātsyāyana. He quotes the sage Bābhravīya (whose name he mentions in the plural to signify the great respect with which the sage is regarded) to say that all this does not mean that the young man should remain speechless like a pillar for three nights with his lady, for in that case he might be taken to be an impotent person and despised by the girl! On the contrary, says Vātsyāyana, he may make advances of love to her and try to gain her confidence without transgressing continence (*brahmacharyam*).[115] Asvalayana says that according to some, this period of self-restraint may be extended to twelve days; or it may be as long as even one year, if the couple desire their offspring to be a *rishi*.[116]

---

[112] Rig. x, 85, 43–47:

"*ā nah prajām janayatu prajāpatir ajarasāya samanaktvaryamā/*
adurmangalīh patilokam āviśa śan no bhava dvipade śam chatushpade//
aghorachakshur apatighnyedhi śivā paśubhyah sumanāh suvarchasah/
vīrasūr devakāmā syonā śan no bhava dvipade śam chatushpade//
imām tvam indra mīḍhvah suputrām subhagām kriṇu/
daśāsyām putrānādhehi patim ekādaśam kridhi//
samrājnī śvaśure bhava samrājnīm svasravam bhava/
nanāndari samrājnī bhava samrājnī adhivrishṇu//
samenjatu viśvedevāh samāpo hridayāni nau/
sam mātariśvā sam dhātā samu deshtrī dadhātu nau//

[113] Sān. G. S. i, 17, 3; Hir. G. S. i, 22, 6; Pār. G. S. i, 8, 19; Āp. G. S. 2, 6, 12: Āśv. G. S. i, 7, 22 (According to this last text, this rite is performed before the couple leave the bride's father's home); etc.

[114] Āśv. G. S. i, 8, 10:
Akshāralavaṇāśinau brahmachāriṇāvalamkurvāṇāvadhah śāyinau syātām; also Śān. G.S. i, 18, 19; Pār. G. S. i, 11, 13; Go. G. S. ii, 5; Kh. G. S. i, 4, 12; Āp. G. S. viii, 8; Hir. G. S. i, 6, 23; 10.

[115] Kām. iii, 2, 1 ff.: *sangatayos trirātram adhah śayya brahmacharyam kshara-lavaṇa-varjam aharas tatha saptaham saturya-maṇgala snanam prasadhanam saha-bhojanam cha prekshā-sambandhinam cha pūjanam iti sārvavarṇikam.* [Yashodhara, in his commentary explains: *kshāra=phaṇita-guḍādi* (jaggery, etc.); *lavaṇa=saindhavadi* (salt, etc.); *prekshāsambandhinām naṭādīnām cha darśanam; samgatayoh=pariṇayāt prāhāsamāgamayoh.*]

tri-rātram avachannam hi stambham iva nāyakam paśyantī kanyā nirvidyeta paribhavet cha tritīyām iva prakritim, iti Bābhravīyah/ upakramet cha visrambhayet cha, na tu brahmacharyam ativarteta, iti Vātsyāyanah.

[116] Āśv. G.S. i, 8, 10; cf. Mānava G.S. i, 14, 14 which says the same thing, without, however, referring to the quality of the offspring resulting out of such penance.

On the fourth day some rites are performed, preparatory to the meeting of the newly wedded couple. These rites are the foetus-laying rites; they are not mentioned in all the *Grihya-Sutras*.[117] The husband offers nine expiatory oblations to Agni.[118] And, after this sacrifice to Agni is completed, he mates with her while reciting the following *mantras*: "United are our minds (*manas*); united our hearts (*hridayāṇi*), united our navel (*nabhih*), united our body and skin (*tanu-tvachah*). I will bind thee (*yujyāmi*) with the bond of love (*kama*); that bond shall be indissoluble (*avimochanāya*)".[119] The husband embraces her while saying the *mantra*: "Be devoted to me, be my companion".[120] Thereafter he seeks her mouth with his mouth while he recites these *mantras*: Honey! Lo! Honey! My tongue's speech is honey; in my mouth dwells the honey of the bee; on my teeth dwells concord. The concord that belongs to *chakravāka** birds, that is brought out of the rivers of which the divine Gandharva is possessed,—thereby we are concordant".[121] He then prays the Gods Vishṇu, Śinīvalī, Aśvins, Agni and Indra, for the birth of a male offspring,—'the most valiant of his kin'; he also recites the verse: "I do with thee the work that is sacred to Prajāpati. May an embryo enter thy womb; may a child be born without any deficiency, with all limbs, not blind, not lame, not sucked out by the Piśāchas."[122] This concludes the ritual part of the after-*vivāha* ceremonies.

These rites and the manner in which they are to be conducted show that mating is regarded as a serious social and personal duty devoid of selfish profligacy or lusty sensual indulgence. Hereafter, the couple start their career as keepers of the home (*griha*) wherein they do their best to fulfil their vow not to fail each other in their pursuit of *dharma, artha*, and *kāma*, for the sake of achieving *mokśa*.*

The above description of the rites performed at the *vivāha* must speak for itself. For the Hindu, then, marriage is a *samskāra*, and as such, the relations between the marrying parties are of a sacramental character, and not a contractual nature. For, apart from the necessity of begetting a son in order to assist the householder in the discharge of his obligations (*riṇas*), it has been ordained by the *Dharma-Śāstras* that the wife is a necessary complement as the *grihapatnī* (i.e. the lady of the house) for the proper and full execution of his *dharmas* as the *griha-pati* (i.e. the lord of the house). Both the terms *patnī* as well as *pati* involve the implication of "guardianship" of the home. This is also emphasised by the words which designate one's wife as his *dharma-patnī* and *saha-dharma-chāriṇī*, i.e. she who has to share all the sacred obligations, and, she who does carry them out in partnership with her husband.

The importance of certain rites in the Hindu *vivāha* should not fail to secure the attention of a student of the Hindu *vivāha* system. A marriage is not regarded as complete unless and until certain important rites which are essential for a *vivāha* are performed. Such are the *Pāṇi-grahana*, joining

---

[117] They are, e.g., in Hir. G.S. i, 6, 23, 11 to 25, 2, in details; and in Bau. G.S. i, 7 and Mān. G.S. i, 14, 1–19 in short.

[118] Hir. G.S. i, 6, 23, 11 to 24, 1.

[119] Bau. G.S. i, 5, 31; Hir. G.S. i, 24, 4.

[120] Hir. G.S. i, 7, 25, 5.

* Mythologically famous for their male and female's strong attachment to each other.

[121] Hir. G.S. i, 7, 24, 6.

[122] Hir. G.S. i, 7, 25, 1.

* The vow taken by the bridegroom at the *vivāha*:

"Dharme cha arthe cha kāme cha nāticharāmi, nāticharāmi, nāticharāmi."

See above, and footnotes 85–86.

of hands of the bride and the bride-groom, and the *sapta-padī* ("seven steps") *mantras*. "The *mantras* of marriage" says Bhīshma, "accomplish their object of bringing about the indissoluble union of marriage at the seventh step. The maiden becomes the wife of him to whom the gift is actually made with water".[123] Again, "Till the hand is actually taken with due rites, marriage does not happen".[124] And, the rites of marriage must take place in the presence of sacred fire.[125]

Nārada has said that once the *mantras* are recited by joining the hands of the bride and the bridegroom (*pāṇi-grahaṇa*), the marriage becomes binding.[126] So also Vasishṭha and Baudhāyana declare that a damsel who is not wedded in accompaniment with sacred rites may be deemed even as a maiden, and she may be lawfully given to another man.[127] "The nuptial *mantras* including those of "*paṇigrahaṇa*" says Manu, "are a certain proof that a maiden has been made a lawful wife; but the learned should observe that they are complete with the seventh step."[128]

Vātsyāyana too has attached great importance to the sacred rites performed in the wedding. He gives an advice of caution, for instance, that in the *Gāndharva vivāha* the nuptials may have to be secretly performed, yet they have to be performed before the sacred fire; and, this fire is brought from the house of a *Śrotriyo* i.e. a gentleman who has been regularly observing his sacred duties; *kuśa* grass is spread before it; and oblations are offered in such a fire according to the rules of the *Smriti* (*yathā-smriti*).[129] The couple is then to go thrice round the fire.[130] The reason for this precaution to perform the rites before the fire is, that marriages performed with the fire as the witness are binding and can never be set aside.[131]

In the opinion of Kauṭilya, the rejection of a bride before the rites of *pāṇi-grahaṇa* is valid amongst the higher *varṇas*. Among the Śūdras, however, the rejection is valid at any time before the last rite of the nuptials. But rejection of the bride even after the *pāṇi-grahaṇa* rite is permitted in the case of a bride whose guilt of having lain with another man has been discovered afterwards. However, rejection of the bride after *pāṇi-grahaṇa* can never be allowed in the case of brides and bridegrooms of pure character and high family.[132]

Now, while Manu regards the first six forms, out of the list already mentioned, as lawful, he gives his particular approval to the *Gāndharva* and the *Rākshasa vivāha* forms in the case of the warrior *varṇa*, i.e., the Kshatriyas, as being permitted by the time-honoured tradition.[133] Baudāyana observes that of all the forms, the *Gāndharva* form is recommended by some since it springs out of mutual love of the two parties.[134] Both Baudhāyana and Nārada say that this form is meant for all the *varṇas*.[135] The *Kāma Śūtras* have also specially recommended the *gāndharva* form of *vivāha* as

---

[123] Mahā. Anu. 44, 55.

[124] Ibid. 44, 35.

[125] Ibid. 44, 56.

[126] Nār. xii, 3.

[127] Vas. xvii, 73; Baudh. iv, 1, 15.

[128] Man. viii, 227: '*pāṇigrahaṇikā mantrā niyatam dāra-lakshaṇam/teshām tu nishṭhā vijneyā vidvadbhih saptame pade/*'. Both Medhātithi and Kullūka, commenting on this verse, explain that this means marriage cannot be revoked or annulled after the seventh step is taken.

[129] Kāma. iii, 5, 11.

[130] Ibid.

[131] Kāma. iii, 5, 13.

[132] Arth. p. 212.

[133] Man. iii, 26. "*gāndharvo rākshasas chaiva dharmyau kshatrasya tau smritau/*".

[134] Nār. xii, 44; Baudh. i, 11, 20, 16 also says '*gāndharvam apyeke praśamsanti sarveshām, snehānugatatvāt'*.

[135] Ibid.

being the most respected form of marriage; because says Vātsyāyana, it is the result of mutual love; and, he adds, mutual love is the true foundation as well as the true goal of marriage.[136]

In the *Mahābhārata*, out of the eight forms of marriage, the *Brāhma, Daiva, Ārsha* and *Prājāpatya* forms of *vivāha* are said to be permissbile for the Brāhmaṇas,[137] and the *Gāndharva* and the *Rākshasa* forms are viewed as proper for the *Kshatriya*.[138] At another place, Bhīshma says that the *Brāhma* form is followed by the righteous Brāmaṇas, and *Kshātra* form by the Kshatriyas,[139] but when referring to the *Gāndharva* form as one in which "the father of the girl, without consulting his own wishes, gives away his daughter to a person whom the daughter likes and who reciprocates her sentiments", Bhīshma does not make mention of any *varṇa* in particular[140] as the *Smritis* mentioned above have done. Indeed, he says in a further passage in the same *Adhyāya* "the *Brāhma, Kshātra* and *Gāndharva* forms are righteous (*dharmyāh*); pure or mixed, these forms forsooth should be followed."[141]

The *Artha-Śāstra* has not said much about this point, and we naturally cannot expect much from it either, since its main concern is the science of government and politics. It permits, in the first instance, the first four forms as ancestral custom, valid on the father's approval. It also permits the other forms, provided the sanction of both the parents is obtained. Ordinarily, according to the *Artha-Śāstra*, "any kind of marriage is approvable provided it pleases all those (that are concerned in it)."[142]

In the *Mahābhārata*, we have just seen how the *Gāndharva* form is defined.[143] The father or the guardian of the girl gives her in marriage in this form in accordance with her wishes, and to a man of her choice. But, it should be noted here, that this passage still visualizes that ultimately, it is the father (or the guardian), who has to give the girl in marriage, though this is to be done in accordance with her own wishes, not his. The passage does not refer to a marriage arranged by the girl and the boy themselves. In another passage greater credence is given to the marriage by the mutual choice of the two parties than even to the engagement made by the bride's father to a man of his choice. "The engagement made by the relatives of a girl is, no doubt binding and sacred; but the engagement fixed by the bride and the bridegroom with the help of *mantras* is much more so."[144]

In Vātsyāyana's book, there are good many references to courtship between the maiden and her young man. Of course, "All the world knows", according to Vātsyāyana, "that a girl however much she may be in love, will not herself make any overtures to the man".[145] The whole skill, therefore, in courtship and winning over the love of a maiden rests with her lover. Vātsyāyana gives many shrewd hints to the suitor in order to enable him to accomplish his heart's desire; and, in these

---

136 Kām. iii, 5, 29–30.

137 Like Manu. iii, 24, above.

138 Mahā. Ādi. 73, 8–13; also 73, 27.

139 Ibid. 44, 4, 5.

140 Ibid. 44, 6: *Ātmābhipretam utsrijya kanyābhipreta eva yat/abhipretā cha yā yasya tasmai deyā Yudhishṭhira/ gāndharvam iti tam dharmam prāhur vedavido janāh//*

141 Ibid. 44, 10: "*Brāhmah kshātro'tha gāndharva ete dharmyā nararshabha/prithag vā yadi vā miśrāh kartavyā nātra samśayah//*". The 'mixtures' of these forms are illustrated by the marriages of Nala-Damayantī, which is a *Brāhma-Kshātra* marriage; of Rukmini-Krishṇa which is a *Rākshasa-Gāndharva* marriage; and of Subhadrā-Arjuna, which is a *Kshātra-Rākshasa marriage.* Comm. of Nīlakaṇṭha.

142 Arth. p. 172.

143 See above and footnote 138.

144 Mahā. Anu. 44, 26.

145 Kām. (tr. by Peterson): B.B.R.A.S. Jour., Vol. xviii, pp. 117–18.

matters, he seems to take a very progressive view of things: The suitor may, for instance, collect flowers and make garlands of these in company of and with the help of his lady-love; or, he may play some indoor games with her (like the game of dice, for example); all such things are to be practised having regard to their age and their degree of acquaintance with each other.[146] Or, the lover is advised to seek their help and guidance for the fulfilment of his quest.[147] He is asked to spare no pains to please her by securing for her (*prayatnena sampādayet*) rare novel articles (*apūrvāṇi*) which she might desire to have.[148] The *Gāndharva vivāha*, as the sage Vātsyāyana envisages it, should be the flowering of such courtship. The young man, after persuading his beloved to be his bride and life-mate, is advised to arrange, through the help of mutual friends, the time and the place for the two to meet together and sanctify their love in the presence of the sacred fire.[149] The two lovers should then go round the fire thrice, with due rites of oblations in accordance with the rules laid down by the *Smritis*.[150] For "marriages performed with the sacred fire as the witness can never be rescinded"—this is the opinion of all Āchāryas".[151] After all this has been accomplished in secret, however, the parents have to be appraised of the happy event.[152] The parents and the relatives may then be won over by the lovers; when their consent is obtained, the formal marriage ceremonies are advised to be performed.[153] Such is the *Gāndharva vivāha* according to Vātsyāyana. In case the girl hesitates to take to this course of action (*aprati-padyamānā*), it is advised that she may be brought to a secret place on some pretext (*anyakāryopadeśena*) with the help of another lady of good family, (of course, provided she is in love with the man, but is hesitant to marry secretly); here the rites before the sacred fire should then be performed. Or, the young man is advised to persuade the mother of the girl, or her brother, and with his or her help, to get the girl at a secret place where, with due rites as described above, the wedding should be effected.[154] According to Vātsyāyana, the Gāndharva form of marriage is the most respected (*pūjita*) form of marriage, because, in the first place, it is founded on mutual love, and secondly, because love is the be-all and end-all of marriage;[155] moreover, it is free from any cumbersome formalities and trouble.[156]

The most emphatically denounced form of marriage is that in which money is paid to the bride or her kinsmen, as the bride-price or dowry. Selling the daughter even for the smallest gratuity, is against all morals.[157] The *Mahābhārata* is quite clear on this point. According to Bhīshma, the sale and purchase of the daughter, though known to be practised by a few human beings for a long time, should never be done by good men.[158] "No one should give his daughter to such a person (who

[146] Kām. iii, 3, 5, (*parichayasya vayasaśchānurūpāt*).

[147] Ibid. iii, 3, 8–9.

[148] Ibid. iii, 3, 11–12.

[149] Ibid. iii, 5, 11.

[150] Ibid. (*Yathāsmriti hutvā cha trih parikramet*).

[151] Ibid. iii, 5, 13: "*Agnisākshikā hi vivāhā na nivartanta iti āchāryasamayah.*"

[152] Kām. iii, 5, 12. '*tato mātari pitari cha prakāśayet*', etc.

[153] Ibid.

[154] Kām. iii, 5, 18–19.

[155] Kām. iii, 5, 20–23:

> '*Vyūḍhānām hi vivāhānām anurāgah phalam yatah . . .*'; and '*. . . anurāgātmakattvāchcha gāndharvah pravaro matah*'.

[156] Ibid. '*sukhatvād abahukleśāt*'.

[157] Man. iii, 51; Āp. ii, 13, 11; Vas. i, 37–38; Baudh. i, 21, 2–3; Mahā. Udyoga. 97, 15–16.

[158] Mahā. Anu. 44, 37.

offers money for the bride); in fact, he is not the man with whom one may marry his daughter. A wife should never be purchased; nor should a father ever sell his daughter."[159] Such money, again, if paid by a person for buying a girl, need not bind her father or kinsmen to give the girl to him only. "The kinsmen of the maiden should bestow her upon him whom they consider proper. There need be no hesitation to do such a thing (*nātra kāryā vichāraṇā*); the righteous act thus without caring for the giver of the money even if he be alive".[160] Continuous sufferings in hell will be the punishment for the man who sells either his son or daughter.[161] We are further told that "In the form of marriage called *Ārsha*, the man who marries has to give a bull and a cow; and the father of the maiden accepts the gift."[162] Some characterise this gift as a purchase price (*śulka*), while others are of opinion that it should not be considered as such. The true view, however, is that a gift for such a purpose, be it of small value or large, should be considered as price, and the bestowal of the daughter under such circumstances should be considered a sale.[163] And, in spite of the fact of its having been practised by a few persons, it can never be taken as the traditional *dharma* practice (*naisha dharmah sanātanah*).[164] Even a human being who is not a relation of blood should never be sold; what need then be said of one's own child? No *dharma* can ever be served with the riches acquired by doing such acts against the dictates of *dharma*.[165]

Regarding the age of marriage of a girl or a boy, there is a great variety of opinions among the Hindu writers; and it is extremely difficult to say anything specific and uniform about their general opinion. The only thing which they agree about is that the age of the bride must be less than that of the boy. And, even to this day, a contrary instance of marriage in which the boy is younger than the girl may be hard to find among the Hindus. Manu has said, for instance, that a man of thirty should marry a girl of twelve; and, a man of twenty-four should marry a girl of eight.[166] Manu's commentators Medhātithā and Kullūka inform us that this rule was not followed to the letter. In the *Mahābhārata* at one place we find Bhīshma, while explaining to Yudhishṭhira about *vivāha*, saying that "A person of thirty years of age should marry a girl of ten years of age wearing a single piece of cloth. Or a person of one and twenty years of age should marry a girl of seven years of age."[167] Of course, at other places, it advocates sixteen years as the age for a girl to marry (see below). All agree upon one point, viz., that the bride must be younger by three years or more than the husband.[168] Vātsyāyana also says that the bride must be at least three years younger than the bridegroom.[169]

In the *Grihya Sūtras*, the marriageable maiden is referred to as a *nagnikā*.[170] And Dr. Ghosh has pointed out in this connection, that Mātridatta's commentary on this word explains it as referring to a girl who is fit to be undressed (from *nagna* = undressed) in privacy with her husband for cohabitation

---

[159] Ibid. 44, 46; cf. Man. iii, 51–52.

[160] Ibid. 44, 50–51.

[161] Ibid. 45, 19.

[162] Ibid. 45, 20; See Manu. iii, 29.

[163] Mahā. Anu. 45, 20: "*Alpo vā bahu vā rājan vikrayas tāvad eva sah*." Also in Manu. iii, 53.

[164] Mahā. Anu. 45, 21.

[165] Ibid, 45, 23: "*Anyo'pyatha na vikreyo manushyah kim punah prajāh/adharma-mūlair hi dhanais tair na dharmo katham cha na*/"

[166] Man. ix, 94.

[167] Mahā. Anu. 44, 14.

[168] Gaut. iv; Yāj. i, 52; Man. iii, 4, 12; Āpa. ii, 6, 13, 1; etc.

[169] Kām. iii, 1, 2:—(*trivarshāt prabhriti nyūnavayasām*).

[170] Gobhi. Gr. S. iii, 4, 6; Man. Gr. i, 7; Hiraṇyakeśi Gri. i, 19, 2; Vaikhā. Gr. iii. 2, 1; etc.

and therefore is one who has attained perfect maturity.[171] "*Nagnikā*, therefore", in Dr. Ghosh's opinion, "in ancient times meant a young but mature girl. It is difficult to believe that *nagnikā* meant a naked girl (i.e. a child too young to put on clothes) having regard to the fact that the *Mahābhārata* advocates the marriage of a *nagnikā* of sixteen"![172] Further, we may note that the *Grihya-Sūtra* rules about the observance of *brahmacharya* by the couple for three days after *vivāha* and of co-habitation on the fourth,[173] positively assume a mature age of marriage, both for the bridegroom as well as the bride.

In Vātsyāyana's *Kāma-Sūtra*, we have a description of the various ways and means employed by wooers to win over young maidens for marriage by showing their skill in the various arts or by giving attractive presents to them.[174] There are also references, in these *sūtras*, of various other means on a more romantic level; for instance, lovers sent messages and love-letters to each other through persons in whom both the lovers could repose their full confidence; or friends of one party praised the virtues and attainments of the lover to the beloved or deprecated and found faults with any other possible suitor, in the interest of the one whom they praised.[175]

Yet it is very difficult to define the attitude of Vātsyāyana's *Kāma-Śūtra* regarding the age of the bride, in spite of the fact that it is a text which concerns itself with problems of sexual psychology and morality rather in details. For, even while talking about a young man's courtship to the maiden (*kanyā*), he refers to a *Bālā* (child), as well as a *Yauvane-sthitā* (adolescent) and a *Vatsalā* (*adult*).* A *bālā* may be won over by plays and games befitting a very young person (*bāla-krīḍanakair*); an adult damsel (*yauvane-sthitā*) may be courted by demonstration of skill in various arts (*kalābhih*); while a *vatsalā*,—by which may be implied a lady of more advanced years, who is capable of offering love (*vatsalam*) herself—may be solicited by winning the confidence of persons in whom the lady puts her faith (*viśvāsya-jana*).[176] But in the description which he gives of the girl who has fallen in love with her suitor as a result of his enthusiastic and untiring efforts, he seems evidently to pre-suppose the young maiden to have attained a fairly mature age. Thus, he gives certain signs (*lakshaṇāni*) from which her love for a man may be suspected and ascertained: The lady who has fallen in love avoids looking straight in the face of her lover (*sanmukham*); or she shows signs of bashfulness when he looks at her.[177] Further on, Vātsyāyana gives a piece of advice to the young maiden that she should choose the man who would truly love her, rather than a man endowed with

---

[171] *Tasmād vastra-vikshepaṇārhā nagnikā mdithunārhā iti arthah.*

[172] Ghosh: *Hindu Law of Partition*, p. 707.

[173] See *supra*, pp. 24–25 above.

[174] Kām. iii.

[175] Kām. iii, 2; 3; 5; etc.

* In the *Ratiśāstra*, the following terms are referred to, and explained thus: "A maiden is called *bālā* till she attains the sixteenth year of her age; she is known as a *taruṇī* till she attains the thirtieth year; thereafter, till the age of fifty-five, she is called a *prauḍhā*; while after the fifty-fifth year of age, she becomes a *vriddhā*—Ch. iv. The author goes on further to describe different ways of courtship of these girls, similar as the above of the *Kāmasūtra*.

[176] Kām. iii, 3, 43–44.

[177] Kām. iii, 3, 25; cf. '*Rati-śāstra*', ch. vi.

many virtues or riches.[178] "Out of many suitors of equal merits (*guṇasāmye'bhiyoktrīṇām*), choose him", the sage advises, "who is in love with thee (*anurāgātmakah*)".[179]

On the whole, we may say, that Vātsyāyana does not seem to have been in favour of child-marriages; for he refers to the bride as *prāpta-yauvanā* (*prāpta*=attained; *yauvana*=youth) and *vigāḍha-yauvanā* (*vigāḍha*=mature). His description of *Gāndharva* form of marriage as a highly respected one, of the love-letters exchanged between the wooer and the wooed, and of the methods to be employed in courting love, perhaps too clearly demonstrate that he was all in favour of mature marriages. In the epics, and in the *Smritis*, the prescribed age of marriage is very low, as will be seen below. The important factor governing the prescription of marriageable age is of course the age of puberty—which is, according to modern scientists, between about twelve to sixteen for girls and between about fourteen to eighteen for boys.[180] However, the permissible age according to law is not the actual age at which every marriage takes place, the latter is usually higher than the former.[181] This fact should always be borne in mind when we consider the legislation on the age of marriage.

In the *Mahābhārata* as well as in the *Smritis* again (even though these prescribe, sometimes, very low age for girls to marry), there are many indications to show that, in fact, the actual age of marriage must have been higher. The various duties prescribed for the housewife in the *Smritis*, as well as in the *Śukra-Nīti*, for instance, are such as could not be performed by too young a girl.[182] Of course this does not give a strong evidence in favour of the position that *Smritis* too expected complete maturity of body and mind in marriageable girls; for the duties may have as well been intended, not for the newly married bride, but for the wife after she has attained maturity of age and intellect in her husband's home. The *Mahābhārata*, on the other hand, gives numerous actual instances where the bride-to-be was maiden, who had attained an adequate physical as well as intellectual status deemed necessary for starting married life. The marriages of Dushyanta and Sakuntalā, Sāvitrī and Satyavana, Subhadrā and Arjuna, Rukmiṇī and Krishṇa, Nala and Damayantī, to mention some only are all marriages where the maiden, out of love, married the man of her own free choice. In the *Svayam-vara* (*svayam*=self; *vara* from *vri*=choose)* of the Epics the bride very often made a selection out of several suitors for her hand. There are also several instances in the dramatic and the poetic literature regarding such choosing by the bride of her own husband; for instance, Bāṇa's *Kādambarī* depicting the romances of two pairs of lovers, viz. Kādambarī-Chandrāpīda, and Mahāśvetā-Puṇḍarīka; and the dramas *Mālātī-Mādhavam, Vikramorvaśīyam* and *Śākuntalam*, give rich and vivid descriptions of such happenings.

[178] Ibid. iii, 4, 52 and 55:—

'*Kanyābhiyujyamānā tu yam manyetāśrayam sukham/*
anukūlam cha vaśyam cha tasya kuryāt parigraham//
varam vaśyo daridro'pi nirguṇo' pyātmadhāraṇah/
guṇairyukto'pi na tvenām bahusādhāraṇo patih//'

[179] Ibid. iii, 4, 59.

[180] Goodsell, W.: *History of Marriage and the Family*, Macmillan 1934, pp. 63–64—cited by Panunzio: *Major Social Institutions*, p. 154.

[181] Panunzio: op. cit. p. 157.

[182] See next chapter.

* It may be pointed out here that the term *svayam-vara* was not always used in its strict meaning of the "individual's own choice" entirely, but in a qualified way. It often meant that the father, or the guardian, did not choose the bride-groom for his daughter, but laid down some difficult test or contest to be passed or won as a qualification for gaining the hand of the daughter.

In connection with the age of marriageability for boys and girls, it should be observed here that a life of sex-experience at too early an age has been found to be harmful to the development of the personality,—physical and intellectual,—of the male as well as the female. It is equally harmful to start sex-life too late. Hamilton and McGowan have shown, for instance, that sexual frigidity of later life in women is due mostly to repressions during childhood, as also to lateness of sexual experience. Therefore, in their opinion, "Early sexual experience is valuable to the mental health and the marital normality and happiness of women".[183] If proper precautions are taken, early marriages,—by which is not meant child marriages, but marriages at a fairly mature age yet not much later—are bound to be happier, both from the point of view of psychological as well as physical compatibility of the partners concerned. Apart from the absence of repressed morbidity already mentioned above, there is a positive advantage of a psychological nature in early marriages. The likes and dislikes and the general mental attitude of men and women become more and more formed and fixed as the individuals advance in age, so that there is often little or no room left for mutual give and take, mutual adjustments and psychological compatibility of a couple which happens to come together at a rather late age. On the other hand, psychological compatibility between the two is certainly more possible and highly probable, if they come together at an age when their mental attitudes are not yet finally formed and hardened but are rather pliable, flexible and mobile in regard to mutual adjustment, so that there is likely to be little room for serious conflicts between the two who become pledged to live together for life. Thus, the problems of the adaptation to each other's tastes, conduct and attitudes are likely to be obviously easier for solution at an early age than later in life. In the words of Williams, "the case for early marriage, from the psychological point of view, lies in the fact that, if married early, the nature of each is still plastic, and there is a greater possibility of congeniality than later when the characteristic attitudes have become fixed".[184]

"On the other hand", however, he proceeds to say, "if marriage is delayed until the character is formed, then both the man and woman are more sure of what their natures are and of the kind of person with whom they will be congenial".[185] But then, even if the adult man or woman reaches the age when his or her character is fixed and when he or she has attained the maturity of judgment to know the kind of person who should be chosen as the life-mate, such persons cannot be said to be free from the dangers of misjudgment and even folly. For, the courtship of the adult need not and in fact in many cases, does not, lead to a really congenial choice of mate. The period of courtship is more or less full of excitement and thrill; so that there is little room for real reflexion and calm and balanced observation. During the period of courtship, when living together is not possible, each is apt to be attracted to the other by favourable points of consideration; this increases the likelihood that each may even overlook or be blinded to the unfavourable ones. In fact, the emotional situations involved in courtship must leave little room for the judicial exercise of wisdom and reason. "The thrills of courtship prove little as to the wisdom of courtship".[186]

But there is more to be said still about a happy marriage: What is essentially required for happiness in wedded life is not so much wise or judicious choice, or agreement of temperament; it is much more the *attitude of mind* towards avoidance of strife, an attitude *not* to magnify minor differences, a willingness to give and take, to seek harmony and to adapt. The two partners are going to face, after marriage, any number of new situations which were unforseen, un-anticipated

[183] Ch. on "Physical Disabilities in Wives", in "*Sex in Civilization*", Ed. by Calverton & Schmalhausen, pp. 235–36.
[184] Williams: *Prin. Soc. Psy.*, p. 288.
[185] Williams: *Prin. Soc. Psy.*, p. 288.
[186] Williams: Ibid. p. 290.

by them, requiring on their part constant efforts at mutual adjustment and compromise of attitude and outlook. "I had never thought you would be or do so-and-so when I married you . . ." and so on . . . is a common complaint between couples who do not find themselves able to adjust their selves to each other.

Panunzio has very well pointed out the advantages and disadvantages of parental guidance or parental choice of the mate, and spontaneous choice of the mate by the parties themselves:[187] "Spontaneous mate choosing has its advantages. It places mating above the economic or social calculations of parents or other relatives, who ordinarily tend to consider their interests first; it gives some measure of self-expression to the choosers and lends greater beauty and romance to mating; and it is free and adventurous.

"On the other hand, spontaneous mate choosing seems disadvantageous in some respects. It is, first of all, scarcely choosing at all. Youthful individuals tend to be drawn to each other by mere accidental propinquity; they do not primarily think but feel; they do not or cannot look ahead; they fail to consider whether they are physically or emotionally fit for one another; often they either do not perceive or ignore their differences in race and culture, in personal habits, in aptitudes, in educational and religious training, and in political background. Consequently, their choice, in so far as they do choose, is largely non-deliberative. In reality they do not choose at all, but merely "fall" in love, and often the fall mars their whole lives. In addition, spontaneous mate choosing mainly being emotional, tends to build the romantic figment of "perfection" which often adds to the likelihood of failure in marriage. Perfect or nearly perfect marriages have been known, e.g., that of Robert Browning and Elizabeth Barrett and that described in *An American Idyl*. But these are rare, very rare. Romantic marriages in which no account is taken of biological and cultural differences and in which practically no preparation has been made for the slow never ending process of adjustment, seem to have a greater probability of failure.

"Although scientific data are not available for a sound generalization, it may be asserted that, all in all, spontaneous mate choosing does not provide a sufficient degree of control of the sex impulse or of guidance in choice. This form of choosing may partly account for the disorganization in marriage, as evidenced in the number of divorces, prevailing in parts of Western culture, particularly in democratic nations. Marriage, even at its best, calls for a profound adjustment; man and woman are in many respects natively so different that when to normal, inherent male-female differences, nonrational selection adds other elements of possible discord, marriage becomes so complex as frequently to be doomed to failure from the outset".

It seems fair, therefore, to conclude from what has been said so far, that in deciding the marriageable age for boys and girls, the chief point to remember is that too late marriages are likely to be as harmful as, or even more harmful than, too early marriages. This is not to say that we are in favour of infant and child marriages. It is only intended to point out that the sponsors of late marriages will have to pause and think over and answer the same difficulties, plus a few more in all probability, before advocating a late age-limit of marriage. And, the question to be answered also is: How late is not too late to marry!

Further, marriage must also be looked upon for the married couple as the first major field of practising the lessons of individual and social adjustment through a series of mutual contacts, and also of contacts jointly as partners in a variety of activities and dealings with others in the family and outside the family. Panunzio even thinks that "It is not unlikely that a greater amount

[187] C. Panunzio: *Major Social Institutions*, p. 180.

of socialization and accommodation occurs in and through marriage than in or through any other institution".[188]

Though we do not have as yet adequate scientific data on the question, the specialists in the subject seem to be generally agreed upon the advisability of comparatively early—not too early—marriage. Such marriage is advantageous in their view, from the individual bio-psychological as well as from the social point of view. Thus, it has been pointed out that "after a girl is 18 or 20, an early marriage tends to remove the emotional strain of celibacy which, if prolonged, may distort her personality. A younger woman has a wider choice of men and therefore is more likely to secure a suitable mate, making it easier for younger couples to adjust themselves to one another in the marriage state. Judges and divorce lawyers have noted less frequency of divorce in early marriages than in the late ones."[189]

The man who marries in the early twenties,[190] has, from the practical point of view, several other advantages too: By beginning married life earlier, he would be able to get more happiness; by giving full expression to his emotional and physical urges at the right time without having to suppress them, he is able to lead a more healthful life, and is therefore likely to live longer. "It is widely alleged that early marriages are not so likely to be happy. This is one of those glib generalizations that is passed around solemnly until it comes to be taken as a gospel truth. There is no real basis for it, when one comes to study the record. . . . The important factor is the quality of the people who are marrying, not their age".[191] In view of this, Paul Popeno* suggests the following broad "formula" for marriage, on the basis of his specialised studies and data: "People should marry *after* they are physically mature, after they are emotionally mature, and *before* they are intellectually mature",[192] and this is in the early twenties which, in his judgment, is the normal time for marriage.[193]

The problems of marital happiness and also of family welfare are now engaging the serious attention of the Universities and also other organisations in the U.S.A. and other advanced parts of the world, with the result that there have been established a number of family welfare centers and also independent departments for the subjects in some of the Universities there. Of the investigations that have been recently made in the field of marital happiness there *by collecting actual data from married couples and treating it scientifically* by statistical and other methods, the following may be mentioned as the most important, viz.,—L. M. Terman: *Psychological Factors in Marital Happiness* (McGraw-Hill, New York, 1939); and E. W. Burgess & L. S. Cottrell, Jr.: *Predicting Success or Failure in Marriage* (Prentice-Hall, New York, 1939). The findings of these investigators agree largely with each other, and, though these studies were made in the American context, our readers may find them interesting in this connection, and hence the following brief note on them is added:

---

[188] C. Panunzio: *Major Social Institutions*, p. 180.

[189] Paul Popenoe: *Modern Marriage*, Macmillan, N.Y. 1925, p. 50.

[190] Paul Popenoe: *Modern Marriage*, 2nd Rev. Ed., Macmillan, 1941, p. 10.

[191] Ibid. pp. 13–14.

* Dr. Paul Popenoe, of the University of Southern California, U.S.A., is the General Director of the American Institute of Family Relations, Los Angeles, California, and is the author of *Modern Marriage* (1925, New Ed. 1940), *The Child's Heredity* (1929), *Applied Eugenics* (2nd Ed. 1937), and other books and a number of research articles on the subject of marriage and family.

[192] Ibid. p. 14.

[193] Ibid.

Terman's study was made on a sample of 792 couples of California and he also had the co-operation, counsel and/or advice from Dr. Burgess, Dr. Popenoe, and others. His conclusion is that the ten background circumstances most predictive of marital happiness are: (1) Superior happiness of parents, (2) childhood happiness of the spouses, (3) lack of conflict with mother, (4) home discipline that was firm without being harsh, (5 & 6) strong attachment to mother and to father, (7) lack of conflict with father, (8) parental frankness about matters of sex, (9) infrequency and mildness of childhood punishment, and (10) premarital attitude towards sex that was free from disgust or aversion (Terman, Op. cit. p. 372).

Burgess and Cottrell begin by observing that in the oriental countries 'the entire course of selection of mates, marriage, and marital adjustment is regulated by Oriental mores with a minimum of personal freedom and initiative and a maximum of familial and social control". On the other hand, "In American society, the mores ensure a maximum of personal freedom in courtship, engagement, and marriage . . . ." (Op. Cit. pp. 43–4). In their investigation, they found that among the several pre-marital factors which show a rather high positive correlation with adjustment in marriage are: approval of marriage by the parents of the couple; similarity of their family backgrounds; husband and wife not only children; husband closely attached to, and having little or no conflict with, his father and mother; wife's close attachment to mother, husband and wife reared in the country; church attendance by husband two or more times a month; couple acquainted with each other two or more years; husband and wife 22 to 30 years old at time of marriage; couple married by priest or rabbi. (Op cit. pp. 354). There are other factors also mentioned by the authors which correlate highly with marital happiness, which the reader should see for himself from the work.

The authors also make the following observations on the basis of their study (p. 349): (1) Contrary to prevailing opinion, American *wives* make major adjustment in marriage. (2) *Affectional relationships in childhood*, typically of the son for the mother and the daughter for the father, condition the love-object choice of the adult. (3) The *socialization* of the person, as indicated by his participation in social life and social institutions, is significant for adjustment in marriage. (4) The *economic factor* in itself is *not* significant for adjustment in marriage, since it is apparently fully accounted for by the other factors (impress of cultural background, psychogenetic characteristics, social type, and response patterns). (5) With the majority of couples, problems of sexual adjustment in marriage appear to be a resultant *not so much of biological factors as of psychological characteristics* and of *cultural conditioning* of attitude towards sex. (Italics ours.)

In a later paper, Dr. Burgess (who, as Prof. Christensen remarks, "is pioneer and Dean in the field of family research") observes that "new findings are becoming available upon the factors which makes for success in modern marriage. These may be briefly summed[194] up: (1) the possession of personality traits such as an optimistic temperament, emotional balance, yielding disposition, sympathetic attitude, self-confidence, particularly on the part of the husband, and emotional dependence; (2) similarity of cultural backgrounds; (3) a harmonious and understanding family environment; (4) a socialized personality as evidenced by number of friends, participation in organizations, educational level; (5) the keeping up of religious observances; (6) an occupation with moderate economic status, superior education, high degree of social control, reasonable security and little or

[194] Burgess, I. W.: "Research", from a symposium entitled "*New Foundations for Marriage and Family*", in *Marriage and Family Living*, Sumner, 1946, pp. 64–5,—quoted by Christensen, H. T.: *Marriage Analysis*, Ronald Press, New York, 1950, pp. 186–7.

no mobility; (7) a love relationship growing out of companionship rather than infatuation; and (8) wholesome growth of attitude towards sex and similarity strength of sex desire of husband and wife.

Concealment of the defects of the bride by her father or her kinsmen is a highly punishable offence.[195] Once, however, the defects or blemishes of the bride are openly declared before marriage, the kinsmen are not liable to any punishment even if the defect consists of such serious disease as leprosy, or such serious blemish as loss of virginity (*sprishṭamaithunā*).[196] If, however, the husband discovers such disease or loss of chastity in the bride after the marriage, and these were not disclosed to him before, he may abandon her.[197] Nay, even the whole agreement of marriage may be annulled, if the girl possesses blemishes which were not declared before.[198] According to Nārada, if any concealed defects in the husband were disclosed after marriage to the woman, who is herself faultless, such marriage also could be dissolved.[199]

Kauṭilya says that the person who marries a girl without declaring his own blemishes shall be punished not only with double the fine imposable upon the father or other kinsmen of the bride for a similar offence on their part in concealing her defects, but he shall also forfeit the *śulka* (money) and the *strī-dhana* (bride's property) that might have been paid by him for the bride.[200] Ordinarily, in the opinion of Kauṭilya, a bride cannot be rejected after the *pāṇigrahaṇa* rite is performed: but she can be rejected even after *pāṇigrahaṇa* if it is afterwards detected that she had been unchaste. "In the case of brides and grooms of pure character and high conduct",[201] however, the question of rejection on any other account can never be raised.

Nārada and Parāśara have laid down that marriage could be dissolved if the husband is found to be impotent (*klība*)[202] Nārada's theory is that woman is the field (*kshetra*) and man is the seed-giver (*bījin*); so the field must be given to one who has seed (*bījavate*).[203] Hence she who finds her husband devoid of virility may, after waiting for six months, choose another man as her husband. There are, according to these two *Smritis*, five cases of legal sanction, wherein the wife is allowed to marry a second husband: She may take a second husband, if the first is missing (*nashṭa*), or dead (*mrita*), or becomes an ascetic (*pravrajita*), or is impotent (*klība*), or is degraded from the caste (*patita*).[204] Nārada further adds that in such cases, the woman shall be enjoined by her relatives to seek another husband, even if she does not herself think of doing so! (Nār. xii, 96). Mādhavāchārya commenting on Parā. iv. 28, quotes an identical verse from Manu which, however, is not to be found in the text of Manu that has come to us today. In case the husband is missing, the wife who has no issue already must wait for his return for four years if she is a Brāhmaṇa, for three years if she is a Kshatriya, and for two years if she is a Vaiśya. But if the wife has already had an issue from the lost husband,

---

[195] Yāj. i, 66 (*uttama sāhasa*, high offence, punishable by a fine of 1,080 *paṇas*); Nār. xii, 31; Man. ix, 224 (fine of 96 *paṇas*).

[196] Man. viii, 205.

[197] Man. ix, 72; Yāj. i, 76; Vis, 162.

[198] Man. ix, 73.

[199] Nār. xii, 16; 96.

[200] Arth. p. 213 (Shamasastry's Tr.).

[201] Arth. p. 212 (Shamasastry's Tr.).

[202] Nār. xii, 16; Parā. iv, 28;

[203] Nār. xii, 18–19.

[204] Nār. xii, 97; cf. Parā. iv, 28; cf/ also *Mahānirvāṇatantra*, xi, 66: "*Shaṇḍhenodvāhitām kanyām kālātīte'pi pārthiva/jānan udvāhayedbhūyo vīdhiresha śivodituh*."

then each of these, respectively, is asked to wait for double the period mentioned above.[205] Gautama suggests that a wife may wait for six years for her husband who has disappeared.[206]

Kauṭilya has permitted the woman to abandon her husband if he is a bad character, or is long abroad, or has become a traitor to the king, or is likely to endanger the life of his wife, or has fallen from his caste or has lost virility.[207] Also in cases of the husband's absence for a long period abroad, the Brāhmaṇa, Kshatriya, Vaiśya and Śūdra wife has to wait for four, two, three and one years respectively, for his return, if she has no issue. But if she has an issue already, she must wait for double the period prescribed above; and during this period, the *jnāti* or the community must provide her with maintenance if she has none. She may wait for less period if she is not provided with maintenance. After this period of waiting is over she may marry any one whom she likes.[208]

Kauṭilya also speaks of divorce (*moksha*). A divorce may be obtained only in the case of mutual enmity and hatred between the husband and his wife. Neither the husband nor the wife could dissolve the marriage against the will of the other party.[209] But even Kauṭilya, who alone of the *Śāstrakāras* goes beyond the repudiation or rejection or abandonment (*tyāga*) as prescribed by *Smritis*, and gives a consideration to the problem of the divorce (*moksha*) of marriage, also stresses, like the *Smritis*, that marriages consecrated according to the Brāhma, Daiva, Ārsha and Prājāpatya forms cannot be dissolved at all.[210]

The remarriage of widows is generally not favoured by the *Smritis*. Or to put it in other words, even though, as we have seen above, the *Smritis* permit the widow to marry again, such re-marrying does not possess the sacramental character as the first marriage; the 're-marrying' is not 're-marriage'! "Once is a maiden given in marriage" seems to be the general rule of observance.[211] The *Smritis* as well as the *Kāmā-Sūtras* refer to a remarried widow as a *punarbhū*.[212] A true wife must preserve her chastity as much after as before her husband's death.[213] She should never insult his memory. Manu declares that the remarriage of widows is nowhere prescribed in the *Sāstras* which treat of marriage.[214] The *Smritis* eulogize the woman who keeps her husband's bed unsullied after his death.[215] Vātsyāyana too, though he makes reference to the *punarbhū*, speaks of her in rather reproaching terms. He refers to a *punarbhū*, as a widow (*vidhavā*) who, because she is unable to control her sex[216] seeks a person who is after enjoyment (*bhogin*).[217] He also calls her as a seeker after pleasure.[218] At another place he says that sexual relations with a *punarbhū* and a *vesyā* (prostitute) are not proper (*na sishṭah*), but they are not forbidden (*na pratishiddhah*), as they are

---

[205] Nār. xii, 98–99; Vas. xvii, 75–79; Gaut. xviii, 15–17.
[206] Gaut. xviii, 15.
[207] Arth. p. 175 (Shamasastry's Tr.).
[208] Arth. pp. 180–81.
[209] Arth. p. 171.
[210] Arth. p. 177.
[211] Man. ix, 47; '*sakrit kanyā pradīyate*'; Yāj. i, 65; also Nār. xii, 28.
[212] e.g., Man. ix, 175; Nār. xii, 46; Vas. xvii, 20; Vis. xv, 8.
[213] Man. v, 151; Yāj. i, 75, 83; Vis. xxv, 13–14.
[214] Man. v, 162: '*na dvitīyaś cha sādhvīnām kvachid bharto-padiśyate*; and in ix. 65: '*na vivāha-vidhāvuktam vidhavā-vedanam punah*'.
[215] Man. v, 151–65; Yāj. i, 75–77.
[216] '*indriya-daurbalyād āturā*'.
[217] Kām. iv, 2, 39.
[218] Ibid.: "*saukhyārthinī*".

meant merely for pleasure (*sukhārthatvāt*).[219] He thus ranks sex relation with a widow in the same category as that with a prostitute. The marriage rites, as we have already seen, require the bride necessarily to be a virgin according to Vātsyāyana also.[220] This means that for a widow, there could be no regular rites of marriage according to him also. If there be a widow, as mentioned above, having intimate relations with a man, then evidently for Vātsyāyana, such relations are not on the same level as those of sacred marriage relations. Manu and Yājnavalkya would say that the widow must not even mention the name of another man after her husband's death; she may spend her days of widowhood by emaciating her body, by living on pure flowers, roots and fruits.[221] The widow who remains chaste (*brahmacharye vyavasthitā*) reaches heaven after her death even though she has no son.[222] A widow who becomes unfaithful to her deceased husband has no claim on the property of her husband,—not even maintenance; she may even be excommunicated.[223]

The *Smritis*, however, give two cases in which a woman can re-marry with recitation of the sacred *mantras*, the first marriage being considered by them as no marriage at all. Thus a damsel, abducted by force, and not wedded with the recitation of the sacred texts, may be lawfully given to another man; for, "she is as good as a maiden."[224] The second case is that of a damsel who is married with the recitation of the sacred texts, but whose husband dies before the consummation of the marriage.[225] If such a woman is still a virgin, she can go through the sacrament of *vivāha*. The *Mahānirvāṇatantra* also mentions a similar situation when a married woman is allowed to marry a second time; it says that a maiden who has been married (*pariṇītā*) but who has not co-habited (*na ramitā*) with her husband till his death, is eligible for marriage again; such is the law among the Śaivas (*śaiva-dharmeshvayam vidhih*).[226]

A man who has entered the *grihasthāśrama* must not, under the rules of the *Smritis*, remain single. After the death of his wife, he should, according to the religious rites, take another wife without delay.[227] The *Mitākśarā*, commenting on this rule of Yājnavalkya, says, that it holds good in case the husband has not obtained any male issue from his first wife. So that, in the latter case, even during the life-time of the first wife, the husband is allowed to take another wife. The *Smritis* permit a man to marry any number of wives from his own *varṇa* or from any of the lower ones, but he has never to take a wife from a *varṇa* higher than his own.[228] Yājnavalkya interprets this regulation as putting a restriction on the number of wives allowed for a man. Thus, a Brāhmaṇa can marry four wives, one from each *varṇa*; the Kshatriya can marry three wives, one from his own *varṇa* and one

---

[219] Kām. i, 4, 3.

[220] See *ante*, Footnotes 30–31.

Also Man. vii, 226: "The nuptial texts are applicable solely to virgins and nowhere among human beings to females who have lost their virginity, for such females are excluded from sacred ceremonies (*pāṇigrahaṇikā mantrāh kanyāsveva pratishṭhītāh/nākanyāsu kvachit nrīṇām lupta-dharma-kriyā hitāh*).

[221] Man. v, 157; Yāj. i, 75.

[222] Man. v, 160; Yāj. i, 75; Parā. iv, 26; Vis. xxv, 17.

[223] Nār. xii, 51 ff.; Parā. x, 26–35.

[224] Vas. xvii, 73; Baudh. iv, 1, 1, 15.

[225] Man. ix, 176: *sā ched akśatayonih syāt . . . paunarbhavena . . punah samskāram arhati/*; also Nār. xii, 46; Vas. xvii, 20; Baudh. iv, 1, 16; Vis. xv, 8.

[226] *Mahānirvāṇatantra* xi, 67.

[227] Yāj. i, 89; cf. Man. v, 167–9.

[228] Man. iii, 13; Yāj. i, 57; Bau. i, 16, 2–5; Vas. i, 24–25; Vis. xxiv, 1–4.

from each of the next two *varṇas*; the Vaiśya can marry two wives; and the Śūdra can marry only one wife.[229]

From the point of view of the Hindu, there is an important question to be considered in relation to the number of wives allowed for a man, viz., the continuity of the family line. It takes us back to the very basis upon which the Hindu *vivāha* system is based. According to it, marriage is necessary because the continuity of the family line is essential,[230] and for the fulfilment of the social and personal duties and obligations (*riṇas*) (See next Chapter on Family). Again, this continuity, depends on the male issue; for the daughter is a member of the family only till her marriage.[231] It is therefore of the very essence of a marriage union that sons should be born of it. *Moksha* is obtainable through sons and grandsons.[232] Therefore, man should marry more than once in case the first marriage fails to promote its main objective of begetting a male offspring. This seems to be the main idea underlying the permissive sanction for more than one wife to the Hindu. This is further evident from a consideration of the demands of mutual relations of fidelity between husband and wife, which we have discussed elsewhere.[233] It is their duty to perform religious rites and sacrifices together. And, so long as a householder (*grihastha*) has already a wife who is able to take part with him in his religious duties as a *grihastha*, and also has borne him issues, he must not take another woman for his wife.[234]

That polygyny, though thus theoretically sanctioned, was looked upon as more or less exceptional event, is evident also from a consideration of the rules laid down for the 'supersession' of the first wife. Thus, according to Manu, a wife who is barren (*vandhyā*) may be superseded by another wife in the eighth year after marriage; she whose children do not survive, may be superseded by another wife in the tenth year after marriage; she who brings forth only female issues may be superseded by another wife in the eleventh year; while a quarrelsome wife may be superseded by another without any delay.[235] But, a wife who is "kind to her husband and virtuous in her conduct may be superseded only with her consent, and must never be disgraced" by such an act even though she happens to be diseased (*rogiṇī*).[236]

The most desirable state of married life is of course that in which both the husband and his wife are mutually devoted to each other till death.[237] "Let man and woman, united in marriage, constantly exert themselves that they may never be disunited and may not violate their mutual fidelity".[238]

The *Artha-Śāstra* lays down slightly different rules in regard to marrying more wives than one, of which the following would be a brief statement:[239] If the first wife has no issue at all, or has no male child, the husband has to wait for eight years; thereafter he may marry another woman. If she

---

229 Yāj. i, 57.

230 Yāj. i, 77; Āp. ii, 5, 11, 12, etc.

231 Excepting in the case of an 'appointed' daughter, which is a remedy for continuity of family line devised by the Hindu lawgivers.

232 Yāj. i, 77; Āp. ii, 5, 11, 12.

233 See next chapter on Family.

234 Āp. ii, 11, 12—(*dharma-prajā-sampanne dāre nānyām kurvīta.*)

235 Man. ix, 81.

236 Man. ix, 82: *Yā rogiṇī syāt tu hitā sampannd chaiva sīl$$ta$$/sānujnāpyādhivettavyā nāvamanyā cha karhichit//*

237 Man. ix, 101: "*Anyonyasyāvyabhīchāro bhaved āmaraṇānt $$/esha dharmah samāsena jneyah strī-pumsayoh parah//*"

238 Man. ix, 102.

239 Arth. pp. 174 f.

ever bore a dead child, the waiting period for the husband is extended to ten years. And, if she is mother of female issues only, the husband has to wait for twelve years before marrying another woman. For, "women are created for the sake of sons".[240] The man who violates the above rule will have to pay the first wife not only her *Śulka* and *Strīdhana* property but also an adequate monetary compensation (*adhiveda-nikam artham*), in addition to a fine of twenty-four *paṇas* to the Government. In fact, he may marry "any number of women", provided he gives his wives proportionate compensation and adequate subsistence (*vritti*).[241]

Vātsyāyana's view about the number of wives allowed for a man is a little different from that stated above. He advises the first wife herself, if she happens to have had no issue from the marriage, to persuade her husband to marry another wife. The man should marry a second wife if the first wife bears no male issue, and if the continuity of the family is not ensured.[242] Though, at one place, he refers to the person devoted to one wife (*ekachārin*),[243] the reference looks like a eulogy bestowed on an exceptional virtue. For, at another place, he advises the young maiden to choose a poor man as a husband who may be solely devoted to herself only (*ātma-dhāraṇa*), rather than a rich man whose riches would probably divide his love between many (*bahusādhāraṇah*).[244] But here it is also probable that Vātsyāyana is perhaps referring not to the love that was divided between more than one lawfully wedded wives, but between the wife and the paramours and mistresses, of whom he gives lengthy descriptions, and which seems to have been a fashion amongst the wealthy of his times.[245]

Continuity of the family, as has been already pointed out, is the primary object of *vivāha*. A man is allowed to marry any number of wives primarily with this object in view. There is also another provision for the purpose mentioned for the widow whose husband dies without bearing her a son. Such a woman is allowed to bear a son to the younger brother of her husband, or any *sapiṇda or sagotra* of the husband.[246] This custom was known as *Niyoga* (levirate); and as will be seen from the stringent regulations prescribed for the same mentioned below, it was actuated with the sole purpose of begetting a son for the son-less widow. The person who was appointed under *Niyoga* to beget a son for the widow was to approach her "anointed with clarified butter, silently, to give one son only, and, by no means second".[247] After the purpose of *niyoga* was attained, the man and the woman had to behave towards each other like a father and a daughter-in-law.[248] If they behaved otherwise, they became guilty of defiling the bed of a *Guru* or of a daughter-in-law.[249] The child born of *niyoga* was regarded as a *kshetraja* son of the deceased husband, i.e. he was obtained in the field (*kshetra* i.e. the wife) of the deceased; therefore he was considered as belonging to the deceased husband.[250] However, this custom has been looked down with distinct abhorrence by the *Smritis*.

---

[240] Arth. p. 174.
[241] Arth. p. 174.
[242] Kām. iv, 2, 3.
[243] Kām. i, 4, 43.
[244] Kām. iii, 4, 55–56.
[245] See Kām. v.
[246] Yāj. i, 68–69; Gaut. xviii, 4; Man. ix, 59–60; Āpa. 20, 27, 2–3; Nār. xii, 80–81.
[247] Man. ix, 60; Yāj. i, 68; Nār. xii, 80–81.
[248] Man. ix, 62: *guruvachcha snushāvachcha varteyātām parāsparam.*
[249] Man. ix, 63.
[250] Ibid.

Manu considers it as beastly behaviour (*paśu-dharma*) and therefore inhuman, and prescribed nowhere in the *Dharma-Śāstra*.[251] Other *Smriti* writers too do not regard it as a proper custom.[252]

This brings us to a close of the survey of the institution of *vivana*. Before concluding, however, a few remarks on the system and institution of *vivāha*, as the Hindu conceives it, would not be out of place.

The various Vedic *mantras* recited by the bride, the groom and other parties concerned at the *vivāha* ceremony reveal some of the vital social implications underlying the Hindu view and aim of *vivāha*. These *mantras* repeat and reiterate the fundamental ideas and ideals of *vivāha*, to fulfil which the couple pledge themselves together. Socially as well as personally, both the husband and wife are conceived as equal, having equally important functions and status. The couple are asked to start their after-marriage career as the joint keepers of the home, in which capacity they are exhorted to strive their best to fulfil their marriage vow of not failing each other in the pursuit of *dharma, artha* and *kāma*. In the home, both the husband and wife are conceived as possessing rights, obligations and status consistent with the nature and the capacity of each of the two; and these rights, obligations, and status, though rightly not regarded as *identical*, are nonetheless viewed as *equal in importance* for the proper nurture of the family, and of its traditions and culture.

Thus, the wife is as much the mistress of the home (*grihapatnī*) as the husband is the master of the home (*grihapati*). Besides, the wife is the supreme ruler (*samrājnī*) of the household. Each of them is repeatedly reminded to regard the other as his and her indispensable complement for the fulfilment of the various social and domestic obligations enjoined on those in charge of a household (*gārhapatyāya*). The newly married couple is exhorted to live in perfect harmony with each other, ever avoiding quarrelling and always happy with each other (*modamānau; mā viyaushṭam*); and the couple on their part pray together that the Higher Powers bless them with a complete union of hearts (*samāpo hridayāni nau*) as well as bodies (*tanvam*). The couple was exhorted not only to fulfil the biological obligations of reproduction and nurture of the children, but to live to be father and mother of heroes and leaders (*vīrasū*). And, they were asked not only to carry out the social obligations connected with the *dharmas* of the *grihasthāśrama* but also to fulfil the individual or psychological obligation of exerting to attain the fullness of each other's personalities in each other's company, till their bodies withered by age and death came to them. From the social side, *vivāha* may be said to be a recognition and acceptance by the bride and the groom of the *āchāras* and *dharmas*, the practices and the ideals, that prevail in and rule the community to which they belong.

Also, our brief survey of the problem of marriage will give a fair indication of the ideas, ideals and purposes underlying the Hindu marriage. In the first place, one of the purposes underlying the *vivāha* seems to be in the endeavour to secure the best progeny for the family, for the fulfilment of which man must take the best bride available and the maiden is wedded to the best groom available. Secondly, the problem of marriage-relationship is not decided somehow or anyhow by the parents; it is sought to be solved, on the contrary, with a view to serving the needs of regulated social behaviour, organization and control; all these are broadly and generally defined by the *Grihya-Sūtras* and the *Dharma-Sūtras*; though later on they were modified or altered by customs of the *varṇas*, and of the times and places (*deśa* and *kāla*), all the same the *Sūtra* tradition may be said to be have been generally followed and practised by all the *varṇas* and the *jātis*. In fact, the problem

---

[251] Man. ix, 66–68.

[252] Brih. Smr. xiv, 12; Baudh. ii, 3, 33 c; Āp. ii, 27, 2 ff.; Hār. xii, 81; and 48; Nār. iv, 17.

of marriage relationship was sought to be solved on the basis of deliberation, choice and selection with reference to certain guiding principles and rules, and not of any personal infatuation or fancy.

And, if in addition to this, we consider the after-marriage relations between the man and his wife as sanctified ceremonially in terms of the *samskāras* that follow the *vivāha*, we may be enabled to see the depth of the seriousness and scrutiny which amounts to sacredness that is attached to married life. In these ceremonials, the vow (*vrata*) of celibacy (*brahmacharya*) has to be observed for a brief period after marriage; and the mating rites presuppose and ordain that the mere satisfaction of sex-impulse of the couple is not the main idea underlying their marriage, and reminds them that they are wedded and they mate essentially in order to live a life of higher purposes. Further, in this connection, we should also consider the other rules laid down in the *Dharma-Śāstras* regarding the control of sex-life, wherein sexual relations are considered lawful only under certain conditions of the body and the mind and the whole being of each of the parties concerned, while all other sexual relations are classified as *vyabhichāra* or misconduct or not becoming human being. And, if we put and co-ordinate all these considerations together, we can well understand how the best interests of the propagation of the species, of the upkeep of the line of *pitris* whose descendants' sacred place of dwelling and doing is to be the home, are expected to be subserved by the institution of *vivāha* by observing a life of self-control by both the man and his wife who become the managers of the home for the while. In fact, the responsibilities, duties and obligations, as also the advantages for the *grihastha* and the *grihinī*, which the groom and the bride are going to become, are summed up during the marriage ceremony and held up before the vision of the new couple, for the fulfilment and satisfaction of which they pledge themselves jointly at the wedding.

CHAPTER VI

THE FAMILY

Though almost everybody is born in a family and seems to know and understand what family is from first hand experience, yet the many special studies which have been devoted in recent years to "The Family"[1] bring out very prominently how very difficult it is to define precisely and briefly the institution of the family. In a recent comprehensive and careful study of the family, Burgess and Locke have defined it as "a group of persons united by ties of marriage, blood or adoption; constituting a single household; interacting and communicating with each other in respective social roles of husband and wife, mother and father, son and daughter, brother and sister; and creating and maintaining a common culture." They also point out that "The two necessary elements in the definition of a phenomena are that (1) it should be wide enough to include all cases to be covered, and (2) it should be specific enough to exclude all marginal cases", like the household, kin, fraternity, etc., if we are concerned with defining the family. And, presumably, in their judgment, the above definition of the family satisfies these conditions. In the view of MacIver and Page, the family is "a group defined by a sex relationship sufficiently precise and enduring to provide for the procreation and upbringing of children", and "It may include collateral or subsidiary relationships, but it is constituted by the living together of mates, forming with their offspring a distinctive unity".[2]

All these generalizations are probably based entirely or very largely upon the family institution as it is known among the western peoples. However, as Dunlap has been careful to point out, it is well-nigh impossible to define the family universally "except in an arbitrary way."[3] It is true that in one of its well-known forms, it consists of a man and a woman with their joint children living together in the same abode during the minority of their children.[4] But even this form has many variations. Thus, there are families without children; or with adopted children; or with the man having a different abode of his own than the woman and the children; or with the grandparents, aunts, uncles, and/or grandchildren as members; or with more than one wife or husband or both; or in which there is the widowed mother with her children; or in which there is the single mother with her adopted children.[5] And, there may be a community, like the Nayars of South India, who have excluded the satisfaction of sexual needs from the functions of the family.[6] Their women marry according to Hindu custom, but the actual father has no control over his children who belong to the mother's group, have no claims over him or his property, and may even use their mother's brother's name

---

[1] Burgess, E. W. and Locke, H. J.: *The Family*, p. 8.

[2] MacIver, R. M. and Page, C. *Society*, p. 238.

[3] Dunlap, K.: *Civilized Life: The Principles and Applications of Social Psychology*, pp.136–7.

[4] Ibid.

[5] Ibid.

[6] Thurston, E.& Rangachar: *Tribes and Castes of South India.* Madras, 1909. See also, Linton, R.: *The Study of Man*, pp. 154–8.

as part of their full name. Further, though most families are characterized by the union of man and woman and their offspring, if any, yet once a family is established it persists even after the man or the woman is dead. In the opinion of Nimkoff, if there is no offspring born, it would be improper to speak of the family, for there is no such thing as a "childless family"; a more correct expression in such a case would be "childless marriage".[7] Domicile and residence together of the members of the family is one other criterion which it is difficult to apply strictly to the Hindu family, which, as we shall see in this chapter, is united mainly not by the so many physical and tangible bonds but much more by the spiritual, religious and psychological bonds between generations after generations as also between the members of the same generation.

Although the family began in its earliest origins as a reproductive or biological association, it has developed into a primary social unit of the highest importance for man. "Of all the organizations, large or small, which the society unfolds" observe MacIver and Page[8], "none transcends the family in the intensity of its sociological significance. It influences the whole society in innumerable ways, and its changes. . . . reverberate through the whole social structure. It is capable of endless variation and yet reveals a remarkable continuity and persistence through change (See Note 8)." As a social institution, it has emerged in order to satisfy certain very basic biological, psychological and social needs of man. And, even though it has gone through many changes during the past centuries and several of its original functions like the educational, the economic, the religious, and the recreational have been gradually taken away by other social and state agencies, yet its basic functions which center around the primary bio-psycho-social needs of man have not been affected. These primary functions are (1) the more stable satisfaction of the sex need of the man and the woman, (2) procreation, care and nurture of the young, and (3) the sharing of a home and all that this involves.[9] "Only in a *successful* family", say MacIver and Page, "are these three functions so united that each of them reinforces and enriches the satisfaction of the others. Sex becomes not a detached phenomenon—as it tends to be in extramarital relations and usually is in prostitution—but part of a larger experience of meeting common problems. And the nurture of the children takes place within the focus of the home which, as considerable evidence seems to indicate, is a more favourable environment for them than that of the state nursery of other public or private agencies."[10] Even in Russia, where the family has undergone by far greater changes than anywhere else in the world during the past thirty years, with nurseries for children and other services being highly developed under the control of the State so as to strip the family of many of its former functions, its primary biological and socio-psychological functions have not been affected.[11] "The central factor of continuity between the old and the new family in Russia," conclude Burgess and Locke after a survey of the Russian family, "is an intangible but very real thing, viz. deep family feeling and the affection and solicitude of parents for children, which survived the Revolution and now again is being expressed freely and openly." This means, therefore, "that the capacity of the family to persist under unfavourable conditions has been dramatically confirmed by the outcome of events in the Soviet Union. The evidence from the great Russian experiment seems to prove that the family can survive without the support of law and even in the face of governmental attempts to weaken and undermine it."[12] As

[7] Nimkoff, M. F.: *The Family*, p. 8.
[8] MacIver, M. R. & Page, C.: *Society*, p. 240.
[9] Ibid. pp. 254; 263–4.
[10] Ibid. (Italics in the original).
[11] Burgess, E. W. and Locke: op. cit., pp. 180–202.
[12] Ibid. p. 201–202.

Helen Bosanquet in her excellent work on the subject pointed out long ago, "Even if the world could carry on without the family, it could not afford to lose the qualities which would go with it. It is a sombre world as it is, and no shade or tone of feeling that makes for depth and variety and richness can be spared from it. To reject the source of so much warmth and beauty because it sometimes fails, would be like banishing the sun from the sky because it is sometimes covered with clouds."[13]

All this goes to prove the deep-rooted and all-embracing socio-psychological significance of the institution of the family for the individual and the society. Man is not born human, nor is he born social; but he becomes so both through association and communication and the family is the first and foremost agency in his "cultural conditioning" in this direction, by providing for him "his earliest behaviour patterns and standards of conduct."[14] The infant at birth is primarily on a biological level. Its first contacts by which it begins to become a social-psychological being are in the family. "The child is surrounded by social definitions in the family. Moral attitudes abound for every situation. Ideas of right and wrong are repeatedly emphasized. The child finds ready-made ways of doing things presented to him almost before the occasion arises for their use. . . . Sentiments built up around certain objects and practices become cogent factors in the lives of individuals. Ritualistic performances on special occasions, family traditions that have become sacred are closely related to sentimental attitudes. There are political, religious and social opinions that are potential forces in the family atmosphere. The pattern of behaviour and attitudes in the family reflect day after day the customs of the larger group in which the family finds itself."[15]

The earliest basic traits of the personality of the individual are formed in the family, which transmits the cultural heritage to him and thus maintains a cultural continuity between the individual and his society, and indeed between generations to generations of the society. It is the most effective link of cultural adjustment between them. "A baby is born, not only into a culture, but also into an environment of interpersonal relations. From the moment of birth the infant is in emotional and mental interaction first with its mother, and then with the other members of the family. These emotional experiences, psychological rather than cultural in their nature, give definitive shape to the initial structure of personality . . . . (which is) the unique configuration of an individual's pattern of responses to others and to himself as determined by psychogenic conditioning."[16] The genic traits and characteristics which are due to the biological inheritance provide the raw material for the shaping of personality; they provide the potentialities on the one hand and the limitations on the other within which personality traits could develop, improve or change. But, their actual "function and meaning develop in the psychogenic interaction and in social experience."[17] They are formed in the early emotional development of the child in the family environment, in the interpersonal relationships of the family. They include "tendencies to extroversion and introversion, dominance or submission, optimism or pessimism, emotional independence or dependence, self-confidence or lack of confidence in self, and ego-centrism or socio-centrism."[18] The interaction of the members of the family in their psychogenic aspects is termed by Burgess and Locke "the family psychodrama", with a psychological stage on which "the players take roles determined by the interplay of the emotions of love, fear, and hate, of the feelings of superiority and inferiority, and of reactions of

[13] Bosanquet, H.: *The Family*, p. 245. Macmillan, London, 1915.

[14] Burgess and Locke: op. cit., pp. 212–13.

[15] Brown, L. Guy: *Social Psychology*, 1934, p. 73.

[16] Burgess & Locke: op. cit., p. 241.

[17] Ibid. p. 243.

[18] Ibid. p. 244.

security, insecurity, adequacy, and inadequacy".[19] In such a psychodrama, the psychogenic reaction patterns of the individual are gradually shaped, moulded and fixed; and they are not likely to change afterwards. "In general, they tend to evolve according to the trends set up in early infancy. If they can be changed significantly it is probably only in the period in which they are being formed; i.e., in the early months and years of life."[20]

The psycho-social influence of the family environment on the child is so deep and so quick, that in the view of the psychologists the child acquired almost all its personality and character traits of later adulthood before five, and according to some, even earlier. Allport tells us of a careful observational study made by two psychologically-minded parents of their infant, keeping records of its behaviour, from the moment of its birth onwards upto four months. on the basis of which the following prophecy was made as to its future character: "ready laughter, well-adjusted i.e. 'normal' and 'introverted', capable of considerable temper, active, sensitive of rhythm, adaptable, wiry and muscular, tall, mischievous, with linguistic superiority."[21] These qualities, of course, could not have been actually observed in the infant at four months, but indications were noticeable in the child which suggested the beginnings of these qualities. Later, other teachers also co-operated in making analyses and records of the character and personality of the child without any knowledge of the previous records and without any knowledge of each other's records. These records, which were continued upto the age of nine of the child, corroborated in an astonishing manner the early prophecy regarding the child's prospective character. Allport concludes that *vague and variable indications of distinctive traits are evident at as early an age as even four months*, and that *from early infancy there is consistency in the development of personality*.[22] This study and other studies have been cited by Allport to show that the innate determinants of personality—since, at birth and upto four months, only innate tendencies would be manifest to a large extent—are very important;[23] but he further observes that they do not imply that the family environment has no effect on the development of the child's personality.[24] Indeed, it is possible that the original tendencies may be supported, modified or even destroyed according as the family environment is supporting, modifying or destructive of these tendencies,[25] though, the limits and scope of such changes are set by the innate tendencies. Environmental forces are bound to affect the child's character and personality development particularly during the first three to five years, by which time its psychogenic personality traits will have been nearly fixed and, as we have already pointed out earlier, no change in the environment later will appreciably alter these basic traits. If a personality appears to have changed dramatically in later life, on closer examination and analysis it would be found to have been changed not in its basic

---

[19] Ibid. p. 245.

[20] Ibid. p. 244.

[21] Allport, G. W.: *Personality—A Psychological Interpretation*, pp. 122–ff.

[22] Ibid. p. 125 (Italics in the original).

[23] cf. the Marāṭhī saying: '*mulāche pāya pāḷaṇyānt distāt*' i.e. 'An infant's feet (i.e. the direction his personality is going to take) are noticeable in the cradle.'

[24] Allport, op. cit., p. 125. Some eminent biologists, however, hold a strong hereditarian view in regard to man's development. For instance, Parker concludes that "we are perhaps about nine-tenths inborn and one-tenth acquired. What we get by education is a small acquisition planted in a very large inborn background"—Parker, G. H.: *The World Expands*, p. 252. Harvard University Press, Cambridge, Mass. Burgess and Locke also note that the biologists are inclined to stress the importance of biological heredity. See Burgess and Locke, op. cit., p. 242.

[25] Allport: op. cit.

psychogenic traits, but in 'social type', i.e., in the social expressions and manifestations of the traits. Thus, say Burgess and Locke:

"St. Paul on the road to Damascus was converted from a persecutor of Christianity to a proselytiser for it. This was a transformation in social attitudes, for in his new role he was the same dominating, self-confident, optimistic personality as of old. All such instances of profound transmutations from sinner to saint, from drunkenness to total abstinence, from radical to conservative, from pauper to millionaire, are changes in attitudes, in character, in ideals, in roles, and in social type, and not variations in psychogenic reaction patterns. These . . . . remain basically the same."[26]

The family, as a social unit, has already assimilated through years and ages, the traditions, the sentiments and the modes of behaviour of the society. It therefore plays the part of a suitable medium to convey these to its individual members. Thus in the family, 'the biological, psychological and sociological forces meet in giving the individual his start in life.'[27] The tremendous influence of the family on the individual is brought out from the negative side by indicating the harms into which a disorganised family is likely to involve the individual. "Families develop moral codes, more or less in conformity to the general sentiments, but with interesting variations. The family, more than any other group perhaps, affects the development of the individual's moral attitudes. It has an almost uncontested control over children in their earlier and most impressionable years. Sensitive to the prevailing culture, it seeks to transmit the moral ideas of the group to its members. When it fails in this task, through disorganization, the child may grow up with distorted sentiments and find itself socially isolated or at war with the community."[28]

Psychoanalysts have also emphasised this aspect of psychosocial influence of the family on the individual. Flügel observes that "Even on a superficial view it is fairly obvious that, under existing social conditions, the psychological atmosphere of the home life, with the complex emotions and sentiments aroused by and dependent on the various family relationships must exercise a very considerable effect on human character and development. Recent advances in the study of human conduct indicate that this effect is even greater than has been generally supposed: it would seem that, in adopting his attitude towards the members of his family circle, a child is at the same time determining to a large extent some of the principle aspects of his relations to his fellowmen in general; and that an individual's outlook and point of view in dealing with many of the most important questions of human existence can be expressed in terms of the position he has taken up with regard to the problems and difficulties arising within the relatively narrow world of the family."[29] Adler's studies of the child in its relation to the family, and Freud's psychoanalytical studies are too well known in this connection. Comte had recognised this deep influence of the family life upon the individual, when he said: "In the family life alone can the social instincts find any basis for growth."[30]

All the altruistic attitudes of man could be traced to their roots in the family life; co-operation, self-sacrifice, service to humanity, universal brotherhood, love of living beings, have been traced

---

[26] Burgess, E. W. & Locke, E. J.: *The Family*, p. 245.

[27] Young: *Social Psychology*, 1931, p. 237.

[28] Kreuger and Reckless: '*Social Psychology*', p. 274.

[29] Flügel, J. C.: *The Psychoanalytic Study of the Family*, p. 4.

[30] Comte: *Positive Philosophy*, vol. II, ch. V. quoted by Ellowed.

back to their origins to co-operation in the family-life.[31] The interaction of each of the members with the others in the family is of profound significance in determining the individual's mental attitudes and his behaviour in society. Dr. Burgess, therefore, has rightly stressed the importance of family as "a unity of interacting personalities"[32], and Walter and Hill refer to it as "an arena of interacting personalities."[33]

The foregoing analysis also indicates the functions which the family institution performs in a society. Among its most important functions are regulating and disciplining the sex impulse and giving it stability and durability, which is principally a function in relation to the two founders and the principal actors in the family psychodrama. Marriage and family are the means used by society to control promiscuous expression of sex and dissipation of man's energy which could be directed and used in many other useful channels, without, at the same time, entirely suppressing the sex. In fact, they make sex a more meaningful, a more enriching experience. "All other things being equal", says Nimkoff, "sex expression in marriage proves to be more satisfying than sex expression apart from marriage. Psychology has made the reason for this fact clear. For civilized human beings, satisfaction in the expression of any fundamental drive depends not merely upon the act of the expression alone, but also upon the factors associated with it. For example, a civilized human being is not satisfied to eat just anything at all. His pleasure varies with the nature of food, the way it is prepared, and the conditions under which it is consumed. Sex is in no way different, unless it be that satisfaction here depends even more upon attending circumstances. Marriage (and family, we may add) makes possible such a conditioning of the sexual relationship as to give to it the greatest significance of which it is capable. In marriage, sex may become enriched by all the sentiments which association in an enterprise affords. Sex acquires a depth and breadth of meaning which it otherwise lacks. Thus marriage regulates sex in order to make it more meaningful".[34]

A most important service of the family is that it provides for the satisfaction of what Thomas regards as the four "fundamental" wishes or desires, viz., the wishes for new experience, for security, for recognition and for response,[35] because these and their combinations perhaps include all other desires and therefore can be used to explain the inner motivations of all social behaviour.[36] These wishes are universal, and represent the fundamental needs underlying all social relationships. The family is the most significant field where every individual takes his first lessons in the satisfaction of these wishes. The actual concrete desires of individuals will vary from time to time and culture to culture, but they will be found to be combinations of two or more of these fundamental wishes which are the ultimate underlying motives of social behaviour. For instance the wish for mastery or power is a combination of the wishes for recognition and security,[37] and so on.

Thus, the new experiences, the new stimuli, the new associations the child meets with in the family environment aid in its mental and social development. The satisfaction of the need for security begins with the physical and emotional security, given to it from birth onwards by embracing, caressing, nursing and other kinds of personal attention. "Typically, the family is a haven of

---

[31] Ellwood: "*Sociology in its Psychological Aspects*", pp. 213 ff.

[32] Burgess, E. W. "The Family as a Unity of Interacting Personalities", in "*The Family*", Vol. VII (March, 1926), pp. 3 ff.

[33] Waller, W. and Hill, R. *The Family: A Dynamic Interpretation*, Ch. 2, Dryden Press, N. Y. 1951.

[34] Nimkoff, M. F.: *The Family*, (1934), pp. 55–56.

[35] Burgess & Locke: op. cit., pp. 302 ff.

[36] Ibid. Also Britt, S.H., *Social Psychology of Modern Life* (1949) pp. 106–8.

[37] Burgess and Locke: op. cit., pp. 318, 327.

security to which its members turn for comfort and reassurance from the troubles and trials of the outside world. . . . in adjustments to the outside world. Two hampering conditions to personal adjustment are the lack of family security or overdependence upon it. The function of family security is to promote rather than interfere with the transition from the stage of dependence to that of independence."[38] The need for recognition is satisfied through the roles the child plays in the family, the attention he secures, the statuses he occupies, the approvals he gets therein. The need for response is satisfied through the affection and the comradeship he receives in the family. In fact, the responses in the family are more intimate than elsewhere and are always reciprocal, between the husband and the wife, between parents and children. Ogburn has rightly stressed the affectional bond as a very important one that holds the family together, and the one bond on which the family must continue to rely for its solidarity even if all the others fail or are reduced in strength.[39] Through the affectional bond in the family, man, woman and child learn the technique and expression of affectional virtues which stand them in service in dealing with the outside world. The "feeling of being alone and apart from others comes much less frequently to those who have families of their own. Even when there is friction between the husband and wife, the desire of each for intimate response may be satisfied."[40]

Apart from economic security, the family in many societies affords a religious security to its members. This is particularly true of the Hindu family. The Hindu parents find a spiritual immortality through their sons. Their future life here and hereafter is blessed through sons and their sons and their religious and social behaviour. Family prayers and rituals have to be gone through by elders with children. The family, the home, is the place to which one can look for personal psychological peace and security. It is the retreat to which man retires after the day's work and his dealings with the outside world to relax, to recoup, and to regain his physical and psychic balance in order to be able to deal effectively with the outside environment again.[41]

We may conclude this section with one or two general observations: The family must have had its origins in the biological phenomenon of reproduction, but, it gradually developed into a socio-psychological phenomenon of the highest significance. On the one hand, several of its functions have been taken away from it by various agencies, and on the other, despite this, its central function of affectional unity has become stronger and stronger in the more complex and civilized societies. And finally, in some civilized societies, and predominantly among the Hindus, as we shall notice below, the original biological functions and the satisfaction of the sex were positively made subservient to the higher values of life, to moral and spiritual life and to life after death.

I

This general background and discussion on the family will help us to understand the Hindu family psychodrama in its proper perspective, and we may now begin our inquiry into the structure and functions of the Hindu Family. The real family life of a *Snātaka*, i.e. one who has completed his

[38] Ibid. 309–10.

[39] Ogburn, W.I.: "Social Heritage and the Family", pp. 24–39 in *Family Life Today*, Houghton Wifflin, 1928—Quoted by Nimkoff, op. cit. pp. 57–60.

[40] Nimkoff: op. cit. p. 56.

[41] Nimkoff: Ibid. pp. 76–7.

course of the *brahmacharyāśrama*, starts with his marriage (*vivāha*). Beginning from the acceptance of the bride's hand, that is, as soon as he is wedded, the man is to prepare himself to undertake "the activities connected with the home" (*grihyam*).[42] Here, according to the Hindu *Dharma-Śāstras*, he has to practice all those rites (*vidhis*) intended for the preservation and continuity of the *kula*, which word may be translated as the 'Family'. With the sacred fire kindled at the wedding, the *grihī* (i.e. the *grihastha*) has to follow, according to the rules and regulations and directions of the *śāstras*, the domestic activities and duties and the "five great sacrifices" (*pancha mahā-yajnas*).[43] These five sacrifices are intended to expiate the sins committed by a *grihastha*, and which, as a *grihastha*, he cannot but help committing, at the five "slaughter-houses",[44] as it were, which exist in each home, viz., the hearth (*chullī*), the grinding-stone (*peshaṇī*), the broom (*upaskarah*), the pestle and mortar,[45] and the water-vessel.[46] While using these implements and tools in the home, he would wittingly or unwittingly cause destruction of so many creatures, like ants, worms, etc. The five great sacrifices are the *Brahma-yajna*, the *Pitri-yajna*, the *Deva-yajna*, the *Bhūta-yajna* and the *Nri-yajna* (or *Manushya-yajna*).[47]

These expiatory sacrifices are performed in terms of the execution of certain social and human duties. Thus, teaching and studying are to be pursued as expressive of the *brahma-yajna*, which is offered to the memory of the distinguished and learned sages of the past (*rishis*); the offering of water and food known as *turpana* and offered at the *śrāddha* ceremony forms the sacrifice to the spirit or memory of the ancestors (*pitri-yajna*); oblations offered to the sacred fire (*homa*) have reference to the sacrifice to the gods (*deva-yajna*); offering of food to alleviate and propitiate the spirits which are supposed to influence human being constitutes the *bhūta-yajna*; and the hospitable offerings of food and shelter to guests and strangers (*atithi-pūjanam*) has to be performed in a spirit of sacrifice to man (*nri-yajna*).[48] Every householder (*kuṭumbin*) must offer these five great sacrifices in order to gain permanent (*nityam*) happiness.[49] Indeed, these five viz., the sages, the ancestors, the gods, the spirits and the strangers look up (*āśāsate*) to him in expectation of these offerings.[50] The *grihastha*-and-his-*grihiṇī* (*dampatī*) should take their meals only after (*śesha-bhug*) they have duly honoured the *rishis, devas, pitris, griha-devatas* (the guardian deities of the home), the *atithis* (guests) and the *bhrityas*[51] (servants). Therefore, a discipline of giving away, of parting with things of worldly value, is sought to be cultivated in the home.[52] Clarified butter, which is one of the most expensive articles of food, has to be poured out into the fire,[53] as a symbol of this. The householder aught never to seek to accumulate or amass wealth; he should live in the manner of a *śilonchha*, i.e. in the manner of one

---

[42] Āś. G.S. i, 9, 1: '*pāṇi-grahaṇādi grihyam paricharet*'; also Pār. G.S. i, 2, 1; Kh. G.S. i, 5, 1; Śān. i, 1; Hir. G.S. i, 7, 22, 2–3; Āp. G.S. ii, 5, 14; etc.

[43] Man. iii, 67; also, Yāj. 1, 97; Śān. G.S. i, 1 ff; Āś. G.S. i, 9; Pār. G.S. i, 2; Go. G.S. i, 1, etc.

[44] *Sūnā=paśuvadhasthānam*—(Kullūka).

[45] *Kaṇḍanī=ulūkhala-musale.*

[46] *Udakumbha.*

[47] Man. iii, 68–69.

[48] Man. iii, 70 and 81; Yāj. i, 102; Āś. G.S. iii, 1, 1–4.

[49] Man. iii, 79–81; Yāj. i, 23, 104.

[50] Man. iii, 80.

[51] Man. iii, 116–17; also Pār. G.S. ii, 9, 12–14; Yāj. i, 105. Pār. G.S. ii, 9, 15, however adds: "The householder, may, however eat before other members of the house".

[52] See the observations on the current use of the term *Yajamāna*, on pp. 63–65, *supra*.

[53] cf. Thoothi: '*The Vaishṇavas of Gujarāt*', p. 32.

who does not accumulate the harvest of the farm, but distributes that to those who are in need of it, while he himself lives on the fallen and abandoned stalks of corn and grain that remain on the farm after the harvest is taken away.[54]

The sacred fire kindled at the time of the *vivāha* has to be kept alive ceaselessly with great vigilance.[55] When the husband is absent from the house (as when he is on journey, etc.), this fire is to be looked after and worshipped by his wife or in her absence, by the son, or daughter or the pupil (*antevāsī vā*) as the case may be.[56] The wife has to undergo a fast if it goes out, in the opinion of some, says *Āśvalāyana*.[57]

The *Grīhya-Sūtras* have prescribed ceremonies and rituals for building a house too. The ceremonies symbolise prosperity of wealth, cattle and progeny in the house. The home is supposed to be the dwelling place not only for the living members of the family, but also for the fathers and fore-fathers who have passed away and for the children and grand-children who are to come. The owner of the house to be built draws, with an Udumbara* branch, three times a line round the building-ground while uttering: "Here I include the dwellings for the sake of food", and sacrifices in its centre on an elevated spot, with the *mantras*, "Who art thou? Whose art thou? To whom do I sacrifice thee, desirous of dwelling in the village? *Swāhā!* Thou art the god's share on this earth. From here have sprung the fathers who have passed away. . . ." etc.[58] There are invocations to the deities asking them to guard the home, that it may be 'prosperous, long-lasting, standing amid prosperity', and to which "may the child come; and the calf."[59] The builder of the house establishes the sacred fire inside the house after it is built,[60] and entering the house offers oblations to the Vāstoshpati (Lord of dwelling) in order that he may be saviour of the human beings and animals that may come to dwell in the house.[61]

In such a home, the *grihastha* (*kuṭumbin*) has to satisfy the *rishis* by studying and learning (*svādhyāya*), worship the *devas* (gods) by burnt oblations, remember the *pitris* (manes) by *tarpaṇa* offerings (*srāddha*), serve men by offering food (*anna*) to them and other living creatures (*bhūtas*) by the *bali* offerings.[62] And, after he has thus attained freedom from all obligations and dues to the society (*ānriṇyam gatvā*), i.e. having satisfactorily fulfilled them in and through the home in accordance with the *śāstras*, he is to make over everything to the son, and dwell in his home without caring for any worldly concern.[63]

The *grihastha* has to do all these activities as a matter of duty; besides, by fulfilling these obligations, he enhances his *dharma*. For, after a householder's (*kuṭumbin*) death neither father, nor mother, nor wife, nor sons, nor relations stay with him to be his companions to help him

---

[54] Yāj. i, 128.
[55] Āśv. G.S. i, 9, 2.
[56] Āśv. G.S. i, 9, 1; Śan. G.S. ii, 17, 3.
[57] Āśv. G.S. i, 9, 3.
* The symbolic significance of using a branch of Udumbara tree in this connection is obvious. Its branches grow rather evenly on all sides. Its life is also rather long, and it bears fruit profusely. When full grown, it covers a wide area under the roofs of its branches, and therefore can afford cool shelter to a large number of people under it.
[58] Śān. G.S. iii, 2, 1–2; cf. also Āśv. G.S. ii, 7 f.; Gobh. Gr. S. iv, 7; etc.
[59] Sān. G.S. iii, 9; Āśv. G.S. ii, 8, 16; Pār. G.S. iii, 4, 4; etc.
[60] Pār. G.S. 4, 5 gives a lengthy ritualistic description of this.
[61] Śān. G.S. iii, 4, 2; Pār. G.S. iii, 4, 7; Kh. G.S. iv, 2, 6–21; Āp. vii, 17; etc.
[62] Man. iii, 81; also Yāj. i, 23; 104.
[63] Man. iv, 257.

(*sahāyārtham*); *dharma* alone remains with him.[64] "Single is each person born, single he dies; single he enjoys the fruit of good deeds, and single he suffers the penalty of sins. Leaving the dead body on the ground like a log of wood or a clod of earth, the relatives depart from him. Only his *dharma* follows him. Let him, therefore, incessantly act for the gradual accumulation of *dharma*, in order that it may be of help to him after death. For, with the help of *dharma*, he will be able to traverse a gloom (*tamas*) which is otherwise difficult to pass through."[65]

The foregoing outline of the Hindu's *griha*, its relation to the householder, and the rites and rituals by which it has to be incessantly hallowed is sufficient to give us some clue into the psychology of the Hindu home. As we have said, the Hindu home is the dwelling place not only of the living members of the family, but also of the *pitris*, the ancestors, under the care and blessings of *Agni*,—the sacred Fire, the presiding deity of the home. The *panchamahāyajnas* have to be performed in the presence of *Agni*. The fathers and fore-fathers are to be remembered every day at the time of *pitri-yajna*. And, even the Śūdra, the lowest class, is allowed to practise the *panchamahāyajnas*, though he has to do this without the recitation of the *mantras*.[66] Thus the psychology of spiritual continuity forms the basis of the Hindu's family and its traditions (*kula-dharma* and *kula-paramparā*). The living members of the family are, so to speak, trustees of the home which belongs to the *pitris*, the ancestors, in the interests of the *putras*,—future members of the family. All the property enjoyed by the members of the family belongs to the home and not to any particular member or members of the family. And the home consists of a continuity of all the members of the family—past members that are no more, present members that are living, and future members that are to come into being. The home therefore is the place wherein there is common kitchen, common property, common god, common weal and common woe. The central idea here is the worship of the family (*kula*) as a temple of sacred traditions (*paramparā*).

Life in this world, for the Hindu, is a sojourn.[67] The individual does not belong to the home, nor does the home belong to the individual. He comes from elsewhere, belongs to elsewhere, where he shall have to go. The individual has to perform his due *dharmas* and *karmas* here, without manifesting any sign of ownership. All the home property belongs, in the social meaning, to the individual's fore-fathers, and his progeny, not to the individual himself. In this sense, we may say, that the home is supposed to belong to the perpetual Agni in the home, the symbol of the continuity of the family.

The home, moreover is the place where the *Dharma-Śāstras* as also the *Artha-Śāstras* and the *Kāma-Śāstras* are practised. It is the place where the *dharmas* and the *karmas* are thought out, practised and idealized. Even though the *grihastha* is free to behave in any way he likes within normal limits, within the four walls of his house, there is always present a divine witness (*sākshī*) to each and every one of his deeds in the form of the Agni, the permanent sacred fire of the home, who keeps watch over, blesses, directs and inspires the *dharmas* and the *karmas* of the inmates of the home. He is also the intercessor between man and his departed forefathers, and between man and the Gods. He is the God's representative to interpret the divine to man and the human to the Gods.[68] The *griha* thus belongs in this sense, to *Agni-Deva*, and to the past and coming members of the family, and partially only—and that in a limited sense—to the *grihastha* himself.

---

[64] Man. iv, 239.

[65] Man. iv, 239–242.

[66] Yāj. i, 121; Man. x, 127, and Kullūka's commentary on it; also cf. Vish. Purā. iii, 8, 33; Mahā. Śānti. 60, 35–37.

[67] See our discussions in chapter II.

[68] Cf. Thoothi: *The Vaishṇavas of Gujarāt*, p. 32.

It is in view of these ideas and ideals that the *grihastha* is asked to live a life of non-attachment in the family; thus a spirit of selflessness, (*aliptatva* or *samnyasta vritti*) even while conducting the affairs of the world, restrains and dominates his thought and action. The *grihastha* should himself feel perfectly at peace in the *griha*, realising that after all the *griha* is really in charge of and under the guidance and supervision of Agni.

We can thus see that there are two kinds of checks upon the Hindu *grihastha:* In the first place, the individual himself does not belong to this *samsāra*. He belongs elsewhere. For him, the *samsāra* is *kshaṇa-bhangura*—a temporary field of action (*karma-bhūmi*). In the second place, his life in *grihasthāśrama* must be lived and directed only in terms of necessary *dharmas* and *karmas*. To the extent to which the individual performs these, he prepares himself for the next stage of life, and then the final goal, viz. *mokśa*.

II

With this preliminary survey of the salient points in the general psychology of Hindu family life, we shall now commence a review of the Hindu family in relation to its members and *vice versa*, and the interpersonal relations of the members among themselves, in order to get a complete view of the socio-psychological implications of the Hindu family. The first thing that strikes us when we consider the Hindu family is its joint nature. All the members of the family live together in the same abode. The family circle is not the narrow one consisting of parents and children only; very often it used to be as wide as could be, there being presumably no limit on its size. But, it seems that normally the joint family included three generations; for, the life-span of three generations is around a hundred years; and it would be extremely rare that an individual may outlive a century. The Hindu law texts have taken note of this fact, since, under the rules of the Law of Partition, any member of a joint family who is removed more than three degrees from the common ancestor can claim a share on partition.[69] Occasionally, however, the family may include in the Hindu society four generations; and, of course, any number of members.[70] "Not only parents and children, brothers and step-brothers live on the common property, but it may sometimes include ascendants, descendants and collaterals upto many generations."[71]

All these members of the joint family lived under the same roof, and shared the property of the family in common;[72] and they do so even now in the more orthodox Hindu families and in the villages of India. Brihaspati speaks of the Hindu family as an association, the members of which share a common kitchen (*ekapākena vasatām*).[73] The members performed their daily sacred *sandhyā* rites before the same fire, and the daily sacrifices and worship of fire used to be performed at the common hearth. Every member of the family has to undergo the *Samskāras*, the sacraments

---

[69] Jolly: *Outlines of an History of the Hindu Law of Partition, Inheritance and Adoption*, 1885, (Calcutta, Tagore Law Lectures), pp. 87 ff.

[70] See Jolly: *Hindu Law and Custom*, p. 168.

[71] Ibid. p. 168.

[72] Nār. xiii, 38.

[73] Bri. xxv, 6.

prescribed by the *Śāstras*, for sanctifying the body; and the sacrificial rites at these *samskāras* are to be performed at the common fire.

According to the Hindu *Dharma-Śāstra*, the individual has to pass through many *samskāras*—*śarīra-samskāras* as Manu and others have called them;[74] for, these are intended to sanctify the body (*śarīra*) beginning from the moment the foetus is laid (*garbhādhāna*) to the death (*antyeshṭī*) of a person. Thus, they are supposed to purify (*pavanah*) the person of a human being in this life and for the life after death.[75] Each of these *samskāras* is preceded by a symbolic sacrifice (*homa*). The number of these *samskāras* differs according to different authorities; the *Grihya-Sūtras* enumerate about forty; while the *Gautama Dharma-Sūtra* names forty-eight.[76] It will be sufficient for us to consider the more important of these in connection with our discussion. These are as follows:[77]

(1) The *garbhādhāna* or the foetus-laying ceremony is performed at the consummation of marriage.[78] This ceremony is in continuation of the pledge taken by the marrying parties at their wedding, viz. to fulfil the obligation of continuing the family line. Also, the mating of husband and wife as identified with the foetus-laying ceremony suggests that mating is conceived as a part of the obligations of the married couple towards the family and the community.

(2) The *pumsavana samskāra*, or the 'male-making' rite is performed during the third month of the wife's pregnancy.[79] It is intended to propitiate the deities which are supposed to govern the sex of the foetus, so that thereby a male issue may be born. The male issue is an important adjunct in the family; for he helps the continuity of the family. In view of this, we may say that in the *pumsavana* rite, the aim of mating is conceived as serving the welfare of the family, and through it, the welfare of the community.

(3) The *jāta-karma* ceremony is performed at the birth of the child: Here the father touches and smells (*avaghrāṇam*) the child and utters benedictory *mantras* into its ears, expressing his wish that it may be endowed with long life (*āyus*) and intelligence (*medhā*). The child is then fed with honey and butter and is thereafter fed on the breast by the mother for the first time.[80] The umbilical cord of the child is cut after this. General care is taken to ensure the safety of the mother and the child.

(4) The *nāma-dheya* rite is performed on the tenth or twelfth day after the birth of the child when it is given a name. The question of naming is important according to some authorities; and certain broad rules have to be followed here in order that the name may refer to the family, the community and the social class to which the person belongs. In Manu's opinion, for instance, the name given to the newborn baby should be such as to signify his *varṇa*. Thus the name of a Brāhmaṇa should denote something auspicious (*māngalyam*) and imply contentment

[74] Man. ii, 27.

[75] Ibid.

[76] These *Samskāras* are treated in minute and lengthy details in the *Grihya-Sūtras*, for these texts are written with the special purpose of describing all the domestic (*grihya*) rites.

[77] e.g. Man. ii, 26–28; cf. Yāj. i, 10–13.

[78] See last chapter.

[79] Ś.G.S. i, 20; Āś. G.S. i, 13; G. G.S. ii, 6; H. G.S. ii, 1, 2, etc.; and in Yāj. i, 11. It is not mentioned by Manu.

[80] Ś.G.S. i, 24; Āś. G.S. i, 15, 14; Pār. G.S. i, 16, 4, etc. (The order of *avaghrāṇa*, touching the child, uttering *mantras*, and feeding the child is not the same in all the *Grihya-Sūtras*).

(*śarmavat*); this last word is taken by some to mean, "ending in *śarman*", as e.g., in 'Vishṇu-Śarmā'. So again, the name of a Kshatriya should denote power (*bala*) and imply his duty of protection (*rakshā*), as e.g., 'Bala-Varmā'. That of a Vaiśya should denote wealth (*dhana*) and express prosperity (*pushṭi*), as e.g., 'Vasu-Bhūti'. Lastly, a Śūdra's name should denote something simple and humble (*jugupsitam*) and his duty of service (*preshya-samyutam*), as e.g. 'Dīna-Dāsa'. The names of women should be easy to pronounce; they should not imply anything dreadful (*akrūram*), possess a plain and unambiguous meaning (*vispashṭārtham*), and must be pleasing and auspicious (*manoharam māngalyam*); besides they should end in long vowels and contain a term of benediction (*aśīvādābhidhāna-vat*), as e.g., in the name 'Yaśodā-devī'.[81]

(5) The *nishkramaṇa* ceremony is performed in the fourth month after the child's birth: Here the child is, as if, presented to the Sun; and thus its first contact with the greatest natural force that weilds power over the world, as also its first contact with the world outside the home, is ritually celebrated.

(6) The *anna-prāśana*[82] (*anna*=boiled rice, cooked food; *prāśana*=eating) rite is performed in the sixth month after birth. The child is now fed with cooked food for the first time. Here the problems of the upkeep and maintenance of the growing body of the child occupies the minds of the parents.

(7) The *chūdā-karma*, or the first tonsure of the hair, for the sake of *dharma*,[83] is performed in the first or the third year, or at any age according to the tradition in the family.[84] This ceremony is perhaps intended to celebrate the child's introduction to the rules of bodily hygiene.

(8) The *upanayana* ceremony when the boy is initiated into the study of the *Vedas*, is performed at different ages for different *varṇas*.[85] With this ceremony the boy is really accepted as a member of the group and of the spiritual life of the community to which his forefathers belong; for, from now onwards, he has a right to know and learn the well-preserved sacred lore of the community. He now enters the *brahmacharyāśrama*, i.e. the first *āśrama* or stage of a life of *dharma*. In fact, the rite of *upanayana* heralds the second birth of the individual,[86]—the spiritual birth of the individual as a member proper of the group and its cultural heritage. It is therefore significant of the appellation *dvi-jāti* (or *dvi-janman*, or *dvi-ja*) i.e. 'twice-born'* given to the members of the first three *varṇas*, in that any one born within any of these *varṇas* must, of necessity, go through the *Upanayana* rites. From now on, he begins his studies of *vedas* including *vedāngas* for a certain period of years, which is different for different *varṇas*, usually at the *āśrama* (hermitage) of *guru* (teacher).

(9) The *sāvitrī* is to be performed, according to the *Grihya-Sūtras*, immediately after the *upanayana*, or during the third year after *upanayana;* according to Manu, it is to be performed some time before the completion of the sixteenth year for a Brāhmaṇa, of twenty-second year in the case

[81] See Man. ii, 31–33; and Kullūka's commentary thereon. Also cf. Pār. G.S. i, 17; Āś. G.S. i, 15, 4–5.

[82] It may be noted here that the *Grihya-Sūtras* recommend flesh of different kinds of fowl and fish for the child at this ceremony—See Ś. G.S. i, 27, 2 ff.; Āś. G.S. i, 16, 3; Pār. G.S. i. 19, 18 ff. etc.

[83] *'dharmatah'—dharmārtham kāryam*—Kullūka on Man. ii.

[84] Man. ii, 35; Āś. G.S. i, 17, 1:—*yathā-kula-dharmam vā.*

[85] See chapter iv.

[86] Man. ii, 68: "*aupanāyaniko vidhih utpatti-vyanjakah*", etc.

* *dvi*=two; *jan*=to be born.

of a Kshatriya, and of twenty-fourth year in the case of a Vaiśya.[87] This rite forms a part of the duties of *brahmacharyāśrama*.[88]

(10) The *samāvartana* rite celebrates the return of the student to his ancestral home after the completion of his studies at the *āśrama* of his *guru*. This *samskāra* is the point, in the individual's career, which marks the completion of his education, and his fitness to enter into and accept the responsibilities of a family life.

(11) The *vivāha* (marriage) ceremony marks the individual's entry into the *grihasthāśrama*. This ceremony may be said to seal the socialization proper of the individual; for here he takes the pledge to assist in the continuation of the race, and actually commences his efforts in that direction. Here, again, he accepts the fundamental doctrine of *yajna* in its fullest sense[89]; he takes a vow, also, to keep on the home Fire (*Agni*) continuously alive.

(12) The *antyeshṭī* or the funeral rite, performed at death, marks the end of the human career of the individual, and his entrance into the realm of ancestors (*pitris*).

This whole series of sacraments has to be performed for the females also in order to sanctify the body (*samskārārtham śarīrasya*), in their proper order and at proper times (*yathā-kālam yathākramam*), but with this difference, that the sacred *mantras* are not to be recited on these occasions (*amantrikā*).[90] So also, so far as woman is concerned, the nuptial ceremony is to be regarded as equivalent to the *Vaidika samskāra* called *Upanayana*.[91] Thus, for a woman, devoted service of her husband is equivalent to residing at the *Guru's* home and serving him; and her devotion to various household duties is but the same as the worship of *Agni* (Sacred Fire).[92]

In the same way, the Śūdras, like women, can go through these *samskāras*, without the recitation of sacred *mantras*.[93]

All these *samskāras* are a part of '*varṇa-dharma*' (the duties of the *varṇas*) as well as of the *āśrama -dharma* (those of the *āśrama*). While the *Varṇa*-scheme approaches the task of regulating the social life of the individual through the community as a whole in the main, the *Āśrama* scheme is essentially devised to the same end, but approaches the task from the individual's side. And between these two stand the *samskāras*, through which the individual becomes, from stage to stage, organised and disciplined into a more and more perfect social being till he retires from active life. Thus, the natural man is raised to the fullest social status step by step, till *vivāha*, when the orbit of his life becomes essentially dedicated to the service of social ends; hereafter, till he retires from his duties as a householder, he is pledged to produce worthy progeny, which becomes the joint duty and interest of the man and his wife for which the two have become united.

And yet, while all efforts are made towards the socialisation of the man, the care of the man himself as a unique individual is not lost sight of. There are several modes and means, prescribed by the *Dharma-Śāstras*, with the help of which the individual is expected to cultivate his personality in spite of, apart from, and yet in the midst of a life that is pledged to serve social ends. This

---

[87] Man. ii, 38.
[88] See chapter iv.
[89] See next section.
[90] Man. ii, 66. See also Āś. G.S. i, 15, 10; 16, 6; 17, 19; Yāj. i, 13.
[91] Man. ii, 67; Yāj. i, 13.
[92] Ibid.
[93] See Man. x, 127; Yāj. i, 121.

is especially apparent from the fact that after all *grihasthāśrama* has to be pursued only as a stage and step to secure the entrance into the next *āśrama* of *vānaprastha* and from thence into the *samnyāsa*.[94]

The various *samskāras* performed in the first half of a man's life are so many stages for the individual in the process of his socialization. All the ritual and ceremonies at these *samskāras* have a reference to the socialization of the individual. The individual is, as it were, carried over from one experience to another in the course of his life, in order that he may feel himself more and more at one with the community of which he is a part. These rituals and ceremonies are common to all members of the Hindu community; thus they signify the common bonds that hold the members of the community together.

The *samskāras* and the elaborate ceremonies performed in association with them signify, both to the individual as well as to the community, that something important is coming to happen to the individual on these particular occasions, in which both the community as well as the individual have their interests. Thus, the *Upanayana* ceremony, for instance, of which we have already spoken in Ch. IV and above, signifies that the individual is now to prepare himself to learn the community lore, for his own good as well as for that of the community. The very elaborate ceremony of *vivāha* again, signifies the most important step taken by the individual for the welfare of the community, in that he accepts the responsibility of reproducing for the increase of the strength of the community. And it also signifies a very important step taken by the individual for his own good, in that he shows readiness to start *grihasthāśrama*, and, through it seeks to accumulate *dharma* for his future welfare towards *mokśa*. The rituals thus signify that the individual is being entrusted with certain obligations and responsibilities for his own welfare as well as for the good of the community, from which latter obligations and responsibilities he was so far free.

III

We shall now proceed to consider specific mores of relations of the members of the Hindu family with each other and with the family. Thus we shall have to consider the relations of the husband, the wife, the son, the daughter, and the parents with each other and of each of these with the rest of the members of the family.

1

Regarding the mutual relations between the husband and the wife, the *Manu-Smriti* has declared that mutual fidelity till death is the "summary" of the highest *dharma* for husband and wife.[95] Manu further adds that once they are united by the nuptial ceremony, they must always exert themselves to see that they are never at variance with each other, and that they ever remain faithful to each other.[96]

---

94 See Chapter III on the *Āśramas*.

95 Man. ix, 101: *Anyonyasyāvyabhīchāro bhaved āmaraṇāntikah/esha dharmah samāsena jneyah strī-pumsayoh punah/ /*

96 Man. ix, 102: *Tathā nityam yateyātām strī-pumsau tu kritakriyau/yathā nābhicharetām tau viyuktāvitaretaram/ / esha strī-pumsayor ukto ḍharmo vo rati-samhitah/ /*

The true goal of marriage lies in "the consciousness of a permanent and unbreakable friendship,"[97] as Urwick would say; this cannot be reached unless marriage itself is made unbreakable. The natural basis of the family is the care of the young;[98] that is the primary function of the family. "The normal function of the family is to secure what is best, or the best available for the nurture of the children, with a view to their preparation as citizens of a larger community."[99] The monogamic family, it follows therefore, is the natural form of association, "being the only one in which both the parents can normally devote themselves whole-heartedly, and with cordial co-operation to the necessary task,[100] of taking care of the young. The Hindu writers have devoted much of their energy not only in praising monogamy (one wife at a time), but they have gone further in eulogising life-long union of one man to one woman, such that after the death of either, the survivor remains single and faithful to his or her memory (i.e. *ekachāritva* or *ekapatnīvrata*). The epic story of Rāma is an example of such ideal realised. So again, is the story of King Aja in Kālidasa's well known epic '*Raghu-vamsa*'. The *Dharma-Śāstras* of Manu and Yājnavalkya instruct the husband to be devoted solely to his wife.[101] He should respect her and please her.[102] Vātsyāyana also speaks of the husband devoted to one wife in highly eulogistic terms.[103] The *Mahābhārata* gives similar instructions to the husband as the *Smritis*.[104] All the daily sacrificial rites, designed to ensure happiness after death, have to be performed by man and wife together.[105] In the family, the husband ought to exert himself to live in harmony with his wife and children.[106] The home, in which the husband is always pleased with his wife as well as the wife always feels pleased with her husband, is indeed the most blessed home.[107] Man is only half human, not complete, until he marries and begets children; then only he becomes a full man.[108]

The primary object of marriage is the continuity of the family line, according to the *Smritis*.[109] And therefore, if the first marriage of a man does not succeed in this objective he is permitted to marry again even while the first wife is alive. Vātsyāyana observes that the wife who bears no child may herself advise her husband to marry another woman; and he advises such a first wife to regard the second wife as her younger sister.[110] The *Smritis* urge that the husband should not marry another wife if his first wife is able to share in the performance of his religious obligations, and has also borne him sons.[111] The wife of the same *varṇa* as the husband only can personally share with her husband and assist him in the performance of religious rites.[112] Such a wife, if she is kind to her

---

97 Urwick: *"The Social Good"*, p. 137.

98 J. S. Mackenzie: *Outlines of Social Philosophy*, p. 77, London: Allen & Unwin, 1918; Reprinted 1952.

99 Ibid. p. 80.

100 Ibid. p. 77.

101 Man. iii, 45; Yāj. 1, 81.

102 Man. iii, 55–60; Yāj. i, 82.

103 Kām. i, 3, 4.

104 Mahā. Anu. 46—the whole *Adhyāya*.

105 Man. ix, 196.

106 Man. ix, 45; Ap. ii, 14, 16.

107 Man. iii, 60: *santushto bhāryayā bhartā bhartrā bhāryā tathaiva cha/yasminneva kule nityam kalyāṇam tatra voi dhruvam/ /*

108 Śat. Br. v, 1, 6, 10.

109 Yāj. i, 78; Āp. ii, 5, 11, 12; etc.

110 Kām. iv, 2, 1–5.

111 Yāj. i, 73; 76; Āp. ii, 5, 11, 12; cf. Man. ix, 95; 80; 81.

112 Man. ix, 86; Yāj. i, 88.

husband and virtuous in her conduct, must never be shown disrespect by her husband by marrying another woman.[113] He may, however, marry another woman if the first wife gives her consent to do so.[114]

Ordinarily, divorce is not known to the Hindu institution of marriage. Husband and wife are bound to each other, not only "till death", but even after death, in the other world.[115] But, the *Artha-Śāstra* makes mention of dissolution of marriage (*mokśa*) in the case of marriages; viz., the *Brāhma, Daiva, Ārsha*, and *Prājāpatya*.[116] Such dissolution of marriages when these marriages had taken place under forms other than these four, again, cannot be availed of against the will of the two parties. It is available only on the ground of enmity of the parties towards each other.[117]

As regards the husband's authority over his wife, we must not consider this in isolation from certain other aspects which are connected with it. It is along with the obligations and duties of the husband towards the wife as the complementary aspect of his authority over her that we must consider the Hindu husband's "dominion" over his wife. He is the lord and master of his wife and as such he should be adored by her, even though he is devoid of virtues.[118] On his side, however, he should realize that pleasure, harmony as well as *dharma* depends upon her, and so he should never get cross with her even though she may happen to do so.[119] He is her guardian in her youth, just as her father guards her in childhood, and her sons are bound to do in her old age.[120] The husband is known as *Bhartri*,[121] because he is the support of his wife; and he is known as *Pati*[122] because he has to protect her.[123] When he fails to discharge these two functions, he ceases to be both *Bhartri* and *Pati*.[124] "This eternal course of *dharma* is ever followed by righteous men,—viz., that the husband, however weak he might be, aught to protect his wedded wife."[125] For, by protecting one's wife, one protects one's own offspring; and, by protecting the offspring, one protects one's own self.[126]

The wife is known as the *Jāyā*, because one's own self is begotten on her.[127] It is further ordained that the woman whose hand is accepted in marriage should be treated with respect and kindness; and all that is agreeable to her should be given her.[128] So also, her elder relatives-in-law, namely, father-in-law, the brother-in-law, the mother-in-law are exhorted to please her with affection;[129] for she is the cause of the begetting of offsprings, their nurture and the fulfilment of other factors, so necessary

---

[113] Man. ix, 82.

[114] Ibid.

[115] Man. v, 160–1; 164; Suk. Nī. iv, 4, 57–9; Kāt. 837 (Kane's Ed.); also Rāmā. ii, 29, 17–18: "She who is given away as wife by her father to the man, with due ceremonies belonging to each class by touching holy water, belongs to him even in her life in the next world."

[116] Arth. p. 177.

[117] Arth. p. 176.

[118] Man. v, 147–54; Yāj. i, 77: Viś. xxv, 12–14.

[119] Mahā. Ādi. 98, 39; *Apriyokto'pi dārāṇām na brūyād apriyam budhah/ratim prītim cha dharmam cha tadāyattam avekshya cha/ /*

[120] Man. ix, 3.

[121] From *'bhri'*—'to support' or 'to maintain'.

[122] From *'pā'*—to 'protect' or 'guard'.

[123] Mahā. Ādi. 104, 28.

[124] Mahā. Śānti. 266, 37.

[125] Ban. 12, 68.

[126] Ibid. 12, 69.

[127] Ibid. 12, 70—(from '*jan*'—to beget).

[128–129] Mahā. Anu. 46, 1–13.

for the good of society.[130] By cherishing woman, one but virtually worships the goddess of prosperity herself; by afflicting her, one but afflicts the goddess of prosperity.[131] A man's half is his wife; the wife is her husband's best of friends; the wife is the source of *Dharma, Artha* and *Kāma;* and she is also the source of *Mokśa*.[132] "No man, even when he is in temper, should ever do anything that is disagreeable to his wife. For happiness, joy, virtue—all depend upon the wife."[133]

Further, in the *Mahābhārata*, the wise and learned Bhīshma gives a piece of sound advice to the husband in regard to his manner of behaviour in the family. "A householder should be satisfied with his own married wife", says he.[134] He should avoid any act such as may cause a breach of peace in the family. He should never fall out with his kinsmen in the family, his brothers, sons, wife, daughter and even his servants.[135] "With endurance," he should "bear without excitement or anxiety every sort of annoyance, and even censure" from these members of the family.[136] In general, in family affairs, "he should keep self-controlled; he should avoid malice and curb his senses."[137] The unity and harmony of family-life is well brought out in the following passage: "The eldest brother is like a father (to all his younger brothers); the wife and the sons are but one's own body; one's menial servants are, as it were, one's shadow; and the daughter is an object of profound love."[138]

Nārada forbids the husband and the wife even from ever bringing their quarrels to the notice of their relatives, or the king,[139]—(i.e., perhaps, to the Court for redress or trial).

The *Mahānirvaṇatantra* gives the husband another striking piece of advice with regard to the treatment to his wife: He should never punish her; rather, he should always protect her with the respect due to his mother (*mātrivat*). A virtuous wife who dearly loves her husband (*sādhvī pati-vratā*) should never be abandoned, even if the husband happens to be in grave peril.[140]

Yājnavalkya, in the *Brihadāraṇyaka Upanishad*, has clearly brought out the psychological unity of man and wife in the family. He explains that man, who was originally one, cleft himself into two, because he felt no pleasure in the loneliness, and wished for a second; these two became the husband and wife. The two separately, he says, are like half of a shell, each; together, they are one whole.[141] We are told in the *Rāmāyaṇa* that the learned sage and Royal Adviser Vasishṭha asked Sītā to remain at home while her husband Crown Prince Rāma would go to forest to fulfil his father's promise, and to rule the kingdom in Rāma's place; for, he argued, "the wife is the very soul (true representative) of him who marries her."[142] This interpretation of the unity of the husband and wife, whereby the wife is to be looked upon as the husband's deputy, possessing all the authority and carrying out all the duties and responsibilities of the husband during his absence even in such important matters as ruling an empire and all that this involves, is indeed a most significant interpretation.

[130–131] Ibid.

[132] Mahā. Ādi. 74, 40.
[133] Mahā. Ādi. 74, 50.
[134] Śānti. 243, 14.
[135] Ibid. 243, 15–16.
[136] Ibid. 243, 21.
[137] Ibid. 243, 14.
[138] Ibid. 243, 20.
[139] Nār. xii, 89.
[140] *Mahānirvāṇatantra*, viii, 39.
[141] Br. Up. 1, 4, 3.
[142] Rāmā. ii, 37, 23–24.

It is further significant to note that Sītā was prevailed upon to take over her husband's duties and authority even though he had three younger brothers.

Here we may also remind ourselves of the ceremonies centering round the *vivāha*, especially the *sapta-padī mantras* in which the bride and the groom walk together before the nuptial altar over seven heaps of rice.[143] The whole ceremony of marriage, indeed, is significant in connection with our present discussion; but the *sapta-padī* rite is specially so, because the seven pledges which the bride takes here perhaps best summarize the whole psychology underlying mutual relationship between the husband and the wife in the family.

2

Next we consider the position of the wife in the Hindu family. In the family, the wife comes as a stranger. All the other members of the family have already imbibed the family traditions, customs and usages; and the family sentiments have become quite a part of their lives. The newly-wedded wife, on the contrary, is in these respects a perfect stranger in the family. Her first important duty on entering her new home, therefore, would be to exert towards adapting herself to the traditions and sentiments of the house of which she now becomes a member. A true adaptation, however, would become the most difficult task if it is one-sided only; it is desirable that the other members of the household too should attempt to be of real help to the newcomer. They have to take a lenient view of her acts of omission and commission until she has become acclimatized to the new atmosphere. The greater part of this responsibility, which falls on the shoulders of the members of the family, has naturally to be shared by the husband. We have already seen what the *Mahābhārata* has to say regarding the husband's part in this matter.[144] In the same passage, the parents-in-law and other relatives-in-law of the new bride are called upon to treat her with respect and kindness, if they desire for happiness in the family; "for such conduct on their part always produces considerable happiness and advantage."[145] The wife is "a friend bestowed on man by Destiny", says Yudhisṭhira to the Yakśa.[146] The wife of King Daśaratha, in the *Rāmāyaṇa*, is described as being to him like "a friend, wife, sister and mother" as well.[147] On occasions of joy, the wife who has a sweet tongue is like a friend who increases the joy by sharing it with her husband; on religious occasions, she is to him what a father should be; in times of distress and worry, she is to him what a mother would prove to be.[148]

The *Mahābhārata* declares that in truth, a householder's home, even if crowded with sons, grandsons, daughters-in-law and servants, is virtually a lonely place for him to live, if there is no housewife.[149]

---

143 See ch. v.

144 Mahā. Anu. 46, 1–13. (See above, footnotes 128–131), etc.

145 Anu. 46, 3.

146 Mahā. Vana. 373, 72.

147 Rāmā, ii, 12, 68–69.

148 Mahā. Ādi. 74, 72.

149 Mahā. Śānti. 144, 5:

putra-pautra-vadhū-bhrityair-ākīrṇam api sarvatah/
bhāryā-hīnam grihasthasya śūnyam eva griham bhavet/

One's home is not the house made of brick and mortar; it is the wife who makes the home. A home without the wife is like a wilderness.[150]

Thus, the very important part played by the wife, has received great attention by Hindu writers. The husband's true attitude towards his wife cannot be better described than what is done by the poet Kālidāsa in *Raghuvamśa* wherein King Aja laments for his deceased wife thus: "She was my *grihiṇi* (the lady of the house), my wise counsellor in intellectual matters (*sachivah*), my *confidante* (*sakhī*) in private, and my dearest disciple in the pursuit of the arts."[151]

All this clearly shows what part the husband is expected to play in relation to his wife. Out of all the relatives by marriage, the husband is the wife's nearest relation. In the task of her adaptation to the family life his co-operation must naturally be the most helpful to her. Of all the family members, it is the husband, first and foremost, who is expected to give the wife a response of heart and mind. And no unity between man and woman can be perfect without the psychological concord of their spirit and emotions. Each must go out in sympathy to the other; each must give the greater part of her or his affection to the other; and, each must, in fact, in every possible way, try to be perfect psychological complement of the other.

And yet, though the Hindu writers expect much from the husband in this direction of mutual sympathy, mutual affection, and mutual congeniality, a great deal is also expected by them of the wife. The wife herself seems to be held by them to be the most responsible of all for her own adaptability into the family. Thus, the mistress of the house is asked by Manu and other *Smriti* writers to obey her lord as long as he lives, and remain faithful to his memory after his death.[152] They sometimes go even farther than that; they declare that she should worship him as a deity even though he happens to be a man of bad character and has no good quality in him.[153] Brihaspati says that the wife, who feels afflicted when her husband is afflicted, and feels happy when he is happy, is the truly devoted wife of her husband.[154] Woman is "the goddess of fortune" in the family, because, she can make or mar the happiness of the family.[155] She is the immediate person concerned with the

---

[150] Ibid. 144, 6:

na griham griham ityāhur grihiṇī griham uchyate/
griham tu grihiṇī-hīnam araṇya-sadriśam matam/ /

See also Ibid. 144, 12–17:

vrikśa-mūle'pi dayitā yasya tishṭhati tad griham/
prāsādo' pi tayā hīnah kāntāra iti niśchitam/ /
dharmārthakāma-kāleshu bhāryā pumsah sahāyinī/
videśa-gamane chāsya saiva viśvāsa-kārikā//
bhāryā hi paramo hyarthah purushasyeha paṭhyate/
a-sahāyasya loke'smin loka-yātrā-sahāyinī//
nāsti bhāryā-samo bandhur nāsti bhāryā-samā gatih/
nāsti bhāryā-samo loke sahāyo dharma-samgrahe//
yasya bhāryā grihe nāsti sādhvī cha priya-vādinī/
araṇyam tena gantavyam yathāraṇyam tathā griham//

[151] *Raghu.* viii, 67: *grihiṇī sachivah sakhī mithah, priya-śishyā lalite kalāvidhau/*

[152] Man. v, 151; Yāj. i, 75; 83; Vis. xxv, 13–14.

[153] Man. i, 154–6; Yāj. i, 77; Vis. xxv, 15; Kāt. 836.

[154] Brih. Smr. xxiv, 8.

[155] Man. ix, 26.

nurture and bringing up of the children; so, she plays the most important part in the family life.[156] On the lady of the house alone, says Manu, depends the due performance of all acts of *dharma* (*dharma-karyaṇi*), heavenly bliss for oneself and one's ancestors, the due care of the offspring, and, on the whole, "the highest conjugal happiness"[157] (*ratir uttamā*). It falls to her lot, therefore, as her important responsibility, to maintain peace in the house and promote happiness in the family. She must do her utmost towards conducting the affairs of the family smoothly by keeping under control her thought, speech and actions (*mano-vāg-deha-samyatā*) and by doing her duty towards her husband.[158] Such a wife is called a sādhvī, a virtuous and chaste woman, in this world.[159]

As a wife, woman has to subject herself to the authority of her husband.[160] She should never, in the opinion of Manu, do anything that might displease him, whether he be alive or dead.[161] As the mistress of the house, she should always possess a cheerful temperament, managing her household affairs cleverly and efficiently, and spending economically.[162] Vyāsa gives a similar account of the house-wife's typical duties: She is to rise up early in the morning before her husband, take her bath, and clean the house, the yard of the house and the utensils of cookery. Then she is to light the fire in the oven, make arrangements for different kinds of tasty dishes for the day, give the servants orders of their work for the day, and make out an estimate of the expenses necessary for the day. She should then pay her respects to the elders in the house. After the meals are prepared, she should first serve the children in the family, then her husband and afterwards take her meals. After the meals are over, she should prepare the daily account of the family income and expenses.[163] Vātsyāyana agrees with the *Smritis* in regard to the duties of the lady of the house.[164] He advises her to exert herself towards gaining the full confidence of her husband;[165] she should obey her husband's elder relations and behave courteously towards the servants of the family.[166] "If the husband sins against her, let her be indeed a little angry and scold him, but not too much."[167] She may engage herself in amusements of every description, but only so far as may please her husband.[168] "Angry words, angry looks, speaking with averted ahead, standing at the door and looking out, talking in the garden, remaining long in a place apart—all these things let her shun;[169] she is not to go out of the house without the husband's permission;[170] and, if the husband is used to spending too much money, or not spending wisely, let her tell him of that in private."[171]

---

[156] Man. ix, 27: *utpādanam apatyasya jatasya pari-palanam/*
pratyaham loka-yātrāyāh pratyaksham strī-nibandhanam/

[157] Man. ix, 2, 8.

[158] Man. ix, 29 and v, 165 (both identical).

[159] Ibid.

[160] Man. v, 148–9; Yāj. i, 85–6; Śukr. Nī. iv, 4, 25; Vis. xxv, 13; Bau. ii, 3, 45; Vas. v. 3.

[161] Man. v, 156.

[162] Man. v, 150; Yāj. i, 83; Vas. xxv, 4–6.

[163] Vyāsa. Smr. ii, 20 ff.

[164] Kām. iv, 1, 1–55;—Peterson's Tr. in *J. Anthr. Soc. Bom.*, Vol. ii, No. 7 (1891), pp. 456–66.

[165] Ibid. v, i.

[166] Ibid. v, 37.

[167] Ibid. v, 19.

[168] Ibid. v, 16.

[169] Ibid. v, 22.

[170] Ibid. v, 25.

[171] Ibid. v, 14.

The *Mahābhārata* also outlines similarly the duties and the attitude of the wife to the husband. Bhīshma reports a conversation between two women Sumanā and Śāṇḍilī. The former wanted to know by what penances the latter was able to attain celestial regions. Śāṇḍilī replied that it was not by virtue of any hard penances at all; but, by virtue of her obedience and devotion to her husband she was able to achieve paradise.[172] In the *Vanaparva* section, Krishna's wife Satyabhāmā desires to know of Draupadī how she was able to "rule the sons of Paṇḍu", her five husbands.[173] How was it that they were so obedient to her and were never cross with her?[174] Satyabhāmā thought it was all due probably to some magic power which Draupadī possessed! Draupadī, however, assured her that it was all entirely due to her obedience and devotion to her husbands. She took her bath, ate and slept after her husbands, and after all the servants and attendants.[175] She was always engaged in assisting her husbands.[176] She renounced whatever her husbands did not enjoy.[177] In her opinion, "the husband is wife's god; he is her (sole) refuge; . . . My husbands have become pleased with me and are at my beck and call on account of my diligence, my alacrity, and the humility with which I serve my elders."[178]

The *Rāmāyaṇa* is full of incidents of the wife's devotion to her husband, its heroine Sītā being herself the chief object of the poet's eulogy. Sītā says that in this world, the wife is the sharer of her husband's destiny; all other relatives are each responsible for his or her own destiny only.[179] The husband is indeed a Deity for the wife.[180] "Women who love their husbands,—whether he treats them well or ill, whether he lives in the city or in forest,—attain high status; and, the husband, whether wicked or lustful, is the highest God to the wife of good morals."[181]

There is of course the more mundane aspect of the duties of the mistress of the house: She is held responsible for the general comfort of all the members of the family. Manu observes that she should undertake the management of household affairs, collection and expenditure of her husband's wealth, preparing for food, keeping everything clean in the house, and fulfilling all the *dharma* obligations.[182] She should not sleep at odd hours; nor should she wander about mixing with wicked people; nor should she ever drink intoxicating liquors.[183] She should rise before the other members of the house and pay her respects to the elder members of the family.[184] She should be always cheerful, and should manage the affairs of the family with cleverness;[185] and, she has to take care to keep everything clean in the home, and should be economical in regard to expenditure.[186] In this regard, Draupadī explains how she followed this duty of the wife as the manager of household affairs. She used to keep all articles and utensils and food in the house clean, to prepare food at

[172] Mahā. Anu. 23.
[173] Mahā. Vana. 232, 4.
[174] Ibid. 5–6.
[175] Ibid. 24.
[176] Ibid. 29.
[177] Ibid. 32.
[178] Ibid. 37 and 39.
[179] Rāmā. ii, 27, 4–18.
[180] Rāmā, ii, 39, 31.
[181] Rāmā. ii, 117, 22–28.
[182] Man. ix, 10–11.
[183] Man. ix, 13; also Br. Smr. xxiv, 7.
[184] Br. Smr. xxiv, 7.
[185] Man. v, 150.
[186] Ibid.

the proper hour, to offer the religious oblations and worship, and to look to the comforts of the guests of the house.[187] Draupadī, indeed, with pride, claims that she alone knew, better than any one else, about what the servants, attendants, and even the cow-herds and shepherds in her palace did and what they did not do; in fact, she alone had the fullest knowledge of the confidential details of the wealth and the income and expenditure of the huge royal establishment of her lord.[188] This illustrates the Hindu conception of the wife's duties and responsibilities in the family.[189]

Vātsyāyana, speaking about the duties of a Hindu wife, likewise describes her as the manager of the home; the wife must look after the household work and arrangements;[190] she is to make purchases of things of domestic necessity, like utensils, oil, salt, drugs etc.;[191] and she has also to keep accounts of income and expenditure, and check them.[192] Vātsyāyana also says that the lady of the house should maintain good garden for vegetables to be used in the kitchen, as well as a garden for fruits and flowers.[193] In the drama *Śākuntalam* of Kālidāsa, the sage Kaṇva's advice to his adopted daughter Śakuntalā, on the eve of her departure for her husband's abode, is similar; Śakuntalā is advised by the sage to obey her husband's parents and behave courteously with servants; and above all, says he "do not fall out with your husband even if he happens to insult you."[194]

In the *Śukra-Nīti*, we find almost similar account of the duties of a housewife.[195] She is expected to get up before her husband, clean all utensils, sweep the house, pay her respects to the elders in the family, cook the food, and so on. Women, according to *Śukra-Nīti*, have no separate right to the use of means for the realization of the three-fold aims of life—*Dharma, Artha* and *Kama*—except in terms of service of the home and the husband.[196] "The wife should be pure in mind, speech and action; she should abide by the instructions of her husband, and follow him like a pure shadow; she must be a friend in all his good activities, and a servant at all his commands."[197] In the home she should be sweet and gentle in spech, and courteous in behaviour.[198] "The father gives measured things, the brother and son also give only limited things. Who does not worship the husband who is the giver of everything?"[199] The wife should practise music and gentle manners, "according as the husband is master of these, and thus practise the fine arts of winning over, with regard to him."[200]

Under the Hindu ideal of marriage, man and wife become united according to the sacred *mantras* and rituals with the blessings of the gods. Indeed, in the *Mahābhārata* we are told that "According to the injunctions of the *śāstras*, the husband should regard his wife as an acquisition due to his own pristine deeds or what has been ordained by God."[201] "The husband is declared to be one with

[187] Mahā. Van. 232 and 233.
[188] Ibid.
[189] Cf. also similar enumeration of the housewife's duties given by Hārīta, in Colebrooke's "*Digest*", Bk. iii, Ch. ii, Sect. 1, p. 141, cii. (Quoted in S. C. Vidyārṇava's "*Yājnavalkyasmriti*", pp. 147–48).
[190] Kām. iv, 1, 3; cf. *Rati-śāstra*, vii.
[191] Ibid. vv, 26–28; cf. *Rati-śāstra*, Ibid.
[192] Ibid. v, 32; cf. *Rati-śāstra*, Ibid.
[193] Ibid. vv, 6–8.
[194] Peterson infers that Kālidāsa is quoting Vātsyāyana here.
[195] Śukra-Nī. iv, 11 to 65.
[196] Ibid. 11.
[197] Ibid. 23–25.
[198] Ibid. 37–42.
[199] Ibid. 64–65.
[200] Ibid. 55–56.
[201] Mahā. Anu. 44, 27.

his wife", says Manu. He adds also, that "he only is the perfect man who consists of three persons united viz., his wife, his offspring and himself."[202] 'Mutual fidelity till death' is, in Manu's opinion, the summary of the highest law for the husband and wife to follow.[203] The harmony of intellect and feeling between the two chief members of the family is of supreme importance in the view of Hindu writers on the subject. The *saptapadī* brings forth most vividly the full significance of this intellectual and emotional unity of the married couple. This psycho-moral harmony is further emphasized by the fact that all daily rites and *dhārmika* duties to be performed in order to win happiness here and hereafter have to be performed by man and wife together.[204] Brīhaspati speaks of the wife as *saha-dharma-chāriṇī* i.e., one who participates with her husband in the pursuit of *dharma*, and also *as ardhāngī*, i.e., half the being of her husband.[205]

The *Smritis* and the *Mahābhārata* refer to the wife by the name *Jāyā*, because, according to them the husband becomes an embryo and is born again (*jāyate*) of his wife as her son.[206] Every family has to take care that its offsprings are of pure blood. *Mokśa* is obtained through sons and grandsons. Continuity of the family line in this world (*ānantyam loke*) was the main object of taking a wife; and with this primary aim of marriage in view, the husband should carefully guard the wife so that the children born out of the union are of pure blood.[207] If the wife is not well guarded, she may bring disgrace on both the families, her husband's as well as her father's.[208] By carefully guarding the wife, the husband is able to preserve the purity of his offspring, his family, himself, and his means of acquiring *dharma*.[209] The use of force is inadvisable in guarding women; moreover, man will not be able to guard them completely by force.[210] Manu suggests that instead of using force against his wife, the husband should try to keep her engaged in the management of the household affairs, so that she may not get idle moments for thinking of or doing any undesirable or shameful act.[211] Thus, for Manu and Brihaspati, the management of household affairs, as we have described before,[212] is in a way, a means of engaging the wife's mind which may otherwise be led astray, since "the empty mind", as they say, "is the devil's workshop."

This reminds us of Charles Cooley's remarks: "Nothing works more for sanity and contentment than a reasonable amount of necessary and absorbing labour; disciplining the mind and giving one a sense of being of use in the world. It seems a paradox to say that idleness is exhausting, but there is much truth in it, especially in the case of sensitive and eager spirits. A regular and necessary task rests the will by giving it assurance, while the absence of such a task wearies it by uncertainty and futile choice. Just as a person who follows a trail through the woods will go further with less exertion than one who is finding his way, so we all need a foundation of routine, and the lack of this among women of the richer classes is a chief cause of the restless, exacting, often hysterical

---

[202] Man. ix, 45; also Āp. ii, 14, 16.
[203] Man. ix, 101–103.
[204] Man. ix, 96.
[205] Brihas. xxiv, 10–11.
[206] Man. ix, 8; Yāj. i, 56; Mahā. Van. 22, 70.
[207] Yāj. i, 78; Āp. ii, 5, 11, 12; and Mahā. Ādi. 74, 35.
[208] Man. ix, 5.
[209] Man. ix, 7.
[210] Man. ix, 10.
[211] Man. ix, 10–11; also Br. Sm. xxii, 4.
[212] See above.

spirit harassing to its owner and every one else, which tends towards discontent, indiscretion and divorce."[213] The *Mahābhārata*, the *Rāmāyaṇa* and Vātsyāyana's *Kāma-Sūtra* and the other *śāstra* writers, however, do not refer to any such motive specifically when they prescribe similar duties for the lady of the house.

Of the very high value placed on the virtue of chastity in women, numerous instances could be adduced from the Epics and other works. After the death of the husband, remark Manu and Yājnavalkya, the wife must not even mention the name of another man.[214] The woman who is unfaithful to her husband suffers disgrace in this world; and, after death, she loses her place by the side of her husband in heaven.[215] But the wife who maintains chastity (*brahmacharya*) after her husband's death attains heaven even though she has no son.[216]

But even here, as in some other cases also when we examine the *Dharma-Śāstras*, we are not treading on smooth grounds free from opposing viewpoints. For, the *Smritis*, at certain places, also require the husband to keep a distance between himself and his wife. For instance, he is not to eat in the company of his wife, nor is he to look at her when she is eating, sneezing, yawning, or sitting at ease.[217] On the other hand, the descriptions in the epics and poetry and drama speak of the housewife as taking part in the husband's affairs on terms of equality. The verse in the *Raghuvamśa* already quoted,[218] for instance, is quite in contradiction to such injunctions of the *Smritis*. In Vātsyāyana's opinion, the wife could take the liberty of rebuking her husband, if he is a spendthrift, or, again, if he commits any wrong against her.[219] In the *Mahābhārata*, Draupadī's advice to her husband Yudhishṭhira, on what his duty was and what it was not, at the time when he declared his intention to renounce worldly engagements and lead an ascetic life, clearly indicates her status of the wife as the advisor of her husband.[220] She even goes to the extent of rebuking him for making his brothers and herself suffer the tortures of forest life, though the rebuke is couched in "soothing and sweet words", as the narrator Vaiśampāyana puts it. "Why…did you say to these brothers, then living with you", she demands, "….these words, viz., 'we will kill Duryodhana and enjoy ruling the Earth'? Having yourself said these words to your brothers then, why do you depress our hearts now?"[221]

Of course, equality of status did not imply identity of rights and functions of the man and the wife. It meant that each of the two was recognized as possessing equal importance as a member jointly in charge of the home. The functions, and therefore also the rights and privileges, of the two sexes towards each other were always considered to be dissimilar in nature. Nevertheless, there was no distinction of degree, in terms of 'higher and lower', superior and inferior, between them. There was only a distinction of kind. And in the drama of family life, woman's place was on the whole as high as man's according to most authorities.

---

213 Cooley: "*Social Organization*", p. 368.

214 Man. v, 157; Yāj. i, 75, 77.

215 Man. v, 161; 164; Vas. xxi, 14.

216 Man. v, 160; Yāj. i, 75; Śukr. iv, 4, 57–59; Kāt. 837; Vis. xxv, 17; Pār. iv, 26.

217 Man. iv, 43; Yāj. i, 131; Vis. lxviii, 46; Vas. xii, 31; Gaut. ix, 32.

218 *Grihiṇī sachivah sakhī mithah, priya-śishyā lalite kalāvidhau*/ see above.

219 Kām., op. cit., (Peterson) verses 19 and 14.

220 Mahā. Śānti. 14, 6–37.

221 Ibid. 7 and 11.

Manu declares that a wife can never be released (*vimuchyate*) by repudiation.[222] But the husband may abandon (*tyajet*) his wife, only in case she possesses some blemish, disease, or faults which were not disclosed to him before marriage.[223] Even if she hate him, he is not allowed to abandon her immediately. He has to bear with her at least for one year; and if she continues to hate him even after that period, he may deprive her of her property, and cease to cohabit with her;[224] she must, even then, however, be maintained by him. If she shows disrespect for the husband who has some vice, or who is given to drinking, she shall be abandoned only for three months and shall be deprived of her ornaments and furniture.[225] But a wife cannot be cast off if she shows disrespect, or even aversion, to her husband who is insane (*unmatta*), or a eunuch, or who is destitute of manly strength (*abījam*), or who is suffering from serious disease (*pāpa-rogiṇam*).[226]

Vasiṣṭha and Yājnavalkya, however, give us somewhat different regulations in connection with abandonment or desertion of a wife. They are not in favour of the husband abandoning her except in cases of certain very serious offences. She shall be abandoned only if she commits adultery with her husband's pupil or his teacher, or with a man of low caste.[227] In no other case should she be absolutely abandoned according to these *Smritis*. The wife who proves unfaithful otherwise than in the cases mentioned above should be deprived of her authority and allowed only sufficient food to maintain her body; she should be treated with disdain and made to sleep on bare ground.[228] But after one month of suffering of this punishment, says Vasishṭha, she becomes purged of the sin.[229] Even if she has committed a sin, or if she is quarrelsome, or has left the house, or if she has suffered criminal force, or has fallen into the hands of thieves, the wife must not be abandoned; the husband should wait till her courses appear, because by her temporary uncleanliness of the menstruation period she becomes pure afterwards when the courses have ceased and after she has taken a bath.[230] Says Yājnavalkya: "Women are pure in all limbs; they never become entirely foul; they are purified of all their sins every month by their temporary uncleanliness; they are always pure, whatever offences they commit."[231]

3

The *śāstras* have given detailed instructions in regard to the days after a woman's monthly sickness during which period only she is supposed to be able to conceive a child.[232] And a married couple is enjoined to desist from sexual union on days other than these. Besides, even on these days, they are enjoined to mate only for the purpose of begetting children. Thus, sexual relation between a

[222] Man. ix, 46.
[223] Man. ix, 72; Yāj. i, 66.
[224] Man. ix, 77; and comm. by Kullūka.
[225] Man. ix, 78.
[226] Man. ix, 79.
[227] Yāj. i, 27; Vas. xxi, 9; cf. Man. ix, 80.
[228] Yāj. i, 70; Vas. xxi, 6.
[229] Vas. xxi, 6.
[230] Vas. xxviii, 9 and 4.
[231] Yāj. i, 71–72; also Vas. xxviii, 9 and 4; cf. Vis. xxiii, 40; Baudh. ii, 2, 4, 4.
[232] Man. iii, 45: *ritu-kālābhigāmī syāt*; also in Śān. G. S. iv, 11, 17; Pār. G.S. i, 11, 7–8; Āp. G.S. ii, 1, 17–18; Yāj. i, 79–81; Vas. xii, 21–24; cf. Kūrma Purā. i, 2, 15, 11 ('*ritu-kalābhigāmī syāt yāvat putro 'bhijāyate*'); etc.

man and his wife is viewed as not proper even when it is had during the right period, if it merely serves as a means for satisfying lust; so also, sexual union between the husband and his wife is not proper, even if it takes place with a view to reproduction, if it is not in the right period prescribed by the *śāstras*.

Regarding the proper time of personal intimacy for the husband and wife, Manu says that the natural season (*rituh svābhāvikah*) of women consists of sixteen days in each month beginning from the first day of menstruation; of these, however, the first four days of menstrual period, the eleventh (*ekādaśi*) and the thirteenth (*trayodaśī*) are forbidden; and the rest are recommended for sexual intercourse.[233] Particular care has to be taken by the husband to avoid such intimacy with his wife when she is passing through the menstrual period; for, if he approaches her in such condition, he is likely to impair his vitality (*āyuh*), his energy (*teja*), his strength (*bala*), his wisdom (*prajnā*) and also his sight (*chakshu*).[234] By avoiding sexual intimacy with the menstruating wife, on the other hand, he will augment these powers.[235] And, the *grihastha* who abstains from sexual relations on all the days forbidden for cohabiting as above is considered as good as a *brahmachārī*[236]—of course in a qualified sense—in whatever *āśrama* he may be!

Manu perhaps finds the above rules a little too rigorous to be followed by all *grihasthas* and at all times; for, he also adds the proviso that the husband may approach his wife on any day except the *parvas*,[237] with the intention of gratifying the desire of his wife.[238] Further, it is also enjoined that the man who does not have sexual relation with his wife in the proper season is a sinner.[239] Lastly, the husband is enjoined to seek sexual gratification through his wife only, and no other woman.[240]

4

Coming now to the position of the son in the family,[241] we may note at the outset, that the acquisition of sons was considered to be the primary aim of marriage. The son rescues the souls of the deceased ancestors from the hell into which they might fall without his birth. "Because the son protects his ancestors from the hell called *Put*, he has been called *Putra*."[242] "A man conquers the world by the birth of a son; he enjoys eternity by that of a grandson; and, the great grand-fathers enjoy eternal happiness by the birth of a grandson's son."[243] This is the religious view in support of the necessity of having a son.

---

233 Man. iii, 46–7; cf. Yāj. i, 79.

234 Man. iii, iv, 41.

235 Man. iii, iv, 42.

236 Man. iii, 50: "*brahmachāryeya bhavati yatra-tatrāśrame vasan*".

237 i.e. *amāvāsyā*, the thirtieth day of the Hindu calendar month, the day of moonless night, regarded as an inauspicious day for certain occasions; and a few such other days in each month.

238 "*tad-vrato rati-kāmyayā.*" "*tadvrato*" is explained by Kullūka as '*bhāryā-prītir-vratam yasya sa tad-vratah*'.

239 Bau. iv, 1, 17; and also Devala, quoted by Mādhavāchārya on *Parāśara-samhitā*, p. 100, (Bombay Sanskrit Series).

240 'sva-dara-niratah *sadā*'—Man. ii, 45; also Yāj. i, 81.

241 This section should be read particularly in conjunction with section 6, which describes the position of the parents *vis-à-vis* their children.

242 Man. ix, 138; Mahā. Ādi. 74, 27; cf. also Rāmā. ii, 107–12.

243 Mahā. Ādi. 74, 38.

The *Mahābhārata* looks at the necessity of a son in the family from another angle also; the child is looked upon as a great bond of affection in the family, the centre to which the love of the parents converges: "What is a greater happiness to a father than what the father feels when his son, running to him, clasps him with his (tiny little) arms though his body is full of dust and dirt,"[244] And, "even the exhilarating or soft touch of the sandal paste, or that of a woman, or of water, is not so pleasing as that of one's own infant son, locked into his embrace;"[245] truly ""there is nothing in the world whose touch is more pleasing than that of a son."[246] The Brāhmaṇas utter the following Vedic *mantras* (on behalf of the father), adds the *Mahābhārata*, at the birthday ceremony of the child: "You are born of my body; you have sprung from my heart. You are myself in the form of my son. . . . My life depends on you. The continuation of my race depends on you. . . . Therefore live in happiness for one hundred years."[247] "The man who, having begotten a son who is his own image, does not look after him, never gains the higher worlds. The *Pitris* (ancestors) have said that the son continues the race and supports the relatives; therefore to give birth to a son is the best of all sacred acts."[248] Manu expresses the view that it is necessary to acquire a son, if one desires to unite with the state of eternal bliss, viz. *Mokśa*.[249]

The position of the eldest son, however, is peculiar in the Hindu family. He has the authority to offer the funeral cake (*piṇḍa*) at the *Śrāddha* ceremony i.e., the religious observances on the death anniversary of the father and the ancestors. On the birth of the first (*jyeshṭha*) son, the father is freed from his debt to the manes.[250] Manu says that the eldest son on whom the father passes his debt (*riṇam*) and through whom he obtains immortality (*ānantyam*) is alone begotten for the fulfilment of *dharma* (*sa eva dharmajah putrah*); all the rest are considered as the offspring of desire (*kāmajāh*).[251] The eldest son can make the family prosperous or bring it ruin; he is worthy of honour, and is not to be treated with disrespect by those who want to follow *dharma*.[252] As long as the eldest brother behaves as an eldest brother ought to behave (*jyeshṭha-vrittih*), he should be honoured and respected by his younger brothers like mother and like father; and, even if he behaves in a manner unworthy of an eldest brother (*a-jyeshṭha-vrittih*), he should yet be honoured like a brother (*bandhu-vat*) at least.[253]

After the father's death, the sons may live under the eldest brother's control, paying him the same reverence and honour which they used to pay to their father.[254] If the brothers want to separate, under the *Smriti* rules, they have to give the best portion of the ancestral property and a large share to the eldest brother.[255] If, however, he is unworthy, he would forfeit this special right of his.[256] In the *Mahābhārata*, Bhīshma gives a discourse on the duties of the younger brothers towards the

244 Ibid. 74, 52.
245 Ibid. 74, 55.
246 Ibid. 74, 57.
247 Ibid. 74, 61–63.
248 Ibid. 74, 96–97.
249 Man. ii, 28.
250 Man. ix, 106
251 Man. ix, 107.
252 Ibid. 109.
253 Ibid. 110.
254 Man. ix, 105; also Gaut, xxviii, 1, 3; Bau. ii, 3, 13; Āp. ii. 14, 6.
255 Man. ix, 112–13; Yāj. ii, 114; Gaut. xrviii, 4–7; Vis. xviii, 37.
256 Man. ix, 213.

eldest, and his obligations in turn towards the younger ones.[257] The eldest brother should always treat the younger brothers in the way in which a preceptor treats his disciples.[258] The eldest brother should at times overlook the faults of his younger brothers; and, though possessed of wisdom, be should at times act as if he is not aware or mindful of their faults; if a younger brother be guilty of any sin, the eldest brother should correct him by indirect ways and means.[259] A great deal of the security of family happiness depends on the behaviour of the eldest brother towards the younger ones. "It is the eldest brother who augments the prosperity of the family or destroys it entirely. If the eldest brother does not happen to be gifted with sense, and is of wicked conduct, he encompasses the destruction of the whole family."[260] After the father's death, the younger brothers should "rely upon the eldest brother, as they did upon their father during his life time."[261] He is to maintain them and protect them.[262] The *Mahābhārata* would deprive the eldest brother of his share in the family property, if he in any way does harm to his younger brother.[263] It further says that, if the brothers wish to partition the family property during the father's life time, the father should give equal shares to all of them.[264]

Thus in the Hindu family, the eldest son is a particularly favoured person as compared to the other relatives. It is of course natural, generally speaking, that the first born child should attract greater part of the attention and affection from the parents.[265] But, in the Hindu family, this natural partiality to the eldest child—provided he is male, of course—is further supported by the added force of moral injunctions to that end. At the same time, *śāstras* have also placed upon his shoulders certain responsibilities; and, according to some authorities, the eldest brother who fails in these duties and responsibilities towards his younger brothers would not only be deprived of his authority, but also of his share in the family property. This shows that they took a serious view of the eldest brother's failure in observing his responsibilities towards his younger brothers.

L. Guy Brown has lucidly pointed out the significance of the position of the first-born child, especially if the child is a son.[266] The experiences connected with each position, i.e., first, second, third child etc., are different, and in each case the individual will develop unique patterns of behaviour. Brown quotes Adler to say that experienced observers "can recognize whether an individual is first born, an only child, the youngest child or the like."[267] This will be particularly pronounced in those cultures, like the Hindu, where the eldest son is recognized as an important individual in the family from the beginning, to whose arrival in the world the whole family has been looking forward. Brown further points out: "Where there are other children, a great responsibility is often thrust upon the eldest child. If he accepts the burden, he usually develops into a stable conservative person. He will have a great reverence for family traditions and heir-looms. It devolves upon

[257] Mahā. Anu. Adhy. 105.
[258] Ibid. 105, 2.
[259] Ibid. 105, 4.
[260] Ibid. 105, 7.
[261] Ibid. 105, 18.
[262] Ibid. 105, 7.
[263] Ibid. 105, 7.
[264] Ibid. 105, 12.
[265] Cf. Young: *Social Psychology* (First Ed., 1937), p. 240 ff.; Brown: *Social Psychology*, pp. 88–92.
[266] Brown, L. G.: *Social Psychology*, McGraw-Hill, N.Y. 1934, page 88 ff.
[267] Adler, A.: *Understanding Human Nature*, p. 149.

him not only to protect his younger brothers and sisters but also to cherish everything connected with the family name. Always and everywhere he must be the perfect example. If he does not rebel and consider himself the family martyr he will be a law-abiding citizen, conforming always to the demands of his family and community. He will develop a great sense of doing things because it is his duty. Security will be his dominant interest.[268]

However, such family and cultural traditions which place a high premium on being the first-born son are also likely to create another type of personality—the eldest son "who feels that he alone can do things right and becomes a chronic critic. . . . No matter how well things are done by the other members of the family, there will always be fault-finding on the part of the eldest. In this case he may become the family martyr in his own estimation and may proceed to make himself into one by playing secondary rôles, then feeling sorry for himself. There is some compensation for him in making cutting remarks, in criticism. These become a means by which he keeps up a high opinion of himself."[269]

It must be remembered, however, that it is not the chronological birth order or position in itself, but the psychological position which the child occupies in the family which is really significant and tells on the development of the child's personality. "His psychological position in the family," observe Murphy and Murphy, "is of the utmost importance for the development of social behaviour, but 'psychological position' is by no means completely dependent on birth order."[270] After representing a digest of fifty birth order studies which indicate inconclusive or contradictory results,[271] they conclude that "the objective fact of ordinal position in the family, without regard to its meaning to the child, to the siblings, and to the parents, is sure to yield meagre psychological results. The question whether the child feels accepted and loved; his emotional relation with his parents; competition or support which brothers and sisters bring to him; and the specific pressures or areas of freedom and stimulus that come along with one position in the family or another are probably more important, than the objective fact of ordinal position."[272]

In a culture like the Hindu, however, in which the importance attached to being the eldest son is hemmed in by *dharma*-injunctions of heavy responsibilities and duties attached to the position, towards the younger as well as towards the elder members of the family, and in which failure to abide by them is threatened with the penalty not only of the loss of that position but also of a share in the family property and of considerable degradation, the position and its attendant glorification is much less likely to lead to the second type of personality as Brown has pointed out above. And, even though no case has been known where the eldest brother's failure to observe his duties and responsibilities towards the younger siblings has resulted in his being deprived of his family share, it is within the knowledge and experience of many a Hindu, even to this day, that he has, in quite a number of Hindu families, even sacrificed personal comforts and achievements in order to support and bring up his younger siblings, to give them better education and help them attain better positions in life, or, if the younger sibling is a sister to be married, to secure a good match for her.

268 Brown, L. G.: op. cit.
269 Brown, L. G.: op. cit.
270 Murphy, G., Murphy, L. B. and Newcomb, T. M.: *Experimental Social Psychology*, 1937, pp. 362–3.
271 Ibid. pp. 348–62.
272 Ibid. p. 363.

5

Let us now try to see the position of the daughter in the family. It is enjoined that the father should look upon his daughters with the tenderest feeling. In the opinion of the *Mahābhārata*, the goddess of prosperity herself always resides in the persons of one's daughters.[273] According to the *Dharma-Śāstras*, the *grihastha* should never quarrel with his daughters.[274] One should regard one's daughter as the highest object of tenderness (*duhitā kripaṇam puram*).[275]

On the other hand, there are also statements which go to show that the birth of a daughter was looked upon with disfavour. Thus, the wife who was successively giving birth to daughters only was allowed to be superseded, after eleven years since marriage, by marrying another wife.[276]

One who has no son is allowed to 'appoint' his daughter (*sutām kurvīta putrikām*), so that her son may perform his funeral rites and *śrāddha*.[277] Manu tells us that the great Dakśa Prajāpati, the lord of all created beings, himself followed this rule and appointed all his daughters to give their sons into his family, in order to multiply his race (*vivridhyartham svavamśasya*).[278] The son of such an appointed daughter inherits the whole estate of the maternal grandfather.[279] If a son is subsequently born to the maternal grandfather, both of them are to share equally in the estate.[280] The separate property of the mother, however, is shared by the unmarried daughter; the son of the appointed daughter has no share in it.[281] A daughter who is not married till her father's death is to receive from each of her brothers, after the father's death, one-fourth of his share.[282]

The daughter must be given in marriage by the father at the proper time.[283] If a proper suitor of good qualities and of the same *varṇa* is found even before the maiden has attained marriageable age, the father should not hesitate to give his daughter to him.[284] The *Mahānirvāṇatantra* says that the daughter should be brought up and educated with care like the son till her marriage.[285] The maiden, on the other hand, is granted the privilege of remaining unmarried till her death in her father's house, rather than marrying a person destitute of good qualities (*guṇa-h. na*).[286] Ordinarily, she is not to take any initiative in regard to bringing about her own marriage. She may wait for three years, after she has attained the proper age, for being wedded. After that time she may take it upon herself to choose her mate from her own *varṇa* and worthy of her (*sadriśam*) without waiting for the help of her father.[287] She incurs no guilt thereby.[288] Only, she is not entitled, then, to take away with

---

[273] Mahā, xiii, 11, 14 (Bombay Ed. by Gaṇpat Ātmāram) *'nityam nivasate Lakshmīh kanyakāsu pratishṭhitā'*.
[274] Man. iv, 180; Mahā. Śānti. 243, 15–16; Yāj. i, 153.
[275] Man. iv, 185 (—*kripaṇam=param kripāpātram*—Kullūka); Mahā. Śānti. 243, 20–1.
[276] See *Supra*; Man. ix, 81; Bau. ii, 4, 6; cf. Nār. xii, 94.
[277] Man. ix, 127; Vis. xv, 5; Vas. xvii, 15–17; Gau. xxviii, 18; Bau. ii, 3, 15.
[278] Man. ix, 128.
[279] Man. ix, 128.
[280] Man. ix, 134.
[281] Man. ix, 133; Yāj. ii, 128.
[282] Man. ix, 118; Yāj. ii, 124; Vis. xviii, 35; Brihas. xxv, 64.
[283] Man. ix, 4; Yāj. i, 64; Vas. xvii, 69–70; Bau. iv, 1, 12, 17–19; etc.
[284] Man. ix, 88; Vas. xvii, 70; Gau. xviii, 21; Bau. iv, 1, 11.
[285] *Mahānirvāṇatantra*, viii, 47.
[286] Man. ix, 89.
[287] Man. ix, 90; Yāj. i, 64; Vis. xxiv, 40; Gau. xviii, 20; Vas. xvii, 67–68; also Mahā. Anu. 44, 16.
[288] Man. ix, 91.

her the ornaments which her parents, or her brothers might have given her.[289] On the other hand, if the young maiden who has attained marriageable age has no father or other guardian to arrange for her marriage, she may approach the King, and with his permission, may herself choose her groom (*varayet svayam*) and marry him.[290] Vātsyāyana also opines that a maiden, who, though possessed of good qualities and born in a humble family or even when well-born, is destitute of wealth, or has lost her parents, and is come of age, should move herself to arrange her own marriage.[291]

Once a daughter is betrothed to a man, she shall be given to him only.[292] "Neither ancients nor moderns who were good men have done such a deed,—that after promising a daughter to one man, they gave her to another."[293] Nārada however lays down some exceptions to this rule: Thus, should a more respectable suitor appearing eligible in point of capabilities to acquire *dharma, artha* and *kāma* is found, then the former engagement may be broken even though *śulka* i.e. financial consideration has been already accepted for the maiden.[294] So also, when a groom goes abroad after having espoused (*pratigrihya*) a maiden, she should wait for him till she passes through three monthly sicknesses, and then choose another husband.[295] On the other hand, if a man, after having plighted his faith to a maiden deserts her, although she is blameless, he shall be fined and shall be compelled to marry the maiden even against his will.[296]

The sale of a daughter in marriage has been forbidden to a Hindu father. Even a *śūdra* ought not to take nuptial fee, when he gives away his daughter; for, he who takes a fee sells his daughter.[297] Again, "No father who knows (what is right and wrong) must take even the smallest gratuity in return for his daughter; for, a man, who, through avarice takes a gratuity (virtually) sells his offspring."[298]

6

Finally, we shall consider the position of the parents in the family. The term *pitarau* (dual of *pitri*) is used to denote father (*pitā*) and mother (*mātā*) collectively. Literally, however, *pitā* (the nominative singular of *pitri*) means "father"; just as *mātā* (the nominative singular of *mātri*) means mother. The term *pitri* is derived from *'pā'* to 'protect' or to 'preserve', and *pitri* therefore etymologically means 'protector'. The derivative meaning of the word thus emphasizes the most important obligation of the father with reference to the offspring, viz., to look after the helpless young one and give it care

---

[289] Man. ix, 92; Gau. xviii, 20.

[290] Nār. xii, 22: *yadā tu kaśchin naiva syāt kanyā rājānam āsrayet / anujnayā varam tasya parīkshya varayet svayam/ /*

[291] Kām. iii, 4, 36.

[292] Man. ix, 47; Nār. xii, 28.

[293] Man. ix, 99.

[294] Nār. xii, 30: *kanyāyām prāpta-śulkāyām śreyānśched vara āvrajet / dharmārthakāma-samyuktam vākyam tatrān-ritam bhavet / /*

[295] Nār. xii, 24: *pratigrihya cha yah kanyām naro deśāntaram vrajet / trin ritūn samatikramya kanyānyām varayed varam / /* (The tr. is Dr. Jolly's).

[296] Nār. xii, 41: *pratigrhya cha yah kanyām adushṭām utsrujet narah / vineyah so'pyakāmo'pi kanyām tāmeva ched vahet / /*

[297] Man. ix, 98; cf. Āp. ii, 13, 11–12.

[298] Man. iii, 51; cf. Bau. i, 21, 2–3; Vas. i, 37–38; Āp. ii, 13, 11.

and protection. The *Rig-Veda* refers to the father as the symbol of all goodness and kindness.[299] He is described as fondly carrying the child in his arms, and playing with it on his lap.[300]

On the other hand, the father's word is to be always obeyed by the son.[301] The *Aitareya Brāhmaṇ*[302] narrates the story of a boy named Sunahsepa being sold by his father; so also there is a story in the *Rig Veda* of Rijrāśva who was blinded by his father.[303] But such acts have been condemned no sooner than narrated in the same passages. As MacDonell and Keith have pointed out in this connection, "to lay stress on . . . isolated and semimythical incidents would be unwise."[304] So, it becomes a really difficult task to judge the extent to which the father exercised dominion over his son in the Vedic period.

There are, though, other instances of the son carrying out the word of the father without even questioning its morality or propriety. Rāma gives his mother some instances of this kind, in support of his own desire to abdicate the throne and go in exile in order to fulfil his father's word of honour given to his step-mother in an unguarded moment.[305] Rishi Kandu, at his father's order, killed a cow even though he knew it was a sinful act on his part to do so; King Sagara at his father's command, started digging the earth till he himself perished in the act. Paraśurāma, again committed the most heinous crime of murdering his own mother at his father's command. Rāma stoutly argues and asserts, therefore before his mother that his duty was to obey his father, even if that meant disobedience of the mother's command. Thus of the two parents, the father's word is the more to be honoured than the mother's by the son. And the *Sukrā-Niti* has said that it was through the strength of their father's penances really that Paraśurāma got back his mother alive, and Rāma got back his kingdom;[306] and, due to the disobedience of their father's commands, the sons of Yayāti, and of Viswāmitra, came to be degraded to the lowest positions in life.[307] "One should always keep up the habit of serving one's father in word, thought and action; one should ever do that by which the father is satisfied; one should not do that by which the father is pained even on a single occasion."[308] Generally speaking, however, both the parents have to be respected by the offsprings with equal reverence.[309]

The *Mahābhārata* inculcates the same spirit of obedience to both the parents on the part of the offspring. The story of Bhīshma remaining a bachelor to the end of his life for the sake of his father's wish is well-known. He was the only son of his father King Santanu at the time the latter fell in love with a beautiful fisher girl and wanted to marry her. To satisfy the girl's father so that he may give his daughter to Santanu without hesitation, Bhīshma renounced his own claims on the throne in succession to his father, and further, took a vow not to marry so that he may have no sons to claim the throne against the sons of his father that may be born to the fisher girl. To carry out the father's word is the supreme duty of the son.[310] The father, the mother and the *guru*—these

[299] Rig. iv, 17, 17; viii, 86, 4, etc.
[300] Rig. i, 38, 1; v. 43, 7.
[301] Rig. i, 68, 5.
[302] Ait. Br. vii, 12 ff.
[303] Rig. i, 116, 16; also 117, 17; (From *Vedic Index*, i, 526).
[304] *Vedic Index*, i, p. 526.
[305] Rāmā. ii, 21, 30 ff.
[306] Śukr. N. ii, 78–79.
[307] Ibid. 83–85.
[308] Ibid. 86–87.
[309] Rāmā. ii, 30, 35, ff.
[310] Śānti. 272, 15.

three are always to be obeyed, and never to be insulted; there is no sinner in the world equal to the son who insults any of these three.[311] The five Pāṇḍava Princes married one wife just in order to carry out the command of their mother, though it was given under complete ignorance of the situation.[312] Whatever any of the five brothers earned or secured was submitted to their mother Kuntī, who would then, as a rule, ask all the five to share it. Arjuna, the third brother, won Princess Draupadī as his bride in an open competition for her hand, and the five brothers arrived home with her and announced joyfully from outside to their mother who was inside that they had brought Draupadī; whereupon Kuntī, without even looking at what was brought, said, as usual, that they should all share it!

Many other instances could be given from the two Epics to show the very high degree of filial reverence expected of the sons and daughters. The story, for instance, is told of a boy Chira-kārin, son of sage Gautama, who was ordered by his father to kill his mother Ahilyā with whom Indra had committed adultery. Chirakārin—he was so called because he would always reflect for a long while (*chiram*) before acting—however, pondered a great deal over the propriety of the order given by his father: He could not commit the sinful act of killing his mother at all; for though obedience to the father was a very high *dharma* for him (*pitur-ādnā paro dharmah*), by his own *dharma* he was also bound to protect his mother (*sva-dharmo mātri-rakśanam*).[313] Who could be happy after killing his own mother? On the other hand, who could ever acquire any prestige (*pratishṭhā*) by disobeying his father?[314] The father is the son's foremost of *gurus* (*gurur agryah*) and his highest *dharma* (*paro dharmah*);[315] the father being pleased, all gods are pleased.[316] On the other hand, the mother too, is equally venerable; she is the principle cause (*hetuh*) of the union of the five elements (*pancha-bhautikah*) which make for the son's birth as a human being.[317] She is the soothing balm against all sorts of calamities that may befall the son;[318] with the mother the man feels protected; without her, he feels deserted.[319] "The man who, though shorn of all prosperity, (*śriyā hīno'pi*), enters his home calling out—'O mother!'—does not suffer from grief; nor does decrepitude (*sthāviram*) ever attack him."[320] A person whose mother is alive, even if he has sons and grandsons and is a hundred years old is for her but a child of two.[321] Able or disabled, lean or robust, the son is always protected by the mother. . . . When his mother leaves him, then does the son become old, then does he become stricken with grief, then does he feel that this world has no interest for him (*śūnyam jagat*). There is no shelter like the mother; there is no refuge like her; there is no defence better than her; there could be no one dearer than her (to the son).[322] The mother is called *dhātrī* of her son, because she has borne him in her womb (*kukshi-samdhāraṇāt*); she is called *jananī*, because she is the principal cause of the son's birth (*jananāt*); she is known by the name *ambā* also,

---

311 Śānti. 108, 29–31.
312 Ādi. 211.
313 Mahā. Śānti. 266, 11.
314 Ibid. 266, 12.
315 Ibid. 266, 17.
316 Ibid. 266, 21.
317 Ibid. 266, 25.
318 Ibid. 266, 26:—'*sarvasyārtasya nirvritih*'.
319 Ibid. 266, 26:—'*mātrilābhe sanāthatvam anāthatvam viparyaye*'.
320 Ibid. 266, 27.
321 Ibid. 266, 28.
322 Ibid. 266, 29–31.

for she rears his limbs (*angānām vardhanāt*); she is *vīrasū* because she gives birth to valiant (*vīra*) children; and she is *suśrū* for she nurses and looks after (*suśrūshaṇāt*) the son.[323] In the person of the father is a combination of all gods; but in the person of the mother, however, is a combination of all gods and also all humanity.[324]—All these and such other thoughts had filled Chira-kārin's mind, and he passed a long time, in fact many days in this manner in an indecisive state of mind, till the father returned back, now repentant of his cruel order given to his son, and burning with grief; he was, however, delighted to find out that his son had not carried out the order as yet!

Under the injunctions of the *Dharma-Śāstras*, the father is the object of the deepest reverence for the sons. He is the first of those in the family to whom respect has to be paid by the children of the family.[325] Manu says that the father, indeed, is the Guru of his son.[326] Some *Smriti* writers have given the father a considerably high position of authority in the family; he rules over his family as a king over his subjects.[327] Vasishṭha has said that the father has the power to drive his son out of the house, and even to sell him.[328] But Maṇu and Yājnavalkya forbid that the father should ever cast off his son, unless he has committed a very serious crime.[329]

The child may be punished by beating only when the parent wants to correct him, not otherwise; and even then, such beating could be done on his back, and never on a noble part of the body.[330] And, the *Mahābhārata* advises that the son should be only "mildly reprimanded by parents for purposes of instruction."[331] Punishment has been one of the chief means with most parents for controlling and canalizing the behaviour of their children. However, too often, it is indulged in by parents to prove their authority and to satisfy their prestige notions rather than for the genuine welfare of the child. Indiscriminate and harsh punishment to children leads to warped and distorted personalities in later adulthood. "Punishment" says Brown, " . . . . is a definite experience that will become part of the organization of past experiences on which all attitudes are based."[332]

In the *Smritis*, at some places, the mother is referred to as more venerable than even the father. She is said to be thousand times more venerable than the father.[333] In general, the *Smritis*, too, emphasize that the mother, the father and the preceptor, as well as the eldest brother must be respected and obeyed by every one.[334] And, one should never offend one's father, mother and Guru.

The reader will be interested in the following account of a modern Hindu family in action, given by a young Hindu student, from the files of case-studies collected by Professors Burgess and Locke:—

"My family is not a very big one. There are three brothers who are married, the widowed mother, and two daughters who are also married but have not gone to live with their husbands. The widowed

---

[323] Ibid. 266, 32–33.

[324] Ibid. 266, 43.

[325] Man. ii, 145; Gaut. vi, 1–3.

[326] Ibid: cf. Yāj. i, 34.

[327] Nār. i, 32–42.

[328] Vas. xv, 2.

[329] Man. viii, 389; Yāj. ii, 237; similarly in Yāj. i, 35; Gau. vi, 51; Vas. xiii, 48, etc.

[330] Man. iv, 164 and viii, 299–300; cf. Vis. lxxi, 80–81.

[331] Mahā. Anu. 104, 37.

[332] Brown, L. G.: *Social Psychology*, p. 69.

[333] Man. ii, 145: "*sahasram tu pitrīn mātā gauraveṇātirichyate*".

[334] Man. ii, 225–37; Vis. xxx, 1–10.

mother is about 50 years old, and the eldest son is about 35 years of age. The youngest son is still in his teens although he has a wife and a child. Both the daughters are little girls of not more than 10.

"All the members of the big family co-operate and work for each other. All cook and eat in the same place. The earnings, savings, and toil are shared by all the family members. One of the brothers looks after their property and supervises the agricultural work. The youngest of them stays at home and attends to business. He works at his big shop with his assistants, selling and buying. He has also the responsibility of seeing that other family members, especially the women, are not in any trouble.

"The women in this family have really no well-defined work. All of them work together. They have their servants who do the hardest work. Usually, the youngest wife is the one who works for the others. The widowed mother does nothing but she manages everything. She has absolute rule over the family members. She sees that the daughters-in-law behave, that the house-father (the eldest son) receives the respect due to him from other family members, that servants of the household are well-behaved and orderly, that the community thinks well of the house, that the family priest is respected and honoured, that enough money is contributed for feeding the Brāhmans, that gods are venerated properly, and that there is some substantial saving in the house every month.

"I was at the wedding of one of my sisters who was 8 years old at that time. The marriage was arranged by the widowed mother. The bridegroom was not more than 12. The bride viewed her husband as a playmate and was told by her mother and the Brāhman priest to place her affection on him, and never think of any other boy."[335]

This family, on the whole, shows not only the influence of the traditional Hindu ideology but also the influence of the later system of early marriage of boys and girls.

These are some of the salient aspects of the Hindu family life. The *kula* or the family was no doubt regarded by the Hindu as the place of nursery where the individual learns his lessons in social life. Here, in the *kula*, were given him lessons in affection, lessons in giving respect to elders, lessons in subserving individual inclinations and even aspirations, for the purpose of the attainment of collective ends. The sex instinct has to be directed to the end of the continuity of the family. The home (*griha*) is primarily the place where the three objects of life, *dharma, artha* and *kāma*—spiritual merit, wealth-earning, and the gratification of the senses—have to be practised in terms of a harmonious synthesis together, towards the end of attaining the final beatitude (*mokśa*); and, as has been observed by Manu, the real good of man consists in a proper aggregate of these three *purushārthas*.[336]

And in this *grihasthāśrama*, again, is *yajna* preached for the *grihastha*. The definition of *yajna* as preached in this *āśrama* is perhaps the most important. Living in the midst of circumstances and situations which are likely to develop the ego and multiply its involvements and of 'mine'-ness and 'thine'-ness, living as a *grihastha*, as a *kuṭumbin*, as a man of the world (*nāgarika*), the individual is yet asked to live and believe that this is not the final end for which he is born.[337] The individual is expected to believe that his life as a man of the world is only a part of his duties (*niyata-karma*) whereby he is to fulfil his obligations to his wife, to his children, to his family, to his departed ancestors and to his community. And, in the midst of all these circumstances, the

---

335 W. E. Burgess and H. J. Locke: *The Family*, pp. 18–19. N.Y., American Book Co., 1950.

336 Man. ii, 224.

337 Cf. Thoothi: "*The Vaishṇavas of Gujarāt*", p. 54.

individual is expected to live out of, and, as if, apart from these, as if he were performing the *yajna*. In the midst of world and worldliness, the *grihastha* is no doubt a part of it; yet he is called upon to behave with a spirit of detachment in all his sense-doings, in the true spirit of a *yajna*. The symbolic fire in the home and its continuity and its worship, the various ceremonials that centre around it,—all these show that the home is only a trust vested in the *grihastha*, a *yajnakuṇḍa* as it were, in which the *grihastha* and those under his care have to pour their lives for the perpetuity of that fire and what it represents and embodies. Not only the *grihastha's* and the *grihinī's* duties and doing have this note of direction; but this note also governs the attitude which the other members of the house are to have towards these two and towards each other.

CHAPTER VII

ATTITUDE TOWARDS THE WOMAN
And Her Place in the Society

The attitude of a community towards the woman has a great social significance in any society. The attitude of the Hindu towards the woman as reflected in the *Śāstrakāras*' and other authorities' writings has already been considered by us in several respects in the course of our discussions on education, marriage and family; but that had necessarily to be restricted to the specific contexts only. Here we shall consider the attitude of the Hindu towards womankind as a whole and in general, so as to give a complete picture of the woman's place in Hindu society.

In the *Rig-Veda*, the husband and the wife are described as taking equal part in the sacrificial rites. The *'dampatī'*—the householder and his wife—with 'one accord' press the Soma (a plant, most important in sacrificial offerings), rinse and mix it with milk, and offer adoration to the God.[1] The Vedic literature mentions many a woman's name who attained eminence as philosophers along with men. Viśvavārā, of the family (*gotra*) of Atri, is described as a philosopher (*brahmavādini*) and well versed in the sacred texts (*mantra-drashṭrī*), and is the author of a hymn in the *Rig-Veda*.[2] Ghoshā, the daughter of sage Kakshīvān, was the author of two hymns of *Rig-Veda*;[3] and Lopāmudrā, wife of Agasti, composed two verses.[4] Queen *Śāśvatī*, wife of King Asanga, is also a philosopher of the Vedic times;[5] so was Apālā, another philosopher (*Brahmavādinī*) well versed in the sacred texts (*mantra-drashṭrī*).[6] Indrāṇī, the wife of Indra, too was a *mantra-drashṭrī*.[7] So again, two ladies, Sikatā and Nivāvarī, composed ten verses of a hymn.[8] The *Rig-Veda* also relates to us the story of Brihaspati and his wife Juhu, which is pertinent in this connection: He left his wife and went away for practising penances; but the Gods explained to him how it was improper to perform penances alone without wife.[9] These are some of the instances from the Vedas which speak for the status of woman during the Vedic period.[10]

Thus, during the Vedic period, we have reasons to believe that so far as education was concerned, the position of women was generally not unequal to that of the men. Woman had similar education as man; she took part in philosophic debates like man and with men; she practised penances like

---

[1] Rig. viii, 31, 5; cf. also x, viii, 27, 7.
[2] Rig. v, 28.
[3] Rig. x, 39–40.
[4] Rig. i, 179, 1–2.
[5] Rig. viii, 1, 34.
[6] Rig. viii, 80; 91.
[7] Rig. x, 86 and 145.
[8] Rig. ix, 86, 11–20.
[9] Rig. x, 109.
[10] See also ch. IV

man. This shows that man and woman were regarded as having equally important status in the social life of the early period.

Similarly, the *Śatapatha Brāhmaṇa* informs us that woman was regarded as an equal sharer with man of the responsibilities and duties in the home. The following passages from the *Śatapatha Brāhmaṇa* will illustrate this: "When the husband is about to ascend (the sacrificial altar), he addresses his wife in these words: 'Come, wife, let us ascend to heavens'; and the wife answers, 'Yes, let us ascend'. The reason why he addresses his wife thus is that she is one half of his own self; therefore as long as he has no wife, so long he does not propagate his species, so long he is no complete individual; but when he has a wife, he propagates his species, and then he is complete. 'Complete I want to go to that supreme goal,'—thus he thinks; therefore, he addresses his wife in this manner."[11] One who has not married is not competent to offer the ritual prayers and sacrifice.[12] In fact, the duty of singing the *mantras* at the sacrificial ceremony was to be performed by the wife.[13] These passages bring out to us that the woman was regarded as having an equally important share in the drama of human life as man. Man without woman was considered as an "inadequate person."

But in the same *Brāhmaṇa* there is another passage which shows that woman is regarded as intellectually inferior to man, or rather, that she is regarded as more emotional and less rational by nature than man; therefore, she is apt to fall an easy prey to external appearances; she lacks the ability for true appreciation or balance of mind and does not possess depth of reason. This passage relates to the story of the theft of *soma* (nectar or elixir) from heaven. While Gāyatrī was carrying *soma* away from heaven, a Gandharva (a celestial demi-god belonging to the class of musicians) stole it away from her. The Gods devised a trick to get *soma* back from the Gandharvas. They knew that the Gandharvas were fond of women. So they sent Vāk (the Goddess of Speech) to them; and she managed to bring *soma* back to the Gods. But the Gandharvas too followed her, and said to the Gods, '*soma* shall be yours and Vāk ours'. 'So be it!' said the Gods; 'but if she would rather come hither, do not carry her away by force; let us woo her.' The Gods accordingly wooed her. "The Gandharvas recited the Vedas to her, saying 'see how we know it, see how we know it!'" The Gods, however, once again decided to take advantage of their knowledge of woman's nature; they created the lute, and sang and played upon it and amused Vāk, whereupon she returned to them. "But in truth, she returned to them vainly; for, she turned away from those engaged in praising and praying (i.e. the Gandharvas), to dance and song (i.e. to Gods). Wherefore, even to this day, women are given to vain things; for, it was on this wise that Vāk turned thereto, and other women do as she did. And hence, it is to him who dances and sings that they most readily take a fancy."[14]

This passage purports to explain that a woman has the weakness of being emotional or sentimental and can be easily deceived by external appearance. It also suggests that the fair sex is more sensitive to expressions of fine arts. As we proceed we shall find somewhat similar views about woman's nature in the *Mahābhārata* and other works.

With such views, we may compare a very recent analysis by Dr. A. A. Roback, formerly of Harvard University, who argues that there is an inborn basis for the disposition of consistency, and that, on the whole, women naturally lack it:—

---

[11] Śat. Br. v, 2, 1, 10.

[12] Śat. Br. v, 1, 6, 10: *a-yajnīyo vaisha yo a-patnīkah.*

[13] Śat. Br. xiv, 3, 1, 35: *patnī-karma eva ete atra kurvanti yad idgātārah.*

[14] Śat. Br. iii, 2, 4, 2–6.

> ". . . . Women, too, are, as many great novelists and essayists have remarked, incapable of acting with consistency, and, unless moved by pity, are prone to commit many unfair acts on various pretexts, chief among which is that, being the weaker sex, or the weaker of two of their own sex, or having 'gone through' more than their rival or expecting to enjoy life less than some one else, they ought not to lose at least this opportunity of making up for the hardship either already endured or in store for them.
>
> "Consistency Lacking in Women:—Such a warm champion of woman's cause as Moll tries to gloss over this character defect by an explanation which leaves much to be desired. 'When women', he writes, 'are so frequently denied the sense of justice, it is. . . .a matter of the present motive preventing other considerations from presenting themselves.' (A. Moll: "*Sexualität und Charakter*": *Sexual-Probleme; Zt. f. Sexualw'ft. u. Sexualpolitik*, 1914, Vol. X). What is this but an admission of the fact that they are not considerate of others, in other words, that they lack the impulse to apply to others the same measure as they apply to themselves?
>
> "We hear it said and repeated almost *ad nauseam* that women are prompted by their feelings rather than by their reason. But such a hollow statement possesses no scientific value. Many women reason well enough at the very time they are supposed to be guided by their feelings. Their reasoning, however, lacks consideration for others. It is the element of consistency alone which is wanting—a gap which is sometimes filled by the substitute of pity. If the above time-honoured and apparently universal belief about the mainspring of woman's conduct is to be invested with any psychological meaning, we should necessarily hold to one or the other of these alternatives; either that women, on the whole, are born with stronger instinctive tendencies, or else the consistency urge is weaker in them than in man. The former alternative does not seem plausible, more especially as the maxim of parsimony would lead us to explain the phenomenon through some weakness in the one factor rather than in the many.
>
> "It is, therefore, not in the relative strength of the instinct that we shall find the reason the lack of objectivity in female conduct, but in the relative weakness of the fundamental principle of conduct which has its root psychologically in some mechanism making for consistency."[15]

With the above quotation from Roback, we may compare Freud's view: "It may be admitted that women have but little sense of justice, and this is no doubt connected with the preponderance of envy of their mental life."[16]

However, recent cross-cultural studies by anthropologists like Margaret Mead[17] seem to indicate clearly that personality and character differences are in general basically influenced by the cultural norms of the society in which an individual is born and bred. Even the character and temperament traits associated with 'maleness' and 'femaleness' are profoundly influenced and are the resultant of the peculiarities of the culture to which its men and women belong. Excepting for the natural anatomical and bio-physiological differences among the sexes, there could be hardly any psychological traits or characteristics, in general, which are not influenced by the peculiar traditions, beliefs and attitudes current in the culture. These traditions, beliefs and attitudes influence the behaviour of men and women born in the culture from early childhood, and mould and shape their behaviour to bring it in conformity with the standards set up in the culture as a result of these beliefs and attitudes. Individuals who deviate from such standards or norms are looked upon as 'queer',

---

[15] A. A. Roback: *The Psychology of Character*, 3rd Ed., pp. 609–611, London, Kegan Paul, 1952.

[16] Freud: *New Introductory Lectures on Psychoanalysis*, (1934), pp. 134 ff.

[17] Margaret Mead: *Sex and Temperament in Three Primitive Societies*, in *From the South Seas*, William Morrow, 1939. Also the same author's *Male and Female*, William Morrow, New York, 1949.

eccentric, unusual or abnormal. But all such judgments are relative to the particular cultural norms accepted and established in the given society.

It thus becomes a circle, 'vicious' or otherwise, of human behaviour: Men and women behave in certain typical ways respectively in a society because their society expects them to behave in these ways; and the society expects them to behave in these ways because all the members of the two sexes in that society are actually found to follow those respective modes of behaviour. Even such traits which are broadly classified as "masculinity" and "femininity", according to our experience in our cultures, and all the many characteristics respectively associated with each of them, may show a complete reversal of expression in different cultures with opposite norms for the sexes than ours, men showing all the feminine characteristics and women all the masculine characteristics.—excepting of course, the natural anatomical and bio-physiological differences,—as for example among the Tchambulis of New Guinea.[18]

Such divergences on a whole cultural or group scale in certain societies are adjudged as exceptional by Helene Deutsch, an eminent Freudian.[19] These exceptions, in her view, cannot affect the general principle relating to the universal personality and temperamental differences which distinguish men from women. She further maintains that "this principle will continue to assert itself until we succeed in influencing the internal, hormonal constitution of the human body", and also until the anatomy of the sexes and the reproductive functions are altered.[20]

It must be said here that Deutch and other Freudians in general have not had any first hand knowledge of the ways of men and women in societies other than their own, viz., the European or the American white groups. Cross-cultural studies and evidence furnished by Mead, Benedict and others is more scientific for general conclusions on the issues concerned.

In the epics of the *Rāmāyaṇa* and the *Mahābhārata*, the question of the position of woman could be studied from so many points of view. And the views expressed are not always free from contradiction of each other, as we shall see presently.

In the *Rāmāyaṇa*, Kausalyā, the mother of Rāma performs the *svasti-yāga*, the sacrifice to ensure good luck to him, on the morning of the proposed installation of her son as the Crown Prince.[21] Sītā is described as offering *sandhyā* prayers, i.e. ritual prayers which are offered with *mantras* in the morning, noon and evening.[22] Rāma had to go in exile for twelve years to fulfil his father's word given to his step-mother; and, on his return home after years of exile, he was given the first *abhisheka*, a symbolic coronation "bath", first at the hands of several unmarried girls, and then by the Ministers and Generals.[23]

The *Rāmāyaṇa* is a glorious illustration for the Hindu of the ideal womanhood. Sītā is prepared to cast off all the luxuries of the palace and accompany her husband to the forest. On the eve of Rāma's departure to the forest to fulfil the word of his father, King DaŚaratha, Rāma declared to Sītā that he had no intention to take her with him and make her suffer so many hardships; against this she argued thus:

---

[18] Ibid.

[19] Helene Deutsch: *The Psychology of Women*, 2 vols. Vol. I, pp. 224–225. Norton, New York, 1944.

[20] Ibid.

[21] Rāmā. ii, 20, 15: *sā kshauma-vasanā devī nityam vrataparāyaṇā/agnim juhoti sma tadā mantravat-krita-mangalā.*

[22] Rāmā. v, 15, 48.

[23] Rāmā. vi, 138, 38; 61.

"My lord, the mother, father and son,
Receive their lots by merit won;
The brother and the daughter find
The portions to their deeds assigned.
The wife alone what'er await,
Must share on earth her husband's fate;
So now the King's command which sends
Thee to the wild, to me extends.
The wife can find no refuge, none,
In father, mother, self or son:
Both here, and when they vanish hence,
Her husband is her sole defence."[24]

Sītā is regarded as one of the five ideal and revered women of India, the other four being Ahalyā, Draupadī, Tārā and Mandodarī; even a mental recital of the names of these five is said to purge one of one's great sins (*mahāpātaka*).[25] It is highly significant to note, in this connection, that each one of these ladies happened to have some blemish or other in her career or behaviour for which, however, she was in no way responsible. And therefore, each one of them was, from the moral standard of purity of motives, regarded as a woman of ideal character. Thus, Ahalyā, the wife of sage Gautama, was seduced by God Indra who disguised himself as her husband and deceived her; Draupadī was married to five husbands, the sons of Kuntī, who unknowingly asked them, as usual, to share like good brothers what really one of them had won in an open contest,—for her hand was won by Arjuna, the third brother, from amongst a number of suitors by fulfilling a difficult test of archery; Sītā was abducted by her husband's enemy Rāvaṇa with a view to violating her chastity, and though she successfully resisted his attempts and remained faithful to her husband, Dame Scandal was busy spreading malicious gossip about her; Tarā was abducted by The Moon who refused to deliver her up to her husband Brihaspati, the *Guru* of the Gods, until God Brahmā compelled the Moon to restore her to Brihaspati; and, Mandodarī was the wife of King Rāvaṇa, supposed to be the villain of the *Rāmāyaṇa* and was the enemy of Rāmachandra. Evidently, these women have been judged, not by their physical failures or blemishes in behaviour for which they were in no way responsible, but by their otherwise exemplary conduct as wives and by the purity of their motives and of their ideals. And even to this day, there is an attitude of deep reverence towards these 'ideal' ladies in the mind of the Hindu.

In the *Mahābhārata*, there are some notable instances which illustrate how women used to take upon themselves the task of counselling and guiding men on religious and social questions. Thus, a lady named Sulabhā discusses the problem of attaining *mokśa*.[26] It is a fairly long discourse: Sulabhā who was "gifted with *yogic* power",[27] had really come to test the knowledge of King Janaka. Both of them exchanged whatever he and she had to say on the problem. After "hearing the words of Sulabhā fraught with excellent sense and reason," King Janaka could not reply thereto.[28] Again, the Brāhmaṇa preceptor (*guru*) of King Senajit cites to him the authority of the verses sung

[24] Rāmā. (Tr. By Griffith) ii. 27.

[25] *Ahalyā Draupadī Sītā Tārā Mandodarī tathā/pancha-kanyam smaren nityam mahā-pātakanāśanam.*

[26] Mahā. Śānti. 321, verses 20–192.

[27] Ibid. 321, 16.

[28] Ibid. 321, 193.

by a courtesan (*veśyā*), called Pingalā (*pingalayā gītā gāthā*) on the problem of life, death, and knowledge.[29] In the Vanaparva, again, Draupadī gives a long lecture to Yudhisṭhira and Bhima upon certain problems of conduct and mortality.[30] She is also called a *paṇḍitā*, a learned lady.[31]

In a later Parva, Draupadī is once more found giving a long discourse[32] to her husband on his duties as a Kshatriya, i.e., a member of the warrior class. Yudhishṭhira, disgusted with war and its evil effects, is in favour of renunciation of all worldly affairs. But Draupadī reprimands him for this foolish idea of his. "If," says she, "these brothers of yours were wise, they would have locked you up with all the unbelievers (in a prison) and taken charge of the government of the earth. The man, who, on account of feeble intellect, acts thus never succeeds in achieving prosperity."

Let us try to find out some more light on the question from the views on woman expressed in the *Mahābhārata* itself. In the Anuśāsana-parva we are told that Yudhishṭhira requested the wise Grandfather Bhīshma to enlighten him regarding the nature of women (*strīṇām svabhāvam*).[33] "It is said that woman is the root of all evil, and that she is narrow-minded," says Yudhishṭhira.[34] Bhīshma replies to him that, in a sense, the female is naturally a temptress and a lurer;[35] moreover, she is not endowed with strength of will enough to resist temptation; therefore, she always stands in need of protection by man.[36] There are two types of women the virtuous (*sādhvī*) and non-virtuous (*a-sādhvī*). The virtuous ones are the mothers of the earth, they sustain the whole earth. The non-virtuous type are given to sinful behaviour and can be recognized by the signs or marks (*lakshaṇa*) expressive of the evil that is in them which appears on their persons.[37] The face or perhaps the body, in Bhīshma's opinion here, seems to be the index of a woman's character.[38]

It is because of this natural weakness of her character that she is not to be held as much responsible as the man for her sins. Woman should not be condemned altogether as a sinner because she naturally lacks the strength of mind to resist temptations. ". . . . Woman commits really no offence", says Chira-kārin, referring to Indra's adultery with his own mother by duping her. "It is man only who commits offences. By committing an act of adultery, only the man becomes sullied with sin. . . . Women can commit no sin. It is man who becomes sullied with sin. Indeed, on account of the natural weakness of the sex as shown in every act, and their liability to solicitation, women cannot

---

[29] Mahā. Sānti 174 (In the Mahābhārata, this story is narrated by Bhīshma to Yudhishṭhira.)

[30] Mahā. Van. 27 ff.

[31] Ibid.

[32] Mahā. Śānti. 14. (The whole chapter).

[33] Mahā. Anu. 38, 1.

[34] Ibid.: *striyo hi mūlam doshāṇām laghu-chittā hi tāh smritāh/.*

[35] Mahā. Anu. 38–39.

[36] Mahā. Anu. 43, 19.

[37] Ibid. 43, 19–21:

> "*striyah sādhvyo mahābhāgāh sammatā loka-mātarah/*
> *dhārayanti mahīm rājan imām sa-vana-kānanam//.*
> *a-sādhvyaś chāpi dur-vrittā . ./*
> *vijneyā lakshaṇair dushṭaih sva-gātra-sahajair nripa//*"

[38] For a modern discussion of the problem, see A. M. Ludovici: "*The Choice of a Mate*", Part II, pp. 239 seq., where he discusses the question of physiognomy, human points and morphology, as avenues of approach from the visible to the invisible in order to know the man or the woman.

be considered as offenders."[39] The Sage Ashṭāvakra, who had gone out in search of knowledge of the nature of the woman, is informed in a similar manner of "the lightness of the female character" by the celestial Lady to whom he approached to obtain the knowledge.[40]

In another Adhyāya in the same Parva we find Bhīshma speaking in terms of high reverence about woman. "Women should always be adored (*pūjyā*) and treated with love (*lālayitavyā*)."[41] Where women are treated with honour, the very Gods are said to be propitiated; and where women are not adored, all acts become fruitless (*aphalāh*).[42] If the women of a family, on account of the treatment they receive, indulge in grief and tears, that family soon becomes extinct.[43] Those homes which are cursed by women meet with destruction and ruin as if scorched by some Atharvan rite; such homes lose their splendour; their growth and prosperity cease.[44] Bhīshma further tells Yudhishṭhira that Manu, on the eve of his departure from this world, made over women to the care and protection of men; for he knew that women are weak, that they would fall an easy prey to the seduction of men, that they possess a sensitive temperament which quickly responds to any offer of love or affection, and also that they excel in sincerity (or truthfulness).[45] "There are others among them who are full of malice, covetous of honours, fierce in nature, unlovable, and impervious to reason. Women, however, generally deserve to be respected. Do ye men show them honour!"[46] The execution of the *dharma* of man depends upon woman; all pleasures and enjoyments also entirely depend upon her; men should therefore serve women and bend their wills before them.[47] In childhood, the father looks after her; the husband looks after her in youth; when she becomes old, her sons protect her; therefore, at no period of her life can a woman enjoy unrestrained freedom.[48] Women are the deities of prosperity; the person who desires affluence and prosperity should honour them.[49]

We are also told in the *Mahābhārata* that the Goddess of Prosperity (*Śrīh*)[50] resides within the woman who is given to truth and sincerity and who pays due respect to the gods and the Brāhmaṇas,[51] who is pleasing and auspicious in appearance, and is gifted with virtues,[52] and the Goddess avoids

---

[39] Mahā. Śānti. 266, 38 & 40:

evam strī nāparādhnoti nara, evāparādhyati/
vyuchcharaṇaś cha mahā-dosham nara evāparādhyati//
nāparādho'sti nārīṇām nara evāparādhyati/
sarva-kāryāparādhyatvān nāparādhyanti chānganāh//

[40] Ibid. 19–21.
[41] Mahā. Anu. 46, 5.
[42] Ibid. 5–6.
[43] Ibid. 6.
[44] Ibid. 7.
[45] Ibid. 8: "*abalāh svalpa-kaupīnāh su-hridāh satya-jishṇavah/*"
("*svalpa=īshad āyāsena apaneyah kaupīno guhyāchchādanapaṭā yāsām, sadyohāryā ityarthah*"—*Nīlakaṇṭha*.)
[46] Ibid. 9.
[47] Ibid. 10: "*strī-pratyayo hi vai dharmo, rati-bhogaś cha kevalah/*
paricharyā namaskāras tadāyattā bhavantu vah//"

[48] Ibid. 14.
[49] Ibid. 15: "*śriya etāh striyo nāma satkāryā bhūtim ichchhatā/*
pālitā nigrihītā cha śrīh strī bhavati Bhārata//"
[50] Mahā. Anu. 11.
[51] Ibid. 11, 11: *"satya-svabhāvārjava-samyutāsu vasāmi devadvija-pūjikāsu/"*
[52] Ibid. 11, 15: "*priya-darśanāsu saubhāgya-yuktāsu guṇānvitāsu/*"

those women who are inclined to sinfulness and uncleanliness or impurity, or who are fond of disputes and quarrelling, or are indolent, sleepy or inclined to laziness, or those who often visit other people's houses, or those who lack modesty.[53]

Umā the wife of God Siva, was once asked to discuss the subject of woman's duties with a view to give an authoritative statement to the world, so that the course of conduct laid down by her "will be followed from generation to generation;"[54] she is then said to have given a detailed description of what a woman should do and what she should not do (*strī-dharmāh*).[55] These *dharmas* are generally in agreement with what has been said already in connection with the wife's duties in the family,—to serve her husband and his elders, to act as her husband's companion in the performance of all *dhārmika* acts, to be sweet in speech and manners, and so forth.[56]

In the Śānti-parva, Bhīshma advises Yudhishṭhira that if any warrior-kings died in the Great War without leaving male issues, their daughters should be crowned as Queens of the respective countries.[57]

In the Anuśāsana-parva we are also told that on the whole the woman cherishes a deeper attachment (*sneha*) for her children than man.[58] The woman, in general, is said to be capable of loving more strongly and more profoundly than man.[59]

The same Epic has opined that woman should not be forced to marry or live with a person whom she does not like. It says: "Manu does not speak highly of the practice of a girl living with a person whom she does not like. Living as a wife with a person whom she does not like produces disgrace and sin."[60] And, there is an instance in *Mahābhārata*, in which a woman was not merely saved from marrying one whom she disliked, but was also given assistance to marry the man of her choice: Bhīshma captured the three daughters of the King of Kāsī (Benares) in order to marry them over to his brother; but the eldest intimated to him that she had already fallen in love with the King of Sauba who had accepted her love and that she would have chosen him only in the *svayam-vara (sayam* =by oneself; *vara*=choice of husband) arranged by her father; whereupon, Bhīshma, who was himself well-versed in *dharma (dharma-jnah)*, after consultation with Brāhmaṇas learned in the *Vedas*, sent her back to the lover of her choice.[61]

If we turn our attention from the Epics to the *Smritis*, we meet with similar conceptions about the nature and the status of the woman.

Thus, Manu says that "women must always be honoured and respected (*pūjyā bhūshayitavyāś cha*) by the fathers, brother, husbands and brothers-in-law who desire their own welfare". And,

[53] Ibid. 11, 12–13: "*parasya veśmābhiratām alajjām/*
pāpām achokshām avalehinīm cha
vyapeta-dhairyām kalaha-priyām cha/
nidrābhibhūtām satatam śayānām
evam-vidhām tām parivarjayāmi/"

[54] Mahā. Anu. 146. 10: "*lokeshveshā gatih sadā*".

[55] Ibid. 12.

[56] Ibid. 33–37.

[57] *kumāro nāsti yeshām cha kanyās tatrābhishechaya/Mahā. Śānti*. 32–33.

[58] Mahā. Anu. 12, 46: "*striyas tvabhyadhikah sneho na tathā purushasya vai.*"

[59] Ibid. 12, 52: "*striyah purusha-samyoge pritir abhyadhikā*"; and 12. 54: "*evam striyā mahārāja adhikā prītir uchyate.*"

[60] Mahā. Anu. 44–23.

[61] Mahā. Ādi. 102.

"where women are honoured (*pūjyante*), there the very Gods (*devatāh*) are pleased, but where they are not honoured, no sacred rite[62] even could yield rewards." The family (*kulam*) in which women (*jāmayah*=female members of the family) are passing their lives in suffering will soon crumble to pieces (*vinaśyati āśu*). One who desires prosperity (*bhūti-kāma*) of family life should always respect the women-folk of the house.[63] In the family (*kule*) in which the wife (*bhāryā*) is pleased with the husband, and the husband feels happy with the wife, prosperity (*kalyāṇam*) always resides.[64] The householder (*grihī*) should always try to maintain peace with the female members of the house.[65] These statements by Manu do not give us much knowledge of the specific social status of the woman, but they give us a knowledge of the general attitude towards her in the family.[66]

In Manu's opinion, women were created by the Almighty to be mothers, just as men were created to be fathers; therefore, he says, it has been ordained by the *Dharma-Śāstras* that all the activities belonging to *dharma* and *yajna* have to be performed by man and wife together.[67] Now, a maiden may be given in marriage, even though she has not attained the proper marriageable age, if a handsome suitor of equal *varṇa* and excellent qualities (*utkrushṭa*) is found. But, on the other hand, a maiden should never acquiesce in her guardian's desire to give her away to a man of bad character or even lacking any good quality (*guṇa-hīna*). She should rather prefer to remain unmarried in her father's house till her death (*ā-maraṇāt*). Or, she may wait for three years after she has attained puberty (*ritumatī*), after which period, if her guardians fail to arrange for her marriage, she may herself (*svayam*) choose her match suited to her (*sadriśam*) and marry him.[68]

This seems to give a good deal of freedom to the young girl in the family at least in the matter of choosing her life-companion. But at other places, Manu and other *Smritikāras* are not prepared to allow any kind of independent activity to women,[69] without consultation or permission of the male members of the family; as already pointed out, she is subject to the guardianship of the father during her childhood, of her husband during her youth, and of her sons after the death of her husband. She is not allowed to do anything independently (*svātantryena*) even in her own home.[70] Vātsyāyana, who generally holds more liberal views than Manu about the fair sex, also looks upon unrestrained independence for women with disapproval; for he gives instructions as to the manner and the ways by which the citizen (*nāgaraka*) should protect his womenfolk (*antah-pura*)[71] and his wife (*dārā*).[72]

We have also seen in a previous Chapter how the *Smriti-kāras* have disposed of some of the *samskāras*, intended to sanctify the human body, in the case of the woman. In her case, they are to be carried out without the recitation of sacred texts (*mantras*).[73] Again, for woman, the marriage ceremony is equivalent to the *upanayana* or initiation ceremony of the boy; serving the husband

---

[62] "*kriyāh=yāgādi-kriyā*"—Kullūka.
[63] Man. iii, 55–59; cf. Yāj. i, 82.
[64] Ibid. iii, 60 ff.
[65] Ibid. iv, 180–81; cf. Yāj. i, 157–8.
[66] See also chapter vi, section 2.
[67] Man. ix, 96.
[68] Man. ix, 88–92; also cf. Yāj. i, 64; Vis. xxiv, 40–41; Vas. xvii, 69–71; Gau. xviii, 20–23; Bau. i v, 1, 11–14.
[69] Man. v, 148: (—*na bhajet strī svatantratām*).
[70] Man. v, 147–48 (*na svātantryeṇa kartavyam kinchit kāryam griheshvapi*); cf. also, Yāj. i, 85–86; Vis. xxv. 12–13; Vas. v, 1–3; Gau. xviii, 1; Bau. iii, 3, 44–5; Kāt. 930; and Man ix, 2–3 (*na strī svātantrayam arhati*).
[71] Kām. v, 6; iv, 2, 72–84.
[72] Ibid. v, 6, 43 ff.
[73] Man. ii, 16; Yāj. i, 13; Vis. xxvii, 13.

(*pati-sevā*) is equivalent to serving the teacher (*guru*), and residing in the husband's house and doing her household duties (*grihārtha*) is equivalent to the daily sacrifices and worship of fire (*agni-parikriyā*) by man.[74] Sacrifice by a woman displeases gods;[75] indeed the woman who offers an *agnihotra* sacrifice (burnt oblation) will sink into hell (*naraka*).[76]

Harīta informs us that in early times there were two classes of women, the *brahma-vādinī*, i.e., those proficient in metaphysical knowledge which was a life-long pursuit for them and the *sadyovadhū* i.e., those who studied only till their marriage and preferred to lead the life of married housewife.[77] Therefore, says Hārīta, women are not on the same level of status as the Śūdras; for, he argues, the three *varṇas* cannot be born from the womb of a Śūdra woman![78] Therefore, he further proceeds, women must also undergo sacramental rites with Vedic *mantras*.[79] But Mādhavāchārya, who quotes the above verses of Hārīta, declares that this applied to women of ancient times. And, in support of this view, he also quotes the sage Yama, saying that women were formerly (*purā kalpe*) entitled to be initiated with the sacred *mantras*, and also to teach the *Vedas* and recite the *Sāvitrīmantra*.[80]

A woman in her monthly course is regarded "untouchable". The husband should not approach (*nāpagachchhet*) his wife, even though he may be mad with desire (*pramatto'pi*), when she is in her courses; nor should he sleep with her in the same bed; if he does so, his wisdom (*prajnā*), energy (*tejah*), strength (*balam*), sight (*chakshuh*) and life-duration (*āyuh*) shall diminish.[81] Such a woman becomes touchable or pure (*vi-śuddhyati*) again by taking bath after the period is over.[82] A person even by merely touching (*sprishṭvā*) a woman in her monthly course himself becomes impure and untouchable; he becomes pure (*sudhyati*) by taking a bath.[83] It is also said that the mouth of a woman is always pure,[84] and this is explained by saying that it is to be regarded as pure for the purposes of kissing or other intimacies.[85] Yājnavalkya has also said that woman inherits purity from the God Soma, sweet speech from Gandharva, and perfect purity again from Agni; therefore, women are always pure (*medhyā*).[86] This again is explained by saying that women should be regarded as pure (*śuddhāh*) for the purposes of touching or embracing (*sparśālinganādishu*).[87]

---

[74] Man. ii, 67; cf. Yāj. i, 13; Vis. xxii, 32.

[75] Man. iv, 206.

[76] Man. xi, 36–37.

[77] Hārīta, xxi, 23 (Quoted by Mādhavāchārya, in "*Parāśarasamhitā",* Ed. by Islampurkar, Vol. i, Pt. ii, p. 82:—

ata eva Hārītenoktam: dvi-vidhā striyah/
brahma-vādinyah sadyo-vadhvaś cha/
tatra brahma-vādinīnām upanayanam agnīndhanam vedādhyayanam svagrihe cha bhikśācharyā iti/
sadyo-vadhūnām tu upasthite vivāhe kathanchit upanayanamāntram kritvā vivāhah kāryah/

[78] Ibid. "*na śūdra-samāh striyah na hi śūdra-yonau kshatriyavaiśyā jāyante*" (Hār. xxi, 20–21).

[79] Ibid. "*tasmāt chhandasā striyah samskāryāh*"/ (Har. xxi, 12).

[80] Ibid. "*purā kalpe tu nāriṇām*" etc.; see footnote No. 172, ch. iv.

[81] Man. iv, 40–42; cf. also Yāj. i, 138.

[82] Man. v, 66, Yāj. iii, 20.

[83] Man. v, 85; Yāj. ii, 30.

[84] Man. v, 130; (*nityam āsyam śuchi strīṇām*), cf. Yāj. i, 187; Vis. xxiii, 49; Bau. i, 9, 2; Vas. xxviii, 8.

[85] See *Mitākśarā*, or Yāj i, 187.

[86] Yāj. i, 71.

[87] *Mitākśarā* on Ibid.

Manu has a rather peculiar opinion about the nature of the fair sex in general. "It is the nature of women to seduce men in this world;[88] for that reason the wise never remain unguarded (*na pramādyanti*) in the company of females (*pramadāsu*).[89] For, women are able to lead astray not only the ignorant, but even a learned man, and make him a slave of lust and anger (*kāmakrodha-vaśānugam*).[90] Therefore, one should not sit in a lonely place with even one's own mother, sister or daughter; for the senses are powerful (*balavān indriya-grāmo*) and master even a learned man.[91] Manu calls woman the temptress, (*pramadā*), a noun derived from the verb *pra-mad*, which means 'to intoxicate', or 'to inflame with passion'. The derivation itself may speak suggestively in respect of the nature of the woman. But we have already seen that there are similar opinions expressed in the *Mahābhārata*, too, on certain grounds and in certain contexts; we therefore cannot accuse Manu, as is done by some, as being the only writer with such a view of the woman-kind for, like the *Mahābhārata*, Manu, too, has shown great regard for womankind in different contexts, as will be seen below.

In the family, says Manu, the *grihastha* should regard his daughters as the highest objects of tenderness; he should bear their offences without resentment.[92] A true householder should respect his elder sister and father's or mother's sister as his own mother (*mātri-vad*).[93] The mother is the most venerable person in this world—even more than the father. More than one *Dharma-Śāstra*-writers have declared that the father is a hundred times more venerable than the teacher, but the mother is a thousand times more venerable than even the father![94] The mother's place in the family affairs is on the same footing as that of the father and the teacher. One should always do what is agreeable to these three, even though one may be grievously offended by these.[95] When these are pleased one gets all the rewards in this world and the next. As long as they live one should always inform and consult them about all that he proposes to do "in thought, word or deed, for the sake of the next world."[96] Every other *dharma* must be regarded as subordinate to the *dharma* of honouring these three.[97] Obedience to father, mother as well as elder brother is expected of every person.[98] These and the *Guru*, the teacher, should never be offended.[99] One who casts off (*tyajet*) his mother has to pay the very high penalty of six hundred *paṇas*;[100] such a man, moreover, should never be invited at any sacrificial ceremonies (*havya-kavyah*).[101]

In this connection, it is highly interesting to note the views of Varāhamihira[102] (or Varāhamihara) on women. Though Varāha-mihira was an astronomer and wrote primarily on *jyotisha-śāstra* (astronomy and astrology), he has also touched upon a few other topics in the course of his

---

[88] (*svabhāva esha nārīṇām narāṇām iha dūshaṇam*).
[89] Man. ii, 213.
[90] Ibid. ii, 214.
[91] Ibid. ii, 215.
[92] Man. iv, 185: "*duhitā kripaṇam param . . . tasmād etair adhikshiptah sahetāsamjvarah sadā*/ /"
[93] Man. ii, 133: '*mātrivad vrittim ātishṭhet*'; cf. Vis. xxxii, 3.
[94] Man. ii, 145; Yāj. i, 35; Gau. vi, 51; Vas. xiii, 48.
[95] Man. ii, 225: '*nārtenāpyavamantavyā*'; cf. Vis. xxxi, 1–3; Gau. xxi, 15; Āp. i, 14, 6.
[96] Man. ii, 235–36: '*tat tat nivedayet tebhyo mano-vāk-kāya-karmabhih*'; cf. Vis. xxxi, 6.
[97] Man. ii, 237: "*esha dharmah parah sākshād upadharmo'nya uchyate.*"
[98] Man. ii, 225–37; Vis. xxxi, 1.
[99] Man. iv, 162; Āp. i, 1, 14; Gau. xxi, 5.
[100] Man. viii, 389: Yāj. ii, 237; Vis. v, 163.
[101] Man. iii, 157; Yāj. i, 224; Vis. lxxxii, 23, 29.
[102] Of the first half of the 6th Century, lived in Ujjaini.

discussion in one of his works.[103] He seems to have felt rather strongly that injustice was done to women by men of his times, or perhaps even before his times. "It is women who adorn jewels, women are not adorned by the splendour of jewels," he remarks, "for, women can capture the hearts of men even without jewels but jewels without being displayed on the bodies of women cannot do this.[104] There is no other jewel created by the Lord of men but the jewel of woman which is capable of giving delight to man by hearing about it, by sight, by touch, and by thinking about it. With her help, *dharma, artha*, son and pleasures of the senses are possible. Hence, the frail fair sex should ever be regarded in the home as the goddess of prosperity (*grihalakshmī*) and treated with respect (*māna*) and dignity (or glory, *vibhava*).[105] I am convinced," adds Varāhamihira, "that those who disregard the qualities (*guṇān*) of women and talk about their short-comings (or faults, *doshān*) in an ascetic (or cynical) mood must be themselves bad men; such talk by them is not inspired by *bona fide* motives (*sadbhāva*).[106] For, tell me honestly," asks Varāhamihira, "what fault do women have which has not been shown in their behaviour by men? Women have been driven into mis-deeds by men shamelessly, but women are superior in virtues. Here is what Manu has said in this connection:[107] *Soma* (The Moon) gave them purity; *Gandharvas* (the Celestial Musicians) gave them cultured speech (*śikshitām giram*); *Agni* (the God of Fire) has granted them freedom to eat anything; hence, they are (as pure) as gold.[108] The Brāhmaṇas are pure in their feet; the cow on her back; the goat and the dog in their mouths; but women are pure (*medhyāh*) all over (*sarvatah*),[109] Women are incomparably pure (*pavitram*); they are never defiled; their menses destroy all their blemishes.[110] Those homes in which virtuous women who are disrespected curse them are destroyed entirely as if struck by the Goddess of destruction.[111] Whether as the wife or as the mother, man is born of woman; hence, oh ungrateful ones who want to slander women (to whom you owe your

[103] In his *Brihat-samhitā*, he has, for instance, written chapters on "The Traits of Women" (*strī-lakshaṇam*, ch. 70); "In Praise of Women" (*strī-praśamsā*, ch. 74); "On Amiability" (*saubhāgya-karaṇam*, ch. 75); "On Union of Man and Woman" (*pum-strī-samāyogah*). See Brihatsamhita, Ed. by Dr. H. Kern, Benares, "Bibliotheca Indica" Series, Asiatic Society of Bengal, Calcutta, 1865. (Eng. tr. by N. Chidambaram Iyer, Madura, 1884. Marathi tr. with text by J. H. Athalye, Jaganmitra Pre Ratnagiri, Bombay, 1874.)

[104] *ratnām vibhūshayanti yoshā, bhūshyante vanitā na ratnakāntyā/ cheto vanita harantyaratnā, no ratnāni vinānganāngasamgāt// Brihatsamhitā*, 74, 2.

[105] *śrutam drishṭam sprishṭam smritam api nriṇām lhādajananam/*
na ratnam strībhyo'nyat kvachid api kritam lokapatinā/ /
tadartham dharmārthau suta-vishaya-saukhyāni cha tato/
grihe lakshmyo mānyāh satatam abalā māna-vibhavaih/ / Ibid. 4.

[106] *ye'pyanganānām pravadanti doshā, vairāgya-mārgeṇa guṇān vihāya/ te durjanā me manaso vi-tarkah, sadbhāva-vākyāni na tāni teshām/ /* Ibid. 5.

[107] *prabrūta satyam kataro'nganānām dosho'sti yo nācharito manushyaih/ dhārshṭyena pumbhih pramada nirastāh, guṇādhikās tā Manuna'tra choktam/ /* Ibid. 6.

[108] *somas tāsām adāchchhaucham gandharvāh śikshitām giram/*
agniś cha sarva-bhakshitvam tasmān nishka-samāh striyah/ / Ibid. 7.

[109] *brāhmaṇāh pādato medhyāh gāvo medhyās tu prishṭhatah/*
ajāśvā mukhato medhyāh striyo medhyās tu sarvatah/ / Ibid. 8.

[110] *striyah pavitram atulam naitā dushyanti karhichit/*
*māsi māsi rajo hyāsām dushkritānyapakarshati/ /*Ibid. 9.

[111] *jāmayo yāni gehani śapantyapratipūjitāh/*
tāni krityā-hatānīva vinaśyanti samantatah/ / Ibid. 10.

very existence), how can you ever gain happiness?[112] Mutual fidelity is enjoined equally for the husband as well as for the wife and its violation by either is censured equally by the *śāstras*; but men disregard this, whereas women do not; hence women are superior to men.[113] The man who becomes faithless to his wife can be purified of his sin if he wears the donkey's skin with the hair outside and begs alms for six months; with the announcement: 'I have been faithless to my wife; please give me alms!'[114] Man's sex desire is not abated even at the age of hundred; it abates in him only by loss of power; whereas in women it is controlled by their own fortitude (dhairya).[115] What an impudence is it on the part of those bad men who indulge in slandering innocent women, which is comparable to the impudence of the robber who accosts the very person whom he robs and cries out at him: 'Halt, you robber!'[116] The sweet talks which man bestows on the woman in privacy he forgets afterwards; on the contrary, the woman, out of deep fidelity, embraces even her dead husband and enters the funeral pyre."[117] Though Varāhamihira has written well-known treatises on the *śāstras* of *jyotisha* (astronomy), he is not regarded as a *dharma-Śāstra* authority; yet his views are striking as those of a thinker of the times; and it may also be that he is voicing the opinion of other thoughtful men of the times too.

Women who have no one to protect them, who are sterile, who have no sons, whose family is extinct, widows who are faithful to their departed husbands, and women afflicted with diseases, have to be given protection by the King. So also, the King must protect the property of such women, and punish their relatives in case the latter misappropriate their property during their life-time.[118]

Sex-union with sisters by the same mother, with unmarried maidens, with females of the lowest castes, with the wife of a friend, or with the wife of a son, is a heinous crime—a *māhā-pātaka*;[119]

---

[112] *jāyā vā syāj janitrī vā sambhavah strī-krito nriṇām/*
he kritaghnās tayor nindām kurvatām vah kutah sukham?/ /Ibid. 11.

[113] *dampatyor vyutkrame doshah samah śāstre pratishṭhitah/*
narā na tam avekshante tenātra varam anganāh// Ibid. 12.

[114] *bahir-lomnā tu shaṇ-māsān veshṭitah khara-charmaṇā/*
dārātikramaṇe bhikshām dehītyuktvā viśuddhyati// Ibid. 13.

It may be noted here that Āpastamba would award the same punishment to the man who proves unfaithful to his wife: '*dāra-vyatikramī kharājinam bahir-loma paridhāya dāra-vyatikramaṇe bhikshām iti saptāgāraṇi charet/ sā vrittih shaṇ-māsān/*

—Āpastamba. i, 9, 8.

[115] *na śatenāpi varshāṇām apaiti madanāsayah/*
tatrāśaktyā nivartante narā dhairyeṇa yoshitah//
Brihatsamhitā, op. cit. 14.

[116] *aho dhārshṭyam a-sādhūnām nindatām anaghāh striyah/*
mushṇatām iva chaurāṇām tishṭha chaureti jalpatām// Ibid. 15.

[117] *purushaś chaṭulāni kāminīnām*
kurute yāni raho na tāni paśchāt/
sukritajnatayānganā gatāsūn
avagūhya praviśanti sapta-jihvam// Ibid. 16.

This indicates that the custom of *satī*, burning herself to death on the funeral pyre of the departed husband by the wife, was in existence in Varāhamihira's times.

[118] Man. viii, 28–29; Vis. iii, 65.

[119] Man. xi, 59; Yāj. iii, 231; Vis. xxxvi, 4–7; Gau. xxi, 1; Bau. ii, 2, 13; Āp. i, 21; 8–9, 17–18.

such conduct is equivalent to violating the *Guru's* bed, and has the same punishment prescribed.[120] Sex union with a woman given to drinking is a sin of the second order (*upa-pātaka*) which must be punished by the expulsion of the man from his caste.[121]

The husband of a widow who has remarried must not be entertained at a sacrifice.[122] Such a woman is called a *punar-bhū*, and has no social status; and her husband would be generally censured in the society.

The one great issue which presents itself to our mind when we consider the position of woman in India is with regard to her place in the scheme of the *āśramas*. It is true that in the early Hindu India, the woman could freely avail herself of the *āsrama-vyavasthā* in the same way as man did, as the mention of a number of learned women of the times shows. But later, women, along with the Śūdra, were not taken into account, so far as the management of life through the *āśrama* stages is concerned, by the *Dharma-Śāstras*. Of course, along with this we must also remember that Vātsyāyana, *Śukra-Nīti* and the *Mahābhārata* mention a scheme of education in the sixty-four arts for women, and *Vātsyāyana* also says that they should be taught the *śāstras* too. This implies that according to these authorities, generally speaking, both men as well as women should be educated, but the content of education was conceived along different lines for men and for women, and further, women were not expected to undergo the hard and rigorous life of the *āśrama*-discipline like boys but to stay at home and pursue studies—at least until marriage. This is as far as *brahmacharyāśrama* is concerned. The *grihasthāśrama* is a joint *āśrama* for both the man and his wife; and here also, the content of the *āśrama* discipline and the modes of behaviour prescribed are naturally bound to be different for the two parties, though generally speaking they are considered to be equal partners in the home. The *vānaprasthāśrama* and the *samnyāsāśrama* do not seem to be meant for women, probably because of the hardship involved in these, though here, too, we have instances in very early literature of women who led the life of *samnyāsinīs*.

The explanation given for the exclusion of women from the *āsrama* scheme is that her life is so much related to man, and that the lives of the *grihastha* and his *dharma-patnī* are mutually adjusted according to the *Dharma-Śāstra*. We have already seen, for example, in the chapter on Education, how the nuptials and the life of a housewife are considered for the woman as equivalent to the *brahmacharya* and the *grihasthāśrama* of man. There is historical evidence, as we have narrated elsewhere, that *vānaprasthāsrama* and *samnyāsāsrama* were available for women; and in actual practice, according to the Hindu theory, with the permission and consent of the husband, a woman could enter the *vānaprastha* or the *samnyāsa āsrama*, just as a man could enter these with the consent of his wife. Usually, of course, the man and wife enter these two *āsramas* together, in theory at least. So far as the first *āsrama* is concerned, however, the great question that presents itself to us is: Why should woman be denied the right and privilege to learn and to teach systematically, which the male individual gets and gathers and may also impart—why should that discipline and purpose of the *Brahmacharyāsrama* be denied to the woman? Apart from the few names of women-teachers that we have noted, almost all teachers were males. Is the natural inherent difference to be regarded as such a defect in the female sex as to be the cause of the absence of such rights in the case of woman?

[120] Man. xi, 171; Yāj. iii, 233; Vis. xxxiv, 2; liii, 1; Vas. xx, 15–16; Gau. xxiii, 12–13, 32.
[121] Man. xi, 67; Yāj. iii, 236–37; 239; Vis. xxxvii, 13, 31, 33; Gau. xxi, 1, 11; Vas. i, 23.
[122] Man. iii, 166; Yāj. i, 224; Gau. xv, 16.

The answer to all this is given by saying, as we have seen, that the āśrama for the woman to learn is the home. Woman's part was perhaps supposed to be in the conserving and propagation of the race; and these functions were probably thought to be naturally inherited by her, and as not in need of training through the *āśramas*. as man required. Also, the burden of maternal duties was probably thought to be too heavy to add any other liabilities upon her. It is extremely difficult to decide to what extent this can be proved to be true. The woman is also denied many of the *samskāras* including that of *upanayana*. Here also, she is supposed to become a *dvijā* when she marries. Now, the explanation offered in support of all this seems to amount to this, that the lives of man and woman after marriage were considered as one and the woman could never be thought of independently of married life. But then, in this connection, the questions of perpetual widowhood, absence of divorce, and absence of a public career for woman are three issues very difficult to answer. Also, if the theory that the life of man and woman who are married to each other is one and sacred be granted as true, how could it be possibly maintained that man may marry, under any circumstances, more than one wife?

In a community like the Hindu which worships more than one deity[123] and has enshrined them, the way in which he has divinized Gods as well as Goddesses and reveres them aught to reflect in a significant manner his attitude towards the female sex. The deities worshipped by him as Gods and the ancient personalities who have risen in his view to the divine status by dint of their virtuous and illustrious deeds and character and in fact are believed by him to be the very incarnations (*avatāra*) of God, and in whose memory there have been shrines and temples erected all over the country

[123] In connection with the idol-worship of the Hindus, the following observations by Stanley Rice in his book *Hindu Customs and Their Origins*, (Allen and Unwin, London, 1937) are well worth quoting:

"Side by side with the higher forms of religion (in India, which Rice has described in the preceding pages) persisted the aboriginal cults and superstitions which are mainly responsible for the branding of Hinduism with the name of idolatry—an accusation about as just as to judge Catholicism by the tawdry images in its churches. The persistence of these cults indicates that at no time did the Aryan religion—and still less the philosophical speculations—ever really capture the popular imagination. The blending of the races led inevitably to the blending of the religion. The great temples grew up dedicated to the greater Gods, Śiva and Vishṇu in their various forms, to their female counterparts and to the deified heroes, Rāma and Krishṇa, incarnations of Vishṇu. With the coming of the *bhakti* movement—at any rate in the eyes of the masses—the religion lost all or nearly all of its esoteric meaning in ecstatic and unreasoning adoration, while in the villages still continued the worship of the minor 'village deities', the *Grāma-devatās*, particularly of those malevolently inclined Goddesses whose special care was the physical ills of mankind……This multiplicity of Gods and godlings has given rise to the idea of polytheism, which, however, is foreign to the true esoteric Hinduism. Properly viewed in that light they are only the aspects of the One God. Even the Hindu Trinity—*Trimūrti*—is only the expression of the same idea. It contemplates Creation, Preservation, and Regeneration which combine the great principles of Nature and therefore of the Universe.

"Thus when Hinduism is spoken of as idolatry, there is only a measure of truth in the accusation; nor is it enough to protest that the Hindu does not worship the idols but only the principles which they represent. That is an accusation which applies equally to certain forms of Christianity, as anyone can testify who has seen the little dolls held out to be blessed by the Pope in the Vatican….

"But it is an entire misconception to suppose that the purer esoteric Hinduism has any part or lot in such worship. Most of what is seen is nothing but the shell; it may be affirmed that very few believe in it. Hinduism properly so-called appeals, unlike Judaism, less to the emotions than to the intellect. Its limitations are the limitations of man's reasoning powers and the very difficulty which has so often been found in defining it is due to this cause. Its intellectualism—its insistence that knowledge is the way of Salvation and that ignorance is the cause of all back-sliding—is indeed its weakness, for that is a state of mind that very few are either inclined or will seek to attain" (pp. 212–14).

throughout the centuries past, are usually worshipped as couples, as Gods together with their inseparable Goddesses. And, indeed, in naming and addressing them jointly, the name of the Goddess has precedence, as for instance, in *Lakśmī*[124]*-Nārāyaṇa,*[125] *Umā*[126]*-Maheśa,*[127] *Sītā-Rāma,*[128] *Rādhā-Krishṇa* and *Rukminī-Krishṇa.*[129] Further, some Goddesses—like some Gods—are also worshipped and enshrined independently in their own rights, as for instance, *Laksmī, Pārvati* (in the name and form of *Durgā*, or *Jagad-Ambā*, or *Kālī*),[130] and *Saraswatī.*

These are the ways in which the womankind was judged in old India. The judgments may often seem contradictory to each other and at places even self-contradictory. She is a *devatā* (Goddess) as well as a *pramadā* (seducer). She is sincere or truth-loving and yet she has weakness of character, lack of judgment and of balance of mind. She is the queen of the house, but she does not deserve freedom and independence, even in the family affairs. What may apparently seem as a contradiction of statement, however, is in truth not a contradiction. The *Śāstra-kāras* and the Epic and other writers have viewed the problem of woman from different points of view and during different periods. And since at each time the universe of discourse is changed, the views expressed appear to be contradictory. Thus, from the point of view of family stability and happiness, the woman is to be respected and honoured; and, in view of the inherent weakness of her nature she is conceived as needing the protection of man, and to that extent, dependent on man. But if we are minded to look at the Hindu conception and treatment of womankind on the whole, we must admit that the Hindu seers have honestly and sincerely made repeated inquiries into the problems of the nature and position of the fair sex for the maintenance, growth and development of the best and the noblest of the human heritage in any society. It may be that due to several reasons, which must have formed the signs and characteristics of the times, they seem to be conservative in one cycle and liberal in another regarding certain aspects of the life of woman. But, along with these and in spite of these strong opinions, or even prejudices, against the nature of woman, the Hindu sages have never failed woman in giving her entire due as a maiden, a wife, a mother, a householder and as a matron in the economy, upkeep and exaltation of the family and its best traditions.

---

124 *Lakshmī*, the wife of *Vishṇu* (or *Nārāyaṇa*), is the Goddess of prosperity and abundance.

125 *Vishṇu* is so called because he preserves the world. The name is thus explained:—

yasmād-viśvam idam sarvam tasya śaktyā mahātmanah/
tasmād evo'chyate vishṇur viśa-dhātoh praveśanāt//

Nārāyaṇa is an epithet of Vishṇu. It is explained thus:—

Āpo nārā iti proktā āpo vai nara-sūnavah/
Tā yad asyāyanam pūrvam tena nārāyaṇah smritah//Man. i, 10.

Brahmā, Vishṇu and Maheśa form the sacred *Trinity*, Brahmā being concerned with creation, Vishṇu with preservation and Maheśa with destruction out of which comes regeneration, of the world. Strict Hinduism regards these as aspects of but one God called *Trimūrti*.

126 *Umā*, the daughter of Himavat (The Himalayas), also called *Pārvatī* (the offspring of *parvata*, mountain). The name *Umā* is explained by poet Kālidāsa thus: *Umeti* (i.e. 'Oh do not' [practise penance]) *mātrā tapaso nishiddhā, paśchād Umākhyām sumukhī jagāma*—Kumāra. i. 26.

127 *Maheśa*=Great God (Maha+*Īśa*), an epithet of *Śiva* (= auspicious).

128 *Sītā* is regarded as an *avatāra* of Lakshmī, just as *Rama* is regarded as an *avatāra* of Vishnu.

129 *Krishṇa*, too, is regarded as an *avatāra* of Vishṇu. *Rādhā* was the cowherdess (*gopī*) who showed exemplary devotion (*bhakti*) to Krishṇa, and so she is divinized and her name immortalized together with that of Krishṇa. *Rukminī* is the wife of Krishṇa.

130 *Jagad*=Universe; *ambā*=mother. Kālī (blackness) is supposed to be a fierce and destrictive *avatāra* of *Pārvatī*.

In connection with this whole question of feminine psychology and the various writers' views on the same, it must be borne in mind, before adjudging a writer as a champion or a hater of women, that his views are based upon and are reactions to the social, cultural and other environmental conditions of his times. What Viola Klein has said about Freud applies to all critical and honest students of feminine psychology. "In Freud's writings" observes Klein, "we find . . . on the one hand the wonder at the enigmatic' woman, the approach to feminine psychology as a 'riddle' to be solved and a theory which views the development of femininity as a particularly 'difficult and complicated process'; on the other hand there is the contempt . . . for her inferior intellectual capacities, her greater vanity, her weaker sexual instincts, her disposition to neuroses and hysteria, and for her constitutional passivity . . . Judgments on the strength or weakness of the sex-impulse in women (passed by Freud and other psycho-analysts) are not based on organic facts but are in accordance with a cultural pattern and milieu. . . . They are also valid, most probably with corresponding modifications, in every society with strong patriarchal traditions."[131] However, even among psycho-analysts, a new school of thought is developing, backed by careful anthropological and sociological studies made in different cultures, which lays stress on the differences in mental development owing to differences in cultural patterns in which individuals are brought up in different regions of the world. "The realization that in different societies women fulfil different social functions and accordingly display different attitudes and mental characteristics has shattered the idea of the all-powerful influence of anatomy and biological facts on character-traits."[132]

We must not, however, commit the opposite error of overstressing the social and environmental influence to the disregard of natural biological and anatomical endowments in the sexes which make a difference in moulding and developing their mental characteristics. The significance of *guṇa* (the natural psycho-biological endowment) is no less important than that of *désa* (region, place) and *kāla* (time, period) here. The potentialities as well as the limitations of both these factors in the psychological development of each of the sexes in their own different way must be reckoned with. In the same period of history, regional and cultural differences may lead to variations in the character traits of the women and of the men of these regions. So also, even in the same region or country different conditions may operate at different periods in history leading to different character traits in the women as well as in the men of that country. Furthermore, in this connection, it should be remembered that the judge no less than the judged are influenced by the conditions of the place and the time and react to the same, each in his own way. It may also be noted that till this day, there has been no full length scientific study of the problem of feminine psychology based on a careful analysis of the natural as well as environmental differences between the sexes. Almost all the studies available are based on observation of female behaviour in the specific cultural contexts in which they were made, and therefore whatever validity they may possess is limited to the respective cultural context. None of them can tell us much about the natural and universal psychological differences among the sexes.

---

[131] Klein, Viola: *The Feminine Character*, pp. 84–89. Kegan Paul, London, 1946. This book presents a study of the ideas of different authorities—Havelock Ellis, Weininger, Freud, Helen Thompson, Terman and Miles, Margaret Mead, W. I. Thomas, etc.—on woman's psychology.

[132] Ibid.

CHAPTER VIII

THE FOUR VARNAS

Honour and shame from no condition rise;
Act well your part, there all the honour lies.

—Alexander Pope: *Essay on Man*, Epistle IV. 1

We have already noted the fact that just as *āśramadharma* is formulated primarily with reference to the conduct of the individual's life in the world, so there is another co-ordinate system, devised by the Hindu, called the *varṇadharma* which is formulated primarily with reference to the society in which the individual lives.[1] Of course, both the kinds of *dharmas* concern themselves with the organisation and management of the individual as well as the group or the society. Together, the two schemes are known as *varnāśrama-vyavasthā*, the organization (*vyavasthā*)-of-*varṇa*-and-*āśrama*; and they are to be looked upon and practised as interrelated and inter-coordinated parts of a composite whole. But the difference between the two may be said to lie in the manner of approach and emphasis in the organisation of man's life and his activities in regard to the two kinds of *dharmas*. In the scheme of the *āśramas* (*āśrama-vyavasthā*), the problem is approached from the point of view of the training or *nurture* (*śrama*) of the individual through specifically provided environments at different stages of his life; in the *varṇa*-organization (*varṇa-vyavasthā*) on the other hand, the problem is considered from the point of view of the larger group, and the individual's position is defined in this group with reference to his innate *nature* (*guṇa*), his tendencies and dispositions. We have considered the *āśrama* scheme and its purpose and method in the preceding chapters. In this chapter we take up the *varṇa*-organisation for our review. We may begin with the views of Hindu thinkers on the problem of *varṇa*-organisation, and then in the light of this and of some pertinent modern views, we shall try to evaluate the same.

I

There are several passages in the oldest Vedic literature dealing with the origin of the *varṇas*. The oldest is the hymn in the *Purusha-sūkta* of the Rig-Veda which says that the *Brāhmaṇa varṇa* represented the mouth of the *purusha*,—which word may be translated as 'the Universal Man', referring perhaps to mankind as a whole,—the Rājanya (i.e. Kshatriya) his arms, the Vaiśya his thighs and

[1] See the opening remarks in Ch. III.

the Śūdra his feet.[2] Zimmer and others have held the opinion that this *Purusha* hymn was a later interpolation and that the institution of caste was not Rigvedic, but of later origin.[3] But it has been shown that there are other passages, apart from the *Purusha-Sūkta*, in which the division of society into *varṇas*, though not in the rigid form of later times, is mentioned. Thus, in Rig-Veda (VIII, 35, 16–18), the three *varṇas*, the Brahma, Kshatram, and Viśah are mentioned; while in Rig-Veda (I, 113, 16), the four *varṇas* are referred to thus: 'One to high sway (i.e. Brāhmaṇa), one to exalted glory (i.e. the Kshatriya), one to pursue his gain (i.e. the Vaiśya) and one to his labour (i.e. the Śūdra),—all to regard their different vocations, all moving creatures hath the Dawn awakened.'[4] Further, the division into four *varṇas* is here correlated to the duties of each *varṇa*. Haug's opinion on the origin of the institution of caste seems to be correct. "It has been of late asserted," he observes, "that the original parts of the Vedas do not know the system of caste. But this conclusion was prematurely arrived at without sufficiently weighing the evidence. It is true that caste system is not to be found in such a developed state; the duties assigned to the several castes are not so clearly defined as in the law books and Purāṇas. But nevertheless the system is already known in the earlier parts of the Vedas, or rather presupposed. The barriers only were not so insurmountable as in later times."[5]

Reverting to the *Purusha-Sūkta*, an allegorical meaning is suggested by the whole *sūkta* with reference to the *Purusha* and the creation of *varṇas* from his limbs. The *Purusha* is described as being himself "this whole universe, whatever has been and whatever shall be".[6] Further, we are also told that the moon sprang from his mind (*manas*), the Sun from his eyes, Indra and Agni were created out of his mouth, and air or wind from his breath.[7] Again, from his navel arose the atmosphere (*antariksham*), from his head the sky, from his feet the earth (*bhūmi*), and from his ear the four quarters (*diśah*); in this manner, the worlds were created.[8]

The *Purusha-Sukta* has been interpreted as having an allegorical significance behind it from another point of view also.[9] Thus, the mouth of the *Purusha* from which the Brāhmaṇas are created is the seat of speech; the Brāhmaṇas therefore are created to be teachers and instructors of mankind. The arms are symbol of valour and strength; the Kshatriya's mission in this world is to carry weapons and protect people. It is difficult to interpret that portion of the hymn which deals with the creation of the Vaiśyas from the thighs of the *Purusha*. But the thigh may have been intended to represent the lower portion of the body, the portion which consumes food, and therefore the Vaiśya may be said to be created to provide food to the people. The creation of the Śūdra from

---

[2] Rig. x, 90, 12:
brāhmaṇo'sya mukham āsīd bāhū rājanyah kritah /
ūrū tad asya yad vaiśyah padbhyām śūdro ajāyata//

[3] Colebroke: *Miscellaneous Essays*, i, p. 309 note.
MaxMuller: *Ancient Sanskrit Literature*, p. 570; etc.
(From Muir: *Ori. Sanskrit Texts*, i, p. 12 f.)

[4] Dutt: "*Origin and Growth of Caste in India*", Vol. I (1931), p. 39. This book collects together relevant material on caste from the Vedas, the *Brāhmaṇas*, the *Sūtras* and the Buddhist *Jātakas*.

[5] Quoted by Dutt: op. cit., i, pp. 38–39. He also points out that Oldenberg and Geldner held similar views.

[6] Rig. x, 90, 2: "*purusha evedam sarvam yad bhūtam yach cha bhāvyam*".

[7] Ibid. x, 90, 13.

[8] Ibid. x, 90, 14.

[9] See Haug. "*On the Origin of Brahmanism*", p. 4 (Quoted by Muir: *Ori. Sansk. Texts*, Vol. i, p. 14).

the foot symbolizes the fact that the Śūdra is to be the 'footman', the servant of other *varṇas*. The whole social organization is here conceived symbolically as one human being—the "Body Social", we may say—with its limbs representing the social classes based on the principle of division of labour. The Mahābhārata states the same thing thus: Our obeisance to That (*Purusha*) who consists of Brahmaṇas in the mouth, Kashtras in the arms, Viśah in the entire regions, stomach and thighs, and Śūdra in the feet.[10]

We also find that in the Vedic times there were no restrictions as regards particular occupations for persons belonging to a particular *varṇa*. Thus, a person born as a Brāhmaṇa could take to the occupation of a physician without thereby in any way degrading his social status. "With Soma as their sovereign lord the Plants hold colloquy and say: Oh King, we save from death the man whose cure a Brāhmaṇa undertakes."[11] A Brāhmaṇa *rishi* (sage) says: 'I am a poet, my father is a physician, my mother a grinder of corn. With our different views, seeking after gain, we ran as after cattle."[12] The Ribhus were skilled artisans; and yet they were given high divine honours.[13] And, of the descendants of the Brāhmaṇa *rishi* Bhrigu, some were reported to be experts in the art of making chariots.[14] There is no trace of heredity defining the occupation of an individual in this early literature.

The Śūdras of the Rigvedic period seem to be no other than the non-Aryans, the Dāsas or the Dasyūs who differed from the fair-skinned Aryas on account of their black complexion (*Krishṇatvach*), flat-nose, unintelligibility of speech, absence of sacrificing among them (*a-yajnan*), absence of the worship of God amongst them, and the prevalence of foreign customs which they followed (*anya-vrata*),—all of which were obviously strange to the Aryas.[15] They were kept by the Aryans as slaves. There is no obvious explanation of the term Śūdra which later came to signify the Dāsas; it is, however, suggested that 'Śūdra' was probably the name of some prominent Dāsa tribe, and, in course of time, the word became synonymous with the whole community of slaves, by usage, just as at Athens the term Karian became synonymous with the word slaves.[16]

It has also been shown that there were no restrictions in the Rigvedic society in the matter of diet and drink between the different *varṇas* such as we find in the later society.[17] Whatever food or drink was usual was common to all the *varṇas*. So too, there was no 'higher' or 'lower' *varṇa* for matrimonial alliances.[18] "There were no definite restrictions on intermarriage between the different classes of the Aryan race; in fact there was no necessity, as the different groups in society, whatever might be their occupations, were by complexion, features, language and creed practically homogeneous. Nowhere in the Rig-Veda is any mention of a Vaiśya being regarded as less pure than a Brāhmaṇa, and of social intercourse between the two as degrading to the latter."[19] There are no instances recorded of mixed marriages in the Rig-Veda; but this happened, perhaps,

---

[10] Mahā. Śānti. 46.
[11] Rig. x, 97, 22; from Dutt: op. cit., p. 59.
[12] Rig. ix, 112, 3; from Ibid. pp. 59–60.
[13] Rig. i, 161, 1–5; from Ibid. p. 6.
[14] Rig. x. 39, 14; from Ibid. p. 60.
[15] Ibid. p. 60–63.
[16] Dutt.: op. cit., and "*Camb. Hist. Ind.*"—Ch. x, "Life and Customs in the Sūtras", by Hopkins, p. 234.
[17] See Dutt, op. cit., pp. 64 ff.
[18] Ibid. pp. 68 ff.
[19] Ibid. p. 68.

as Dutt observes, due to the fact that the castes as separate communities prohibiting intermarriages did not exist in the Rigvedic period.[20] Several instances, however, occurring in the Rigvedic period and recorded in later literature, of such mixed marriages, are in fact known to us, like those between Yayāti, a Kshatriya King and Devayānī, the daughter of a Brāhmaṇa; of Dushyanta, a Kshatriya King and Śakuntalā, supposed to be the daughter of a Brāhmaṇa sage. Similar are the cases, mentioned by the commentator,[21] of a *rishi* Syāvāśva marrying the daughter of Kshatriya King Rathavīti; of the marriage of King Asanga with a woman of Angirasa family;[22] and of a rishi Kakshīvan marrying the daughters of King Svanaya.[23]

From the above account during the Vedic period, the *varṇas* seem to have been 'open classes', to use a term of Cooley.[24] They were not watertight compartments, the membership of which was determined by virtue of heredity only; they were, to use Cooley's words again, "more based on individual traits and less upon descent."[25]

Gradually, however, the *varṇas* came to be distinguished from each other. Each *varṇa* became more and more marked off and separated from the other. The four *varṇas* came to be addressed in four different ways, differing in degrees of politeness as indicated by the terms *ehi, āgachchha, adrava* and *adhava* respectively to be used for welcoming persons of the four different *varṇas*.[26] Different sizes of funeral cakes (*piṇḍa*) were prescribed for different *varṇas*.[27]

When reciting the *Gāyatrī Mantra* the three *varṇas* were to start each with different word: the Brāhmaṇa with 'Bhūh', the Kshatriya with 'Bhuvah' and the Vaiśya with 'Śvah'.[28] Indeed, the Śatapatha Brāhmaṇa says that the *varṇas* are created from these words in their order, the Brāhmaṇa being created from the word *Bhūh*, the Kshatriya from *Bhuvah* and the Vaiśya from *Svah*.[29] Further, the Brāhmaṇa is asked to use Palāśa wood for sprinkling purposes at sacrifices, the Kshatriya to use *Nyagrodha* wood, and the Vaiśya to use *Aśvattha* wood.[30] According to the *Aitareya Brāhmaṇa*, the Brāhmaṇa *varṇa* must recite the *Gāyatrī Mantra*, the Kshatriyas the *Trishṭubh mantra*, and the Vaiśyas the *$$agati mantra* at the initiation rite.[31] According to the *Taitirīya Brāhmaṇa*, the Brāhmaṇa *varṇa* should perform their sacrifice during the spring, the Kshatriya *varṇa* during summer, and the Vaiśyas during autumn.[32] Thus, a gradual increase in the distinction between the different *varṇas* in terms of different rights and privileges is noticeable as we pass on from the Rigvedic literature to the Brahmanic literature, viz., in the *Samhitās*, the *Brāhmaṇas*, and the *Upanishads*.

In this later period, the Śūdra still held the position of a menial labourer or slave; and, he was still a non-Aryan. Even then, there was less restriction upon him; and, he was at times allowed the liberty of even taking part in sacrificial ceremonies.[33] Instead of the three *varṇas*, mention is now

[20] Ibid.
[21] On Rig. v, 61.
[22] Rig. viii, 134.
[23] Rig. i, 126; (from Dutt: op. cit., pp. 68–69).
[24] See his '*Social Organization*', Ch. xxi.
[25] Ibid. p. 239.
[26] Śatapatha Br. i, 1, 4, 12; (from Dutt: op. cit., pp. 85 ff.).
[27] Śat. Br. xiii, 8, 3, 11 (from Ibid.).
[28] Śat. Br. ii, 1, 3, 4, (from Ibid.).
[29] Śat. Br. ii, 1–4, 11, ff. (Muir: *Ori. Sansk. Texts*, i, p. 17).
[30] Śat. Br. v, 3, 2, 11; (from Dutt: op. cit.).
[31] Ait. Br. i, 5, (from Ibid.).
[32] Taitt. Br. i, 1, (from Ibid.).
[33] Śat. Br. i, 1, 4, 11 (from Ibid.).

usually made of the four *varṇas* together, the Śūdra also finding a place along with the three other *varṇas*. The prayer goes, for instance: "Bestow splendour on our Brāhmaṇas; bestow splendour on our Kshatriyas; bestow splendor on our Vaiśyas and Śūdras; bestow splendour upon me."[34] In the *Śatapatha Brāhmaṇa*, a Śūdra attenda to a *Pitri-medha Yajna*;[35] the *Chhāndogya Upanishad* relates a story about a Brāhmaṇa teaching the sacred knowledge to a Śūdra, and accepting in return from him rich gifts and also his daughter.[36] Even in the account of the creation of the *varṇas*, the Śūdra finds a place equal to the other *varṇas* in position. "He lauded with one (*ekayā astuvata*)—living beings were formed; . . . . He lauded with three,—the Brāhmaṇa was created. . . . . He lauded with fifteen,—the Kshatra was created. . . . . He lauded with nineteen,—the Śūdra and the Arya (i.e. Vaiśya) were created."[37] In another passage again, the four *varṇas* are referred to as having sprung from the divine element of Agni (Fire) in each of the *varṇas;* through the divine Brāhmaṇa a human Brāhmaṇa was created; through the divine Kshatriya a human Kshatriya sprang; through the divine Vaiśya a human Vaiśya was originated; and through the divine Śūdra a human Śūdra was created.[38]

Though the Śūdra was now accepted as belonging to a fourth *varṇa* along with the three other *varṇas* and though he was given some freedom with regard to attendance at sacrificial parties, he was not yet quite free from many of the old disabilities. Thus, he had for himself no right to perform a sacrifice like the three higher *varṇas*.[39] His duty continued to be, as in older times, to serve the other *varṇas*. He might attend a religious ceremony only to wash the feet of persons of the other *varṇas*, and that because his very origin was out of the feet of Prajā-pati (Creator of Men).[40] He had no God; and consequently he could not perform sacrifices.[41] He would not be even spoken to directly by any person who is engaged in performing important sacrificial rites. "Every one cannot obtain this, for the Gods do not associate with every man but an Arya, a Brāhmaṇa or a Kshatriya or a Vaiśya; for, these can perform a sacrifice. Nor should one talk with every body except only with an Arya, a Brāhmaṇa or a Kshatriya or a Vaiśya; for, these can sacrifice. If any one has occasion to speak to a Śūdra, let him say to another person; 'tell this man so and so'. This is the rule for an initiated man".[42] Even the touch of a Śūdra to articles like milk, meant for the use of a sacrifice, was prohibited.[43]

There seem to be no restrictions during this period of the *Brāhmaṇas* and *Samhitās* as regards marriages between the *Varṇas*, excepting perhaps the restriction upon marriage with a Śūdra male or female by a member of another *varṇa*. There are not, however, many instances recorded specifically showing the absence of such restrictions; but that may be due to the fact that no particular attention was attracted by inter-*varṇa* marriages, as in all probability they must have been quite frequent and not exceptional. The Atharva Veda declares at one place that a Brāhmaṇa's claim to marry a Vaiśya girl must be given priority to the claims of a Vaiśya youth.[44] Of course, cases are

---

[34] Taitt. Sam. v, 7, 6, 4, (from Ibid.).
[35] Śat. Br. xiii, 8, 3, 11, (from Ibid).
[36] Chhānd. Up. iv, 2 (from Ibid.).
[37] Vājasaneya Samhi. xiv, 28 ff. (= Taittiriya Samhi. iv, 3, 10, 1)—Muir: *Ori. Sansk. Texts*, i, p. 18.
[38] Śat. Br. xiv, 4, 2, 27 (= Br. Up. i, 4, 11, ff.)—Muir: Ibid. Vol. i, p. 19.
[39] Śat. Br. iii, 1, 1, 10 and Panchavimśa Br. vi, 11;—from Dutt: op. cit., p. 104.
[40] Tatt. Sam. vii, 1, 1; (from Ibid.).
[41] Panch. Br. vi, 1, 11; (from Ibid.).
[42] Śat. Br. iii, 1, 1; (from Ibid. p. 104).
[43] Taitt. Br. iii, 2, 3; (Ibid. p. 105).
[44] Ath. Ved. v, 17, 9; (Ibid. p. 109).

pointed out where marriage of a man of a higher *varṇa* with a Śūdra woman was looked upon with disfavour. Kavaśa Ailuśa was expelled from a sacrifice because his mother was a *dāsi*, i.e. slave; but he was re-admitted after the Gods had shown him special favour.[45] Another man Vatsa, in order to prove himself as born of Brāhmaṇa parents, had to walk through fire unharmed, before he was admitted to be present at a sacrifice.[46]

Of the Upanishads, the *Brihadāraṇyaka* gives us an account of the origin of the *varṇas* in this way: In the beginning there was *Brahman* only. But alone, he could not prosper well (*na vyabhavat*) Therefore, he further created a form [or a pattern or type] (*rūpam*) with a view to welfare (*śreyo*), viz. the *Kshatra;* this consisted of the Gods Indra, Varuṇa, Soma, Rudra, Parjanya, Yama, Mritya and Iśāna . . . Still, however, *Brahman* found that it could not fare satisfactorily; therefore, it created the *Vaiśya*-hood (*viśam*) in the form of the Gods Vasus, Rudras, Adityas, Viśve-devas and the Maruts. Even then, *Brahman* could not make good progress; so it created *Śūdra Varṇa* in the form of the God Pūshan. In spite of these creations, again, *Brahman* did not develop well; therefore, he still further created the form (*rūpam*) of *Dharma* for welfare [of Brahman, or of human beings.]. The earthly *varṇas* are, in the opinion of *Brihadāraṇyakopanishad*, thus created out of these divine *varṇas*.[47] This theory does not refer to any social gradation amongst the *varṇas*. On the contrary, each *varṇa*, as also the *dharma* for them, were conceived as also created with a view to contributing to the social welfare. Regarding birth in a particular *varṇa*, the *Chhāndogya* tells us that this depends upon the nature of our deeds in the former birth. Those who are of good conduct here, will attain good birth as Brāhmaṇas or as Kshatriyas or as Vaiśyas. But those who are of bad conduct here, will be born again as dogs, swines or outcastes.[48] Here, only the first three *varṇas* are mentioned.[49] In all these views, however, there seems to be no reference to any idea of status or an idea of 'higher or lower' involved between the three *varṇas*.

II

(1)

There is a great deal of theorizing in the *Epic* and the *Dharma-Śāstra* literature on the problem of the origin and development of *varṇas*: There were no distinct castes or classes of men in the *Krita Yuga*,[50] according to the Mahābhārata.[51] At another place, the sage Bhrigu says that only

[45] Ait. Br. ii, 19; Kaush. Br. xii, 1, 3; (Ibid. p. 110).

[46] Panch. Br. xiv, 6, 6; (Ibid.).

[47] Brih. Up. i, 4, 11–15. Professor Ranade, in "*A Constructive Survey of Upanishadic Philosophy*", p. 60, observes in this connection: "In this unorthodox theory, we have the origin of the earthly caste system on the pattern of a heavenly caste system almost in the manner in which the ectypes in Plato's Theory of Ideas are merely replicas of the archetypes."

[48] Chhānd. Up. v, 10, 7.

[49] In Chhānd. viii, 14, also, only Brāhmaṇa, Rājan, and Viś, are mentioned.

[50] There are said to be four *yugas* (ages), *Krita* or *Satya*, also called the 'golden age'; *Tretā; Dvāpara*; and *Kali yuga*, i.e. the present age, also called 'iron age'.

[51] Mahā. Vana. 149, 18: (cf. also Rāmā. Uttar. xxx, 25–26) "*ekavarṇā mayā buddhyā prajāh srishṭāh tathā prabho/ ekavarṇah* . . ." and, *"tāsām nāsti viśesho hi darśane lakshaṇe' pi vā//"*; and Bhāg. Purā. ix, 14, 4: "*eka eva purā vedah . . . eko'gnir varṇa eva cha//"*.

a few Brāhmaṇas were first created by the great Brahman.[52] But later on, the four divisions of mankind—Brāhmaṇa, Kshatriya, Vaiśya and Śūdra developed. The complexion (*varṇah*) of the Brāhmaṇas was white (*sita*),[53] that of Kshatriyas red (*lohitah*), that of the Vaiśyas yellow (*pītakah*), and that of the Śūdras black (*asitah*)—thus does the *rishi* Bhrigu explain his theory of the origin of the *varṇas* to Bharadwāja. But Bharadwāja asks: If the various *varṇas* had to be distinguished simply by means of the colour of their complexion, then surely this must have been found to be an impossible task! For there are endless varieties of men and colour! How could so many different varieties (*vividha*) be classed under four orders only? To this Bhrigu replies that there is no distinction between the different classes.[54] At first the whole world consisted of Brāhmaṇas. Created equally by Brahman, men have, on account of their acts, been divided into various *varṇas* (see Note 54). The theory goes on to explain how the four *varṇas* and other castes (*jātayah*) arose out of the one original class of *Dvijas* (twice-born). Those who found excessive pleasure in enjoyment, became possessed of the attributes of harshness and anger; endowed with courage, and unmindful of their own *dharma, (tyakta-sva-dharmah*), those Dvijas possessing the quality of redness (*raktāngāh*),[55] became Kshatriyas. Those again, who, unmindful of the duties laid down for them, became endued with both the qualities of Redness and Darkness (*pītah*)[56] and followed the occupations of cattle-breeding and agriculture, became Vaiśyas. Those Dvijas, again, who were given to untruth and injuring other creatures, possessed of cupidity (*lubdhāh*), who indiscriminately followed all sorts of occupations for their maintenance (*sarva-karmo'pa-jīvinah*), who had no purity of behaviour (*śaucha-paribhrashṭah*), and who thus nursed within them the quality of Darkness (*krishṇah*)[57] became Śūdras. Thus "divided by these occupations, the Dvijas, (who were, in the first instance, all Brāhmaṇas) due to falling away from the duties of their own order, became members of the other three *varṇas*. None of them, therefore, is prohibited from carrying out all the activities of *dharmas* and *yajnas*."[58] Further, those who, through their ignorance, fell away from their prescribed duties and led a loose life (*svachchandāchāracheshṭitāh*), ended in reducing themselves to the various lower castes (*jātayah*), viz. the Piśāchas (feinds), the Rākśasas (goblins), the Pretas (the evil-spirited), and the various *mlechchha* (barbarian or outcast) *jatis* (castes).[59]

The theory of the origin of the *varṇas* from the various parts of the Creator's body also finds a place in the Mahābhārata. Thus, the Brāhmaṇa is said to have originated from the mouth of the Brahman (the Creator), the Kshatriya from his arms, the Vaiśya from his two thighs, and the Śūdra

---

[52] See Mahā. Śānti. 188, 1–17, for the views of Bhrigu given here.

[53] Nīlkaṇṭha comments: "*varṇah sāttvikam rājasam tāmasam miśram cheti svachchhatvādisāmyāt guṇavrittam varṇa-śadbena uchyate/*" Thus, "*Sitah=sattva-guṇah; lohitah=rajo-guṇah; pītakah=rajas-tamo-vyāmiśrah; asitah=tamo-guṇah.*"

[54] Ibid. 188, 10:

> *Na viśesho'sti varṇānām sarvam brahmam idam jagat/*
> *brahmaṇā pūrva-srishṭam hi karmabhir varṇatām gatam//*

[55] '*raktāngah=rajo-guṇa-mayah*'—Nīlakaṇṭha.

[56] '*pītah=rajas-tamo-mayah*'—Nīlakaṇṭha. However the word *pītah* literally means 'yellow'.

[57] '*krishṇah'—kevala-tamo-mayah*—Nīlakaṇṭha.

[58] Ibid. Śānti. 188, 10–14:

> *ityetaih karmabhir vyastā dvijā varṇāntaram gatāh/*
> *dharmo yajna-kriyā teshām nityam na pratishiddhyate//*

[59] Ibid. Śānti. 188, 17–18.

from his feet.[60] The Brāhmaṇa was created to preserve the Vedas and the other scriptures, the Kshatriya for ruling the earth, holding the rod of punishment and protecting all other creatures, the Vaiśya for supporting the two other orders and himself by cultivation and trade, and the Śūdra to serve the three orders as a servant.[61]

But theorizing about the origin and the distinction between the four *varṇas* does not end with these views only. King Janaka asks a pertinent question to the sage Parāśara on this subject: The whole of mankind has sprung from *Brahman*. Now, it is a law of nature, and the *Śrutis* too say the same, that the offsprings share in common the nature of that from which they are created. Therefore, all the men on earth must have been of one *varṇa* when they were created! Whence, then, did the distinction start? Parāśara replies thus: It is true that the offsprings begotten by one "is none else than the begetter himself"; but, if "the soil and the seed are inferior, the offspring born of these will be inferior". Now, proceeds the sage, though mankind originated from the Great Brahman himself, all did not spring from the same part of his body; the Brāhmaṇas sprang from his mouth, the Kshatriyas from his arms, the Vaiśyas from his thigh and the Śūdra from his feet. But it is to be remembered again that originally only these four *varṇas* were created; all other classes besides these "are said to have originated from an intermixture of these" (*samkarajāh smritāh*). In this manner, for instance, were the sub-sections in the Kshatriya *varṇa* created.[62] Parāśara then gives a list of fourteen such sub-classes like the *stenas* (robbers), *sūtas* (charioteers), *nishādas* (hunters, fishermen), *śvapākas (chāṇḍālas*) and others.

Finally, there is the theory, advanced by the great Bhīshma himself as to the origin of several castes apart from the four *varṇas*. The theory, in short, is this: Originally Prajā-pati (the Lord of Men) created the four *varṇas* only (*chātur-varṇyam cha kevalam*) and laid down their respective duties (*chātur-varṇyasya karmam*) for the sake of *Yajna*.[63] However, a person from any of these *varṇas* was allowed to marry women from his own *varṇa*, and from the *varṇas* below his own. Now, the offspring begotten of a wife of his own *varṇa* and of a wife from a *varṇa* immediately below his own belong to their father's *varṇa;* but the offspring begotten of a wife remoter than one *varṇa* below his own should belong to the *varṇa* of his mother. Thus, for instance, a Brāhmaṇa may marry wives from all the four *varṇas*; the sons from his Brāhmaṇa and Kshatriya wives would be Brāhmaṇas like their father, while his sons of his Vaiśya wife or wives would be Vaiśya, and those of his Śūdra wife or wives would be Śūdra. In this way, again, a Vaiśya's son from either a Vaiśya or Śūdra wife would be a Vaiśya like his father. So far it is all without much complexity; but even this does not explain the rise of more than four castes. For the offspring born in any of the ways so far enumerated would find a place either in his father's *varṇa* or in his mother's *varṇa*. To explain the existence of the various other castes, Bhīshma advances the other part of his theory: It is when a man cohabits with a woman of higher *varṇa* than his own that the offspring so born is regarded as being outside the pale of the four *varṇas*.[64] Such a son is the object of censure from the four principal *varṇas*.[65] Sin lies therefore, in a woman's marrying a man of a *varṇa* lower than her own, not in a man's marrying a woman of a lower *varṇa*. So, Bhīshma

---

[60] Ibid. Śānti. 72, 4–5.

[61] Ibid. 72, 6–8.

[62] Śānti. 297, 2–9.

[63] Mahā. Anu. 48, 3.

[64] Anu. 48, 4–28.

[65] Ibid. 48, 9: "*chātur-varṇya-vigarhitam*".

explains, by permutations and combinations of marriages of the former type, the several castes have come into existence.[66]

(2)

The theory that the four *varṇas* proceeded from the limbs of the Creator is also held by *Manu-Smriti*.[67] And, in order to protect this whole universe (*sarvasya*), differential duties and occupations have been assigned to the different *varṇas (prithak-karmāṇi)* by him.[68] Manu then goes on to eulogise the Brāhmaṇa *varṇa* as the supreme creation of God.[69] He further positively asserts that the Brāhmaṇa, Kshatriya, Vaiśya and Śūdra are the only *varṇas* in existence; there is no fifth *varṇa*; and with this, Yājnavalkya, Baudhāyana and Vasishṭha also agree.[70]

Manu's theory of the origin of mixed castes is, in certain respects, different from that of the Mahābhārata. Sons begotten by twice-born men (*dvijas*, i.e. Brāhmaṇas, Kshatriyas and Vaiśyas) of wives from the immediate lower class belong no doubt to the *varṇa* of their fathers respectively but they are censured on account of the fault inherent in their mothers (*mātri-dosha*).[71] Such is the traditional (*sanātana*) law (*vidhih*) applicable to children of a wife from a *varṇa* only one degree lower than her husband's.[72] The real 'mixture' of *varṇas (varṇas-samkarah)* therefore arises with offsprings born of a woman two or three degrees lower. Thus the son born of a Brāhmaṇa father and a Vaiśya mother would be called an Ambashṭha; that born of a Brāhmaṇa father and a Śūdra mother would be called Nishāda, and so on.[73] The mixture of *varṇas* takes place in other ways also. Of a Kshatriya father and Brāhmaṇa mother spring issues belonging to the Sūta caste; children born of a Vaiśya father and Kshatriya mother or a Brāhmaṇa mother belong to Māgadha and Videha castes respectively; and so on.[74] And, inter-marriages between these new castes give rise to newer and newer castes, so that the process goes on multiplying.[75] Here in this *śloka* (X, 11), Manu has used the word *Jāti* as distinct from *varṇa*. This *śloka* opens the topic concerning offsprings begotten on a woman of higher *varṇa* by a man of lower *varṇa*. Thus, the Sūta, the Māgadha and the Vaideha are so named according to their "*jāti*" (*jātitah*). And, in the next *śloka*, Manu also uses the term *Varṇa-samkarah*, mixture of *varṇas*, in this connection.[76] Though Manu refers to four *varṇas* only, he mentions about fifty-seven *jātis*, as a result of *varṇa-samkarah*.

Here, it would be advantageous for us to firmly fix in our mind that the '*varṇa* theory' of society is not to be confused with the '*jāti*-system' which we meet with today in the Hindu society, and which is usually described by the term 'caste-system'. The word caste was first

---

66 Anu. 48, 4–29.
67 Man. i. 31.
68 Man. i, 87.
69 Ibid. 92–96.
70 Man. x, 4; also Yāj. i, 10; Bau. i. 16, 1; and Vas. ii. 1–2.
71 Man. x, 6; Such children are *apasadas* (base-born)—x, 10.
72 Man. x, 7.
73 Man. x, 11–13; See also Yāj. i, 93–94; Vis. xvi, 4–6.
74 Man. x, 18–45.
75 Man. x, 11.
76 Man. x, 12; See also Yāj. i, 90–91.

used in India by the Portuguese to denote the several *jātis*[77] which they found existing here, and which have continued to exist since then, perhaps with additions. Dr. Dutt summarizes the most apparent features of the Hindu caste-system of to-day by pointing out that "the members of the different castes cannot have matrimonial connections with any but persons of their own caste; that there are restrictions, though not so rigid as in the matter of marriage, about a member of one caste eating and drinking with that of a different caste; that in many cases there are fixed occupations for different castes; that there is some hierarchical gradation among the castes, the most recognized position being that of the Brāhmaṇas at the top; that birth alone decides a man's connection with his caste for life, unless expelled for violation of his caste rules, and that transition from one caste to another, high or low, is not possible. The prestige of the Brāhmaṇa caste is the corner-stone of the whole organization."[78] These are the most salient features of the *jāti* system or the caste-system into which the original *varṇa* scheme of the Hindus has come to be evolved. The word *'jāti'* originates from the Sanskrit word *'jan'* 'to take birth,' while the word *'varṇa'* would mean 'colour'. *Varṇa* has also been derived from *'vri'* 'to choose', meaning accordingly, 'choice of vocation'. Anyway, it has nothing to do, in its origin, with the purely family lineage principle involved in the word *'Jāti'*.

The view that *'varṇa'* and *'jāti'* are distinct and "essentially independent", though "by the reaction of principles on fact the two institutions may have become fused together" later on,[79] was put forward by E. Senart; this is generally accepted by both Iranian and Vedic scholars like Geldner and Oldenberg, as well as by Indologists like Barth and Jolly.[80] This theory "supposes a distinct value for the terms", *jāti* and *varṇa*.[81] Senart has shown how the Aryans first used the term *'Ārya Varṇa'* in Rigvedic literature to distinguish themselves from the *'Dāsa Varṇa'*, the enemies of the Aryans.[82] In the opinion of Senart, the word *varṇa* was used to denote the distinction between the *Āryas* and the non-*Āryas;* but it "was later split up, if I may so express it, so that it might apply no longer to these two primitive *varṇas*, but to more numerous categories. It has not lost all traces of its origin. It does not signify caste in general and in the strict sense, but only 'the four castes',[83] while the castes which are actually found in practice and which do not truly correspond with this theoretical fourfold division into *varṇas*, were designated only by the law-books by the term "*jāti*".[84] The water-tight compartments of the *jāti*-system therefore are due to later Brāhmanic interpretation of the term *varṇa*, and, "to interpret the Vedic testimony by the Brāhmanic theory of a more recent age, is to reverse the true order of things."[85]

---

[77] N. K. Dutt: op. cit., p. 1. Also, P. Masson-Oursel & Others: *'Ancient India and Indian Civilization'*, p. 78; J. A. Hutton: *Caste in India*, 2nd Ed. 1951. pp. 47 ff.

[78] Dutt: Ibid. p. 3.

[79] Senart: *Caste in India* (Tr. by Ross. 1930), p. 153.

[80] Masson-Oursel: op. cit., p. 83.

[81] Ibid. p. 83.

[82] Senart: op. cit., pp. 122–123 (following Zimmer).

[83] Senart: Ibid. p. 128.

[84] Senart: Ibid. pp. 128–129.

[85] Senart: Ibid. p. 126.

III

(1)

Let us next take into consideration the classification of *dharmas* with reference to the *varṇa* scheme. With an obeisance to the Dharma Deity before proceeding to deal with this question, the wise Bhīshma gives his views as follows: Control of anger, speaking the truth, justice (or equity or fair-mindedness, *samvibhāgah*), forgiveness, begetting children of one's own married wife, pure conduct, avoiding quarrel, uprightness (*ārjavam*), and the maintenance of one's dependents (*bhritya*), these are the nine duties, common to all the four *varṇas (sārva-varṇikah)*.[86] Then follows the familiar division of *dharmas* among the four *varṇas*. Thus, teaching, self-control and the practice of *tapas* (austerities) are the specific (*kevalam*) duties of the Brāhmaṇas; study, protecting people, performing sacrifices, making gifts, are the specific duties of a Kshatriya; study, making gifts, celebrating sacrifices and acquiring wealth by fair means are the specific duties of a Vaiśya; and the Śūdra, created "as the servant of the other three *varṇas*" should never amass wealth (*samchayam*) for himself, for then "he makes the members of the three superior orders obedient to him. By this he would incur sin."[87] He is to be maintained by the three other *varṇas*.[88] Whatever he possesses, belongs to his master.[89] Sacrifice, the Śūdra can perform; but he is not held competent to recite *svāhā* and *sadhā*, or any other Vedic *mantra*.[90] "Sacrificing, of course, is as much sanctioned for the Śūdra as for the other three."[91] There are two kinds of sacrifices which are common to all *varṇas*, the sacrifice in the form of faith or belief (*śraddhāyajna*) in god and *dharma*, and what may be called the mental sacrifice (*yajno manīshayā*)[92] in the sense of cultivating a discipline of non-attachment to material possessions.[93] Therefore, says Bhīshma, the moral (*nirṇayah*) of *varṇa-dharma* is that members of all the *varṇas* should always, and by every possible means in their power, perform *yajna*.[94] There is nothing in the three worlds (i.e. Heaven, Earth and the Low World) equal to *yajna*; therefore, it is said that every one, with his heart free from malice, and with faith as the holy foundation for his acts, should perform *yajna* to the best of his abilities and fullest satisfaction.[95]

---

[86] Śānti. 60, 7.

[87] Ibid. 60, 8–29.

[88] Ibid. 60, 31.

[89] Ibid. 60, 36.

[90] Ibid. 60, 37.

[91] Ibid. 60, 40.

[92] Ibid. 60, 44–45.

[93] Nīlakaṇṭha comments: "*tathā cha manase devato'ddeśena dravya-tyāgātmake yajne sarve varṇā adhikriyante, ity-arthah*", i.e., all the *varṇās* are entitled to make sacrifices by way of donating money or property with the intention of attending upon God.

[94] Ibid. 60, 53:

sarvathā sarvadā varṇair yashṭavyam iti nirṇayah/
na hi yajnasamam kinchit trishu lokeshu vidyate//

[95] Ibid. 60, 54:

tasmād yashṭavyam ityāhuh purusheṇānusūyatā/
sraddhā-pāvitryamāśritya yathāśakti yathechchhayā//

The Great God Maheśvara gives a similar account of the division of duties for the *varṇas*. The duties common to all the *varṇas* are: hospitability towards all (*sarvātithyam*), the pursuit of the three-fold objectives of life (viz., *Dharma, Artha* and *Kāma*), and giving alms and gifts according to one's means.[96] Then, some of the specific duties of the Brāhmaṇa are: observance of fasts, listening to the intricacies of *dharma*, observance of courses of conduct laid down in the Vedas, attention to the Sacred Fire in the home, constant recitation of the Vedas, performance of sacrifices, and complete abstension from injuring any creature.[97] In addition to the specific duties of the Kshatriya already referred to above as mentioned by Bhīshma, he should also have "perseverance in acts that have been undertaken"[98] by him, he should give punishment to offenders proportionate to the offences committed, and he should not hesitate to interfere in order to help the distressed.[99] The Vaiśya's main duty is honest trade; and, as usual, the Śūdra's duty consists in attendance upon the three other *varṇas*.[100]

For the *Smritis*, the common *dharmas* of the four *varṇas* are: abstention from injury to any living creature (*a-himsā*), pursuit of truth (*satyam*), abstaining from unlawfully appropriating what belongs to another (*a-steyam*), purity of conduct and life (*śaucham*) and control of sense organs (*indriya-nigrahah, indriya-samyamah*);[101] to these are also added self-restraint (*damah*), forgiveness (*kshamā*), uprightness (*ārjavam*) and generosity (*dānam*).[102] The specific *dharmas* of each of the *varṇas* are the same as noted above by us from other sources.[103] Manu summarizes them by saying: "Among the several duties, the most commendable (*viśishṭāni*) are, teaching the Veda for the Brāhmaṇa, protecting the people (*rakshaṇam*) for a Kshatriya, and trading (*vārtā*) for a Vaiśya."[104]

In times of adversity or distress (*āpad*), however, the Brāhmaṇa may follow the occupations of the Kshatriyas; or he may even follow the occupations of the Vaiśyas, if he is not capable to perform the duties of Kshatriya (*asaktah kshātra-dharmeṇa*).[105] Only, there are certain reservations in this rule; the Brāhmaṇa should not, even when following the Vaiśya's occupations, sell wines, salt, sesamum seeds, animals having manes, bulls, honey, meat and cooked food, under any circumstances.[106] It follows, of course, that a Kshatriya could follow the Vaiśya's occupations in times of adversity or distress. Whether the three higher *varṇas* could follow the Śūdra's occupation of service in such conditions is not mentioned at all; but, it seems that they could not do so under any circumstance. In all such relaxations of rules of *dharma*, the relation of observable duties to the conditions existing in the particular time and place is viewed as of fundamental importance. For,

---

96 Mahā. Anu. 141, 61–79.
97 Ibid. 141, 36–41.
98 Ibid. 141, 49.
99 Ibid. 141, 51–52.
100 Ibid. 141, 55–57: "*Śuśrūshā cha dvijātishu*"/. *Śuśrūshā* means, literally, 'desire to hear', i.e., obedience.
101 Man x, 63; Yāj. i, 122; vis. ii, 16–17.
102 Yāj. i, 122.
103 Man. i, 88–91, and x, 74–80; Yāj. i, 118–19; Vis. ii. 5–9, etc. of *supra* footnote 86 ff.
104 Man. x, 80.
105 Mahā. Śānti. 78. 1–2.
106 Ibid. 78, 4–5.

says Bhīshma, "*dharma* may become *adharma* and *adharma* may become *dharma* according to time-and-place (*deśa-kāla*); such is the significance and power of time-and-place."[107]

The *Dharma-Śāstras*, too have similar relaxations on the prescribed occupations and duties of the four *varṇas* in times of adversity. Thus, a Brāhmaṇa who cannot maintain himself by means of the occupations specially prescribed only for him may adopt the Kshatriya's mode of life. If he is unable to subsist even by this, he may adopt the Vaiśya's mode of life, i.e., trade, agriculture and cattle-rearing. The Kshatriya, of course, can adopt the Vaiśya's mode of living during times of adversity. But here again there are reservations; the Brāhmaṇa and the Kshatriya, when living upon agriculture, must carefully avoid injury to animals; and, when he has to take to commerce, he may sell the commodities which the Vaiśya sells, but he must never sell cooked food and seasamum, stones, salt, cattle, human beings, dyed cloth as well as cloth made of hemp or flax or wool, fruits, roots, medical herbs, water, weapons, poison, meat, *soma* (wine), perfumes of all kinds, milk, butter, oil, wax, sugar, beasts of the forest, birds, liquors, indigo, lac, and all one-hoofed beasts.[108] Further a Vaiśya who is unable to subsist by following his own duties and occupations (*sva-dharmeṇa*) of trade and agriculture may maintain himself by following the Śūdra's mode of life.[109]

But the noteworthy point for Manu is that one should under no circumstances adopt the mode of life prescribed for the *varṇa* or *varṇas* higher than his own.[110] In general, "it is better to discharge one's own *dharma* incompletely (or imperfectly) (*viguṇah*), than to perform completely that of another (*na pārakyah swanu-shṭhitah*)."[111]

During times of famine or in dire necessity when one is in danger of dying for want of food, acceptance of such a thing as a dog,[112] or a cow,[113] from even a Chāṇḍāla,[114] for the purpose of eating, is no sin. A person accepting such food under such circumstances "is no more tainted by sin than the sky by mud."[115] Manu further gives "ten sources or means of subsistence" (*daśa jīvana-hetavah*) open to all men in adversity or distress; these are; learning, mechanical arts, work for wages (*bhritih*), service (*sevā*), rearing cattle, trade (*vipaṇih*), agriculture, contentment (or fortitude, *dhritih*), begging (*bhaikshyam*) and receiving interest on money (*kusīdam*).[116]

The *rishi* Mārkandeya narrates the story of how a Brāhmaṇa ascetic named Kauśika was taught the principles of the *varṇas* and the *dharmas* by *Dharma-Vyādha* ("Dutiful Hunter") of Mithilā.[117] This man, whose occupation was selling meat, was actually found "selling venison and the flesh of the buffalo."[118] The Brāhmaṇa was surprised to find that this person was acclaimed to have

---

[107] Ibid. 78, 32:

"*bhavatyadharmo dharmo hi dharmādharmāvubhāvapi/*
kāraṇād deśa-kālasya deśa-kālah sa tādriśah//"

[108] Man. x, 81–89; Yāj. iii, 32–39; Vis. liv. 18–21.

[109] Man. x, 98.

[110] Man. x, 95–96:—*na tveva jyāyasīm vrittim abhimanyeta karhichit/*

[111] Man. x, 97.

[112] Man. x, 106.

[113] Man. x, 107.

[114] Man. x, 108.

[115] Man. x, 104.

[116] Man. x, 106; also Yāj. iii, 42.

[117] Mahā. Vana. 205, 44.

[118] Ibid. 206, 11.

been a most virtuous man even though he followed "such a dishonourable profession!"[119] But Dharma-Vyādha retorts to the Brāhmaṇa that he was only carrying out the *dharma* prescribed for him by his *karma*. "Fulfilling the duties of my own trade, to which I am already destined by the creator, I carefully devote myself, O best of the twice-born ones (*dvija*), to the service of my superiors as well as the elders;"[120] besides, this hunter always spoke the truth, never envied any one, used to make gifts according to his means, and lived upon what was left after the service of the Gods, the guests and his dependents. He never spoke ill of any one; and he hated none.[121] "A person, even thou'gh born of low lineage, may yet be a man of good character. Again, he may turn out virtuous even if he be a slayer of animals by birth or profession."[122] Therefore, virtue does not altogether depend either on the birth or on the calling of a person.

The reason why one is born in a family which has adopted a low profession is of course summed up in the word *karma*. "Destiny is all powerful" says this hunter to Kauśika. "It is difficult to overcome the consequences of our past deeds. This is (i.e., his profession is due to) *karma*-evil, arising from sins committed in a former life."[123] Whatever is killed by one, moreover, is also killed by its own *karma* too, the killer being only an "agent in consequence of his *karma*."[124] Each of us is under the influence of his *karma;* and each of us must always try to see in what way he can atone for his *karma* and extricate himself from an evil doom ahead.[125] There are so many ways of expiating this *karma*, viz., by gifts, truthfulness, service of the *guru*, faithfully following the *varṇa-dharma* in which one is born, virtuous conduct, freedom from pride, abandoning of idle talk and so forth.[126] "There can be said many things as regards the goodness or badness of our actions. But he who sticks to the *dharma* of his own *varṇa* acquires great glory."[127]

The ascetic Brāhmaṇa, to whom Dharma-Vyādha was expounding this *varṇa-dharma*, became soon convinced of the truth and wisdom of the latter's interpretation, and finally admitted to Dharma-Vyādha that he was indeed no Śūdra at all but a real Brāhmaṇa by virtue of his dutifulness. "For the Brāhmaṇa who is vain and haughty, who is sinful and evil-minded, and who indulges in degraded practices, is no better than a Śūdra. The Śūdra, on the other hand, who is endued with righteousness, self-control and truthfulness," continues the ascetic, "is considered by me as a Brāhmaṇa. A person becomes a Brāhmaṇa by his own good deeds; and by his own evil *karma*, he meets with an evil and terrible doom.[128]"

All this suggests a rather different meaning to the principles of the *varṇa* system as based on one's *karma*. It means that if one is born in a lower *varṇa*, then by following the *dharma* of his own *varṇa* in this birth, he may be able to be born again in a higher *varṇa* in the next birth; and, one who is born in a higher *varṇa* must live up to the duties and obligations of his *varṇa* if he does not want to be degraded in the next birth.

---

[119] Ibid. 106, 19.
[120] Ibid. 206, 21.
[121] Ibid. 206, 22–23.
[122] Ibid. 34.
[123] Ibid. 207. 2–3.
[124] Ibid. 207, 4.
[125] Ibid. 207, 20.
[126] Ibid. 207, 21–22.
[127] Ibid. 207, 39.
[128] Ibid. 215, 13–15.

Later, in the same *parva* in the *Mahābhārata*, we are explained the meaning of *Dharma* in an allegorical manner. Here *Dharma* comes in person to meet his foster-son Dharma-Rāja or Yudhisṭhira, the eldest of the five Pāṇdava Princes.[129] He tells Yudhisṭhira: "Fame, truth, self-control, purity, simplicity, modesty, steadiness, charity, asceticism, and *Brahmacharya* are my very limbs. Be sure that absence of cruelty, impartiality, peacefulness, restraint, purity and want of pride are the so many avenues of attaining to me."[130]

In Maheśvara's opinion, also, a person of lower *varṇa* may attain the status of a higher *varṇa* in the next birth by following his own *dharma* in this birth.[131] The person who does not follow his own *dharma* will be born again in a lower *varṇa*. Thus, good (i.e. relative to one's *varṇa*) deeds may succeed in securing higher *varṇa* for one, but not in this life, according to this theory. The duties which befall one in this life are due to one's past deeds; therefore they must be carried out and also atoned for by discharging the present *dharmas* in a just manner, if a better life is desired in the next birth. This means a higher *varṇa* is attainable through an evolution of births through which the individual attains higher and higher merit by dint of his pursuit of *dharma*. However, we shall revert to Maheśvara's opinion again below.[132]

(2)

But there is another view also in the Mahābhārata itself, expressed in very clear and unmistakable terms by King Yudhishṭhira, —who was also known as *'Dharma-Rāja'*, because he was known to abide by *Dharma* in all his conduct,—that the *varṇa* of the person is to be judged and assigned by what he does here and now, and not just with reference to the family in which he may have been born. Bhīmasena, the second of the Pāṇḍava brothers and a man possessing exceptionally great physical strength, was caught by a Python, who was no other than the Pāṇḍavas' own ancestor, King Nahusha, fallen into the species of serpents because of his sin of highly insolent behaviour towards the *rishis* who were made to draw his chariot, one of whom pronounced a curse on him that he would be born as a serpent; the Python would not release Bhīmasena until correct answers were given to his querries which Bhīmasena, who had entire confidence in his physical strength only, was unable to answer! So, Yudhishṭhira was asked the same questions: "Tell me", the Python asked, "Who is a Brāhmaṇa?" "He in whom are noticeable truthfulness, charity, forgiveness, good character, mercy, ascetic tendencies, and compassion is regarded by the authorities (*smritah*) as a Brāhmaṇa," replied Yudhishṭhira.[133] But, retorted the Python, these traits may be found even in a Śūdra![134] To this Yudhishṭhira replies: "The Śūdra in whom these traits (*lakśma*) are found is no Śūdra (but a Brāhmaṇa), and the Brāhmaṇa in whom these are lacking is no Brāhmaṇa (but a

---

[129] Vana. Adhyāyas 311 to 313.

[130] Ibid. 313, 7–8.

[131] Anu. 143, 1–47.

[132] See below.

[133] *satyam dānam kshamā śīlam ānriśamsyam tapo ghriṇā/*
driśyante yatra nāgendra sa brāhmaṇa iti smritah// Vana. 180, 21.

[134] Ibid. 23.

Śūdra).[135] It is regarded by the authorities that one in whom the characteristic mode of life (*vrittam*) of a Brāhmaṇa is seen is a Brāhmaṇa; one in whom it is not to be found should be assigned to *Śūdra varṇa.*"[136] "If, however, a Brāhmaṇa is to be recognized by his mode of life", argues the Python, "then the distinction of caste (*jātih*) is useless so long as a man's activity does not correspond to the mode of life of his *varṇa!*"[137] Yudhishṭhira replies: "In my opinion, it is very difficult to ascertain the caste (*jāti*) of a man owing to the intermixture (*samkara*) of all *varṇas*. Men of all *varṇas* are begetting children of women of all *varṇas.*[138] Besides, (overt manifestations like) speech, cohabitation, birth and death are the same for men of all the *varṇas.*[139] The proof of this difficulty in ascertaining one's *varṇa* is also found in such utterances of the *rishis* as, "whatever *varṇa* we may belong to, we celebrate the sacrifice"! It is therefore that those who have grasped the essentials (*tattva—darśinah*) [of *dharma*] have known that character (*śila*) is the principal desirable thing."[140]

On this theory, further, every person, at birth, is no better than *śūdra;* his character-traits as expressed in his behaviour later show him to belong to the Brāhmaṇa (or any other) *varṇa*. "The postnatal rituals immediately on birth (*jāta-karma*) are performed for every male prior to the severance of the naval chord; and on that occasion, his mother is, as it were, his *Sāvitrī*, and the father his *Āchārya.*[141] But until his initiation into the Vedas (i.e. until the initiation ceremony—see ch. iv) is gone through, every man is just like a Śūdra. In view of the difference of opinion on this point, Manu, the Self-Created, himself has laid down that if, having gone through the various *samskāras* the members of the *varṇas* do not observe their respective modes of behaviour (*vrittam*), then those members of intermixture of *varṇas* (who may be adhering to their respective modes) should be considered as superior to the former.[142] "As I have already said," repeats Yudhishṭhira again, "him in whom is found the mode of life in line with the various *samskāras (samskritam vrittam)*—him I would consider to be a Brāhmaṇa."[143] The Python—i.e. King Nahusha—was so pleased with these answers that he complimented Yudhishṭhira as "a man who knows what ought to be known" (*viditavedyah*)[144], and released his brother.

---

[135] *śūdre tu yaḍ bhavel-lakshma dvije tach-cha na vidyate/*
*na vai śūdro bhavech-chhūdro brāhmaṇo na cha brāhmaṇah//*Ibid. 25.

[136] *yatraital-lakshyate Sarpa vrittam sa brāhmaṇah smritah/*
yatraitan-na bhavet Sarpa tam śūdram iti nirdiśet// Ibid. 26.

[137] *yadi te vrittato rājan brāhmaṇah prasamīkshitah/*
vrithā jātis tadā'yushman kritir yāvan-na vidyate// Ibid. 30.

[138] *jātir atra Mahā-Sarpa manushyatve mahā-mate/*
samkarāt sarva-varṇānām dushparīkshyeti me matih// Ibid. 31.

[139] *sarve sarvāsvapatyāni janayanti sadā narah/*
vāṅ-maithunam atho janma maraṇam cha samam nriṇām// Ibid. 32

[140] *idam ārsham pramāṇam cha ye yajāmaha ityapi/*
*tasmāch-chhīlam pradhāneshṭam vidur ye tattva-darśinah//*Ibid. 33.

[141] *prāṅ-nābhi-vardhanāt pumso jāta-karma vidhīyate/*
tatrāsya mātā sāvitrī pitā tvāchārya uchyate// Ibid. 34.

[142] *tāvach-chhūdra-samo hyesha yāvad vedam na jāyate/*
tasminnevam mati-dvaidhe manuh svāyambhuvo'bravit//
krita-krityāh punar-varṇā yadi vrittam na vidyate/
*samskāras tvatra nāgendrabalavān prasamīkshitah//*Ibid. 35–36.

[143] *tatredānīm mahā-sarpa samskritam vrittam ishyate/*
*tam brāhmaṇam aham pūrvam uktavān bhujagottama//*Ibid. 37.

[144] Ibid. 38.

This incident is also supposed to have meant as a lesson of humility for Bhīmasena, who had become too vain about his own physical strength, but found that all his physical might and vitality came to nought and he realized that ultimately it is only the strength of character (*śīla*) of a man that is the most potent force in this world.

In the *Bhavishya-Mahā-Purāṇa* we are told that there can be no such thing as *jāti*-distinction amongst human beings, since they are all sons of One Father; and just as the *udumbara*[145] tree grows numerous fruit at the bottom, in the middle and at the end and yet all of them are similar in colour, shape, touch and taste (or juice), similarly men belong to one *jāti*.[146] And, in the *Bhāgavata-Purāṇa* also we are reminded of the fact that *varṇa* is to be known and designated by the deeds of a person rather than his birth. Persons who have grasped the essential meaning of the Vedas (*Veda-drig*) have declared that the *dharma* of men which is by and large determined (*vihitah*) on the basis of native temperaments or tendencies (*svabhāva*) in accordance with the times (*yuga*) is conducive to the welfare of men, in this world as well as hereafter.[147] A person carrying out his *karmas* and following the occupation in accordance with his *svabhāva* will gradually attain the state of quality-less-ness (*nirguṇatā*) by exhausting or destroying the *karmas* born of his *svabhāva*.[148] Just as a field that is being continually tilled loses all capacity of fertility and is unable to yield corn and even destroys the seed sown in it, so does our mind which is the source of all desires become satiated by an over-indulgence in them;—fire may be extinguished by a continuous pouring of clarified butter, though it flashes forth if the butter is poured in drops.[149] If the distinctive characteristics or signs of conduct (*lakshaṇam*) explained as indicative of the *varṇa* of a man be (absent in one person and) found in another, then call that person by the *varṇa* as denoted by these characteristics (*lakshaṇa*),[150] and not by that of his birth. These "*lakshaṇas*" are: Peaceful (or quiet) nature, self-restraint, austerity, purity, contentment, forgiveness, uprightness, knowledge, kindness, firm devotion to God, and truthfulness—these are the characteristic traits of a Brāhmaṇa.[151] Bravery, valour, courage, fire (*tejas*), char-

---

145 The Indian fig tree. It has a long life which may extend to hundreds of years. Also, its branches spread out over a very large area so that hundreds of people could sit under its shade at a time.

146 *Bhavishyamahāpurāṇa, Brāhma-parva*, 42, 45–46:

chatvāra ekasya pituh sutāś cha teshām sutānām khalu jatir ekā/ evam prajānām hi pitaika eva pitraikabhāvān na cha jātibhedah// phalān yatho' dumbara-vriksha-jātāh yathāgra-madhyānta-bhavāni yānti/ varṇa-kriti-sparśa-rasaih samāni tathaikato jātir atiprachintyā/ /

147 Bhāg. Purā. VII. xi, 31:

prāyah svabhāva-vihito nriṇām dharmo yuge yuge/
veda-drigbhih smrito rājan pretya cheha cha śarma-krit//

148 Ibid. 32: *vrittyā śvabhāva-kritayā vartamānah svakarmakrit/*
hitvā svabhāva-jam karma śanair nir-guṇatām iyāt/ /

149 Ibid. 33–34:

upyamānam muhuh kshetram svayam nir-vīryatām iyāt/
na kalpate punah sūtyā uptam bījam cha naśyati/ /
evam kāmāśayam chittam kāmānām ati-sevayā/
virajyeta yathā rājannāgnivat kāma-bindubhih/ /

150 Ibid. 35:

yasya yal lakshaṇam proktam pumso varṇābhivyanjakam/
yad anyatrāpi driśyeta tat tenaiva vi-nirdiśet/ /

151 Ibid. 21:

śamo damas tapas śaucham santoshah kshāntir ārjavam/

ity, self-control, forgiveness, friendliness towards Brāhmaṇas, graciousness and (inclination to give) protection (to others), are the characteristic traits of a Kshatriya.[152] Devotion to God, to *guru* and to the Firm (Principle? or to God Vishṇu?), sustenance of the three classes, belief in God, industry, and dexterity (or skilfulness or shrewdness)—are the characteristic traits of a Vaiśya.[153] Humility, purity, unaffected service to masters, sacrificing without *mantras*, absence of tendency to steal, truthfulness and preservation of the cattle and the Brāhmaṇas—are the characteristic traits of a Śūdra.[154]

The *Śūkra-Nīti* gives us similar bases of the four *varṇas*. Thus, "Not by birth are the Brāhmaṇa, Kshatriya, Vaiśya, Śūdra and Mlechchha[155] differentiated, but by their respective qualities and deeds."[156] And further, in the description of the *dharmas* of different *varṇas*, the *Śukra-Nīti* classifies men in accordance with what they do, and not their duties in accordance with their predetermined position by the accident of birth. Thus, one who can protect men, who is valorous, is a Kshatriya for the *Śukra-Nīti*. And similarly about the other *varṇas*.[157]

We have already referred to Maheśvara's view of how good deeds would lead to higher *varṇa*, by evolution, in the next birth. But during the course of the same discussion on *varṇa*, Maheśvara has also opined that "all the Brāhmaṇas in this world could be really called Brāhmaṇas only on the merit of their conduct or mode of living (*vrittam*); and, a Śūdra, if he is of good conduct, is considered to have attained to Brāhmaṇahood."[158] Even a Śūdra, we are told, who has purified his soul by pure deeds and who has controlled all his senses, deserves to be waited upon and served with the respect due to a Brāhmaṇa—this is what is said by Brahmā himself;[159] and his own opinion also, says Maheśvara, is the same.[160] Neither birth, nor *samskāra*, nor learning, nor being born in a particular family could be considered as cogent grounds for conferring a *varṇa* of the *dvija* kind (i.e.

---

jnānam dayā'chyutātmatvam satyam cha brahma-lakshaṇam/ /

[152] Ibid. 22:

śauryam vīryom dhritis tejas tyāga ātma-jayah kshamā/
brahmaṇyatā prasādaś cha rakshā cha kshatra-lakshaṇam/ /

[153] Ibid. 23:

deva-gurvachyute bhaktis trivarga-pariposhaṇam/
āstikyam udyamo nityam naipuṇam vaiśya-lakshaṇam/ /

[154] Ibid. 24:

śūdrasya samnatih śaucham sevā svāminyamāyayā/
a-mantra-yajno hyasteyam satyam go-vipra-rakshaṇam/ /

[155] A fifth "*varṇa*" is here added. *Mlechchha*= barbarian outcast
[156] Śukra. i, 75–76.
[157] Ibid. i, 77–78.
[158] Mahā. Anu. 143, 51:

"*sarvo'yam brāhmaṇo loke vrittena tu vidhīyate/*
vritte sthitas tu śūdro'pi brāhmaṇatvam niyachchhati/ /"

[159] Ibid. 143, 48:

"*karmabhih śuchibhir devī śuddhātmā vijitendriyah/*
śudro'pi dvijavat sevya iti brahmā'bravīt svayam/ /"

[160] Ibid. 143, 49:

"*svabhāvah karma cha śubham yatra śūdre'pi tishṭhati/*
viśishṭah sa dvijāter vai vijneya iti me matih//".

one of the first three *varṇas*) upon a person; his mode of behaviour (*vritti*) only could be the basis of conferring such dignity upon him.[161]

In the Mahābhārata, once more, we find *Rishi* Bhrigu lecturing on *varṇa-dharma* to Bharadvāja; and his view is noteworthy here in that he explicitly bases the *varṇas* on the *dharmas*, and not the *dharmas* on the *varṇas*. Thus for Bhrigu, he who has been sanctified (*samskritah*) by *jātakarma* and other *samskāras*, who is pure in conduct, who is devoted to the Vedic study, and who is always mindful of his own modes of behaviour (*nitya-vratī*) and of truth,—he with whom truth, charity, abstention from malice or injury to others (*a-drohah*), mercy, modesty (*trapā*), benevolence, and penance are associated—such a person is called a Brāhmaṇa.[162] He who follows the duties proper for a Kshatriya, studies the Vedas, makes gifts, and captures wealth, is called a Kshatriya.[163] He who tends cattle, is engaged in agriculture and the means of acquiring riches, who is pure in conduct and attends to the study of the Vedas is called a Vaiśya.[164] Lastly, "one who accepts any sort of food indiscriminately (*sarva-bhaksha-ratih*), who is prepared to do any work (*sarva-karma-karah*), who does not study the Vedas, and whose conduct is generally indiscriminate (*an-āchāra*) and impure (*a-śuchih*)[165] is a *Śūdra*. Bhrigu further adds: If those characteristics as described so far of a Śūdra are not to be seen in a so-called Śūdra, and those characteristics described regarding a Brāhmaṇa are not observable in a so-called Brāhmaṇa then, such a Śūdra is no Śūdra, and such a Brāhmaṇa too no Brāhmaṇa at all.[166] This last, is a clear declaration to the effect that a man's *varṇa* has to be measured by his deeds and mode of behaviour, and not merely by his descent or birth.

The Sage Parāśara too gives similar criteria for the basis of *varṇa* as Bhrigu has given above, when he advises King Janaka on the *varṇas*. "Brāhmaṇas learned in the Vedas", says he, "regard a virtuous Śūdra as a model of a Brāhmaṇa himself. I, however, regard such a Śūdra as the effulgent Vishṇu of the universe, the foremost one in all the worlds."[167] Members of the lower *varṇas (nihīnāh)* may, with the intention and purpose of raising their own souls to higher levels (*ud-didhīshavah*), follow the conduct of the higher *varṇas*, though without *mantras*.[168] To the question of Janaka, whether it is birth (*jāti*) or the deed (*karma*) which defiles or taints (*dūshayati*) man, Parāśara answers, that in a sense, both may equally defile or taint man.[169] However, there is a difference (*viśesham*) between the two: The man who is tainted owing to birth in a low family but does not commit low acts (*pāpam*), is not really defiled personally by the taint of mere low birth; on the other hand, the man who, though born in a high family (*jātyā pradhānam*), yet perpetrates censurable

---

161 Ibid. 143, 60:

"*na yonir nāpi samskāro na śrutam na cha santatih/*
kāraṇāni dvijatvasya vrittāveva tu kāraṇam//".

162 Śānti. 189, 2–4.

163 Ibid. 189, 5.

164 Ibid. 189, 6.

165 Ibid. 189, 7.

166 Ibid. 189, 8.

167 Śānti. 297, 28:

"*vaidehakam śūdram udāharanti dvijā mahārāja śruto'pa pannāh/*
aham hi paśyāmi narendra devam viśvasya vishṇum jagatah pradānam//"

168 Śānti. 297, 29–30.

169 Ibid. 297, 31–32—(*ubhayam dosha-kārakam*).

(*dhik-kritam*) deeds, is tainted by such deeds.[170] Of the two, birth and deed, therefore, it is by and large the deeds that defile man.[171]

There are various instances recorded of the *varṇa* of persons being known by their deeds as against the *varṇa* of the family in which they were born:

The story of Viśvāmitra, a Kshatriya, becoming a Brāhmaṇa by dint of his own efforts (*balāt*), is recorded both in the *Mahābhārata*[172] and in the *Rāmāyaṇa*.[173] It has been suggested that the great difficulties which Viśvamitra had to undergo in order to attain the position of a Brāhmaṇa are indicative of the fact that such a change of *varṇa* was not countenanced with much favour by the society and by the privileged class of Brāhmaṇas themselves. But, if we take into consideration the division of *varṇas* as based on the dominance of one or the other natural psychological tendencies called *sattva, rajas* and *tamas*, the difficulties which Viśvāmitra had to undergo will have to be interpreted and assessed in psychological terms rather than in terms of the social colour and prejudice which is usually given to them.[174] It is indeed not an easy task to change one's innate tendencies, inclinations and aptitudes. The actual barriers described as being against Visvāmitra's change were not social but psychological, since he had to undergo severe mental discipline and training in order to transform his *rajas* nature into a life of *sāttvika* qualities. It was not merely the question of change of functions or occupations, nor even of undergoing rigorous physical hardship and discipline; it was rather a problem of fundamental spiritual transformation, of a change of heart. And, this view is further confirmed by the nature of the several 'tests' which Viśvāmitra had to undergo in order to prove his Brāhmaṇa-hood.

The story of Parasurāma, a Brāhmaṇa, who became a Kshatriya by profession is too well known to be related here.[175] There are other notabilities in the Mahābhārata, who were Brāhmaṇas by birth but were Kshatriyas by deeds, viz., Droṇāchārya, Kripāchārya and Ashvatthāman. All these three attained the position of Commanders-in-Chief in the Kaurava army. Two Kshatriya princes, Devāpi and Sindhudvīpa attained Brāhmāṇahood.[176] So also, prince Vītahavya was able to attain Brāhmāṇahood.[177] Indra, again, though son of a Brāhmāṇa by birth, became a Kshatriya due to his deeds (*karmāṇa*).[178]

In the *Bhāgavata Purāṇa*, many other instances of change of *varṇa* are recorded: Gārgya, the son of a Kshatriya attained Brāhmaṇahood.[179] Duritakshaya, Pushkarāruāṇi, Traiyyāruṇi and Kavi became Brāhmaṇas likewise.[180] So again, King Śaryāti rose to the eminence of a great Brāhmaṇa (*brahmishṭha*) and officiated as a sacrificial priest.[181] And Nābhāga, another Kshatriya Prince became Vaiśya owing to his deeds (*karmaṇā*).[182] Prishadhra, a Kshatriya prince, became a Śūdra.[183]

[170] Ibid. 297, 32–34.

[171] Ibid. 297, 34.

[172] Ádi. 71, 79.

[173] Bālakāṇḍa, lvii, ff.

[174] The implications of these qualities are discussed below, in section IV.

[175] Mahā. Vana. 115.

[176] Mahā. Śalya. 40.

[177] Mahā. Anu. 30.

[178] Mahā Śānti. 22, 11.

[179] Bhāg. Pu. ix, xxi, 19.

[180] Ibid. ix, xxi, 20.

[181] Ibid. ix, iii.

[182] Ibid. ix, ii.

[183] Ibid. ix, ii.

Not only individuals, but whole families and communities are said to have attained a change of *varṇa* in this manner. Thus in the same Purāṇa, a whole clan or group of people (*gotram*) known by the name Maudgalya is recorded to have attained Brāhmaṇahood, though it descended from one Mudgala who was a Kshatriya.[184] Then, out of the hundred sons of King Rishabha-deva, eighty-one became Brāhmaṇas. And, a whole community of Brāhmaṇas is said to have descended (*brahmakulam jātam*) from a Kshatriya named Dhrishṭa. The *Padma-Purāṇa* tells us that Vyāsa and Vaibhāṇḍaka, though born of very low origin (*asat-kshetra-kula*), were respected and honoured as *dvijātis;* and so was Vasishṭha who was the son of a courtesan (*veśyā-putrah*).[185] And, indeed, the names of Vyāsa (considered to be the author of the *Mahābhārata*) and Vasishṭha have been hallowed by the Hindu tradition as the most revered ones for the Hindu.

There are several other instances recorded of change of *varṇa*, for instance, in the *Matsya Purāṇa*,[186] the *Vāyu Purāṇa*,[187] and in the *Harivamśa*.[188]

In the *Mahābhārata*, there are instances recorded of inter=marriages also between the *varṇas*. King Śantanu married Satyavatī, who was apparently the daughter of a Śūdra. King Dushmanta (or Dushyanta) married Śakuntalā, supposed to be the daughter of *rishi* Kaṇva[189] who was a Brāhmaṇa. And, King Yayāti married Devayānī, the daughter of a Brāhmaṇa priest Śūkrāchārya.[190] *Rishi* Chyavana married princess Sukanyā.[191] And two *rishis*, apparently Brāhmaṇas, called Nārada and Parvata have a quarrel over the daughter of a Kshatriya King Srinjaya whom both of them sought to marry.[192] Such instances of intermarriages are many in the Mahābhārata, and once more indicate that the *varṇa*-barriers were not regarded as insurmountable even in regard to such an important question as marriage.

IV

Of all the ideologies of the Hindu thinkers concerning social organization on the *varṇa* basis (*varṇa-vyavasthā*), the statement made in the *Bhagavad-Gītā* is perhaps the most outstanding and specific; we shall therefore review this theory of the *Gītā* here. The theory classifies society into four *varṇas* (*chātur-varṇyam*) in terms of the dominant *guṇas*, that is to say, in accordance with one or the other of the synthetic moulds arising out of different psychic tendencies and energies innate in the biological and psychological make-up of man. In this sense, the *guṇas* may be said to be the psycho-moral bases of the *varṇa* organization. Before we proceed further in analyzing the *varṇas* as social classes, therefore, let us here try to envisage the *guṇa*-theory as propounded by the *Gītā*:

---

184 Ibid. ix, xxi, 33.

185 Padma-Purā. xlvi, 47–48:

asat-kshetra-kule pūjyau Vyāsa-Vaibhāṇḍakau tathā/ kshatriyāṇām kule jāto Viśvāmitro'sti tat-samah//
. . . veśyā-putro Vasishṭhaś cha anye siddhā dvijātayah//

186 Matsya-P., 1, 88.

187 Vāyu-Purā. xcix, 278; lvii, 121.

188 Hari. xxvii, 1489; xxxvii, 1773.

189 Mahā. Ādi. 71.

190 Ibid. 81.

191 Ibid. Vana. 122.

192 Ibid. Dorṇa. 55.

The whole *karma-kāṇḍa* or "the world of activities" is said to be a result of the complex intermingling of the three *guṇas*, viz., *sattva, rajas* and *tamas*,[193]—roughly, Goodness (or Light or Truth), Passion, and Dullness (or Darkness or Ignorance) respectively, according to Śrī Krishṇa in the *Gītā*. He also says: "The whole world does not recognise Me, since they are deluded by the effects produced by these *guṇas*."[194] The world of human beings is but a part of the whole creation, and, as such, it is also fettered by these three *guṇas*.[195] Now, of the *guṇas*, *sattva* is characterised by purity (*nirmalatva*); consequently, it is of an enlightening and healthy nature; and, it binds one by an attachment to ease (or peacefulness) and to knowledge.[196] *Rajas* is in essence passion; it is the source of yearnings and clingings; and it fetters the embodied one by attachment to activity.[197] *Tamas* is born of ignorance; it is the source of delusion of all embodied beings, binding them by the qualities of carelessness, sloth and sleep.[198] *Sattva*, then, bids for a life of ease and peacefulness, *rajas* for restless activity, and *tamas*, veiling right perception, leads to carelessness (or negligence).[199] By overpowering *rajas* and *tamas, sattva* prevails; by overpowering *sattva* and *tamas, rajas* predominates; while *tamas* dominates in man by overpowering *sattva* and *rajas*.[200] The *sattva* quality can be known to have been fully developed in a man when the light of knowledge shines in his body, through all its 'gates' (i.e., sense-organs);[201] that is to say, all his activities show him to be a man

---

[193] Gī. ii, 45:
"*traiguṇya-vishayā vedā nis-traiguṇyo bhavārjuna/*"
Ibid. vii. 12:
"*ye chaiva sāttvikā bhāvā rājasās tāmasāś cha ye/*
matta eveti tān viddhi na tvaham teshu te mayi//".

[194] Ibid. vii, 13:
"*tribhir guṇa-mayair bhāvair ebhih sarvam idam jagat/*
mohitam nābhijānāti mām ebhyah param avyayam//".

[195] Ibid. xiv, 5:
"*sattvam rajas tama iti guṇāh prakriti-sambhavāh/*
nibadhnanti mahābāho dehe dehinam avyayam//".

[196] Ibid. xiv, 6: "*tatra sattvam nirmalatvāt prakāśakam anā mayam/*
sukha-samgena badhnāti jnāna-samgena chānagha//"

[197] Ibid. xiv, 7:
"*rajo rāgātmakam viddhi trishṇā-samga-samudbhavam/*
tan nibadhnāti kaunteya karma-samgena-dehinam//".

[198] Ibid. xiv, 8:
"*tamas tvajnānajam viddhi mohanam sarva-dehinām/*
pramādālasya-nidrābhis tan nibadhnāti bhārata//".

[199] Ibid. xiv, 9:
"*sattvam sukhe sanjayati rajah karmaṇi bhārata/*
jnānam āvritya tu tamah pramāde sanjayatyuta//".

[200] Ibid. xiv, 10:
"*rajas tamaś chābhibhūya sattvam bhavati bhārata/*
rajah sattvam tamaś chaiva tamah sattvam rajas tathā//"

[201] Ibid. xiv, 11:
"*sarva-dvāreshu dehe'smin prakāśa upajāyate/*

with understanding. On the other hand, a man in whom *rajas* has waxed full shows signs of greed, undertakes (too much) activity and expresses restlessness and longings.[202] And *tamas*, when it gets the upper hand in an individual, manifests itself in obscurity, stagnation (inactivity), carelessness and delusion.[203]

Śrī Krishṇa tells us further about the effects of the influence of the *guṇas* upon the individual: The person who dies with the *sattva-guṇa* fully developed in him will attain the pure worlds of the most exalted who know the highest.[204] If, however, he dies with the *rajas* quality developed in him, he will be born again amongst those that are bound down to *karma*.[205] And, if he dies full of *tamas*, then he would be born amongst the most deluded.[206] The fruit of good deeds, it is said, is *sāttvika* and pure; of actions full of *rajas*, the fruit or end is misery; and, the result of actions full of *tamas* is ignorance.[207] From *sattva*, again, arises knowledge, from *rajas* arises greed, and from *tamas* only carelessness, delusion and ignorance can spring.[208]

Now, when a person is able to realise that the (true) agent of actions is not himself but the interplay of the *guṇas* within him, and he also fathoms That which is beyond the *guṇas*, then, says the Lord, is he able to attain to His Being.[209] When the soul of such a person rises above the three *guṇas* which spring from the body, he enjoys immortality and becomes free from birth, death, age and sorrow.[210] Śrī Krishṇa further describes the characteristics (*linga*), the ways of life (*āchāra*)

---

jnānam yadā tadā vidyād vivriddham sattvam ityuta//".

[202] Ibid. xiv, 12:

"*lobhah pravrittir ārambhah karmaṇām a-śamah sprihā/*
rajasyetāni jāyante vivriddhe bharatarshabha//".

[203] Ibid. xiv, 13:

"*aprakāśo'pravrittiś cha pramādo moha eva cha/*
tamasyetāni jāyante vivriddhe kuru-nandana//".

[204] Ibid. xiv, 14:

"*yadā sattve pravriddhe tu pralayam yāti deha-bhrit/*
tadottamavidām lokān amalān pratipadyate//".

[205] Ibid. xiv, 15:

"*rajasi pralayam gatvā karma-sangishu jāyate/*
tathā pralīnas tamasi mūḍha-yonishu jāyate//".

[206] Ibid.

[207] Ibid. xiv, 16:

"*karmaṇah sukritasyāhuh sāttvikam nirmalam phalam/*
rajasas tu phalam dukham ajnānam tamasah phalam//".

[208] Ibid. xiv, 17:

"*sattvāt sanjāyate jnānam rajaso lobha eva cha/*
pramāda-mohau tamaso bhavato'jnānam eva cha//".

[209] Ibid. xiv, 19:

"*nānyam guṇebhyah kartāram yadā drashṭānupaśyati/*
guṇebhyaś cha param vetti mad-bhāvam so'dhigachchhati//".

[210] Ibid. xiv, 20:

"*guṇān etān atītya trīn dehī deha-samudbhavān/*
janma-mrityu-jarā-duhkhair vimukto'mritam aśnute//".

and the manner of overcoming the *guṇas* of such an individual who has transcended the *guṇas* *(guṇātīta)*: Such a man hates not enlightenment, activity or delusion,—i.e., from the context, *sattva, rajas* and *tamas*,—when they arise, nor longs for them when they have ceased their operations: he is, in fact, unconcerned, undisturbed by the *guṇas*, remains unshaken, unperturbed, knowing that the *guṇas* do and must but act according to their natures; for him, happiness and misery are alike; he abides in himself, i.e., is self-contained and content with what he is and has; for him a clod of earth, a stone and gold are all alike; to such a man, the pleasant and the unpleasant, praise and censure, are the same; he is the same in honour and dishonour, the same with friends and foes; he has renounced all initiative of action; and, he serves Me with the unswerving discipline of devotion (*bhakti-yogena*)—Such a person is said to have transcended the rule and sway of the *guṇas*; thereafter he becomes fit to attain the eminence of *Brahman*.[211] *Tyāga* (renunciation) of *karma*, again, does not mean the absolute giving up of doing anything (*pari-tyāga*) or inaction; it is not avoidance or evasion; such a giving up of all activity would partake the quality of *tāmasa* nature.[212] On the other hand, when *karmas* are abandoned from fear of physical sufferings and pain, it is called *rājasa tyāga*, and will never yield the fruit of a bona fide *tyāga*.[213] The real *tyāga* is the *sāttvika tyāga*, which is accomplished when *karmas* are performed because they have but to be performed, abandoning all attachment as also the desire for their fruit.[214]

This is the general outline of the *Gītā* theory of the individual's psychological make-up,—of his tendencies, dispositions, inclinations, interests and aspirations,—in terms of the *guṇas* innate in him. And, this theory is closely related to the problem of social relations, group characteristics, and social organization. The *guṇas* basically determine the tendencies and aptitudes, the potentialities and the limitations, and directions of successful social contribution by the individual. They also determine the trends of his traits and character. And these factors are to be taken into account when the individual's relations with the society and for the purposes of social order and organization are to be considered. All the *karmas* i.e., activities and occupations necessary for the social organization, upkeep and progress are classified in accordance with these psychological apparatuses in the individual called *guṇas (guṇa-karma-vibhāgash)*.[215]

Again, just as the predominant *guṇa* in an individual determines the general trend of his nature, so also the different types of *karmas* are differentiated and classified, and are expected of and imposed (*karmāṇi pravibhaktāni*) upon different types of men according to the *guṇas* with which each type is naturally endowed and influenced (*svabhāva-prabhavair*).[216] Thus, the *karmas* of a

---

211 "*prakāśam cha pravrittim cha moham eva cha pāṇḍava/*
na dveshṭi sampravrittāni na nivrittāni kānkshati//".
"*udāsīnavad āsīno guṇair yo na vichālyate/*
guṇā vartanta ityeva yo'vatishṭhati nengate//".
"*sama-duhkha-sukhah svasthah sama-loshṭāśma-kānchanah/*
tulya-priyāpriyo dhīras tulya-nindātma-samstutih//".
"*mānāpamānayos tulyas tulyo mitrāri-pakshayoh/*
sarvārambha-parityāgī guṇātītah sa uchyate//".
"*mām cha yo'vyabhichāreṇa bhakti-yogena sevate/*
sa guṇān samatītyaitān brahma-bhūyāya kalpate//". Ibid. xiv, 22–27.

212 Ibid. xviii, 7.

213 Ibid. xviii, 8.

214 Ibid. xviii, 9.

215 Gī. iv, 13.

216 Gī. xviii, 41.

Brāhmaṇa in accordance with his natural inclinations are, leading a life of serenity, self-restrain, austerity, purity, forgiveness, straightforwardness, knowledge, wisdom and belief in God;[217] the Kshātra-*karmas*, in view of the natural inclinations of a Kshatriya, are connected with expressions of valour, prowess, courage, alertness, bravery, generosity, and giving protection to the weak.[218] The Vaiśya-*karmas*, again, considering his nature, are connected with agriculture, trade and merchandise; and the *karmas* of the Śūdra are of the nature of service and attendance of the other *varṇas*[219] and assisting them in the fulfilment of their *karmas* as noted above (*parichyātmakam karma*).

We have also seen, elsewhere, how in the Mahābhārata too there are theories according to which *varṇa* was determined according to the *karmas* and not by the mere fact of one's birth. There is an essential semblance of this way of determining the *varṇa* with the *varṇa* theory based on the psychological principle of *guṇas*. In the *Vishṇu Purāṇa*, once more, we meet with this psychological basis of *varṇa*. It is said there that when the Creator Brahmā desired to create, those in whom *sattva guṇa* was predominant sprang from his mouth and were known as Brāhmaṇas. Those in whom *rajas* predominated originated from his breasts and were known as Kshatriyas. Those in whom both *rajas* and *tamas* predominated originated from his thighs and were known as *Vaiśyas*. Lastly the Śūdra sprang from his feet, and their predominant psychological characteristic was *tamas* (*tamah-pradhānah*).[220] The *Vāyu Purāṇa* gives the account of the *varṇas* again in the same psychological terms.[221] In the same *Purāṇa*, the division of means of subsistence or of livelihood or professions (*vārttā*) between the four *varṇas* is said to have been done by the Svayam-bhū (i.e., the Self-Existent, the Self-Created) according to their propensities (*yathā-rabdhāh*).[222] "Those of them who were rapacious and destructive, he ordained to be Kshatriyas, the protectors of others. The men who attended on these, fearlessly speaking the truth, and propounding the sacred knowledge with exactness (*yathā-bhūtam*), were made Brāhmaṇas." Those engaged in cultivation, etc. were Vaiśyas, the providers of subsistence (*vritti-sādhakān*); and, those who did menial work were Śūdras.[223] Similarly, in the Bhāgawata- Pūrāṇa we are told that the four *varṇas* are meant to follow the four classifications of duties and obligations such as we have already noted elsewhere.[224]

The *Śukra-Nīti* speaks the same thing in different words. Men are said to be of three classes according to their nature and characteristics—*sāttvika, rājasika*, and *tāmasa*.[225] It is these characteristics, and not mere birth, that determine a man's *varṇa*. But, for *Sukra-Nīti*, these characteristics determine a man's *varṇa* even before his birth, influencing his destiny (*prāk-tana*), and yielding for him birth in a particular *varṇa*.[226] What the *Śukra-Nīti* really seems to say, therefore, is that an individual's birth in a *varṇa* is not the *original* determinant of his *varṇa*, but that this birth itself has been determined by his *sāttvika, rājasika* or *tāmasa* kind of *tapas* (discipline) of his activities in his former births! And what is more, his 'intellectual disposition' in this birth, too, is determined

---

[217] Gī. xviii, 42.
[218] Ibid. xviii, 43.
[219] Ibid. xviii, 44.
[220] Vishṇu-Purā. i, 6, 3–5, (—from Muir's *Ori. Sanskr. Texts*, Vol. i, p. 60).
[221] Vāyu-Purā. ix, 36–42; (Muir's *Ori. Sanskr. Texts*, i, pp. 81–82).
[222] And, the Mārk. Purā, has *'yathā-nyāyam yathāguṇam'*, 'according to fitness and other qualities'.—As noted by Muir. op. cit., i, p. 97 note.
[223] Vāyu-Purā. ix, 160–165—from Muir: *Ori. Sansk. Texts*, i, pp. 86–87.
[224] Bhāg. Purā. vii, 11, 14–24.
[225] Śukra. i, 69–72; etc.
[226] Ibid. 73–92.

'according to the effects of his deeds in the previous births' (*prākkarma-phala*).[227] This is similar to the theory that we have met with at one place in the Mahābhārata, where it is explained by Maheśvara in like terms.

V

Most of the basic ideology on *varṇa* theory and its relation to *karma, dharma, guṇa* and other broad principles mentioned in the preceding pages still persists in the mind of the average Hindu. Recent field studies in India, especially in the village communities, seem to bring this out very clearly.[228] According to a most recent study made by a psychiatrist-anthropologist[229] in a village community in Rājasthān though there are many sub-castes in the villages as in all over India, there is also a broad classification of the villagers, often referred to and recognized as such by them in their conversation and social relations, into the four main *varṇas*, viz., Brāhmaṇas, Kshatriyas (Rajputs), Vaiśyas (Banias), and Śūdras (menials, etc.),—and one more added to these, viz., the Untouchables. "The traditional pattern of caste-interrelationship seemed indeed to be the most stable feature of village social life"[230] in the community. Caste, however, was determined by birth, which, in turn, according to the villagers, was the result of the accumulated virtues and sins during one's previous births (his *karma*). One's *dharma* consisted in carrying out the duties and obligations and enjoying the prerogatives assigned to one's caste. There was also a recognition of the fact, sometimes mentioned by the people, that men belonging to the four different castes were now-a-days not keeping to their duties and obligations and have been behaving in ways not appropriate to their caste-*dharmas*. There was also admiration and respect for those who were true to their caste modes of *āchāra* (behaviour) and *vichāra* (thought). Though the members of the three upper castes (which were studied in the investigation under reference), strongly criticized each other's caste for its members' failures, shortcomings and pretences, no one expressed the wish to have been born in another caste than his own. The caste-roles were unquestionably taken for granted. This, in the author's view, discouraged ambition and initiative of the individual. The younger members of the community were beginning to take up professions and occupations which did not fit in with the traditional hierarchical patterns of hereditary occupations.[231] Each Hindu learnt the traditional fundamentals of *karma, dharma* and *moksha*, the inevitability of the cycle of births and re-births, the need to lead life without attachment to worldly things, the value of selflessness, equanimity, and so forth from the older men's repeated sayings, listening to the songs in praise of gods which are sung at the several festival days and to the dissertation with which they are accompanied, attending religious discourses and enactments of episodes from the *Rāmāyaṇa* and *Mahābhārata* in the temples, and in other informal ways.[232]

---

[227] Ibid. i, 89–92.

[228] E.g., the studies of Carstairs, Dube, Marriott, and Srinivas mentioned in the Bibliography. See also, in this connection, Risley's observations quoted on pp. 5–6 *ante*.

It may be mentioned here that out of a total population of 357 million of India, 82 per cent lives in its village.

[229] G. M. Carstairs: *The Twice-Born: A Study of a Community of High-Caste Hindus*. Hogarth, London, 1957.

[230] Ibid. p. 57.

[231] Ibid. pp. 58. 146.

[232] Ibid. pp. 144 ff. See also, pp. 89–124 for current beliefs in the village concerning God, *varṇāśrama dharma, moksha, bhakti*, etc.

VI

We may now consider the modern thought on the classification of a society into different groups in general, and on the castes in particular. This will serve on the one hand, to enlighten us regarding the genesis of social classes and their effect upon the social organization; on the other hand, our view of the Hindu conception and theory of the *varṇas* may also offer criticisms against the opinions generally held in modern times on the problem of social classes. A mutual criticism of the Hindu view of social classification into the *varṇas* and the modern views on social classification may thus enable us to arrive at a common understanding of the organization of society such as is likely to function with the best possible results.

Modern students of social institutions have been recently pointing out that some sort of social classification has always been present and is found to exist in any society, ancient or modern, which is not too crude or primitive.[233] Ward, for example, pointed out how social classes similar to castes in India were in existence in European society. "The four so-called 'Estates' of European History, so clearly recognised in the eighteenth century, correspond so well to the four great castes of India."[234] Thus, the First Estate which consisted of the clergy, the Second Estate consisting of the warrior or ruling class—the nobility, the Third Estate consisting of the merchants and the business-class, and the Fourth Estate consisting of the commons of England or the bourgeoisie of France—the labourers and artisans, correspond to the Brāhmaṇa, Kshatriya, Vaiśya and Śūdra *varṇas* of India. In Ward's view, castes exist in all countries which have undergone the struggles between different races through history. In support of this view he adduces evidence from the forms of social organization in Greece, Rome, Polynesia and other countries. Similarly, Small also opines that in every society, there exists the tendency to create social classes and further their stratification into castes—especially into the three rigid classes, viz., the privileged, the middle class, and the lower unprivileged class without property rights or influence.[235] The privileged classes make all attempts and methods to perpetuate this kind of social differentiation in order to retain their privileges; and thus, the process of social stratification, once started, continues to persist for a long time and is even intensified by passage of time.[236] Said Sumner: "I have sought diligently in history for the time when no class-hatreds existed. . . . I cannot find any such period."[237] And, MacIver, and also Cooley have pointedly drawn our attention to the fact that in the West today 'wealth' is a determinant of social classes as against 'birth' in the East; and we may add, that to some extent at least, in the West today, birth also is a determinant of the social class to which the individual is to belong. However, wealth may be said to be a less rigid determinant of social class than birth; because wealth is concrete, acquirable and alienable, while birth is not so.[238] But wealth is also heritable!

And here, therefore, may be said to be the fundamental distinction between social class and caste, more or less similar to the distinction between *varṇa* and *jāti*. A caste is comparatively a more rigid social class, to which transition from another class becomes well-nigh an impossibility. The

---

[233] cf. e.g. R. M. MacIver: "*Community*", pp. 124–5; also C. H. Cooley: "*Social Organization,*" pt. iv—"Social Classes".

[234] L. F. Ward: "Social Classes and Sociological Theory" in *Amer. Jour. of Socio.*, Vol. xiii, pp. 617–27. Cf. also Ralph Linton: "*The Study of Man*", pp. 127–128, Appleton Century, 1936.

[235] A. W. Small: *General Sociology* (1920), pp. 275 ff.

[236] Ibid.

[237] *The Forgotten Man and Other Essays*, Ed. by A. G. Keller, 1913, Yale, p. 253.

[238] MacIver: *'Community'*, p. 124, note.

still-prevailing distinction between the nobility and the common people in some Western countries is an instance of caste-consciousness, where even wealth or intellect could not yield that status which birth may yield. As Kroeber has said, "castes are a special form of social classes which, in tendency at least, are present in every society."[239] While social classes are comparatively flexible, castes are rigid groups, permanently separated from each other by tradition, custom or even law.

An interesting study of an originally "classless" society which gradually gave rise, in the course of a short period of about 40 years, to social stratification was made recently by Eva Rosenfeld under the sponsorship of the Social Science Research Council of U.S.A.:[240]

> The social system in question was the collective settlements in Israel (called '*kibutz*' or '*kibbutz*,' a term which means "group"), the first of which was established in 1910, and all of which have been mainly agricultural, though industrial branches are gradually developing. Each collective consists, on an average, of about 200 members or about 500 souls, but there are some large ones with over 1,500 souls. The collectives belong to the General Federation of Trade Unions (The *Histadrut*). Here, all property belongs to the commune, and members who leave it have no claim on any part of it. Members are assigned to work by an elected Work Committee. All administrative officers are elected by the general meeting or by the workers of the organisation concerned for certain periods, and positions and duties keep changing hands.[241] "The basic norm is: 'from everyone according to ability, to everyone according to need'".[242] One's first assignment may be that of a manager of a farm; his next one may be connected with kitchen duty. It may also happen "that the manager of an important branch . . . lives in a smaller room, has primitive furniture, worse clothes, and eats less well than some of the unskilled workers who happen to be sickly and need special food and housing. All commodities are distributed centrally and in kind; food is eaten in the communal dining hall. Children are brought up, from birth, in communal children's houses."[243]
>
> The forty-year old history and development of social life in these collectives is revealing. At least two social strata have emerged "out of an initially undifferentiated group of young adults living in an equalitarian and democratic system and bent upon preventing the crystallization of fixed social strata",[244] especially of "the emergence of economic differentiation." There are no economic classes, and consequently, no 'class struggle', in the *kibutz* society. Yet, the social strata that have emerged "have different vested interests with respect to institutional change, and the roles they play in the actual process of change reveal this conflict of interests."[245] Members with high and low status regard each other with a set of stereotype attitudes, and in their relations the awareness of being a disinct social type is clearly expressed. The high and low strata play distinct roles in the process of institutional change and the difference in their *Weltanschauungs* is well known."[246]

[239] "*Ency. of Soci. Sc.*" Ed. by E. R. A. Seligman and A. Johnson, Vol. iii—Art. "Caste", by A. L. Kroeber.

[240] Rosenfeld, Eva: 'Social Classification in a 'Classless' Society", *Ameri. Social Rev.* Dec. 1951, 16, 6, 766–74. *See also*, Weingarten, Murray: *Life in a Kibbutz*, pp. 173. The Reconstruction Press, New York, 1955. In this book, which is a more recent account than the above one, the author, who himself helped to found and develop a *kibbutz*, describes the agricultural type of social settlement that has developed in Israel in recent years. The members of the *kibbutz* are expected, on joining the collective, "to transfer all their wealth to the *kibbutz* treasury", which "then undertakes to be completely responsible for their needs".

[241] Ibid.

[242] Ibid. p. 767.

[243] Ibid. p. 767.

[244] Ibid. p. 766.

[245] Ibid. p. 767.

[246] Ibid. p. 774.

The type of stratification emerging is, however, a very special one. Individuals possessing ability, initiative, and leadership qualities have come up. "Functional necessity forces the group to keep these highly valuable and esteemed members within a narrow range of important, managerial positions. Prestige becomes associated with these positions, which are, then, used as an index of high social status."[247] However, high social status does not bring economic or material reward, but only emotional rewards. The individuals in high positions feel a satisfaction in their ability to identify with larger social interests and with the future of the group. There is a tendency for the children of the top class to rise up rather easily because "their parents' intelligence and abilities (and often also personal integrity and a very high standard of values) are often transmitted" to them, "whether through heredity or through personal contact and influence," and also because "some of the 'halo effect' of the parents does fall on their children. The sons and daughters of 'big shots' in the *kibutz* movement are regarded as the aristocracy among the growing crop of second generation youth." And this, despite the fact that the original criteria of status, viz., intelligence, ability, devotion to collective values and good work performance are still applied to the second-generation members. Hence, it seems that once social stratification makes its start in any form, there are self-perpetuating forces also generated along with it.[248]

As we have said, then, some kind of classification is bound to exist in all societies. Social classification is a phenomenon which it would be impossible to abolish in any society. Men differ from each other in their natural endowments, in their intelligence, special abilities and talents, moods, personality traits and other innate characteristics. Even twins differ from each other in these characteristics. Howsoever much we may cry for equality amongst humanity, we cannot avoid differences between man and man in terms of natural abilities, capacities, intelligence, and aptitudes. In social affairs and social communications, such individual differences are apt to give rise to the formation of social groups, each of which consists of individuals who find themselves agreeable to each other because of general similarity of tastes, vocations, likes and dislikes, social status, and such other factors.[249] Apart from this general similarity of views and tastes which brings individuals together, there is another factor referring to social utility that binds men together into different groups. A human being is able to accomplish skill, mastery and success better and more efficiently in company and in co-operation with a group of persons engaged in common occupations. Such co-operation of a group of minds is, on the one hand, due to common calling, common problems, common solutions; and, on the other hand, it is fostered and nurtured by all these and by a *feeling* of common bond underlying their activities and their minds. Here, we must also reckon with another factor which is closely allied with the above, viz., a *feeling* of being different from other social groups on account of differences in callings, giving rise to different problems and difficulties from those other groups.

There is yet another force which may foster and perpetuate class-differentiations. This force works through the family institution. It is not only most likely that the father may transmit his occupation and calling to his children, but it is in many cases also ordinarily advisable that this should be so, unless any of the children show a positive disinclination towards the family occupation, or a positive inclination towards a different occupation, or they are not, as in most cases in modern times, in touch at all with their father's occupation. The father is conversant with the secrets, the hidden intricacies as well as the difficulties of his own occupation or craft and with their solutions, due to

---

[247] Ibid.

[248] Ibid.

[249] See, e.g., R. S. Ellis: "*The Psychology of Individual Differences,*" (1930), Ch. xvi—"Individual Differences and Social Differentiation," pp. 386–404. Also, A. Anastasi: *Differential Psychology*, Rev. Ed., MacMillan, N. Y., 1958.

long experience; and the child can take advantage of his knowledge and experience without any special efforts or trouble or expense of energies on his part. So again, the children's constant contact with the family occupations is naturally likely to create in them a predisposition towards them. It is therefore natural as well as desirable, in the ordinary course of events, that family trades and occupations should be carried over from father to son. But this should not be a compulsory tradition.

The phenomenon of social classes can be viewed from two sides in order to get a full perspective of the issues involved, from the *social-psychological* side on the one hand, and from the *individual-psychological* side on the other; though, it must be remembered, that such classification of the viewpoints is more or less arbitrary and academic; for, in regard to the phenomenon of social classes as in regard to most others, the social and the individual aspects merge into each other at various points in such a complex manner as to be inextricable from each other excepting in an artificial way. At the same time, also, such distinctions are more than a mere intellectual exercise, for they do afford valuable insights into societal phenomena which are useful when we are faced with the problems of social change,—the desirable and needed change as well as analysis of the accomplished changes in the history and social life of man for a proper perspective of the same.

Looking at the question, then, from the social side, as we have seen, no society can remain classless. Classes emerge in society out of a *functional necessity*, as Kingsley Davis and W. E. Moore have pointed out in a penetrating analysis of social classes. "Curiously, the main functional necessity explaining the universal presence of stratification", observe these writers, "is precisely the requirement faced by any society of *placing* and *motivating* individuals in the social structure."[250] As a functioning system, society must distribute its personnel into groups according to the duties and the contribution of activities it expects from these respective groups for its own stability and progress, largely the former. And, for this purpose it must devise ways and means for inducing the right type of individuals into the right groups and fill in the right positions. These means and inducements constitute the motivating devices for individuals to go into those positions and places such as they can attain readily and accept these as their due positions. In addition, society must also devise ways and means to induce the individuals, who have found themselves into their own suitable positions, to perform their duties of the respective positions and do their utmost by way of creative efforts in the given positions. As the authors further point out, this is true of competitive as well as non-competitive societies; only, in competitive societies, individuals will strive to attain positions which they desire, and therefore the motive to compete with others in order to rise in one's status attains greater importance in such societies; while in non-competitive societies, the motive to perform the duties of one's position to the best of one's abilities is given greater importance.[251]

Now, obviously, there is a variety of social duties requiring a variety of abilities, talents and training; and there is also a variety of talents to be found among the members of the society. Therefore, it is the responsibility of the society to have a system whereby individuals are placed in proper

---

[250] Davis, Kingsley & Moore, W. E.: "Some Principles of Stratification". *Ameri. Social. Rev.* April 1945, 10, 2, 242–49. (Italics ours). These authors' thesis that the universality of social stratification is the inevitable consequence of the functional importance of some social roles and positions and the necessity for placing the right type of individuals with the right type of abilities in these positions for achieving social ends has been confirmed by Rosenfeld's study mentioned above, pp. 324–326.

[251] Ibid.

positions in accordance with the kind of talents and training each of them have. This is essentially the problem of personnel placement, or 'social placement', as Davis and Moore call it. Having placed the individuals, it is further the responsibility of the society to see that their respective duties are diligently performed by the individuals; and this leads to the inevitable "system of rewards that can be used as inducements"[252] and, we may add, also a system of punishments for failure to carry out expected duties. Further, since all duties are not functionally of equal importance for the social sustenance nor do they require equal amounts of abilities and training, society must also have a system of distributing the rewards (and punishments) differentially according to the social importance of the abilities and positions. "The rewards and their distribution become a part of the social order, and thus give rise to stratification."[253] The reward that society can offer are of three kinds, the material things which contribute to individual's sustenance and comfort, those which contribute to "humour and diversions", and those which contribute to the individual's self-respect and ego-expansion. This last, though largely a matter of other peoples' attitude and opinion, is yet as important as the first two, as Davis and Moore have pointed out.[254]

It seems that in the Hindu view, the first, that is, the economic and material means of sustenance were never a measure of reward or of superiority of social status; and in fact these were very often far from enough for the highest social class; and, the means of comfort were practically absent, at least so far as the highest class was concerned. In fact, members of this class were expected to find comfort in the most uncomfortable material things of life, viz., huts for living in jungles or outskirts of the cities, towns and villages; simple, coarse and sparse clothing; simple food; and on the whole a very austere life. And, even though all of them were perhaps not leading lives in huts in the jungles or outskirts of villages, they were generally living a life of simple habits and less material wants. The same may be said to be generally true of the amenities of humour and diversion. Reward in terms of social prestige, of esteem of the high and the low, was the only thing available to this class for the due performance of their duties in society.

Looking at the picture of class-phenomenon from the side of the individual's attitude and outlook and the psychology governing the same, we must at once reckon with, first of all, the feeling of "consciousness of kind"[255] which plays a fundamental role in all group activities of man. Ginsberg

---

[252] Ibid. p. 243.

[253] Ibid.

[254] Ibid.

[255] This term was first coined by Giddings and explained by him in his *Principles of Sociology* (pp. 16, ff.). T.N. Carver in his *'Essential Factors of Social Evolution'* remarks that this is "one of the most clarifying concepts ever introduced in sociological discussions. It is the key to understanding a great many problems of both theoretical and practical nature" (p. 164). The phrase was coined by Giddings to express his conception of the basis of group life. Giddings explains the term thus: "The original and elementary subjective fact in society is the 'consciousness of kind.' By this term I mean a state of consciousness in which any being, whether low or high in the scale of life, recognizes another conscious being as of like kind with itself . . . In its widest extension, the consciousness of kind marks off the animate from the inanimate. Within the wide class of the animate it next marks off species and races. Within racial lines the consciousness of kind underlies the more definite ethnical and political groupings, it is the basis of class distinctions, of innumerable forms of alliance, of rules of intercourse and of peculiarities of policy. Our conduct towards those whom we feel to be most like ourselves is instinctively and rationally different from our conduct towards others, whom we believe to be less like ourselves". (Giddings: *Principles of Sociology*, pp. 17–18 quoted by T. N. Carver, op. cit.).

has analysed and interpreted the psychology of classes from the subjective side in terms of the theory of "sentiments". Sentiments are "systems of emotions or emotional dispositions centering around a common object or having a common nucleus".[256] The sentiments which form the bases of class-formation are of three kinds: First, of course, is the 'consciousness of kind', that is, an awareness of resemblance or similarity with the other members of a class in the possession of certain common ways of behaviour, conduct and outlook, and of difference from those of the members of other classes than one's own; a feeling of *equality* with them, of being at one with them; sharing a number of important social interests, ideas, ideals and aspirations in common with them; a feeling of 'belonging' to that group naturally, as it were, mostly by sheer birth and without any conscious effort or striving on the part of the individual to belong to the class; and a feeling of "being at ease with them."[257] Secondly, there is a feeling of *inferiority* in relation to those belonging to the social classes which stand higher in the social hierarchy, the degree of inferiority being proportionate to the distance between one's class and the higher one. And thirdly, there is a feeling of *superiority* in relation to the members of the classes which stand below one's own in the social hierarchy, the degree of superiority being proportionate to the distance between one's class and the lower one.[258] These psychological factors play their part in aggravating feelings of class differentiation and strengthening and deepening their roots, and thus lead to more and more rigid castes in course of time.

The foregoing analysis will enable us to visualize clearly the dangers and evils of a system of social classes which is directed towards or has developed into a rigid stratification based on a *concentration* of power, authority, prestige and economic and material rewards all together for the 'higher' classes. Yet, it should also be clear that criticisms which are applicable to the social classes that have attained permanence and fixity purely on the basis of descent or family lineage cannot be applicable to the strict *varṇa* theory. For, it has to be specially noted, that the *varṇa* organization is so conceived that there could be no room for any *varṇa* to consider itself as being placed in a position of greater or less advantage or disadvantage with reference to another. Each *varṇa* is designed to occupy a particular position in the society, not with reference to any advantages or special rights, but with reference to its capability and likelihood to carry out a particular portion and aspect of social obligations; and what may appear to be advantages or special privileges of a *varṇa* are primarily intended only to secure the best possible environment and circumstances in order to enable that class to carry out its obligations to the best of its abilities. To take a concrete illustration: The Brāhmaṇa is entrusted with the duty, pre-eminently, of transmitting the intellectual and the spiritual culture of the people, and also to keep it unsullied by generally maintaining its sterling quality. With this end in view, he may have been granted certain apparently advantageous rights and privileges, as say, for instance, a right to start education at an earlier age than members of the other *varṇas*, or an easy access to the King, or a general respect and honour at the hands of all the other *varṇas*. But it would be wrong therefore to suppose that he stands in a specially advantageous position as compared to the other *varṇas*, when we take into consideration the *dharmas* of a *Brāhmaṇa* defining his obligations and duties which refer almost entirely to the general, material and spiritual well-being

[256] Ginsberg, M.: Art. "Class-Consciousness" in *Ency. Soci. Sc.*; also in his book *Sociology*, Home Uni. Lib., London, 1934, ch. vi.

[257] Ginsberg: *Sociology*, p. 161.

[258] Ibid. pp. 159–61.

of the whole group; and also that he is called upon, more than any other *varṇa*, to cultivate a spirit of selflessness and self-surrender with a view to maintaining general social stability. Upon his shoulders rest the highest responsibilities; and failures, and errors of omission or commission on his part in certain respects make him more severely liable to punishments than any other *varṇa*.[259] Similar responsibilities with their attendant privileges and liabilities are defined for each of the other *varṇas*. In fact, the entire *varṇa*-scheme is devised to coordinate and assemble the best and the utmost of group welfare, by yoking each section of the group on to duties and responsibilities in terms of the efficiency of the specific work and service each of the sections is able to render unto the community life.

The *varṇa*-scheme could be said to be intended to promote social organization in another direction also. It seeks to build up and promote social equilibrium and solidarity through a special kind of economic organization. Thus, the *varṇa-dharma* denies the accumulation of wealth to the Brāhmaṇa; his main *dharma* lies in spiritual and intellectual quests. The Kshatriya may accumulate wealth so much as is necessary for the upkeep and protection of the people dependent upon him and has to use it for the same purpose; his principal *dharma* lies in directing his energies towards expression of valour, bravery and even might, but with a view to giving protection to the weak. The Vaiśya is allowed to accumulate wealth, but with a view to strengthening mainly the economic resources of the society of which he is a member and not for the purpose of hoarding merely for personal use. In this way, the three *varṇas* are expected to make their efforts towards a constructive contribution to the social well-being. But there is always bound to be, in any society, a class of individuals, which is by nature incapable of contributing directly in any very constructive manner for the society; such a class, designated as the Śūdra, may yet assist the others who are doing actual constructive work, by directing their energies towards the service of the *varṇas*. That there was no question of prestige and dignity involved in such classification is evident from the fact that according to the theory, *each person is said to be born a Śūdra*; and, we may say, he *should* be so regarded unless and until he shows his hand in any of the superior modes of constructive social contribution. On the whole, therefore the *varṇa*-theory was devised with a view to engaging the different types of human energies in different channels suitable to each of them, and all towards the one end of social organization, social stability and social progress.

The one big difference between the origin, development and stability of social classes in India and anywhere else also is that elsewhere, class-status is acquired as a concomitant or corollary of wealth, and is accompanied by power and authority, whereas in Hindu India a perfect dissociation was attempted and even achieved between wealth and status, between power and authority, between disinterested pursuit and achievements in science on the one hand, and temptations of worldly comforts on the other.

---

[259] See, e.g., Man. viii, 337–38, where, in the case of theft, the Śūdra is required to repay eight times more in value of the goods stolen, the Vaiśya sixteen times more, the Kshatriya thirty-two times more, while the Brāhmaṇa is to repay "sixty-four times, or a hundred-times, or even twice sixty-four times" in value. Cf. also Gaut. xii, 15–17, Yāj. ii, 260.

VII

Now the question before us is: if it is not possible to demolish the natural human tendency to create classes in society, could it be possible in any way to demolish or check the segragative and separatist tendencies to which these social classes may give rise? In other words, if the rise of social classes is an unavoidable phenomenon in the society, in what way could it be possible, in the interest of social solidarity and social organization, to avoid the stratification of the classes, to check the tendency to turn these classes into watertight compartments with rigid restrictions on the mobility between the classes?

The remedy, one may be allowed to say, could be found in our own 'socio-psychological heritage'. If only we try to look back, through the hundreds of years, to the original spirit in which our social institutions were conceived and formulated, we shall find much light on the very vexed problems confronting the stability of our society today.

The first point to be made in this connection is that the greater evil of the present caste-system is a product of the uncompromising rigidity of the heredity principle involved in it. In the system of castes now in vogue,—in India, and all over the world in some form or other,—we have gone far astray from the original principles which governed the *varṇas*. The original principles on which the *varṇas* used to be based were, as we have already noted, either the principle of choice of the duties prescribed for any of the *varṇas*, or the principle of the *guṇas*—the innate psychological disposition of man determining his inclination towards one of the four broad groups of vocations and duties. We must try to fix *varṇa* on the basis of what man does, or rather what he is actually capable of doing, amongst his fellow-beings and for them, and not merely on the basis of whom he is born of. Social classes, on such understanding, should be so flexible, so open, as to admit transition of individuals from one to the other *if desired and deserved* without any undue premium upon mere descent.

There is another very pertinent and noteworthy consideration in this connection. The idea of 'rank' and the consequent ideas of status ought not to be associated with the idea of *varṇa*. There ought to be no special rights, no special privileges and no special dignities which may be considered as advantageous prerogatives over others, associated with any *varṇa*. The ideas of 'social distance', of 'higher' and 'lower', among the *varṇas* ought never to find place in the practice of *varṇa*-theory. In other words, if the formation of social classes is an inevitable phenomena in any society, it must work on the basis of cooperation and equality and not of competition and inequality. A cooperation among the *varṇas* based on the principle of division of labour in accordance with natural capacities and aptitudes will preserve the social energy and therefore is sure to make for progress. On the other hand, the separatist tendencies at present working among the castes are sure to create disruption in society. Social utility, and not class-dignity, should be the principle governing social differentiation into classes.

One thing must be made very clear here. It must be remembered that here, as elsewhere, equality of status does not mean and has not to be confused with identity of occupation, calling or vocation. Any honest occupation is to be deemed as worthy of respect and honour as any other. We must try to forget entirely the idea of associating particular vocations with special respect, and particular other vocations with disrespect. All persons must be deemed equal in the eyes of law and morality. There must be equality of opportunity to all in the social, political as well as economic fields,—opportunity such as is consistent with each individual's aptitudes and abilities and inclinations. That there exist individual differences in natural and inherent traits, abilities, talents, interests and aptitudes is now accepted by science; and the task of socially organizing and mobilizing these for their maximum use and contribution to the society as well as for maximum personal satisfaction to the individual is undertaken in the civilized countries by the 'vocational guidance' programmes now operating in many of these countries. In the place of degenerate descent and heredity, honour must be given to ability and intelligence, to potentialities and performance. Descent should not be allowed to come in the way of any person's achieving or desiring to rise to the social status he may aspire for, if he shows the ability to do so. In order to achieve these results, we must take the aid of knowledge. The spread of education and knowledge, irrespective of caste and on equal bases, will cure many a social disease.

CHAPTER IX

EPILOGUE

The study in Hindu social organization and institutions which we have made in the pages that precede has been offered in the hope that thereby we may be enabled to envisage, in answer to contemporary social quest, the material, moral and spiritual background of the drama of social life and institutions as conceived by the Hindu.

And, as the main purpose we have set to ourselves concerns with a scientific consideration of the fundamental ideology and spirit around which social order, institutions and purposes have been sought to be formulated and reared, the sources of our presentation must, of necessity, be limited to the older Sanskrit lore. What specifically that lore is, has already been dealt with by us in the Prologue, the introductory part of our survey.

In addition to what is said in the Prologue, the considerations which have persuaded us to undertake the task may be noted here as below: There has been a hue and cry, during recent days, on the one hand, by some of us who have been openly seeking to effect drastic changes in our social institutions by considerably or altogether doing away with Hindu ideas, traditions and forms; this they call 'Social Reform'. On the other hand, there are many amongst us who have been vehemently crying against such rejections; they proclaim: Whatever is Hindu in practice, in ideas, in ideals, and in institutions, must be kept up and preserved as the most sacred heritage of our forefathers. The conflict between these two opposed groups has become extremely pointed and acute during our own times. To add to this, issues like untouchability and inter-caste marriages have been creating bitterness between these two extreme groups; each group has its own *pandits* to hold up its doctrines and justify them. At such a juncture, a cool-headed, dispassionate, scientific piece of work that investigates into the basic ideology that implicitly and explicitly governs the Hindu's social psychology and cultural pattern, and a systematic presentation of the same, should be the first essential step for all of us who are interested in the progress of our society. Such a systematic presentation should considerably help the clarification of ideas and issues, and may even point us the way for the future.

It would be wrong to suppose that we would deprecate the efforts of the social reformers in this work. We admit that, in view of the enthusiasm created by the new learning of the West, the old type of Hindu life and institutions must have been proving, for these men, rather a groundless, formalistic, insipid and deadening mass of traditions, formalities and impositions, thwarting the expression and expansion of the innermost longings of the individual and the group. At the same time, we must not hesitate to state that the ideological and mental apparatus with which these reformers worked was rather shallow and superficial; nor was the spiritual basis behind Western life and learning sufficiently understood and appreciated in all its bearings by these well-intentioned men. Their understanding of Western thought and culture was mainly on the mere intellectual plane, and mostly of very selective sections of the Western society with which they happened to come in contact or about which they happened to read or learn. And, the deeper spiritual and psychological background behind that thought and culture, if and when at all attempted to be understood, was only superficially discerned by them. Therefore, the ideology of our Social Reformers has proved to be vague, shows lack of basic psychological understanding and content, though it is full of enthusiasm and even good will on the part of those that thought it out and tried to foster it. Without fully grasping the implications of European values which have evolved out of spiritual struggles for centuries of human effort, our Social Reformers wanted forthwith to abandon the institutions of their forefathers, in whatever decadent conditions they found them, without sufficiently understanding or delving into the basic psychological principles underlying the foundations of their own social heritage. All this has resulted in creating additional social problems which Hindu India has now to solve; for, the 'Reform Movement' has failed to tackle the evils it sought to remedy; and, it has rather created complexities and angularities in social life and outlook which have really become very acute during our own days.

On the other hand, let us also point out that the champions of orthodoxy were not altogether without their own shortcomings. They could not and would not understand the incoming and the onrush of the new issues that contact and even conflict with a strange civilization was incessantly bringing on Hinduism, in terms of a new learning and a strange economic order which was slowly but surely seeking to hold its sway on the mind and ideology of the best and the most enthusiastic members of the Hindu community. The Hindu priest had lost his power of vivifying and revivifying the spiritual life of his flock due to the decadence of the old learning with a great deal of which he was often not even himself well acquainted. Due to such decadence of knowledge, *Sāstric* injunctions tended to be misconstrued and misinterpreted as if they were inflexible masses of taboos, heaven-born and therefore un-modifiable; and yet they were hailed as spiritual inspite of this inflexibility.

The result of all this was that the Hindu social institutions of today are not exactly, even generally, in accordance with the picture of human life, conditions and control, presented by the original *śāstras*. They deviate from their original *Śāstric* concepts, sometimes in fundamental respects, and sometimes in details. Such deviation is particularly noticeable in the matter of regulations regarding the *āśrama* system and the *varṇa*-organization. The deviation of the actual Hindu social institutions of today from the original *Śāstric* bases became the more magnified, in view of the disparity, and sometimes even opposition, between precept and practice in the actual life of those that loudly upheld orthodoxy and the social institutions that it supported. Orthodoxy had, and has, little understanding or care that something has been wrong with itself, that underneath its citadel of learning and life, its religion, morals and practices, lay a foundation that was decaying or that was tending towards decay. Their fundamental mistake seems to be their comfortable and undisturbed attitude towards things that should have really mattered out of the cry of reform, even though that cry came from the 'Social Reformers'. They should have tried to look into every bolt and nut, every nook and corner, every piece of their social and spiritual structure from its foundation to roof, to find out if the good old house was quite in order, if it needed repairs, even if drastic, in answer to the call of the human spirit that hungered and thirsted for solutions of the innermost problems of life, generated by the new Western intellectual enlightenment.

There is also another criticism that has been levelled by some against orthodoxy. They believe that orthodoxy's upholding of the older modes of life and conduct were a reflection of the feeling of inferiority in the face of superior Western modes of behaviour and of the West's acknowledged technological progress and superiority. They see, in the attempts of the orthodoxy to revivify the 'old' Indian cultural heritage, in the cry to go 'back to the ancient ways', a psychological mechanism to compensate such feeling of inferiority by professing that, after all, we are not quite so 'backward' as compared to the more advanced peoples! Especially, when orthodoxy tries to insist, in season and out of season, upon the 'spiritual' superiority of the East, and decry the 'material' outlook of the West, one can discern this kind of attitude among them. However, the cry to 'go back to ancient ways' may also have been voiced by orthodoxy because of the vested interests that these people have come to have—in the caste hierarchy and privileges, in the men's privileges over women, and so on.

All this would be true to a great extent of many of those who thoughtlessly want to return to the ancient days and ways *in toto*—which, of course, they certainly cannot possibly do in reality—and to refuse to move with the times. As against this, however, those who want to justify orthodoxy may as well say that the 'reformers' were anxious to abandon their own ways and ape those of the Westerner merely because they wanted to identify themselves with the latter who were occupying superior position economically and politically in the world today, and were on the whole more powerful and more prosperous.

While the criticisms mentioned above may generally stand well against orthodoxy, we may point out that the reformers, on their part could not, did not and would not put their case either properly, that is to say, in terms understandable to orthodoxy and their followers, or with any faith at least in the ideals of the forefathers. In the midst of hurry and enthusiasm, the Reformers failed to realize what the *śāstras* have actually done towards preserving the best and the noblest in the Hindu culture. It is true, though not without important qualifications, that every phase of the individual's life was sought to be prescribed by the *Śāstras* in all its details. Apparently little was left for the individual to think out for himself or herself. Coupled with this, there was the demand of meek obedience to the letter of these injunctions, taking them to be unmodifiable and unalterable, under any circumstances. All this seemed to be so oppressive and unjust to the votaries of the new learning. In the midst of these circumstances, the virtues and excellences of the traditional Hindu theory and conception of human life and organization came to be overlooked. In their attempts to do away with some of the degenerated practices and theories in Hindu life of their own days, the Reformers ignored the possibilities of resuscitating and revitalizing the historically evolved lore of the forefathers and of taking advantage of their wisdom, preserved, accumulated and enriched by experience and reflection through centuries; and instead, they sought to adopt the ways and outlook of the West in great haste and more or less half-heartedly.

Thus they failed to estimate the value of the *Dharma-Śāstras* on the intrinsic merits of their contents, without understanding that the undesirable forms into which Hindu practices have come to be what they are today was due, of course, to certain historical causes. The intrinsic merit, even in practical life, of our ancient heritage, has the testimonies of foreign travellers in India like Megasthenes and Houen-tsang, at a time when the real spirit of Hindu *Dharma-Śāstra* was actually translated into practice in many ways. To this may also be added the evidence afforded by our literature of old times, i.e., in the drama, the poetry and the folklore which mirror the conditions of the times when they were written. The *Dharma-Śāstras* were obeyed not under coercion, but with a high sense of duty, and with a view to maintaining and furthering the good of the community. And, it is evident that the good of the community was made quite practicable by this attitude of the ancients as envisaged by the *Dharma-Śāstras*. It is no wonder, therefore, that the *Śāstras* should have such a great influence over the psychology and ethos of our forefathers. Instead of reminding ourselves of our noble heritage, and trying to live up to it, we have been either misconstruing it, or otherwise trying to ape blindly the ways and methods of strange cultures and peoples.

There is also another very important consideration which all social reformers have to bear in mind. "Nothing is more certain" says Bartlett, "than that every culture has its 'hard' and 'soft' points; if change is first sought at the former, it will provoke resistance and very likely open discord, while the latter are yielding, and it is from them that reformation will spread".[1] He further points out that "items . . . of material culture are 'hard' in proportion to the intimacy and number of their relations with psychological possessions . . . (and that) material culture is easiest to change at those points which have become most dissociated from psychological possessions. This would carry the further implication that if any newly introduced feature of material culture is to stand a reasonable chance of persistence, it must be linked up with desires, beliefs, ideals, or the like," which have become a part of basic ideology of the concerned people. Every change "must itself fit into some existing pattern of material and psychological culture".

Now, the material and psychological patterns can hardly be distinguished in any culture, excepting in a few matters, perhaps. By and large, all overt behaviour springs from or is the result of or is bound up with the needs and desires, the psychological pattern, of the group. But, some of them are more strongly imbedded into or more basically connected with its psychological pattern,—these would be the 'hard' points, in Bartlett's terminology. Those behaviour modes which are less closely related to the psychological needs are the 'soft' points of the culture.

In terms of the interpretation in the paragraphs above, there is hardly any chance for a new reform to be implemented in a society without resistance, conflicts and disruptive consequences unless the innovation is psychologically and otherwise found or made compatible with the existing pattern of behaviour of the society, or unless that society itself is already seriously feeling the need for the innovation or the reform. "There is, as yet", observes Bartlett, "no general recognition of the fact that the speed, permanence and harmony with which any change of culture can be affected . . . depend more upon how it is related to what I have called the group's 'psychological possessions' than upon anything else."[2] "The social anthropologist who sets out to see methods for deciding hard and soft points in particular cultures is almost at once brought up against historical problems. The psychological expressions of culture usually, maybe always, have roots deep down into the past."[3]

I

We may now direct our efforts to state shortly and in general what a useful and valuable heritage the Hindu seers have given us towards the solution of human problems which we are now facing even more acutely than the ancients must have done.

The first thing that should strike the student of social science here is the deliberative planning, organization and system, a whole thread of an ideology running through, a consistent social philosophy underlying all the institutions and knitting them together into a social pattern or social fabric. At the same time, room has been sought to be left for suitable innovations and changes in accordance with regional and temporal conditions (*deśa-kāla*).

It must be said, however, that the Hindus have not fully realized in history the significance and importance of both these provisions together—the need for the systematic planning of life and

[1] Sir F. C. Bartlett: *Anthropology in Reconstruction*. Huxley Memorial Lecture, Royal Anthrop. Insti., London, 1943, pp. 12–13.

[2] "*Anthropology in Reconstruction*"—Reprinted from *Nature*, 152, (Dec. 18, 1943), p. 710. This article consists substantially of the lecture as it was delivered. The previous citation refers to the Lecutre as printed in advance of the delivery of the lecture.

[3] Ibid.

conduct on the basis of certain values on the one hand, and the necessity of freedom to accommodate or adjust to changing conditions on the other; and, not infrequently, the comprehensiveness of the system was so much stressed as to lead to regard it as a closed system, and rigidity and formalism in life and social inter-relationships and behaviour were developed. Especially, in Hindu India's social history, the orthodoxy and the learned *Śāstrīs* have been largely responsible for overemphasising the adherence to the letter and the rigid form of the *Śāstras*, which themselves were hardly properly understood by them in all their comprehensiveness.

It is, however, very necessary and important to note that the *dharma* concept embraces, as its essential part, not only a comprehensive planning out of man's behaviour in terms of several prescriptive regulations, but it also embraces as an equally essential part, the principle of dynamic growth, of flexibility and modifiability, of relaxability in the prescriptive regulations in accordance with the changing conditions and times (*deśa and kāla*). This dynamic quality of *dharma* has been expressed by the Hindu thinkers in a variety of ways and at many places.[4] It is also apparent in the provisions they have made by way of what they call the *āpad-dharmas*, the *dharmas* in times of distress. But, owing to historical reasons largely and also due to the apathy and the lack of sincerity of the orthodoxy, this dynamic aspect of Hinduism and its relativity to the conditions and the times have been overlooked and even neglected. Yet, history has witnessed that the sheer inherent force of these accommodative principles in *dharma* have occasionally triumphed, as if by self-propelling, when, for instance, Hinduism accepted, eventually and without very serious resistance, apparently even rebellious sections and movements like Buddhism whose founder is deeply venerated by the Hindus universally, Jainism, and several other smaller movements too, and recently, the Ārya-Samāj, the Brāhmo Samāj, and so on; when it accepted as its most illustrious gods Sri Rāmchandra who was a Kśatriya by birth and Śrī Krishṇa who was apparently a milkman; when it accepted as its illustrious sages and saints Vasishṭha,* born of a prostitute, Vālmīki, a fisherman, and later Tukārām, a Śūdra,

---

[4] See pp. 28 ff., 73–74, 302 ff., et seq., *supra*. And also:—

deśa-kālau tu samprekśya balābalam athātmanā/
nādeśa-kāle kinchit syāt deśa-kālau pratīkśitam//
—*Māha. Vana.* 28

adharma-rūpo dharmo hi kvachid asti narādhipa/
dharmaś chādharma-rūpo' sti tach cha jneyam vip$$śchitah//
—Ibid. *Śānti.* 33

sa eva dharmah so' adharmas tam tam prati naram bhavet/
pātra-karma-viśesheṇa deśa-kālāvavekśya cha//
—Ibid. *Śānti.* 35

anyo dharmah samasthasya vishamasthasya chāparah/
pratishṭhito deśa-kale dharmo' hyāvasthikah smritah//
—Ibid. *Śānti.* 314

dharmā bahuvidhā loke śruti-bheda-mukhodbhavāh/
kula-jāti-vayo-deśa-guṇa-kāla-svabhāvatah/
etad dharmasya nānātvam sampad-āpad-vibhedatah//
—Ibid. *Anu.*

deśam kālam vayah śāktim pāpam chāvekśya yatnatah/
prāyaśchittam prakalpyam syād yasya choktā na nishkritih//
—*Atri.* 248

kevalam śastram āśritya na kartavyo vinirṇayah/
yukti-hīne vichāre tu dharma-hānih parjāyate//
—Brihas., in *Pārāśaramādhavīya.* See *supra*, pp. 27–28

Mirābāi, a Kśatriya lady. Dnyāneśwara, born of Brāhmaṇa parents but outcasted in the beginning, Nāmdev, a tailor, Chòkhā Melā and Rohidās, untouchables, Kabīr, a Moslem, and many others irrespective of their low caste and even alien religion.** And, in fact, this accommodativeness and adjustability of Hinduism, because of its inseparability from the very basic tenets that constitute the texture of *dharma*, has spontaneously expressed itself and has been demonstrated throughout history,

---

* See pp. 313–14, footnote No. 185, *supra*, where the names of some other revered sages, born of low parentage, are mentioned.

** In this connection, the following news item which appeared in the *Times of India*, Bombay, (February 4, 1954) may be of interest to the reader:—

Hindu Temple Has Muslim as a Priest

The Times of India News Service, Rajkot, February 13.

"A Muslim, a Brahmin and a Sadhu are the priests of a unique temple in Saurashtra, which attracts scores of pilgrims every week.

"Located at Kalawad, an obscure village 20 miles from here (i.e. Rajkot), the temple is dedicated to Shitalāmātā, offerings to whom are said to cure small-pox. Kalawad is miles away from civilization. The nearest railway station, Jam Vanthali, is 18 miles from Kalawad.

"The temple came into prominence when a community project was inaugurated near Kalawad on October 2 last year. To reach this temple from Jam Vanthali, pilgrims either trek 10 miles or use bus service introduced by the community projects administration.

"Legend gives a historical twist to the origin of the peculiar custom in this temple. . . . Shitalāmātā Temple is one of a few that escaped the ravages of the iconoclast, Allauddin Khilji, who ruled India many centuries ago. Six Jain and Hindu temples fell before dusk on the day Allauddin mounted an assault on Kalawad. In a desperate bid to save Shitalāmātā Temple, its Brahmin priest approached a Muslim fakir through a mendicant friend. He persuaded the fakir to intercede with the Mohammedan Emperor on behalf of the Brahmin priest. Allauddin did not relent.

"Legend has it that the fakir then used his supernatural powers and rendered Allauddin blind till he left Kalawad. The Emperor retreated without sacking the temple. As a token of their gratefulness, the people of Kalawad are said to have conferred upon the Muslim fakir and the mendicant the right to be priests and to share the revenues of the temple they helped to save. The Muslim priest and the Sadhu who enjoy this right today are the lineal descendants of the fakir and the mendicant who shielded Shitalāmātā from the onslaught of Allauddin Khilji centuries ago.

"As time marches on, Shitalāmātā Temple continues to stand as a monument to Hindu-Muslim brotherhood that subjugated bigotry in days gone by".

Here is another news item from the *Sunday Standard*, dated July 4, 1954:—

In Krishna She Sees Allah

From Our Correspondent

Ahmedabad, July 3

Many scenes of Hindu-Muslim amity were witnessed here yesterday during the '*Ratha-Yātrā*' procession.

The ninety-two-year-old priest, Mushidasji of Jagannath Temple, who was walking on foot with the procession, was greeted by Muslims in Chandantalvadi area. The Muslims gave Rs. 101 as a gift to the priest, who added Rs. 101 and returned the amount to them.

An eighty-year-old Muslim woman, who was trying to have the *darshan* (i.e., view or sight) of Lord Krishṇa (who was being carried in the *Ratha*, i.e., the chariot), said it was a procession of Allah. "Ram and Rehman are one and the same. Please let me have the *darshan* of Ram in whom I shall see Rehman", she said.

And here is an extract from a recent article in the *Illustrated Weekly of India*, dated October 20, 1957, pp. 26–27, with photographic illustrations, by A. K. Karekatte:—

The Shirdi Shrine

"An obscure village, 52 miles from Ahmednagar, in Bombay State, Shirdi is a spiritual centre where some believe an answer can be found to life's many sorrows and problems.

beginning from the earliest times when all alien groups which came into contact with the Hindu society were sought to be absorbed and merged into the society along with several of their ways, too, which were absorbed in a spirit of tolerance and accommodation, down to modern times, in many directions. However, there was hardly anything ever done by way of deliberative, thoughtful and careful analysis of conditions and circumstances facing the society at a given time, with a view to re-thinking and discovering the directions and aspects in which the *dharma* prescriptions need to be revised, modified or discarded, and the most effective and least disruptive modes of realizing such changes. And this has resulted in the decadence of our social organization.

If our description of the *āśrama* and the *varṇa* schemes in the preceding pages has sufficiently made out that both these schemes were devised as instruments of life, as the best means towards the fulfilment of what was conceived to be the fullest and the most efficient management of the individual, and of the social and economic orders as a whole, then, in this sense, these two schemes are the unique gifts of Hinduism to the world.

"It was here that the saint, Śrī Sāi Bābā, lived and died. And around his *samādhi* has been built a temple, which attracts pilgrims from all corners of India. Loved in his life-time for his simplicity, catholicity and compassion for human suffering, Sāi Bābā continues to hold sway over the hearts of the multitude even after his death, nearly 40 years ago. . . .

"The cult of Sāi Bābā transcends religious distinctions and the temple doors are open to all. . . .

"The story of Sāi Bābā itself is interesting. About a hundred years ago he came to Shirdi, a young stranger, with a Muslim marriage party. He stayed on to make the hamlet famous as a spiritual centre. He was tall, wore a *kafni* (long robe) in the fashion of a fakir, walked barefooted, maintained himself on alms, practised medicine and accepted nothing from his grateful patients.

"A dilapidated mosque in the village was his home. Was this stranger a Hindu or a Muslim? Even his biographers have not found an answer to this question. But they are one in proclaiming that in the large picture of tolerance and love preached by Sāi Bābā there is no room for distinctions of caste and creed. He uttered the words *Allah Malik* ("God is Lord") as fervently as he sang *bhajans* (Hindu devotional songs in praise of God). Under his mellow influence, the village people agreed to hold the Muslim *urus* (fair) and the Hindu festival of Rām-Navamī (i.e., the ninth day in the first half of the month of Chaitra according to the Hindu calendar, which is the anniversary of the birth of Shrī Rāmachandra) on the same day in a spirit of cordiality. When disciples raised funds to repair the mosque which Sāi Bābā had made his home he insisted on all the temples in the village being renovated first.

"His compassion for those in pain and misery became widely known and soon he was acknowledged a saint. People drawn from many faiths flocked around him and heard his discourses, described by his biographers as containing profound spiritual truths. . . ."

Finally, we may add the observations of a British psychiatrist-anthropologist, G. M. Carstairs, who was born in India and had the Rajasthan dialect of Hindustani as his native language during his early childhood, and after completing University education in Britain and America returned to India in 1949 for a ten-month stay and again in 1951 and 1952 for study in the personality of high-caste Hindus in village, fictitiously called Deoli, in Rājasthān. About the general relations between the different religious groups in Deoli, this is what he has to say:—

". . . In Deoli, as is the case throughout southern Rajasthan, almost all of the Banias were Jains, only two families being *Vaishṇavi* or orthodox Hindus; but they all took part in the festivals of the Hindu religious year, and worshipped at Hindu temples both in Deoli and at pilgrimage-places nearby. These Jains who could boast of more schooling than the majority of their neighbours in the bazar, were more familiar than those with the stories of the *Gītā*, the *Mahābhārata* and the *Rāmāyaṇa,* which contain so much of the inspiration of popular Hinduism. The eclectic attitude influenced even the relations between Moslems and Hindus in the village. Though neither community would enter the other's temple or mosque, there was considerable sharing in communal and family religious festivals. Thus the Moslems would dress well and give feasts like their neighbours on the Hindu high holidays, and prominent Brahmins and Banias followed the procession of the Tazzia at Moharram, the most important celebration of the local Moslems' year." (*The Twice-Born*, Hogarth, London, 1957, pp. 25–26.)

It may be that to us of the present age the scheme of the *āśramas* in all its detailed curricula as laid down by the seers may not be fully acceptable. But if order, progress and social equilibrium have to be sought, the modern world may profitably accept the spirit behind the thinking out and formulation of the *āśrama* system as a whole in order to solve problems connected with the nurture of the individual with reference to the specific and general conceptions of human life and labour which forms the background of community-life. It may be, that details will differ with different peoples, and, in different regions. But, without doubt, the general framework of the scheme will prove efficient and of eternal values. The young boy-student would be certainly well-advised to live a disciplined, orderly life, like the one laid down for the *brahma-chārī*. He particularly learns to begin living with fewest comforts, with fewest wants. He begins to think not of what he can have, but of what and how he can do without some of the comforts and pleasures and conveniences of life, if need be, and learns to get used to conditions lacking ease and comfort. These habits always stand one in good stead in later life, whenever the need arises.

After his studies are over, he is enjoined to marry, and enjoy the gifts of life, but only within the meaning and limits of the obligations and duties expected of a *grihastha* as member of a family and of a community. After these obligations and duties are executed in the midst of the fulness of the joys of living, the person may well spend his declining years in retirement, in a spirit of less and less of attachment to the things of the world; instead of struggling through the strifes of existence and achievements, he should now quite advisedly direct his attention more and more to a life of inward peace and meditation; he should now leave the field of activities and achievement for younger people; at the same time, he must always be willing to give the benefit of his experience of the world, and of his moral presence, to the younger folk when they need it and seek it. If this is the general statement of the *āśrama*-scheme, there must be a universal acceptance of the moral and the higher basis of the *āśrama-dharma*. If properly grasped and worked out, it should be reasonably acceptable to any society, at any level of its development, in any age and country.

Coming to the *varṇa*-organisation:

The question of the basic importance and influence of heredity in the creation of individuals of superior or inferior ability was first specifically and prominently raised by Francis Galton[5], who tried to show that superior or inferior ability is hereditary, and that among humanity, there is a genius class which contributes to the real progress of the society. Karl Pearson[6] continued to collect further evidence and proof by his method of correlation to strengthen the same thesis, and showed that between the two, heredity and environment, the influence of heredity is very much greater in determining individual differences in abilities and intellectual as well as moral excellence. This has been and is being followed by many scientific studies. It is true that nothing like finality can be achieved by such studies[7], even in the years to come, because of the impossibility of experimentally controlling the one or the other of these two factors in order to observe the effects of the remaining

[5] Galton, F.: *Hereditary Genius*, 1869; *Natural Inheritance*, 1889.

[6] Pearson, K.: *Treasury of Human Inheritance, Nature and Nurture*, (1910), and other papers in the Eugenics Laboratory Lecture Series, London.

[7] On the question of heredity vs. environment, see particularly the books of Anastasi, Newman, Freeman and Holzinger; Hogben; Holmes; Jennings; Schwesinger; Osborn; and Woodworth mentioned in the Bibliography; and the Twenty-Seventh and the Thirty-Ninth Yearbooks of the National Society for the Study of Education of U.S.A. For a simple, non-technical and lucid and also sound analysis of the problems, see Amram Scheinfeld: *The "New" You and Heredity*. Chatto and Windus, London, 1952.

factor. In all the studies that have been made with greatest possible care and scientific objectivity[8], it has been found that, even in the cases of identical twins reared apart (where apparently heredity is the same but environments differ), and of children born with different heredity but reared in same environment, the two factors heredity and environment still operate in conjunction with each other, and the results could only give some trends and general indications which are yet far from entirely dependable scientific conclusions.

However, these studies do indicate that the problem of heredity has been increasingly occupying the attention of scientists for the purpose of control and direction of human affairs. And, what was the *varṇa*-theory of the Hindus if not, broadly speaking, a huge experiment in the management and direction of human affairs towards the perfecting of human ability in terms of the principle of heredity?[9] It may be that sometimes, genius arises out of low or otherwise unwarranted origins; nevertheless, it would be but wise and proper for any society to fix certain general principles of selection in terms of heredity, for carrying out the various social responsibilities in the most efficient manner possible and practicable. At the same time, however, it should be remembered that though the presumption would ordinarily be along the lines of these general principles of heredity, yet, of course, no undue importance need be given to mere heredity so as to thwart human ability from expression. In fact, the *varṇa* theory in essence did emphasize heredity, but *heredity properly understood*, in the sense of natural biological equipment. It did not look upon heredity in the more superficial sense of family status or ancestry or lineage. It is necessary to grasp this essential meaning of the *varṇa* theory very clearly.

Here, then, the confusion between 'heredity' and 'descent' (or lineage) must be cleared up, in order that the issues may be understood in their proper perspective. 'Descent' refers to the lineage, that is, the parentage, ancestry, and their manifest and known characteristics and traits, and the status and position of the family. Heredity refers to the natural tendencies, talents, capacities, aptitudes, and dispositions of the individual which are native in the constitution of the individual as the result of the inherited biological genes carrying those tendencies and capacities from parent to offspring. Ordinarily, heredity could be judged in advance by descent, i.e. the parentage and ancestry; but such judgement may not always be borne out by facts as the individual grows. An individual's tendencies and talents are not necessarily traceable or related to the behaviour, traits and tendencies manifest in the activities of the parents or their ancestors, for these ancestors might also have been carrying the latent or recessive seeds of many other traits which may later be reinforced and get the chance of becoming manifest in a descendant or descendants. This may apply to traits which are considered undesirable as well as to those considered desirable in a given society. Heredity provides the individual with certain potential traits, some of which become patent in the individual; but the seeds of other traits also may be carried over latently, and may be transmitted from generation to generation latently or recessively. In the possession of these potentialities, individuals differ from each other, some have superior potentialities, others have inferior ones; or an individual may have superior ones of certain type and inferior ones of certain other type; and so on. These potentialities constitute 'the given', the datum, the nature, the *bīja* of the individual. Thus,

[8] A careful scrutiny of the studies of fraternal twins and identical twins reared together and those reared apart shows "the futility and artificiality of the idea of untangling nature and nurture influences in the sense of ascertaining the percentage contributions of each in any general sense". H. D. Carter, in *Intelligence: Its Nature and Nurture*. The Thirty-Ninth Yearbook of the Nat. Soc. for the St. of Ed., Vol. I, p. 248.

[9] cf. pp. 321 ff.

the importance and significance of heredity lies, mainly, in the fact that it is the *given* endowment, and consists of dominant traits, as well as recessive ones which are not manifest in the individual but may be transmitted to offspring.

In contrast with this, the importance and significance of the environment or the *kśetra* (the field of individual's life and activities) lies in the fact that it is, to a greater or less extent, man's *creation*. A given material could be shaped and moulded, but the extent of such moulding and shaping depends upon the quality and the quantity of the given material. Even inferior material could be shaped and moulded better than it would otherwise be, by proper processing and under proper conditions; but superior material could be turned into still better forms through suitable conditions and processing. The same seems to be true of human potentialities too. They have their own limits, set up by the hereditary nature, for change and improvement; and improvements are possible, under favourable conditions, within those limits. For, even to the same objective environment, individual's will react in a variety of ways, each in his own ways in accordance with his own temperaments, tendencies, needs and capacities. As a matter of fact, no environment could ever be the same for two individuals psychologically, even though physically it appears to be and is the same. On the other hand, with same or closely resembling heredity, differences in environment would affect the individuals differently and are, again, likely to lead to the development of different personality patterns.

This 'given' or the hereditary equipment of the individual however, cannot be fully and unfailingly judged in all cases by the mere knowledge of the descent, i.e., the parentage and the ancestry of the individual on the father's and on the mother's side. For, any of them may have been the carrier, in their constitution, in addition to their known biological and psychological characteristics, of any other characteristics also which were latent or recessive and hence were not manifest but may have been transmitted to their successive generations, and therefore, still have the chance of attaining dominance in any of them. Also, all the characteristics of the ancestors are not necessarily transmitted to every one of the descendants. Hence, lineage by itself is not a sufficient and invariable guarantee of the kind of potential abilities and traits an individual may be born with; though, ordinarily, it may be presumed for many practical purposes that roughly and broadly we may expect individual's potentialities and dispositions in accordance with the lineage, until the contrary is found. As Leonard Darwin put it: "The fact that each hereditary quality of any individual is passed on to some but not to all his descendants shows its results in the following way also. . . . We cannot foretell what will be the qualities of a man before he is born. But if we know the qualities of his near relations we can tell a good deal about what his qualities will probably be. This means that, though we should make many bad shots, we should be generally far nearer the truth than if we went by chance."[10]

Now these potentialities of the individual require suitable environmental conditions (*kśetra*) and scope for their unfoldment and development. They do not develop in vacuum; they unfold and develop in response to stimuli. And, suitable stimuli in the environment will assist their development, whereas unsuitable or thwarting stimuli in the environment will not only keep them in abeyance but may even stunt them and damage them, and may further lead to frustration and consequent maladjustments in the individuals concerned. This is where the *āśrama* theory, as envisaging a plan for the proper training and disciplining of the individual, a scheme for the *śrama* (effort) of man in proper environment, comes in.

---

[10] L. Darwin: *What is Eugenics?*, Watts & Co., London, 2nd Ed. 1937, p. 18.

Until, however, the individual differences in potentialities are revealed clearly, we have no sure means of judging them in advance; and therefore, as far as possible, equal opportunities, scope and environment at least of a minimum sort should be provided for all young children, along the lines of the *āśrama* plan, so that the differential abilities and potentialities are allowed to flower forth. Hence, according to the theory, every individual at birth is to be considered as no better than a *Śūdra*[11] until his potentialities manifest themselves in one or the other of the four broad groupings of qualities or tendencies known as the *varṇa-lakśaṇas*, the characteristic traits of the *varṇas*. As young trainees, therefore, it is desirable to provide for the prince and the pauper the same kind of conditions and environment as far as possible.[12]

At the same time, it may be noted that when it is claimed that a Brāhmaṇa's son will make a good Brāhmaṇa (which is basically similar to expecting an engineer's or doctor's or a soldier's or a businessman's son to continue or take up respectively his father's vocation, and is very commonly done in modern times), it is not the heredity in the sense of "descent' or lineage so much as it is really the environment whose influence is actually implicitly accorded a high premium. It is not so much the mere fact that the son is born of a Brāhmaṇa or an engineer etc., but essentially because he is bred up, since his birth, in the surroundings and atmosphere which are surcharged with conditions favourable to the creation and development of interests and of easy information pertaining to the respective parental vocation that he is expected to be fit for taking up the same. And yet, this expectation, which is ordinarily reasonable, may be stretched too far to an unjustifiable extent, by insisting that he must invariably be born fit for the parental vocation, contrary indications notwithstanding—to which length the extreme *varṇa* or *jāti*-adherents went. The *āśrama*-scheme, therefore, will have to be so worked out, in practice, as to allow due scope in terms of common environment for every individual to give unmistakable indications of his potentialities of traits, talents and temperaments.

All this means that it is unscientific and also unnecessary to extol the claims of either of the two, heredity or environment over the other. And, it is possible to look to the improvement of both without neglecting any one of them. Hence it is asserted that the *varṇa* theory and the *āśrama* theory are closely linked up together as *varṇāśrama-vyavasthā*. Emphasis on any one of these to the exclusion or neglect of the other is bound to result in undesirable and harmful results, socially and morally. No modifications or changes in any one of these systems could lead to desirable results unless due account is taken also of its interrelations with the other and corresponding modifications are also made in the second.

Writers on social science have often understood the caste-system as dependent solely upon descent, which, of course, it is in its degenerate form. But, to say, therefore, that heredity should be no consideration in social organization is to confuse heredity with descent. Charles Cooley, for instance, in his brilliant analysis of social organization, which is a classic treatise on the subject and has retained much of its suggestive and thought-provocative quality through the years after its first publication[13], refers to caste as "an organization of a social mind on a biological principle. That functions should follow the line of descent instead of adjusting themselves to individual capacity and preference evidently means the subordination of reason to convenience, of freedom to order." According to him, the "ideal principle" would be "not biological but moral, based that is,

[11] See pp. 306 ff. Also *janmanā jāyate śūdrah samskārād dvija uchyate*. And, in the Atharva Veda it is declared: *na dāso nāryo mahitvā vratam mimāya*=I do not take anyone as a low-born (*dāsa*) or high born (*ārya*), but I judge him by his qualities.

[12] See ch. iv on Education, especially pp. 115 ff. etc.

[13] C. H. Cooley: *Social Organisation*, Scribner's, New York. First published in 1909. The reference here is to the 1927 edition.

on the *spiritual gifts of the individual* without regard to descent." (Italics ours). This ideal principle would be successfully achieved, says he, "when the population is so mobilized by free training and institutions that just and orderly selection is possible."[14]

Here again, there is, apparently, a confusion between biological heredity and family lineage. Cooley proposes to discard considerations of heredity in the management of social affairs. He thinks that a social classification based on heredity is but an organization of the social mind on biological principles; he sees, underneath such a social classification, a subordination of reason to convenience, a subversion of freedom in the mere interest of maintaining the existing social order; and he asserts that the ideal principle must not be biological but moral,—as if the biological is necessarily antimoral! And, yet, he also talks of individual 'capacity' and 'preferences', 'spiritual and moral gifts' of the individuals, without any regard to descent! Heredity considerations are for him subversive of morals, freedom and reason, and are ministrant only to convenience and the upkeep of existing social order,—as if reason and convenience cannot go together, freedom and order are opposed to each other, and heredity and mobilization of population by free training and institutions are contradictories of each other! We would, on the contrary, say that these can be seen to be complementaries of each other, the more we look into the nature and functions underlying these pairs of supposed opposites. We would assert that a just and orderly selection is possible and attainable only if society looks after *both* biological and nurtural questions relating to the individual and the social group to which he belongs.

To be fair to Cooley, it appears that he wants to attack the social system or systems in which mere lineage or descent in a particular family is taken as the blind and invariable basis for assigning status, position and vocation. And, when in his strictures he refers to 'heredity', he means such lineage or descent. On the other hand, when he refers to individual capacity, gifts, preferences, etc.—which is also closely related to heredity or biological inheritance—he seems to imply that individuals showing abilities or talents in certain directions or of certain type should be allowed scope to express them irrespective of their parents' occupation or status. This means, then, that for social good, we *must* take biological factors into consideration, contrary to Cooley's first stated view. We may ordinarily infer biological factors from lineage or parentage; but, we must not insist that the potentialities of the individual will necessarily be like the manifest qualities of the parents and ancestors; we must be prepared to take cognizance of a difference, if and when such difference is shown by the individual, and must be ready to provide suitable scope for his own qualities.

In fact, the *varṇa*-scheme has taken into consideration not merely the biological but also the moral, not merely the social but also the individual, not merely the material but also spiritual issues into consideration. The *varṇa*-organization was based not only on biological, but also on psychological and even ethical grounds, after a reasoned integration of the various aspects of life, individual and social, so that a coordination of all these factors may be made concretely available in terms of organized social institutions. In this manner, the *varṇa* theory along with the *āśrama* system seeks to achieve social efficiency consistent with, and for the sake of, the physical, mental and moral well-being of the community and its members. The *varṇa* and *āśrama* schemes were thus conceived to enable the society to make the best of the potentialities in the individual, so that through the functioning of the best and the finest that individuals are capable of, the best may be formulated and inherited by the group. While the *āśrama*-scheme pre-eminently conceives the proper nurture of the individual through life, so that the best and the noblest may be born out of it, the *varṇa*-scheme dominantly envisages a proper coordination of the natures of the individual and the group in the interest of social efficiency.

[14] Ibid., pp. 226 ff.

It may be that, due to certain historical causes, while the hereditary aspect of the individual has come to be overemphasised, the nurture of the individual in terms of the *āśrama* scheme has come to be overlooked and even neglected. And, we humbly suggest that it is due to this mishap more than to anything else, viz., the neglect of the individual's nurture, that the hereditary principle seems to have been over-emphasized and has therefore been misunderstood as even failing us, as if on account of some anti-social element which is supposed to be an essential part of the same.

In the *āśrama*, the foundations of proper cognition and perception of the world order and man's place in it are sought to be laid down in the individual's mind from early childhood through the procedures of learning (*vidyā*) independently, as far as possible, of the family and other influences, under the care and direct and entire control of a trusted master, who was known not only for his learning but also for his character. The *āśrama* training also sought to provide the individual with the socially desirable set of goals and motivations in terms of *dharma* which he was expected to pursue in life after completion of his training period. And, on the whole, for the Hindu, the *dharma* and the *karma* ideology, rightly understood, did provide a forceful matrix of motivation in an inter-related manner comprising of the mainsprings of all his activities. Like the cultural ideology of any other people, again, the Hindu cultural ideology has taken deep roots in the culture pattern of its people through several generations.[15] Those of us who are anxious to reform the Hindu pattern of life must reckon with the deep strength of this *dharma* ideology, and, when trying to introduce new ideas and forms of behaviours, must see that the right sort of motivation compatible with this ideology is engendered in the Hindu mind, leading to the right sort of behaviour.

As we have already said, the degeneration of *varṇa* and *āśrama* organizations has come to be so due to historical causes; and therefore, that in no way can be said to be the fault of the basic ideology behind the *varṇa* and the *āśrama* institutions at all. In fact, the early Hindu thinkers had envisaged the possibility of degeneration and even of the divorce and separation of these two schemes as it has come about. Throughout the Hindu scriptures, the possibilities of deviation from and degeneration in all the well-intentioned plans of *dharma* is an oft-recurring theme of discussion. Śrī Krishṇa himself talks of the cycles of degenerations of *dharma* and its repeated resuscitation and revivification being undertaken and accomplished by the Divine Hand from time to time. And, if the *varṇa* and *aśrama* schemes were formulated essentially for the practice and upkeep of *dharma*, certainly the degeneration or mal-adjustments of these two schemes in any period of history is part of the theory of *dharma* as laid down by Śrī Krishṇa and other Hindu seers. Thus, Hinduism can entertain every hope for the survival of its social institutions since its basic ideology is rather comprehensive and well coordinated, and it can also be assured of adaptability to the changing conditions of time, space and economy since this basic ideology does not rigidly predetermine its course of development but leaves room for flexible adjustments consistent with the primary laws of human nature and good living.

The Hindu thinkers saw no opposition between social good and social ends on the one hand, and of individual good and individual ends on the other. The basis of the Hindu social order is *dharma;* in terms of *dharma*, all human activities—biological and psychological, economic and moral, personal and social—are defined, and coordinated in terms of the *varṇa* and *āśrama* schemes. The Hindu seers had clearly understood the intimate relation and mutual interdependence of these two

[15] An idea of how deeply rooted this cultural ideology is even to this day in the mind of the average Hindu could be obtained by studying some of the very recent studies on the village communities in India, like the one by the psychiatrist-anthropologist G. M. Carstairs: *The Twice-Born*; Hogarth Press, London, 1957.

schemes of *varṇa* and *āśrama* with each other; and, unless the pristine balance between these two fundamental contributions of the Hindu sages is secured and maintained hereafter, it will not be possible to live life to its fullest stature, not merely for the Hindus but also for the peoples of all the world. We venture to suggest that the conflict between man and man, community and community, occupation and occupation, politics and economics, economics and ethics, philosophy and life, religion and science, that we are witnessing today in terms of a variety of social tensions—between different groups in terms of conflicts of interests, and between nations in terms of wars,—could be effectively dissolved and resolved in terms of harmony and peace, if these two great instruments of life, of *āśrama* and *varṇa*, that the Hindu thinkers found out and practised, are adopted by all peoples with due modifications in accordance with modern life and in accordance with the specific regional conditions for each different group; if the theory of *dharma* which these two institutions manifested in the concrete is accepted by them; and if the *dharma* that defines human existence as an opportunity of self-understanding and self-conquest through a self-rendering life of service and devotion to duty runs incessantly through their hearts.

With such findings and belief, we may fittingly conclude this work with the memorable *Bhārata-Sāvitrī* verses with which the sage Vyāsa concludes the writing of the Great Epic, the *Mahābhārata*:—

"Raising up my hand,
I declare with all my might:
From *dharma* follow *artha* and *kāma;*
Why not, then, practice *dharma?*
However,
None pays heed to me!
But, be it remembered
That *dharma* should never be abandoned
To fulfil the demands of *kāma*,
Or, through fear or avarice,
Or, even when one's life is at the stake;
For,
Dharma is eternal,
While the joys and sorrows of life
Are but fleeting and transitory,
Even as the soul is eternal,
Though the means and instruments it uses
Are but frail and transient."[16]

---

[16] Mahā. Svargā. 5, 62–63.

Ūrdhva-bāhur viraumyesha na cha kaśchich-chhruṇoti me/
dharmād arthaś cha kāmaś cha sa kim-artham na sevyate/
na jātu kāmān na bhayān na lobhād
dharmam tyajet jīvitasyāpi hetoh/
nityo dharmah sukhe-duhkhe tvanitye
jīvo nityo hetur asye tvanityah//

BIBLIOGRAPHY

1. Original Sources

Rigvedas: (Sanskrit) with Sāyana's Bhāshya. Ed. by M.M. Rājārām Śāstrī Bodas, and Śivarām Śāstrī Goré. 8 Volumes. Bombay.
Griffith, R. T. H.: (Tr.) *Rigveda*, Vols. I & II. Benares: E. J. Lazarus & Co. 1896.
Griffith, R. T. H.: (Tr.) *Yajur Veda*, Vols. I & II. Benares: E. J. Lazarus & Co. 1896.
Griffith, R. T. H.: (Tr.) *Sāma Veda*, Vols. I & II. Benares: E. J. Lazarus & Co. 1896.
Griffith, R. T. H.: (Tr.) *Atharva Veda*, 2 Vols. E. J. Lazarus & Co. 1896.
Bloomfield, M.: *Hymns of the Atharva Veda*. Clarendon Press, Oxford. (Sacred Bks. of the East) 1897.
Whitney, W. D. & Lanman, C. R.: *Atharva Veda*, 2 Vols. Har. Or. Ser. 1908.
Muir, J.: *Original Sanskrit Texts*. Vols. I to V. 2nd Ed. Trübner & Co., London, 1868–70.
Roer, Rajendralal Mitra & E. B. Cowell: *The Twelve Principal Upanishads*, 3 Vols. Theosophical Publishing House, Adyar, Madras, 1931–32.
Hume R. E.: *Thirteen Principal Upanishads*. Ox. Uni. Pr., London.
Aiyar N. K.: *Thirty Minor Upanishads*. Madras, 1914.
Jacob, Col. G. A. (Ed.): *Mahānārāyaṇa Upanishad*. (Bom. San. Ser.) 1888.
Keith, A. B.: *Rig-Veda Brāhmanas—The Aitareya and Kaushītakī* (Tr.). Harv. Ori. Ser. 1920.
Macdonnell, A. A. and Keith, A. B.: *Vedic Index*. 2 Vols. John Murray, London, 1912.
Volumes of translations in the Sacred Books of the East Series (Edited by F. Max Müller):—
The Śatapatha Brāhmaṇ. (Tr. by J. Eggeling) Vols. xii & xxvi.
The Laws of Manu (Tr. by G. Bühler) Vol. xxv.
The Dharmasūtras of Vasishṭha and Baudhāyana (Tr. by G. Bühler) Vol. xiv.
The Sūtras of Āpastamba and Gautama (Tr. by G. Bühler) Vol. ii.
The Institutes of Vishṇu (Tr. by J. Jolly) Vol. vii.
Nārada and Some Minor Law Books (Tr. by J. Jolly) Vol. xxxiii.
The Grihya-Sūtras. (Tr. by H. Oldenberg) Vols. xxix & xxx. *Āśvalāyana-Grihyasātra*: Ed. by Dinkar Keshav Gadgil (*Pothī*)
Pub. by Pt. Nārāyan Mulji, (Tattvavivechak Press), Bombay, *Śaké* 1817.
Āpastamba-Grihyasūtra: Ed. by A. Chinnaswāmī Sāstrī, (Kāśī Sanskrit series), Benares, 1928.
Baudhāyana-Grihyasūtra: Ed. by R. Shāma Śāstrī. Mysore, 1920.
Kāṭhaka-Grihyasūtra: Ed. by Dr. W. Calland. (Dayānanda Mahāvidyālaya Sanskrit Granthamālā), Lahore, 1925.
Khādira-Grihyasūtra: Ed. by A. M. Śāstrī and L. Śrīnivāsāchārya. Government Oriental Library Series. Mysore, 1913.
Mānava-Grihyasūtra: Ed. by R. H. Śāstrī (Gaekwad's Oriental series), Baroda, 1926.
Pēraskara-Grihyasūtra: Ed. by Mahadeva Gangadhar Bakre. (Gujarati Printing Press), Bombay, 1917.
Āpastambiya Dharmasūtram: Ed. by G. Bühler. Third Ed. passed through the Press by M. G. Shastri (Bombay Sanskrit Series). 1932.
Gautama-Dharmasūtram: Ed. by L. Śrīnivāsāchārya (Government Oriental Library Series). Mysore, 1917.
Manusmritih: Ed. by P. H. Pandya (Gujarati Printing Press) Bombay, 1913.
Nāradīya Manusamhitā: Ed. by K. Sāmbaśiva Śāstrī (Trivandrum Sanskrit Series). 1929.
Parāśaradharmasamhitā, or *Parāśarasmritih*: With the Bhāshya of Sāyaṇa Mādhavāchārya. Ed. by Pt. V. S. Islāmpūrkar (Bombay Sanskrit Series). 3 Vols. 1893.
Dutt M. N.: Tr. of the *Dharma Sāstras of Angiras, Atri, Daksa, Hārīta, Kātyāyana, Likhita, Samvarta, Sankha, Sātātapa, Uśanā, Vrihaspati, Vyāsa, Yama*, 2 Vols. Calcutta.
Yājnavalkya Smriti—Tr. by S. C. Vidyabhushan.
Yājnavalkya Smriti—(Sanskrit) Ed. by Wāsudeo Laxman Sāstrī Panśikar. 3rd Ed. Bombay, Nirṇaya-Sāgar Press, 1926.

Kātyāyanasmritisāroddhārah: with Tr. by P. V. Kane. Bombay. 1930.

Mitra Miśra, Mm. Pt.: *Viramitrodayah*, Ed. by Pārvatīya Nityīnanda Śarmā. Chowkhamba Sanskrit Series, Benares, 1913.

Bhaṭṭa Gopīnātha Dīkshita: *Samskāra-ratna mālā*. Ed. by *Kaśīnātha* Śāstrī Āgāśé, and Bābāśāstri Phadké. Ānandāśrama Sanskrit Series. 2 Vols. Poona.

Chaṇḍeśvara Ṭhākura: *Grihastha-Ratnākara*, Ed. by Mm. Kamalākarakrishṇa Smritітīrtha (Bibliotheca Indica, Work No. 249) Calcutta, 1928.

Kauṭilīyam Arthaśāstram: Ed. by R. Shama Shastri. Mysore, 1919

Arthaśāstra. Tr. by R. Shama Shastri, 3rd Ed. 1929.

Śrīmād-Bhāgawata Purāṇa: Tr. by S. Subba Rao, 1928.

Śrīmād-Bhāgawata Purāṇa: With Marāthi Trans. Pub. by Dāmodar Sāvalārām & Co., Bombay.

Vishṇu Purāṇa: Tr. by H. H. Wilson. 5 vols. 1864–77.

The Mahābhārata: by T. R. Krishnacharya. Nirnaya-Sagar Press. Bombay.

The Mahābhārata. English tr. by M. N. Dutt.

Śrī-Mahābhāratam: (Sanskrit). With the commentary of Nīlakaṇṭha. Ed. by Pandit Rāmachandraśāstrī Kinjawadekar. 7 vols. Chitraśālā Press, Poona, 1929–1936.

The Rāmāyaṇa (Tr. by R. T. H. Griffith). 1870–74. (1915 Ed. Benares).

Vālmīki- Rāmāyaṇam: Ed. by T. R. Krishṇācharya. Nīrṇaya-Sagar Press, Bombay. 1911–13.

Nītisāra of Kāmandaka: Ed. by T. Gaṇapati Śāstrī (Trivandrum Sanskrit Series). 1912.

Kāmandakīya Nītisāra: Eng. Tr. by M. N. Dutt, Calcutta, 1896.

Sukranītisāra: Eng. Tr. by B. K. Sarkar. Allahabad, Pāṇinī Office.

Kāmasūtra of Vātsyāyanamuni: Ed. by Goswāmī Dāmodar Śāstri. (Kāśī Sanskrit Series), Benares, 1919.

Patanjali: Yoga System of Patanjali, Ed. by J. H. Woods, Har. Or Ser. Vol. 7.

Patanjali: Yogasūtras. Tr. by Rāma Prasāda, with Intro. by S. C. Vasu. ('Sacred Books of the Hindus', Vol. IV). Allahabad, Pāṇinī Office, 1912.

Brihatsamhitā of Varāhamihira. Ed. by H. Kern. Roy. Asi. Soc. of Bengal, Calcutta, 1865.

Brihatsamhitā: Eng. Tr. by N. Chidambaram Iyer, South Ind. Press, Madura, 1884.

The Yoga-Darśana. By Mm. Ganganath Jha. Tattva-Vivechak Press, Bombay, 1907.

The Yoga-Sāra-Samgraha of Vijnāna-Bhikśu. By Mm. Ganganath Jha. Tattva-Vivechak Press, Bombay, 1923.

Bhagawad-Gītā.

(1) *The Bhakti-Sūtras of Nārada;* (2) *Śāṇḍilya-Sūtram*; and (3) *Bhakti-Ratnāvali:* Tr. by Nandlal Sinha (Sacred Books of the Hindus), Allahabad, 1917–18.

2. General

A list of selected books in English on social psychology, organization and institutions in general, and on Indian problems in particular:

Abbott, J.: *The Keys of Power: A Study of Indian Ritual and Belief*. Methuen, London, 1932.

Adams, Sir J.: *The Teacher's Many Parts*. University of London Press, 1930.

Aiyangar, K. V. Rangaswami: *Consideration of Some Aspects of Ancient Indian Polity* (Sir Subramani Aiyar Lects., 1914) Madras University, 1935.

Aiyar, K. Narayanaswami: *The Purāṇas in the Light of Modern Science*. Theosophical Society, Madras, 1916.

Akhilānanda, Swāmī: *Hindu Psychology: Its Meaning for the West*. Harper, N.Y., 1946.

Akhilānanda, Swāmī: *Mental Health and Hindu Psychology*. Allen and Unwin, London, 1952.

Allport, G. W.: *Personality—A Psychological Interpretation*. Holt, New York, 1937.

Altekar, A. S.: *Education in Ancient India*. The Indian Book Shop, Benaras, 1934.

Altekar, A. S.: *A History of Village Communities in Western India*. Oxford University Press, Bombay, 1927.

Altekar, A. S.: *The Position of Women in Hindu Civilization*. The Culture Publication House, Benares Hindu Univ., 1938.

Anastasi, A.: *Differential Psychology*. 3rd ed., Macmillan, New York, 1958.

Barnett, L. D.: *Antiquities of India*. Philip Lee Warner, London, 1913.

Barnett, L. D.: *Bhagawad-Gīta* or *The Lord's Song*. Dent. London, 1928.

Barnes, H. E.: *Social Institutions in an Era of World Upheaval*, Prentice-Hall, New York, 1942.

Barnes, H. E., and Becker, H.: *Social Thought from Lore to Science*. 2 Vols., 2nd ed., Harren Press, Washington, D.C. 1952.

Barnes, H. E., and Becker, H.: *Contemporary Social Theory*. Appleton-Century, New York, 1940.

Bartlett, F. C.: *Psychology and Primitive Culture*. Macmillan, London 1923.

Bartlett, F. C.: "Group Organization and Social Behaviour". *Inter. Jour, of Ethics*, (1925), Vol. 35, pp. 346–67.

Bartlett, F. C.: "The Co-operation of Social Groups". *Occupational Psychology*, XII, 1, 30–42.

Bartlett, F. C.: *Anthropology in Reconstruction*. Huxley Mem. Lecture, 1943. Pub. by Roy. Anthrop. Insti. of Gr. Br. and Ire., London, 1943.

Bartlett, F. C.: *ibid*., in *Nature*, 152, p. 710, which publishes the Lecture as it was delivered.

Basham, A. L.: *The Wonder That Was India: A Survey of the Culture of the Indian Sub-Continent Before the Coming of the Muslims*. Macmillan, London, 1954.

Basu, P. C.: *Indo-Aryan Polity (Rigvedic)*. 2nd Ed. 1925.

Bear, R. M.: *The Social Function of Education*. Macmillan, New York, 1937.

Belvalkar, S. K., and Ranade, R. D.: *History of Indian Philosophy. Vol.* II—*Creative Period*. Bilvakunja Publishing House, Poona, 1927.

Benedict, R.: *Patterns of Culture*. Houghton Mifflin, Boston, 1934. Betts, G. H.: *Foundations of Character and Personality*. Bobbs-Merrill, New York, 1937.

Bhagwan Das, Babu: *The Essential Unity of All Religions*. Theos. Pub. House, Adyar, Madras, 1932.

Bhagwan Das, Babu: *Krishna—A Study in the Theory of Avatāras*. 3rd Ed. Revised, Theos. Pub. House, Adyar, 1929.

Bhagwan Das, Babu: *The Science of Social Organization*. 2 Vols. 2nd Ed. Theos. Pub. House, Adyar, Madras, 1932–35.

Bhandarkar, D. R.: *Some Aspects of Ancient Hindu Polity*. Benaras Hindu Uni., 1929.

Bhandarkar, D. R.: *Some Aspects of Ancient Indian Culture*, Sir Wm. Meyer Lectrs., University of Madras, 1940.

Bhandarkar, R. G.: *Vaishṇavism, Śaivism and Minor Religious Systems*. Strassburg, 1913.

Bhattacharya, J. N.: *Hindu Castes and Sects*. Calcutta, 1896.

Blunt, E. A. H.: *The Caste System of Northern India*. Oxford University Press, London, 1931.

Bosanquet, Helen.: *The Family*. Macmillan, London, 1915.

Bose, P. N.: *Survival of Hindu Civilization*. Newman, Calcutta, 1913.

Bossard, J. H. S.: *The Sociology of Child Development*. Rev. Ed. Harper, New York, 1954.

Bowden, A. O., and Melbo, I. R.: *Social Psychology of Education*. Mc-Graw-Hill, New York, 1937.

Briffault, R.: *The Mothers: A Study of Origins of Sentiment and Institutions*, 3 Vols. Macmillan, New York, 1931.

Britt, S. H.: *The Social Psychology of Modern Life*, New Ed. Farrar and Rinehart, New York, 1949.

Brown, L. Guy: *Social Psychology: The Natural History of Human Nature*. McGraw-Hill, New York, 1934.

Burgess, E. W. and Cottrell, L. S. Jr.: *Predicting Success or Failure in Marriage*. Prentice-Hall, New York, 1939.

Burgess, E. W. and Locke, H. J.: *The Family—From Institution to Companionship*, Rev. Ed. American Book Co., New York, 1953.

Burlingame, L. L.: *Heredity and Social Problems*. McGraw-Hill, New York, 1940.

Calverton, V. C., and Schmalhausen, S. D. (Eds.): *Sex in Civilization*. Macaulay Co., New York, 1929.

Calverton, V. C., and Schmalhausen, S. D. (Eds.): *The New Generation*. Macaulay Co., New York, 1930.

The Cambridge History of Ancient India, Vol. I. Ed. by E. J. Rapson. Cambridge University Press, 1922.

Cantril, H.: *The Psychology of Social Movements*. Wiley, New York, 1940.

Cantril, H.: 'Social Psychology of Everyday Life': *Psychological Bulletin*, Vol. 31, 1934, pp. 297–330.

Cantril, H.: *The "Why" of Man's Experience*. Macmillan, New York, 1950.

Carver, T. N.: *The Essential Factors of Social Evolution*. Harvard University Press, 1935.

Carr-Saunders, A. M.: *Eugenics*. Home Uni. Library, 1926.

Carstairs, G. M.: *The Twice-Born: A Study of a Community of High-Caste Hindus*. Hogarth Press, London, 1957.

Carstairs, G. M.: "Attitudes to Death and Suicide in an Indian Cultural Setting"; *Inter. J. Social Psychiatry*, I (Winter, 1955), 3, 33–41.

Cattell, R. B.: *Psychology and Social Progress*. C. W. Daniel, London, 1933.

Cattell, R. B.: *The Fight for our National Intelligence*. P. S. King, London, 1937.

Cavenagh, F. A. (Ed.): *James and John Stuart Mill on Education*. Camb. Uni. Press, 1931.

Chakladar, H. C.: *Social Life in Ancient India; Stuches in Vātsyāyana's Kāmasūtra*. Greater India Society, Calcutta, 1929.

Christensen, H. J.: *Marriage Analysis—Foundations for Successful Family Life*. Ronald Press Co., New York, 1950.

Conklin, E. S.: *Heredity and Environment in the Development of Men*, 6th Rev. Ed. Princeton Uni. Pr., 1939.

Cooley, C. H.: *Social Organization—A Study of the Larger Mind*. Scribner's, New York, 1929. First pub. 1909.
Cooley, C. H.: *Human Nature and the Social Order*. Scribner's, New York, 1922.
Cooley, C. H.: *Social Process*. Scribner's, New York, 1918.
Cox, O. C.: *Caste, Class and Race*. Doubleday, New York, 1948.
Cressman, L. S.: "Ritual, the Conserver". *American Journal of Sociology*, Vol. 35. Jan. 1930, pp. 564–72.
Cunningham, B. V.: *Family Behaviour: A Study of Human Relations*. 2nd Rev. Ed., W. B. Saunders Co., Philadelphia, 1940.
Darwin, L.: *What is Eugenics?* Watts, London, 1937.
Das, A. C.: *Rigvedic India*. Vol. I. R. Cambray, Calcutta, 1920.
Das, A. C.: *Rigvedic Culture*. R. Cambray, Calcutta, 1925.
Das, S. K.: *The Educational System of the Ancient Hindus*. Mitra Press, Calcutta, 1930.
Das Gupta, S. N.: *Yoga as Philosophy and Religion*. Kegan Paul, London, 1924.
Das Gupta, S. N.: *Yoga Philosophy*. Calcutta University, 1930.
Davids, Mrs. Rhys: *Indian Religion and Survival*. Allen and Unwin, London, 1934.
Davids, Mrs. Rhys: *The Birth of Indian Psychology and Its Development in Buddhism*. Luzac, London, 1936.
Davids, T. W. Rhys: *Buddhist India*. T. Fisher Unwin, London. 1911.
Davis, K.: *Human Society*. Macmillan, N. Y., 1948.
Davis, K.: *The Population of India and Pakistan*. Princeton Univ. Press; Princeton, New Jersey: 1951.
Davis, K. and Moore, W. E.: "Some Principles of Stratification", *Ameri. Sociol. Rev.* (April 1945), 10, 2, 242–49.
Deploige, S.: *The Conflict Between Ethics and Sociology*. Tr. by C. C. Miltner. B. Herder Book Co., London, 1938.
Deutsch, Helene: *The Psychology of Women*, 2 Vols. Grune & Stratton, New York, 1944.
Dewey, John: *Human Nature and Conduct: An Introduction to Social Psychology*. 9th Imp. Holt, New York, 1927.
Dewey, John: *Democracy and Education*. 19th Imp. Macmillan, New York, 1930.
Dewey, John: *Interest and Effort in Education*. Riverside Educational Monographs, Boston, 1913.
Dewey, John: Educational Essays. Ed. by J. J. Findlay, Blackie, London (no date).
Dewey, John: *Moral Principles in Education*. Houghton Mifflin, Boston, 1909.
Dewey, J.: *The School and Society*, Univ. of Chicago, Pr., 1949.
Dewey, J. and others: *The Authoritarian Attempt to Capture Education*. King's Crown Press, N. Y., 1945.
Dubois, A. J. A., and Beauchamp, H. K.: *Hindu Manners, Customs and Ceremonies*. Clarendon Press, Oxford, 1906.
Dunlap, K.: *Civilized Life: The Principles and Applications of Social Psychology*. George Allen, London, 1934.
Dutt, N. K.: *The Origin and Growth of Caste in India*. Vol. I. The Book Co., Calcutta, 1931.
Ellis, Havelock: *Man and Woman*. 8th Rev. Ed., Wm. Heinemann, London, 1934.
Ellis, Havelock: "Studies in the Psychology of Sex"; Vol. VI—*Sex in Relation to Society*. F. A. Davis, Philadelphia, 1928.
Ellis, Havelock: *Psychology of Sex: A Manual for Students*. Wm. Heinemann, London, 1933.
Ellwood, C. A.: *The Psychology of Human Society*. Appleton, New York, 1931.
Encyclopaedia of Religion and Ethics. Ed. by J. Hastings, 13 Vols. Clark, Edinburgh, 1925–1934.
Encyclopaedia of the Social Sciences. Ed. by E. R. A. Seligman and Alvin Johnson, 15 Vols., Macmillan, New York, 1930–35.
Erikson, E. H.: *Childhood and Society*. Norton, New York, 1950.
Farquhar, J. N.: *The Crown of Hinduism* Ox. Uni. Pr., London, 1913.
Farquhar, J. N.: *Religious Life in India*. Ox. Uni. Pr., London, 1916.
Farquhar, J. N.: *An Outline of the Religious Literature of India*. Oxford University Press, London, 1920.
Farquhar, J. N.: *Modern Religious Movements in India*, Macmillan, London, 1929.
Fick, R.: *The Social Organization in N. E. India in Buddha's Time*. Tr. by S. K. Maitra. University of Calcutta, 1920.
Flügel, J. C.: *A Psychoanalytic Study of the Family*. The International Psychoanalytic Press, London, 1921.
Ford, C. S. and Beach, F. A.: *Patterns of Sexual Behaviour*. Hoeber, New York, 1951.
Freud, S.: *Group Psychology and the Analysis of the Ego*. Tr. by J. Strachey. Inter. Psychoana. Library, London, 1922.
Freud, S.: *Psychopathology of Everyday Life*. Macmillan, 1917.
Freud, S.: Civilization and Its Discontents. Inter. Psychoana. Li., 1930.
Freud, S.: *Introductory Lectures on Psychoanalysis*. London, 1922. Freud, S.: *New Introductory Lectures on Psychoanalysis*. Tr. by W. J. H. Sprott. Hogarth, London, 1933.
Fuller, J. L.: *Nature and Nurture*. Doubleday, New York, 1954.
Garratt, G. I. (Ed.): *The Legacy of India*. Clarendon Press, Oxford, 1937.

Gates, R. R.: *Heredity and Eugenics*. Constable, London, 1923.

Gates, R. R.: *Heredity in Man*. Rev. Ed. Macmillan, London, 1929.

Geddes, A.: "The Social and Psychological Significance of Variability in Population Change, with Examples from India, 1871–1941." *Human Relations*, 1, 2, 1947.

Ghose, Sri Aurobindo.: *Essays on the Gita*. Two Series. Arya Publishing House, Calcutta, 1927–1942.

Ghose, Sri Aurobindo.: *The Yoga and Its Objects*. Arya Publishing House, Calcutta, 1938.

Ghose, Sri Aurobindo.: *Bases of Yoga*. Arya Publishing House, Calcutta, 1936.

Ghose, Sri Aurobindo.: *Light on Yoga*. Arya Publishing House, Calcutta, 1935.

Ghose, Sri Aurobindo.: *The Ideal of the Karma-Yogin*. Arya Publishing House, Calcutta, 1937.

Ghose, Sri Aurobindo.: *The Renaissance in India*. Prabartak Pub. House, Chandernagar, 1920.

Ghose, Sri Aurobindo.: *The Ideal of Human Unity*. Aurobindo Asram, Pondicherry, 1950.

Ghose, Sri Aurobindo.: *A System of National Education*. Arya Publishing House, Calcutta, 1924.

Gillin, J. L. and J. P.: *Cultural Sociology*. Macmillan. New York, 1948.

Ginsberg, M.: "Class Consciousness", in *Ency. of The Social Sciences*, Vol. III, 1930.

Ginsberg, M.: *Studies in Sociology*. Methuen, London, 1932.

Ginsberg, M.: *The Psychology of Society*. 4th Ed. Methuen, London, 1933.

Girth, H. and Mills, C. W.: *Character and Social Structure: The Psychology of Social Institutions*. Harcourt, Brace, New York, 1953.

Gode, P. K.: *The Bhaktisūtras of Nārada and the Bhagawadgītā*. Bhandarkar Oriental Research Institute, Poona, 1923.

Goodsell, W.: *A History of Marriage and the Family*. Rev. Ed. Macmillan, New York, 1935.

Goodsell, W.: *Problems of the Family*. Rev. Ed. Appleton-Century, New York, 1936.

Groves, E. R.: *Marriage*. Holt, New York, 1933.

Groves, E. R.: *The Family and It's Social Functions*. Lippincott, Philadelphia, 1940.

Groves, E. R. and Groves, Catherine: *Sex Fulfilment in Marriage*. Emerson Books, New York, 1942.

Hart, Hornell, and E. B.: *Personality and the Family*. Health 1935.

Healy, W., Bronner, A. E., and Bowers, A. M.: *The Structure and Meaning of Psychoanalysis as Related to Personality and Behaviour*. Knopf, New York, 1930.

Hertzler, J. O.: *Social Institutions*. Univ. Nebraska Press, Lincoln, 1946.

Hertzler, J. O.: *Social Thought in Ancient Civilizations*. Mc-Graw-Hill, New York, 1936.

Hetherington, H. J. W. and J. H. Muirhead: *Social Purpose*. Allen and Unwin, London, 1918.

Hocart, A. M.: *Caste—A Comparative Study*. Methuen, London, 1950.

Hogben, L. T.: *Nature and Nurture*. Norgate, London, 1933.

Holmes, S. J.: *Human Genetics and Its Social Import*. McGraw-Hill, 1936.

Honigmann, J. J.: *Culture and Personality*. Harper, New York, 1954.

Hopkins, E. W.: *The Great Epic of India*. Scribner's, New York, 1902.

Hopkins, E. W.: *India, Old and New*. Scribner's, New York, 1902.

Hopkins, E. W.: *The Ethics of India*. Yale Uni. Press, New Haven, 1924.

Hopkins, E. W.: *The Mutual Relations of the Four Castes According to Mānava-dharma-Śāstram*. Leipzig, 1881.

Hsu, F. L. K.: *Aspects of Culture and Personality*. Abelard-Schuman, New York, 1954.

Hsu, F. L. K.: "An Anthropologist's View of the Future of Personality Studies," *Psychiatric Research Reports*, Ameri. Psychiatric Assn., December, 1955.

Hutton, J. H.: *Caste in India*. 2nd Ed., Oxford Uni. Press, 1951.

Intelligence: Its Nature and Nurture, 39th Yearbook of the National Society for the Study of Education. Public School Publishing Co., Bloomington, Ill., U.S.A., 1940.

Ibbetson, D.: *Punjab Castes*. The Punjab Govt. Printing Press, Lahore, 1916.

India and Pakistan Yearbooks. Times of India Press, Bombay.

Jacobi, H.: *Gleanings from Kauṭilya—Cultural, Literary, Linguistic and Historical*. Tr. by N. P. Utgikar, in *Indian Antiquary*, 1924. from *Proc. of the Roy. Pruss. Aca. of Sciences*, 1911–12.

Jayaswal, K. P.: *Hindu Polity.*: Butterworth, Calcutta, 1924.

Jayaswal, K. P.: *Manu and Yajnavalkya*. Butterworth, Calcutta, 1930.

Jennings, H. S.: *The Biological Basic of Human Nature*. Faber, London, 1930.

Jennings, H. S.: "Heredity and Environment." *Scientific Monthly*, Vol. 19, pp. 225–38.

Jolly, J.: *Hindu Law and Custom*. Tr. by B. K. Ghosh. Greater India Society, Calcutta, 1928.

Jones, E. (Ed.): *Social Aspects of Psychoanalysis*. Lects. Delivered Under the Auspices of the Sociological Society, by E. Jones, J. Glover, J. C. Flugel, M. D. Eder, B. Low and E. Sharpe, Norgate, London, 1924.

Judd, C.: *Education and Social Progress*. Harcourt, New York, 1935.

Kallmann, F. J.: *Heredity in Health and Mental Disorder*. Norton. New York, 1953.

Kane, P. V.: *A History of the Dharmaśāstras: Ancient and Mediaeval Religious and Civil Law*. 3 Vols. Bhandarkar Oriental Research Institute, Poona, India, 1930 ff.

Kane, P. V.: "Gotra and Pravara," *Jour, of the B.B.R.A.S. New Series*, Vol. XI (August 1935).

Kapadia, K. M.: *Marriage and Family in India*. Oxford Uni. Press, Bombay, 1958.

Karve, Irawati: *Kinship Organization in India*. Deccan College Post-graduate Research Institute, Poona, 1953.

Katz, D. and Schanck, R. L.: *Social Psychology*. Wiley, New York, 1938.

Keay, F. E.: *Ancient Indian Education*. Oxford Uni. Press, London, 1918.

Keith, A. B.: *A History of Sanskrit Literature*. Clarendon Press, Oxford, 1928.

Keith, A. B.: *The Religion and Philosophy of the Veda and the Upanishads*. 2 Vols. Harvard University Press, 1925.

Ketkar, S. V.: *The History of Caste in India*. Taylor and Carpenter, Ithaca, New York, 1909.

Ketkar, S. V.: *An Essay on Hinduism: Its Formation and Future* Luzac, London, 1911.

Kilpatrick, W. H. (Ed.): *The Teacher and the Society*. First Yearbook of the John Dewey Society, Appleton-Century, New York, 1937.

Kirkpatrick, C.: *The Family: As Process and Institution*. Ronald Press, New York, 1955.

Kline, Viola: *The Feminine Character*, Kegan Paul, London, 1946. Klineberg, O.: *Social Psychology*. Rev. Ed., Holt, New York, 1954.

Klineberg, O.: *Tensions Affecting International Understanding*. Soc. Ss. Res. Council, N. Y., 1950.

Kluckhohn, C. and Murray, H. A. (Eds.) *Personality in Nature, Society and Culture*. 2nd Ed., Knopf, New York, 1953.

Kolnai, A.: *Psychoanalysis and Sociology*. Tr. by E. and C. Paul. Allen and Unwin, London, 1921.

Krech, D. and Crutchfield, R. S.: *Theory and Problems of Social Psychology*. McGraw-Hill, N. Y., 1948.

Kroeber, A. L.: "Caste", in *Ency. of the Soc. Sci.* Vol. III, 1930.

Kroeber, A. L.: *Anthropology—Race, Language, Culture, Psychology, Prehistory*. New Rev. Ed., Harcourt, Brace, New York, 1948.

Linton, Ralph: *The Study of Man*. Appleton-Century, New York, 1936.

Linton, Ralph: *The Cultural Background of Personality*. Appleton-Century-Crofts, New York, 1954. Brit. Ed., Kegan Paul, London, 1945.

Locke, John: *The Educational Writings of John Locke*. Ed. by J W. Adamson. Camb. University Press, London, 1922.

Locke, John: *Some Thoughts Concerning Education*, by John Locke. Ed. by R. H. Quick. Cambridge University Press, London, 1913.

Lowie, R. H.: *Primitive Religion*. Boni and Liveright, New York, 1925.

Lowie, R. H.: *Are We Civilized?* Harcourt, Brace, New York, 1929.

Lowie, R. H.: *Social Organization*. Routledge and K. Paul, London, 1950.

Ludovici, A. M.: *The Choice of a Mate*. (The International Library of Sexology and Psychology. Ed. by Norman Hair). John Lane, London, 1935.

Lyall, A. C.: *Asiatic Studies: Religious and Social*. 2 Vols. 2nd Ed. John Murray, London, 1907.

McCrindle, J. W.: *Ancient India as Described by Magasthenese and Arrian*. Chuckervertty, Chatterjee & Co., Calcutta, 1926.

Macdonell, A. A.: *A History of Sanskrit Literature*. 4th Imp. Heinemann, London, 1913.

Macdonell, A. A.: *Vedic Mythology*. V. Von K. J. Trübner, Strassburg, 1897.

Macdonell, A. A.: *Lects. on Comparative Religion*, University of Calcutta, 1925.

Macdonell, A. A.: *India's Past*. The Calendon Press, Oxford, 1927. Maclver, R. M. and Page, C.: *Society: An Introductory Analysis*. Farrar and Rinehart, New York, 1949. British Ed. Macmillan, London, 1949.

McKenzie, John: *Hindu Ethics*. Oxford University Press. London. 1922.

McKenzie, J. S.: *Outlines of Social Philosophy*. 2nd Ed. Allen and Unwin, London, 1927. Reprinted, 1952.

McKenzie, J. S.: *The Fundamental Problems of Life*. Allen and Unwin, London, 1928.

McKown, H. C.: *Character Education*. McGraw-Hill, New York. 1935.

MacNicol, Nicol: *Indian Theism*. Oxford University Press London. 1915.

Maine, H. S.: *Ancient Law*. 10th Ed. Reprinted. John Murray London, 1911.

Maine, H. S.: *Lects. on Early History of Institutions*. John Murray, London, 1875.

Maitra, S. K.: *The Ethics of the Hindus*. Cal. Uni. Pr., 1925.

Malinowski, B.: *Myth in Primitive Psychology*. Kegan Paul, London, 1926.

Malinowski, B.: "Marriage", in *Ency. Brit.*, 14th Ed. Vol. 14, pp. 940–50.

Marriott, Mck. (Ed.): *Village India*. Chicago University Press, 1955.

Masson—Oursel, P., H. De William Grabowska, and P. Stern: *Ancient India and Indian Civilization*. Tr. by M. R. Dobie. Kegan Paul, London, 1934.

Max Müller, F.: *India, What Can it Teach Us?* Longmans, London 1910.

Max Müller, F.: *Chips from a German Workshop*. 4 Vols. Longmans, London, 1868–75.

Mayne, J. D.: *A Treatise on Hindu Law and Usage*, Ed. by N. C. Aiyar, 11th Ed., Higginbothams, Madras. 1950.

Mead, Margaret: *From the South Seas*. William Morrow, New York, 1939.

Mead, Margaret: "On the Institutional Role of Women and Character Formation", *Zeitschrift für Sozialforschung*, Vol. 5 (1936), pp. 69–75.

Mead, Margaret: *Male and Female*. William Morrow, New York, 1949.

Mees, G. H.: *Dharma and Society*. Luzac, London, 1935.

Meyer, J. J.: *Sexual Life in Ancient India*. 2 Vols. Routledge, London, 1930.

Monier-Williams, M.: *Indian Wisdom*. 4th Ed. Luzac, London, 1893.

Monier-Williams, M.: *Brahmanism and Hinduism*. 3rd Ed. John Murray, London, 1887.

Mookerji, Radhakumud: *Democracies of the East*. P. S. King, London, 1923.

Mookerji, Radhakumud: *Nationalism in Hindu Culture*. Theos. Pub. House, London, 1921.

Mookerji, Radhakumud: *The Fundamental Unity of India*. Longmans, London, 1914.

Mookerji, Radhakumud: *Ancient Indian Education*, Macmillan, 1947.

Motwani, K.: *Manu: A Study in Hindu Social Theory*. Ganesh & Co., Madras, 1937.

Motwani, K.: *India: A Conflict of Cultures*. Nagpur University Lectures, 1947.

Motwani, K.: *India Can Lead*. Phoenix Pub., Bombay, 1946.

Motwani, K.: *Science and Society*. Hind Kitabs, Bombay, 1945.

Mukerjee, Radhakamal and Sengupta, N. N.: *Introduction to Social Psychology*. Heath, London, 1928.

Murdock, G. P.: *Social Structure*. Macmillan, N. Y., 1949.

Murphy, G. and L. B., and Newcomb, T. M.: *Experimental Social Psychology*. Harper, New York, 1937.

Murphy, G.: *Personality: A Bio-Social Approach*. Harper, N. Y. 1947.

Murphy, G.: *In the Minds of Men. A Study of Human Behaviour and Social Tensions in India*. Basic Books, New York, 1953.

Nature and Nurture: Their influence upon Intelligence. Twenty-Seventh Yearbook of the National Society for the Study of Education. Public School Publishing Co., Bloomington, Ill., U.S.A., 1928.

Nehru, Jawaharlal: *The Discovery of India*. 3rd Ed., Signet Press, Calcutta, 1947.

Newcomb, T. M.: *Social Psychology*. Dryden Press, New York 1950.

Newman, H.: *Education for Moral Growth*. D. Appleton, New York, 1923.

Newman, H. H., Freeman, F. N., and Holzinger, K. J.: *Twins—A Study of Heredity and Environment*. Univ. of Chicago Press, 1937.

Nimkoff, M. F.: *The Family*. Houghton Mifflin, New York, 1934.

Nimkoff, M. F.: *Marriage and the Family*. Houghton Mifflin. Boston, 1947.

Notes and Querries on Anthropology. Pub. by the British Association for the Advancement of Science. 6th Ed., 1950.

Nunn, Sir T. P.: *Education: Its Data and First Principles*. Rev. Ed. Edward Arnold, London, 1935.

Northropp, F. C. S.: *Ideological Differences and World Order: Studies in the Philosophy and Science of World's Cultures*. Yale Univ. Press, 1949.

Northropp, F. C. S.: *The Meeting of East and West*. Macmillan, N. Y., 1950.

Northropp, F. C. S.: "How Asians View the United States". *The Annals of the American Academy of Political and Social Science*, 276, (July, 1951), Philadelphia, 118–127.

O'Malley, L. S. S.: *India's Social Heritage*. Oxford Uni. Press, 1934.

O'Malley, L. S. S.: *Indian Caste Customs*. Cambridge Uni. Press, London, 1932.

O'Malley, L. S. S. (Ed.): *Modern India and the West: A Study of the Interaction of their Civilization*. Oxford University Press, London, 1941.

Osborn, F.: *Preface to Eugenics*. Harper, New York, 1940.

O'Shea, M. V.: *Social Development and Education*. Houghton Mifflin, Boston, 1909.

Pai, D. A.: *Monograph on the Religious Sects in India among the Hindus*. Times of India Press, Bombay, 1928.
Panunzio, C.: *Major Social Institutions*. Macmillan, New York, 1939.
Pargiter, F. E.: *Ancient Indian Historical Tradition*, Oxford Uni. Press, London, 1922.
Parmelee, M.: *Oriental and Occidental Culture*, London, 1929.
Paul, R.: *The Hindu Philosophy of Law in Vedic and Post-Vedic Times*. Bishvabhandar Press, Calcutta.
Peters, C. C.: *Foundations of Educational Sociology*. Rev. Ed. Macmillan, New York, 1930.
Pinkham, Mildreth W.: *Woman in the Sacred Scriptures of Hinduism*. Columbia Univ. Press, New York, 1941.
Popenoe, Paul: *Modern Marriage*. Second Edn., Macmillan, New York, 1941.
Popenoe, P. and Johnson, R. H.: *Applied Eugenics*. Macmillan, New York, 1933.
Porteus, S. D.: *The Psychology of a Primitive People*. Edward Arnold, London, 1931.
Prabhu, Pandharinath H.: "Fact and Theory in the Social Sciences", *The Socio-Economist*, Bombay, II, ii, 1940.
Prabhu, Pandharinath H.: *A Survey of Research in Indian Sociology During Twenty-Five Years:* 1917–1942. Bhand. Ori. Res. Insti., Poona, 1943.
Prabhu, Pandharinath H.: *Lectures on Hindu Social Institutions*. Maharaja Sayaji Rao Memorial Lectures. Baroda Govt. Press, 1942.
Prabhu, Pandharinath H.: *Hindu Social Philosophy*. Reprinted from *Bhāratīya Vidyā*, Bharatiya Vidya Bhavan, Bombay, 1941.
Prabhu, Pandharinath H.: *The Role of Mental Attitude in Culture-Contacts*. Reprinted from *The Eastern Anthropologist*, 1954.
Prabhu, Pandharinath: *Social Effects of Urbanization*. Unesco Research Centre, Calcutta, 1956.
Prabhu, Pandharinath H.: *Social Psychology of Community Dev*elopment. Ind. J. Social Work, XXI, 1, Tata Institute of Social Sciences, Bombay, 1960.
Prabhu, Pandharinath H.: *Transactional Psychology of the Indian Approach*. Presidential Address to the Psychology Section of the International Academy of Philosophy, 1961.
Pradhan, Sita-Nath: *Chronology of Ancient India*. Calcutta University, 1927.
Prasad, Beni: *Theory of Government in Ancient India*. Indian Press, Allahabad, 1927.
Prasad, Beni: *The State in Ancient India*. Indian Press, Allahabad, 1928.
Proceedings and Transactions of the All-India Oriental Conferences.
Radhakrishnan, S.: *Indian Philosophy*. 2 Vols. Allen and Unwin, London, 1927.
Radhakrishnan, S.: *The Hindu View of Life*. Allen and Unwin, London, 1927.
Radhakrishnan, S.: *An Idealist View of Life*. Allen and Unwin, London, 1932.
Radhakrishnan, S.: *The Heart of Hindustān*. Allen and Unwin, London, 1932.
Radhakrishnan, S.: *Religion and Society*. Allen and Unwin, London, 1947.
Radhakrishnan, S.: *East and West in Religion*. Allen and Unwin, London, 1933.
Ranade, M. G.: *Religious and Social Reforms*. Collected and Compiled by M. B. Kolaskar, Gopal Narayan & Co., Bombay, 1902.
Ranade, R. D.: *A Constructive Survey of Upanishadic Philosophy*. Oriental Book Agency, Poona, 1926.
Ranade, R. D.: *Mysticism in Mahārāshṭra*. Aryabhushan Press Office, Poona, 1933.
Rao, C. Hayavadana: *Indian Caste System: A Study*. Bangalore City Press, 1931.
Rapson, E. J.: *Ancient India, From the Earliest Times to the First Century* A.D. Cambridge Uni. Press, 1914.
Rawlinson, H. G.: *India: A Short Cultural History*. Praeger, N.Y., 1952.
Rice, Stanley: *Hindu Customs and Their Origins*. Allen and Unwin, London, 1937.
Risley, H. H.: *The People of India*. 2nd Ed., Thacker, Bombay, Calcutta and London, 1915.
Roback, A. A.: *Psychology of Character*, 3rd Ed. Kegan Paul, London, 1952.
Rosenfeld, Eva: "*Social Stratification in a 'Classless' Society Ameri. Sociol. Rev*., (Dec. 1951), 16, 6, 766–774.
Russell, R. V.: *The Tribes and Castes of the Central Provinces of India*. 4 Vols. Introductory Essay on 'Castes', in Vol. I. pp. 3–197, Macmillan, London, 1916.
Samaddar, J. N.: *The Glories of Magadha*. 2nd Ed. Pub. by the Author, Patna, India, 1927.
Sargent, S. S. and Williamson, R. C.: *Social Psychology*. 2nd Ed. Ronald Press, New York, 1958.
Sarkar, B. K.: *Śukranīti* (Tr.) Panini Office, Allahabad, 1914.
Sarkar, B. K.: *The Political Institutions and Theories of the Hindus*. Leipzig, 1928.
Scheinfeld, A.: *Women and Men*. Harcourt, Brace, New York 1944.
Scheinfeld, A.: *The New You and Heredity*. Chatto and Windus, London, 1952.

Schwesinger, Gladys: *Heredity and Environment: Studies in the Genesis of Psychological Characteristics*, Macmillan, New York, 1933.
Senart, E.: *Caste in India* (Tr. by E. D. Ross). Methuen, London, 1930.
Seward, Georgene H.: *Sex and the Social Order*. McGraw-Hill New York, 1946.
Shastry, Bhagat Kumar: *The Bhakti Cult in Ancient India*. B. Banerjee & Co., Calcutta, 1922.
Sherif, M.: *The Psychology of Social Norms*. Harper, New York, 1936.
Sherif, M. and Cantril, H.: *The Psychology of Ego-Involvements*. Wiley, New York, 1947.
Sorokin, P.: *Social Mobility*. Harper, New York, 1927.
Sorokin, P.: *Social and Cultural Dynamics*. 4 Vols. Amri. Book Co., N. Y., 1937.
Sorokin, P.: *The Reconstruction of Humanity*. Beacon Press, Boston, 1948.
Sorokin, P.: *The Crisis of Our Age*. Dutton, New York, 1946.
Sorokin, P. A.: *Man and Society in Calamity*. Dutton, N. Y., 1943.
Sorokin, P.: *Society, Culture and Personality*. Harper, New York
Spate, O. H. K.: *India and Pakistan*. 2nd Ed. Methuen, London, 1957.
Spear, Percival: *India, Pakistan and the West*. Oxford Uni. Press, N. Y., 1952.
Speier, H.: "Honour and Social Structure", *Social Research*, Vol II (1935), pp. 74–97.
Stern, B. J.: *The Family: Past and Present*. Appleton-Century, New York, 1938.
Sumner, W. G.: *Folkways*. Ginn, New York, 1906.
Sumner, W. G.: *What Social Classes Owe to Each Other*. Yale Uni. Press, 1925.
Symonds, P. M.: *The Psychology of Parent-Child Relationships*. Appleton-Century, New York, 1939.
Tansley, A. G.: *The New Psychology and Its Relation to Life*. 11th Imp. Allen and Unwin, London, 1929.
Taylor, W. S.: "Basic Personality in Orthodox Hindu Culture Patterns". *J. Abn. and Soc. Psych.* 43 (1948), 3–12.
Terman, L. M.: *Psychological Factors in Marital Happiness*. McGraw-Hill, New York, 1938.
Terman, L. M. and Miles, C. C.: *Sex and Temperament*. McGraw-Hill, New York, 1936.
Thomson, G. H.: *A Modern Philosophy of Education*. Allen and Unwin, London, 1929.
Thoothi, N. A.: *The Vaishṇavas of Gujarat*. Longmans, London and Bombay, 1935.
Thorndike, E. L.: *Human Nature and the Social Order*. Macmillan, New York, 1940.
Thouless, R. H.: *Conventionalization and Assimilation in Religious Movements as Problems in Social Psychology—With Special Reference to the Development of Buddhism and Christianity*. Riddell Memorial Lectures delivered before the University of Durham in March 1940, Oxford Uni. Press, London, 1940.
Thouless, R. H.: *General and Social Psychology*. 3rd Ed., Univ.
Tutorial Press, London, 1951. Thurston, E. and Rangachari, K.: *Tribes and Castes of South India*. Madras, 1929.
Tuttle, H. S.: *A Social Basis of Education*. Crowell, New York, 1935.
Urwick, E. J.: *The Social Good*. Methuen, London, 1927.
Urwick, E. J.: *A Philosophy of Social Progress*. 2nd Rev. Ed. Methuen, London, 1920.
Urwick, E. J.: *The Message of Plato*. Methuen, London, 1920.
Urwick, E. J.: *The Values of Life*. (Ed. by J. A. Irving). Univ. of Toronto Press, 1948.
Venkateswara, S. V.: *Indian Culture Through the Ages*. Vols. I and II. Longmans, London and Bombay, 1928.
Waller, W. and Hill, R.: *The Fanily: A Dynamic Interpretation*. Dryden Press, New York, 1951.
Weber, Max.: *From Max Weber: Essays in Sociology*. Tr. and Edited by H. H. Gerth and C. Wright Mills. British Ed. Kegan Paul, London, 1947.
Webster, H.: *Taboo: A Sociological Study*. Stanford Univ. Press, 1942.
Wesley, E. B.: "A Socialized Education for a Socialized Age" in the *Annals of the American Academy of Pol. and Soci. Sc.*, Vol. 182, November, 1935.
Westermarck, E.: *Origin and Development of Moral Ideas*. 2 Vols. 2nd Ed., Macmillan, 1924.
Westermarck, E.: *History of Human Marriage*. 3 Vols. 5th Ed. Rewritten, Macmillan, London, 1921.
Westermarck, E.: *A Short History of Human Marriage*. Macmillan, London, 1926.
Westermarck, E.: *Three Essays on Sex and Marriage*. Macmillan, London, 1934.
Westermarck, E.: *The Future of Marriage in Western Civilization*. Macmillan, London, 1936.
Westermarck, E.: *Ethical Relativity*. Macmillan, London.
Wiese, Leopald von. and Becker, H.: *Systematic Sociology*. Wiley, New York, 1932.
Wiese, Leopald von.: "DIE KLÁSSISCHEN DER SOZILORGANISATION DER INDER", *KYKLOS*, An International Review of Social Sciences, Basel, Switzerland, Fasc. 1, 1955, pp. 72–81.

Williams, J. M.: *The Foundations of Social Sciences: An Analysis of their Psychological Basis*. Knopf, New York, 1920.
Williams, J. M.: *Principles of Social Psychology*, Knopf, New York, 1920.
Woodworth, R. S.: *Heredity and Environment*. Social Science Research Council, New York, 1941.
Young, Kimball: *Social Psychology*. 3rd Ed., Crofts, New York, 1956.
Young, Kimball: *Personality and the Problem of Adjustment*. 2nd Ed., Kegan Paul, London, 1952.
Zubeck, J. and Solberg, P.: *Human Development*. McGraw-Hill, New York, 1954.

AUTHOR INDEX*

Adler, A., 245
Allport, G. W., 206–207
Anastasi, A., 326, 348

Ballard, L. V., 147
Barnes, H. E., 147
Bartlett, F. C., 341–342
Beale, Howard, 135
Belvalkar, S. K., and Ranade, R. D., 20
Benedict, Ruth, 262
Bhandarkar, R. G., 46, 57
Bosanquet, H, 204
Briffault, R., 145
Britt, S. H., 210
Brown, L. G., 205, 244–247, 254
Burgess, E. W., 189, 209
Burgess E. W. and Cottrell, L. S., 188–190
Burgess, E. W. and Locke, H. J., 201, 203–205, 207, 209–210, 254–255

Calverton, V. F. and Schmalhausen. 145, 183
Carstairs, G. M., 321–322, 347
Carter, H. D., 349
Carver, T. N., 3–4, 330
Cattell, R. B., 129
Christensen, H., 189
Colebrooke, H. T., 235, 285
Comte, A., 208
Cooley, C., 237–238, 288, 322, 353
Counts, G. S., 102, 104

Darwin, L., 351–352
Dasgupta, S. N., 39
Davis, K., 5
Davis, K. and Moore, W. E., 328, 329
Deploige, Simon, 77
Deutsch, H., 262
Deussen, P., 83
Dewey, J., 102, 129
Dunbar, G., 10
Dunlap, K., 201–202
Dutt, N. K., 285–291, 297
Durkheim, E., 77

Einstein, A., 134
Ellis, Havelock, 13, 282
Ellis, R. S., 326
Ellwood, C., 106, 209

Flügel, J. C., 208
Freud, S., 260–261, 282

Galton, F., 348
Geldner, 286, 298
Ghosh, Dr., 180
Giddings, F. H., 330
Gillin, J. L. and J. P., 147
Ginsberg, M., 330
Goodsell, W., 182

Hall, C. S., 136
Hamilton, G. V., and McGowan, K., 183
Hamilton, W. H., 147
Haug, H., 286
Hertzler, J. O., 147
Houen-tsang, 340
Hogben, L., 348
Holmes, S. J., 349
Hopkins, E. W., 287
Hutton, J. H., 297

Inge, W. R., 72
Irving, J. A., 69–71

Jennings, H. S., 349
Jolly, J., 218
Jones, Sir Wm., 13
Judd, C., 106

Kane, P. V., 79, 156
Keith, A., 43, 86
Keller, A. G., 323
Klein, V., 282–283
Kolb, W. L, 77
Kreuger, E. T. and Reckless, W., 208
Kroeber, A. L., 324

LaPiere, R. T. and Farnsworth, P. R., 147
Lenard, P., 134
Levy-Bruhl, L., 77
Linton, R., 202, 323
Locke, 132
Lowie, R. H., 102, 104
Ludovici, A. M., 265

Macdonell, A. A., 11, 43, 57
Macdonell, A. A. and Keith, A., 84, 155, 156
Maclver, R. M. and Page, C., 69, 147, 148, 201, 203, 322–323
MacKenzie, J. S., 224
Malinowski, B., 146
Mantegazza, P., 146
Masson-Oursel, P., and others, 297
Max-Müller, F., 285
Mead, M., 261–262, 282
Megasthenese, 340
Modi, P. M., 84–85
Moll, A., 260
Murdock, G. P., 159
Murphy, Gardner, 9
Murphy, G., Murphy, L. B. and Newcomb, T. M., 246

Newcomb, T. M., 80
Newlon, Prof., 134
Newman, H. H., Freeman and Holzinger, 348
Nimkoff, M. F., 202, 209–211

* Joint authors' names are not listed separately but jointly, as they appear on their books.

Nunn, T. P., 103, 105, 111, 130

Ogburn, W. I., 211
Ogburn, W. F. and Nimkoff, M. F., 157
Osborn, F., 349
O'Shea, M. V., 103, 105, 132

Panunzio, C., 103, 147, 157–158, 182, 185, 186
Parker, G. H., 207
Pearson, K., 348
Plato, 69–71, 75
Popenoe, P., 157, 187
Prabhu, P. H., 77

Radhakrishnan, S., 38, 56
Ranade, R. D., 19, 58, 85, 292
Rangachari, K., 156
Rice S., 279–280
Risley, H., 6, 49, 321
Roback, A. A., 260
Rosenfeld, E., 324–326
Ross, E. A., 117, 122–223
Russell, B., 125, 135

Scheinfeld, Amram, 349
Schmidt, R., 13
Schwesinger, G., 349
Sénart, E., 298
Small, A., 323
Sorokin, P., 75, 77–78
Spate, O. H. K., 5
Sumner, G., 104, 136, 148, 153–154, 323

Tansley, A. G., 136–137
Terman, L. M., 188
Terman, L. M. and Miles, C., 282
Thomas, W. I., 210
Thoothi, N. A., 57, 61, 66, 80, 82, 213, 217, 256
Thouless, R. H., 158–159
Thurston, E. and Rangachari, K., 202

Urwick, E. J., 31, 69–72, 75, 224

Vaidya, C. V., 84, 156
Venkatesan, N. K., 56
Venkateswara, S. V., 140
Vidyarnava, S. C., 235

Waller, W., and Hill, R. 209
Ward, L. F., 323
Weingarten, M., 324
Westermarck, E., 147, 149
Wiese, L. von, 75
Williams, J. M, 106, 115, 118, 184,
Winternitz, M., 10–11
Woodworth, R. S., 349

Young, K., 104, 157, 208, 244

Zimmer, H., 285

SUBJECT INDEX

Agni-pariṇayana, 166–167
artha, 12–13, 79ff, 165, 256
as one of the psycho-moral bases of the *aśramas*, 79ff.
Artha-Śāstra, as a source of Hindu social thought, 12–13
āśmārohaṇa, 167
āśramas, ch. iii; 221–223, 346ff. *See also: varṇas*
the ages for entrance, 87–89
brahmacharya, 84, 89. *See also*: ch. iv
grihastha, 89
special praise for, 93–96. *See also*: chs. v and vi the group and the individual in, 96–100
originally three, 84–86
psycho-moral bases of, 78–83, 96–99
and *purushārthas* of *dharma, artha, kāma* and *mokśa*, 78–83, 96–99
samnyāsāśrama, 85–89, 91–92
the social psychology of, ch. iii
theory and practice of, 83ff.
vānaprastha, 83, 89–90
and *varṇas*, see *varṇa*
and the woman, 277–279
and the *yajna-paramparā*, 97–99

bhakta, jnānī, 55–56
bhaktī as a *mārga* of *mokśa*. *See: mārga*
Bhārata-Sāvitrī verse, 358
brāhma marriage, 151–154, 163, 175–176
brahmacharya, after marriage, 171–172, 199–200
brahmacharyāśrama see 'Education.' and *yajna*, 97

Caste, modern views on, 322ff.
Castes and *varṇas*. *See: jātis* and *varṇas*.
Chastity, pre-nuptial, 153–154
Classes, 'open', 294
social, forces fostering, 326ff. *See also: varṇas*
'Classless' society, class emerging from, 324ff.
Concept of human existence and its mission
in the *Brāmaṇas*, 19
in the *Gītā*, 42ff.
in the *Mahābhārata*, 22ff.
in the *Nītis*, 36ff.
in the *Smritis*, 31ff.
in the *Upanīshads*, 19–22
in the *Vedas*, 18–19, 21
in the Yoga-Sūtras, 38ff.See also: karma, development of the theory of

daiva (destiny or fate), in relation to *karma*, 29–31, 36–38, 48
Daughter, 'appointed' 160, 247–248
dowry in marriage of, forbidden, 178–179, 249–250
when free to arrange her own marriage or not to marry, 151, 248–249, 268–269, 270
position of, in the family, 247ff.
'Debts', (individual and social obligations). *See: riṇas desa* and *kāla* (Place and Time), in man's behaviour, 73–75, 301, 342–345
and the nature of sexes, 283
dharma, 12–13, 18, 25, 26ff., 31.,ff., 44ff., 47, 49, 50, 63, 65, 67–68, 73, 74, 79ff., 124, 125, 126, 132, 142, 143, 165, 166, 173, 215–217, 252, 253, 292–294, 299ff., 304ff., 332, 342–345, 356ff.
and its different forms, 26ff., 34–36, 67–68, 301, 342ff.
and nature and nurture (*guṇa* and *śrama*), 74–76.
See also: varṇa-and-*āśrama; guṇa* and *śrama; varṇa* and *dharma*
as psycho-moral basis of *āśramas*, 78ff.
and time and place, *See: deśa* and *kāla*
Yājnavalkya's classification of, 35–36
Dharma-śāstras, sources of Hindu social life and thought, 4, 10ff.
Divorce (*mokśa*) of marriage, *See*: marriage, dissolution of

Education, *See*: ch. i age of initiation (*upanayana*) 111–113
aims of, social and personal, 102–108
brahmacharya (celibacy) during, 130–131, 137, 143, 144
and character training, 118, 122–129 as a *dharma*, 124ff.
external control on, 134–136 and the family influence on, 115ff., 136
female, 137–142, 257–258, 277ff.
free tuition and its effects, 123–125
and individual differences in pupila' abilities, 133–135
initiation into (*upanayana*), 108–111

intellectual and moral together, 126–131
lessons in simple living in, 113ff.
personal attention of the teacher in, 115ff.
place of punishment in, 131–133
Locke on 132
pupil's duties towards teacher, 121ff.
rites of initiation and their social significance, 111 and self-control, 126ff. social and individual aspects of, 102–108
social-psychological implications of, 102ff.
teacher's qualities and duties, 121ff.
and *vidyā* (knowledge) 33, 119ff. as a *vrata* (discipline), 126–131, 143–144
'End', and the 'means' of life, 66ff.
Endogamy, and exogamy, 154–160 Epics, the, as source of Hindu
social life and thought, 9–10
Eugenics, and marriage, 158–163 and *varṇa-organizatīon*, 348ff
Exogamy and endogamy, 154ff.
Family. *See* ch. VI
continuity of the, 215ff. *See also: riṇas* ('debts')
definition, 201–202
eldest in relation to younger
brothers in the, 243ff. father's position in the, 250ff. the 'five great *yajnas*' in the, 212ff., 256
the four basic wishes (Thomas'), 210ff. husband and wife in the, 224ff., 271ff.
interpersonal relation in the, 224ff.
joint nature of the Hindu, 217ff. position of the daughter, 247ff. position of the parent, 250ff. 273–274
position of the son, 242ff. psychoanalytic interpretation, 208
and the *purushārthas (dharma, artha, kāma* and mokśa), 256
the *samskāras* in the, 218ff.
social-psychological implication of, 203ff.
structure and function of the Hindu, 212ff. *See also*: Home
Fatalism. *See: daiva*
Father in the family *See* Parents
Female education. *See* Education, female
Female deities, 279ff.

Gīta, the *Bhagawad-*, and the problem of existence, 42ff. *gotra* and *pravara*, 154–156 *See also*: Endogamy and exogamy *griha-praveśa*, 169–171
Grihasthāśrama. See chs. v and vi; āśramas high praise for, 93–96 and *yajna*, 97, 212ff., 256 *Grihaya-Sūtras*, as source of domestic and social life, 10–11 *guṇas,* as the bases of *varṇa*-system, 35, 73–75, 314–317, 318ff. *See also: lakshaṇa vrīttim* and sex, 283
and *śrama*, 73–79, 284–285

'Hard' and 'soft' points in a culture, 341–342
Heredity, in marriage. *See* marriage, biological considerations and *varṇa. See: varṇa* Hindu-Muslim amity, 344–347 Home, the, and *dharma*, 212ff.
See also: Family and the 'five great *yajnas*', 212ff. rituals for building the, 214–215, 263ff.
Husband and wife, 224ff., 258
authority over wife, 226ff.
permitted days of intimacy, 240–242, 271–272

Idol worship, 279–281 Indian culture and Western impact, 7–8
Interpersonal relationship in the family, 228ff.

jāti, and *varṇa*, 284ff., 303–308, 311, 324
jnāna, as a *mārga. See: mārgas* full meaning of, 32–34. *See also: vidyā*
kāma, 12–14, 78–83, 164, 261
kāma, as a psycho-moral basis of *āśramas*, 78ff.
Kāma-Śāstra, as a source of Hindu life and thought, 12–14
Kāma-Sūkta, hymn to God of Love, 164–165
kanyā-dāna, 164–165
karma, and its atonement, 19ff.
development of the theory of,
in the *Brāhmaṇas*, 19
in the *Gītā*, 42ff.
in the *Mahābhārata*, 22ff.
in the *Smritīs*, 31ff.
in the *Upanishads*, 19–22
in the *Yoga* Sūtras, 38ff.
See also: Concept of human existence
kinds of, according to Patanjali, 39–40
as a *mārga* of attaining final
liberation, 42ff.
theory not fatalistic. *See: daiva kula. See*: Home
lājā-homa, 164, 166
lakśaṇa, and varṇa, 309ff., 352ff.
and woman's character, 265 *See also: guṇas, vrittim*
Levirate (*nīyoga*), 197

Mahābhārata,
the problem of human existence in, 22ff.
as a source of Hindu social life and thought, 10ff.
mārgas, kárma-, jnāna-, and *bhakti*, as ways of attaining the goal of existence, 43–60, 63–66
and *yajnas*, 52ff
Marriage, ch. v; 221–222, 224–225
age of, 179–187
biological considerations in, 154–163
brahmacharya after, 171–172, 199–200
chastity of the bride and groom
before, 153–154
consequences of concealment of defects in the bride or groom, 190–191
and courtship, 180–187
dissolution of, when allowed, 190–192, 226 and eugenics. *See:* Marriage.

biological considerations in
exogamy and endogamy,
154ff. factors in marita
happiness, 183–190
foetus-laying rites after, 172–173,
219
forms of Hindu, 151–153, 174–179
girl to arrange her own, 151
importance of certain rites in,
173–178 as an institution, 147–149
kauyādāna, 164–165 a necessity, 149–151, 194–197, 227
number of wives allowed,
194–197, 225–226, 239–268
and purushārthas of (*dharma, artha, kāma* and *mokśa*),
149–150 164–166, 173,
198–200, 227ff.
qualifications in the bride and
groom for, 153–163
remarriage of widows, 192–194,
277
rites and ceremonies after,
171–173, 198–200
rites and ceremonies in 163ff.
some Western views of Hindu,
145–146
wife, when entitled to seek
dissolution and marry again,
190–192, 226
'Means' and the 'end' of life. 66ff.
mokśa, 12–13, 18, 23, 24, 65ff.,
79–83
mokśa (= dissolution of marriage).
See: Marriage, dissolution of
mokśa, and knowledge, 32
Mother's position in the
family, 250ff.

Nature and nurture. *See: varṇa-*
and-*aśrama* Nayars, of South
India, 202
Nīti-Śāstra, and the problem of
human existence, 36ff. *niyoga. See:*
Levirate

pancha-mahāyajnas, 212ff.
pāṇi-grahana. 165–166, 173–174
its importance, 173–174, 190–191
Parents, in the family, 250ff.,
273–274
patita-sāvitrīka, 112
pravara. See: gotra and *pravara*
Punishment of the child, by parents,
254 place of, in education,
131–133 Locke on, 132
purushārthas and *dśramas.*
See: 'dśramas' and marriage,
See: Marriage
and purushārthas as the psycho-moral bases of *dśramas*,
78–33, 96–99
Purusha-Sūkta hymn, interpreted,
285–287

Rāmāyaṇa, as a source of Hindu
social life and thought, 10
Reform movement, 336ff.
Religious tolerance of the Hindus,
344–347
Remarriage of widows, 192–194,
277
riṇas (individual and social obligations), 83, 87, 173, 213ff. of
the *grihastha* (householder),
173, 195, 213ff.

samnyāsāśrama. See: 'āśramas,'
samnyāsa
and *yajna*, 98–99 *samnyāsāśrami*,
as beyond the
āśramas, 86 *samskāras. See:*
Family, *samskāras* in the
and the *Sūdras*, 222 and the
varṇa and *āśrama*, 222ff. and
women, 222, 277–279 *saptapadī*, 167–168, 229, 236
its importance, 173–174 *Sāstras*,
sciences of life, 12 *Sāvitrī*
mantra, 109–110
patita-sāvitrīka, 112 *Smritis*,
and the problem of existence, 31ff.
as sources of social thought and
life, 9–12
Social class, and caste, *See: varṇas*
modern views, on 322ff.
Social institutions, 147–148
Social organization, based on conception of human existence
and its mission. *See*: Conception of human existence
Social reformer, 2ff. vs. orthodoxy,
336ff.
Social science and values, in India
and the West, 76–79
Son,
his position in the family, 242ff.
the eldest son in the family,
243ff.
Sources, original, of Hindu social
thought and life, 8ff.
Sūtras, Dharma- and *Grihya-*, as
sources of Hindu thought on
domestic and social life. 9, 10ff.

trivarga, dharma, artha and *kāma*,
12, 79ff., 300

upanayana, 89, 108ff.
Upanishads, and human existence,
18–21

Values, and social science, in India
and the West, 76–77
vānaprasṭhāśrama See: āśramas
and *yajna*, 98–99
varṇa-and-*āśrama*, 15, 35–36,
74–76, 111–112, 194, 222,
284ff., 346ff
in the *Bhagawad-Gīta*, 314ff
change of *varṇa*, 312ff. and *dharmas*,
in adversity (*āpad), See: dharma*,
and its different forms.
guṇas as the bases of, 318ff. and
heredity and descent, 333ff.,
348ft.
intermarriage among *varṇas.* and
jāti. See: jāti and *varṇa*. and
karma, 303–305
known by deeds, 305ff., 319 by
lakśaṇas (characteristic
traits), 303ff., 352ff.
mixture (*samkara*) of, 296ft., 307–308
Origins of, in the *Brāhmaṇas,*
Samhitas and *Upanishads*,
289, 292
in the *Gītā*, 314ft.
in the *Mahābhārata*, 292ft.
in the *Smritis*, 296ff.
in the *Vedas*, 285–288
varṇāśrama-vyavasthā. See: varṇa-
and-*āśrama*
vidyā, the concept of, 119–121.*See*
also: jnāna
vivāha. See: Marriage

as *dharma*, 149ff.
as a *samskāra*, 221–222
vivāha-homa, 165–186
vrittam, or *vritti*, 307ff.

Widow, remarriage of, 192–194, 277 Wife,
and husband, relation between, 224ff., 258–259, 263ft. her duties in the home, 231ff
Women and the *āśramas*, 277–279
female deities, 279–281
at home and in society, ch. vii
judgments on their psychology, influenced by cultural context, 281–283
learned, in Vedic and later times, 137ff., 257ff., 271
nature of, 259 et. seqq. and *samskāras. See samskāras.*

Yajamāna, 64, 212ff.
yajna,
evolution of the concept of, 51ff.
the 'five great *yajnas,*' 212ff. faith (*śraddhā*) as, 299 metal (*manīshayā*), 299
yajna-paramparā, 64 and the *āśramas*, 97–99, 212ff., 216
as a spirit of sacrifice, 51ff., 256
Yoga-Sūtras, and the problem of existence, 37ff.